History of the
Second Seminole War
1835–1842

A Model of Fort Lauderdale
A typical Florida fort during the Second Seminole War

History of the
Second Seminole War
1835-1842

Revised Edition

John K. Mahon

UNIVERSITY PRESSES OF FLORIDA
University of Florida Press / Gainesville

UNIVERSITY PRESSES OF FLORIDA is the central agency for scholarly publishing of the State of Florida's university system, producing books selected for publication by the faculty editorial committees of Florida's nine public universities: Florida A&M University (Tallahassee), Florida Atlantic University (Boca Raton), Florida International University (Miami), Florida State University (Tallahassee), University of Central Florida (Orlando), University of Florida (Gainesville), University of North Florida (Jacksonville), University of South Florida (Tampa), University of West Florida (Pensacola).

ORDERS for books published by all member presses should be addressed to University Presses of Florida, 15 NW 15th Street, Gainesville, FL 32603.

Library of Congress Cataloging-in-Publication Data

Mahon, John K.
  History of the Second Seminole War, 1835–1842.

  Bibliography: p.
  Includes index.
1. Seminole War, 2d, 1835–1842. I. Title.
E83.835.M3   1985   973.5'7   85–16443
ISBN 0-8130-1097-7
Copyright 1985 by the Board of Regents of the State of Florida

Original edition 1967.

Second paperback printing 1992

Printed in the U. S. A.

Contents

List of Illustrations

Preface to 1985 Reprint

TWENTY YEARS have passed since I gave the typescript for the *History of the Second Seminole War* to the University of Florida Press. For the first time in a decade, I have reread the text and, have found it to be free of typographical errors. In this reprinting, two or three pages are slightly changed, but more extensive alterations, to fill in an omission or two, have been avoided because of expense. Aside from the limited omissions, the original contains no errors of fact, and the text stands as it is.

I have added in an appendix a bibliography of printed and manuscript materials that have come to light since the original edition was published. I included only those items that add to what is known of the war and the era. There are a few that I simply missed the first time around. The entries in the appendix are annotated, and the annotations point to materials by means of which serious students can fill in gaps not fully covered in the 1967 edition.

In the two decades since the original publication, I have become increasingly convinced that had the Second Seminole War been fought by other-than-Indians, it would have been in the mainstream of American history as one of the great struggles of a people—less numerous and less powerful than their foes—to remain in their homeland. As history got written, however, this conflict, apart from the thrust of so-called

white progress, was neglected. One of the most moving statements of love of homeland ever made came from Tuckose
Emathla, a Florida Indian leader: "Here our navel strings
were cut, and the blood sunk into the earth and made the
country dear to us" (p. 62). No white person of the 1820s
would have stated love of country in that way or with equal
power.

John K. Mahon
June 1985

Preface

THERE IS an expanding tendency to re-examine the American past. Naturally this tendency has operated for the most part upon the more important aspects of our history, for example, Jacksonian Democracy, which has attracted large numbers of "revisionists." Apart from the main currents, there still remain some important corners where few historians have chosen to take a second look. Among them are the wars against the forest Indians of the eastern United States. These wars have been pushed out of view by an almost psychopathic preoccupation with the fights against the plains tribes, fights enlarged to monstrous proportions by fiction, radio, the movies, and television.

The little known Second Seminole War is beyond doubt one of the most dramatic episodes in our history. It has been represented on library shelves for 120 years by one credible history, John T. Sprague, *Origin, Progress, and Conclusion of the Florida War,* published in 1848. This book, standing alone for more than a century, has become like a bible to those who bother to concern themselves with the Second Seminole War. Unfortunately, it is out of proportion: Sprague used 150 pages to tell the story of the first five years, and 250 for the last eighteen months. The resulting disproportion came about not through a willful desire to distort, but because Sprague himself reached the theater of war in November, 1840, and thereafter had at his command much more extensive data than for the period from 1835 to that November. For the last year and a half of the conflict, in other words, his history has the weight of a contemporary document.

Sprague had to be careful not to offend officers who remained his superiors, for he continued in the army until 1870. The reader must also know that he was the son-in-law of the last commanding officer in the Florida War, William Jenkins Worth. I do not mean to imply that he slanted the record in favor of his father-in-law and his professional colleagues; he did not. But, bound to be careful, he avoided all critical analysis. Moreover, he made no effort to set the Second Seminole War in its broad historical context, or to demonstrate forcefully the close connection between the coming of this Indian war and the general issue of Negro slavery, which was then the central problem of the United States. In spite of these omissions, his history is a superior accomplishment.

With the passage of years, additional data have come to light. Also, our relationship with native peoples of all sorts has become a matter of prime importance, and has tended to bring out of the shadows the history of such relationships in earlier eras. The time seems right to look again at the history of the Second Seminole War. I have leaned on Sprague where I could—for there is no sense in doing over what has already been well done—but, in addition, I have read everything in print known to me concerning the war, and have examined as many manuscripts as lay within my reach.

I have tried to embed this conflict in national, in military, and in Florida history. The attempt may have clogged the narrative at times, yet even so, it seemed to be an obligation.

Errors of fact or interpretation are my sole responsibility. That being understood, I express thanks to Dr. Rembert W. Patrick, Dr. Samuel Proctor, and Dr. Herbert J. Doherty, three experts in Florida history, for reading and criticizing the typescript. I am grateful to Dr. Donald E. Worcester for his labor in trying to brighten up the writing and to Dr. Kenneth Wiggins Porter, an expert in Seminole history, for his painstaking study of the whole work and valuable suggestions and corrections. I cheerfully acknowledge an obligation to three anthropologists, the late Dr. John M. Goggin, Dr. Charles

H. Fairbanks, and Dr. William C. Sturtevant, for their attention to the chapter on the origins of the Seminoles. It remains for me to thank my wife, Enid, who typed the entire work with unequaled accuracy. But I thank her, more than for this mechanical task, for becoming interested in what she was reading, leading me to hope that others might do the same.

JOHN K. MAHON

Gainesville, Florida

To the late MAJOR EDWARD T. KEENAN, a student of Seminole history, friend of the Seminoles, and friend of all honest students of Seminole history

I

Origins of the Seminoles

ON JUNE 13, 1842, when the Second Seminole War had been in progress six years, six months, and sixteen days, David Levy, the delegate from the Territory of Florida, addressed the House of Representatives of the United States. He was a handsome man of Portuguese and Jewish lineage, with a high forehead and long hair parted on the left and falling to the lobes of his ears. Indignantly he said, "Sir, the sympathies of the public have been enlisted by the supposition that these Indians were about to be torn unwillingly from the hunting-grounds of their ancestors, and the graves of the past generations of their people. Nothing can be more mistaken. No part of the Indians found in Florida at its cession were aborigines of that peninsula; and most of them were very recent refugees and stragglers from other parts. . . . Thus it will be seen, sir, that whatever of sympathy has been excited in behalf of the Seminoles upon the score of their attachment to the land of their fathers is altogether misplaced."[1]*

"These Indians" had a totally different view of their roots. Twenty-two years prior to Levy's address, Seminole representatives had told white negotiators, "An hundred summers have seen the Seminole warrior reposing undisturbed under the shade of his live oak, and the suns of one hundred winters have risen on his ardent pursuit of the buck and the bear, with none

* Citations to sources begin on page 328.

to question his bounds or dispute his range."[2] Although this statement was obviously couched in the language of the nineteenth-century white Romantics who heard the talk through interpreters, it did demonstrate that the Seminoles believed their roots in Florida to be both deep and venerable. Nor were they careless about their attachment to the soil. In the nation's capital itself, where a delegation of Florida Indians had gone in 1826 to try to see President John Quincy Adams, Tuckose Emathla, called John Hicks by the white men, vividly stated the pull of their connection, "here our navel strings were first cut and the blood from them sunk into the earth, and made the country dear to us."[3] In 1827 Micanopy used almost exactly the same pledge of his loyalty.

Levy was correct when he said that the Seminoles were not aborigines, for other Indians had been in the peninsula before them. The precursors of these earlier Indians had come to Florida perhaps as much as 10,000 years ago. When the Spaniards came, certain tribes were soon identified and named, tribes which remained in contact with white men for nearly two centuries. In western Florida as far east as the Aucilla River were the Apalachees. Throughout the balance of northern Florida, and southward to a line from Cape Canaveral to the southern tip of Tampa Bay, were various tribes of Timucua-speaking Indians. In the southern portion of the peninsula the dominant strain was Calusa. All of these groups were virtually extinct by the middle of the eighteenth century.[4] When the English took over Florida in 1763, most of the remaining Indians were evacuated with the Spaniards: 83 individuals from St. Augustine, 80 families from southern Florida, and 108 Catholic Yamassees and Apalachees from Pensacola. These were almost the only survivors of an Indian population of about 25,000 a century earlier.[5]

Some writers have assumed that a sprinkling of the Calusas lingered on into the nineteenth century, in southwestern Florida along the Caloosahatchee River and Pease Creek. Recent research proves, however, that these so-called Spanish Indians were not Calusas at all; they were an isolated band of Seminoles.[6]

By 1710 northern Florida had become that rare sort of vacuum, a habitable environment, recently peopled, now devoid of population except for a thin fringe of white men principally along the east coast.[7] Into this inviting void there moved from time to time during a century groups of Indians from the territories north of the peninsula. Nearly all of them were of the Muskogean family and were affiliated with the Creek Confederation. This repopulation of Florida was both a by-product of the struggle for empire among the European colonizing powers and an aspect of Creek expansionism. After Queen Anne's War, 1701-13, the Spaniards felt the need for a buffer of natives to replace the Apalachees and Timucuas destroyed by English and Creek raids. The governor of Florida accordingly sent Lieutenant Diego Peña on three expeditions to the Creek country to induce some of the bands to settle in Apalachee, west of the Aucilla River. There lay inviting Apalachee "old" fields, all cleared and waiting for use. His proselyting apparently helped bring action, for a few bands of Lower Creeks did migrate during the second decade of the eighteenth century. The Tamathli group, for example, moved about in southern Georgia and northern Florida, and in time became a part of the tribe known as Mikasuki.[8]

A remarkable Indian, the "Emperor" Brim of the Lower Creeks, had visions of a combination of all southeastern Indians to expel the white man. In order to realize his dream, he exploited Indian-white dissension wherever it cropped up. One of his projects was to incite the so-called Yamassee War against the British in 1715. For it to succeed, Brim needed the support of the Cherokees. When that support was not given, he abandoned the Yamassees to their own devices. They were defeated and driven from their hunting grounds along the coast of South Carolina. Migrating to the vicinity of St. Augustine, they took the side of the Spaniards in the colonial strife, and in return expected protection. However, even the Spaniards could not save them from their deadly enemies the Creeks. Because the Yamassees were the only really effective Indian allies the Spaniards had in Florida, the English encouraged and aided the Creeks. The Yamassees in the long run, therefore, were greatly reduced, and some of them were enslaved by the Creeks. The conquerors impregnated the women of the defeated, and perpetuated the Yamassee strain in the Creeks, and through them in the Seminoles.[9]

The founding of Georgia by the English in 1732 upset the balance in the Southeast. By opening the way for further conflict, it indirectly channeled additional Creek migration into Florida.

The next settlement there resulted from the War of Jenkins' Ear and King George's War, 1739-48. While General James Oglethorpe concentrated his attention on St. Augustine, his Lower Creek allies ranged over north-central Florida, and some bands stayed in Florida or came back there soon after the war. One of these bands was the Oconee, led by the "Cowkeeper." This tribe had once lived on the Oconee River in central Georgia, but as a result of the Yamassee War had migrated to the lower Chattahoochee River. From that point one group moved into the Alachua region of Florida. Well established there by the year 1750, it became the nucleus of the principal Seminole tribe, the Alachua band.[10]

At about the same time that Cowkeeper's Oconees were settling the Alachua district, 1739-50, other Lower Creeks were moving into the old Apalachee territory. Among those was a band led by Brim's son, named Secoffee.* He and his people favored the Spaniards, while Cowkeeper and his group inclined to the English. This unfortunate division was typical of what the European struggle for empire was doing to the southeastern Indians. Differences between pro-British and pro-Spanish factions were to cause various bands from time to time to migrate to Florida.

Movement into West Florida brought migrants near to the small band or bands of aborigines called Apalachicolas. The Apalachicolas were among the few tribes who had managed to survive the English and Creek raids of the eighteenth century. Now, again under pressure, some of them were driven into peninsular Florida, where they mingled with the migrant bands and contributed to the Seminole amalgam. Prominent

* The narrative in this and the previous paragraph does not introduce the division among scholars over the identities of the Cowkeeper and Secoffee. I have weighed the printed evidence and have included what seems to me the soundest account of events and of the identities of these two chiefs. Swanton, *Early History*, 398, treats Cowkeeper and Secoffee as the same person; so does Sprague, *Origin*, 18-19. The matter is examined in greater detail in Fairbanks, "Report," 101, 131-32; Porter, "Founder"; and Porter, "Cowkeeper Dynasty."

among the newcomers into West Florida were the Chiahas, who settled primarily in the area which later became Jefferson and Madison Counties. They were an important element in the formation of the Mikasuki group. As noted earlier, the Tamathlis were also absorbed into this group. A town named Mikasuki was recorded for the first time during the British Period, 1763-83. The name has been perpetuated in Lake Miccosukee and a town of the same designation. But the formation of the Mikasukis did more than add a name to the land. This group showed more determination than any other to remain in Florida. If the Mikasukis were not the dominant element among the Florida Indians by 1835, they were far and away the most militant.[11]

In 1767 a band of Upper Creeks from the town of Eufaula on the Chattahoochee River settled northeast of Tampa Bay and established a center, known as Chocachatti, in what is now Hernando County.[12] This marked a new departure and introduced a language complication. There were two major tongues used in the Creek Confederation. All those Creeks who had migrated to Florida prior to 1767 spoke some variation of Hitchiti. In the dim past this language had been in general use from the Chattahoochee River eastward to the Atlantic Ocean, but at the time of the Florida migrations the area had been infiltrated by several groups speaking other dialects. The second major tongue in Florida was Muskogee, which was introduced into the area with the arrival of the Eufaulas in 1767. These two languages were derived from a common root, but were different enough to be mutually unintelligible.[13]

With the passage of years, other Muskogee-speaking Indians formed towns in the general vicinity of Tampa Bay. All appear to have come from the Upper Creeks. But Upper Creeks found other zones to their liking besides the Tampa area. Some of them, called Tallassees, or Tallahassees, entered West Florida and settled in the middle of what had been Apalachee country. Their name, it goes without saying, has been perpetuated in that region.[14]

Around 1778 a fresh wave of migration carried additional Hitchiti- and Muskogee-speaking bands into Florida.[15] These remained loyal to England, with relative safety in loyal Florida, during the American Revolution.

At some point a small band of Yuchis came to West Florida, but after Andrew Jackson invaded that region in 1818, they migrated eastward to the Spring Garden area in what is now Volusia County. Never numerous, they made various associations among the Florida Indians. Although not Muskogean in language, they found intercourse with other bands easy, since they shared the Creek culture and were members of the Creek Confederation.[16]

It is not surprising that diverse bands were attracted to Florida. In that country there were deer in abundance, even bison for awhile, to say nothing of the herds of cattle running wild from abandoned Spanish ranches. In addition to the ample and varied supply of meats, there were a wide variety of vegetables, berries, and fruits. Those Indians who wished to get as far away from the white man as possible could find adequate nourishment there.

The last major movement of Indians into Florida resulted from the Creek War in Alabama Territory, 1813-14. Starting in part as a civil war between Upper and Lower Creeks, it did much to wreck the Creek Confederation. The war faction known as Red Sticks (because red sticks were their symbol of war) came largely from the Upper Creeks. Their fighting at length brought a three-pronged white invasion into the very heart of the Upper Creek country. One prong was made up of Georgia militia; another, commanded by Major General John Cocke, came from East Tennessee; but the decisive column was the Tennessee militia led by Andrew Jackson. This force under Jackson's command crushed the Red Sticks at the Battle of Tohopeka, or Horseshoe Bend, on the Tallapoosa River, on March 27, 1814. Thus Jackson won a commission in the regular army and a national reputation, and started on his way upward toward the presidency. In killing no less than 800 Red Stick warriors, he virtually wiped out the fighting power of the most formidable of all the Indians of the Southeast.* As a result, the Creek Confederation could do nothing but submit to the severe treaty which Jackson imposed on them on August 9, 1814. He forced the Creeks to cede two-thirds of their land, and was not at all concerned that some of the ceded part be-

* Adair, *History*, 358, says that the Creeks were the most warlike of all the tribes.

longed to friendly Creek bands which had sided with him.[17]

Numbers of the Red Sticks, unable to reconcile themselves to the terms of Jackson's treaty, migrated southward into Florida. Mostly Upper Creeks, they cherished a hatred of the Lower Creeks, who had largely aided Jackson and contributed to their ruin. In Florida, nevertheless, the Red Sticks joined bands which had come from Lower Creek towns. But the bitterness between those who had collaborated with Jackson and those who had not did not die away. Moreover, the arrival of no less than 1,000 warriors and their families in the peninsula at least doubled the local Indian population. That population which had been estimated at 25,000 in 1650, but had shrunk to nearly nothing by 1710, now rose to somewhere in the neighborhood of 5,000 Indians residing in from twenty to twenty-five villages. The Red Stick migration also brought with it a boy, later called Osceola, who was to become the most famous figure of the Second Seminole War.[18]

If the Red Stick migration encouraged fragmentation among the Indians in Florida on the one hand, on the other it tended to separate them from the Creek Confederation. The Red Sticks joined other bands who during half a century had been splitting away from the Creek center. As early as 1765 the "Alatchaway" band had refused to attend the treaty talks at Picolata between the British and the other Creeks. Instead they chose to parley with the English later by themselves. Already, in short, there was a measure of differentiation. A special term to designate some of the bands was first used by John Stuart, British Indian Agent, in 1771. He called them "Seminolies," a name meaning "wild people," because they wanted to draw apart and be by themselves. William Bartram used a similar title a few years later. Nevertheless, the Florida Indians remained associated with the Creek Confederation—even though usually remote from its doings—until the second decade of the nineteenth century. But by the end of Andrew Jackson's Florida campaign in 1818, they had made a complete separation.[19]

As first applied to Indians in Florida, the term "Seminoles" designated only the Alachua band and its numerous offshoots. In this narrative, however, the name refers to all Florida Indians after 1810. Considering that sharp differences among

the fragmented bands persisted even into the Second Seminole
War, when the military officers spoke of Seminoles, Tallahassees, and Mikasukis as separate strains, such a grouping may
seem arbitrary. But whether Muskogee- or Hitchiti-speaking,
whether Upper or Lower Creek, whether Apalachicola, Apalachee, Chiaha, Eufaula, Tallahassee, Tamathli, Oconee, or
something else in origin, all but the Yuchi were of the Muskogean family, all shared the Creek culture, and all had earned
the designation of Seminole because they had broken away
from the settled northern towns and migrated southward.

There were two geographical divisions of the original
Creeks: Upper and Lower. The Upper Creeks lived along the
valleys of the Coosa, Tallapoosa, and Alabama rivers. The
Lower Creeks, when first identified by white men, were settled
in what is now central Georgia, but migrated, probably early
in the eighteenth century, to the vicinity of the lower Chattahoochee and the lower Flint rivers. Although there were
marked differences between these divisions, both had the same
culture pattern.[20]

The Yuchis came from a different background and linguistic
group. Whatever they shared of the Creek culture was picked
up through association with other bands within the nation.
But by the end of the eighteenth century they were thoroughly
saturated with Creek culture. The same was true of other
groups who were non-Muskogean, but who had been admitted
to the Confederation because the Creeks recognized that there
was strength in numbers. Of these outsiders only the Yuchis
figure in our history.

What were the dominant characteristics of the Creek culture? Each band in the Confederation lived in a separate town
and governed itself. Every town was built in conformity with
a common pattern developed because of ritualistic needs, leadership, and the clan system. Usually there was almost no
central machinery to draw the several towns together into any
sort of common policy, but, once at least, a dominant personality made of the Confederation a true political unit. Alexander
McGillivray, part-French, part-Scotch, part-Creek, for a decade before his death in 1793 played off the European powers
against the United States in an attempt to strengthen the
Creeks.[21] Soon after he was gone, centrifugal forces whirled

again among the towns. Benjamin Hawkins, the agent of the
United States to the Indians south of the Ohio River, tried to
halt this trend and strengthen the central authority of the
Confederation so that his government would have a responsible counterpart to deal with, but his success was limited.[22]

Authority at the town level was clearer than at the center
of the Confederation. Each town had a chief, or head man,
called a "mico." His power was considerable, yet it was seldom
exercised without consulting the council of principal men. In
many cases all the men of the tribe were present when crucial
decisions were made. Writing at the time of the American
Revolution, James Adair said, in praise of the democracy of the
Creeks, that they breathed nothing but liberty. Half a century
later George Stiggins insisted that their system was really an
oligarchy, and that when the whole tribe assembled, it was not
to participate in making decisions but to hear decisions handed
down.* John R. Swanton, who quoted Stiggins, suggested that
Adair's views were based on observation of the town government, Stiggins' on that of the Confederation. Certainly there
was more democracy in the former than in the latter. In any
case, the proved men of a town chose the chief but confined
their choice to one hereditary strain as long as it produced a
qualified leader.[23] In the numerous cases when several towns
were associated, the chieftanship followed similar hereditary
lines. Thus, relatives of Cowkeeper headed the Alachua band
and its numerous offshoots for more than a century.

The Seminoles continued to elect town chiefs in the manner
of the Creeks. It is not easy, however, to determine what degree of democracy came to them from the Confederation.
There is no doubt that warriors with qualities of leadership
could rise among the Seminoles regardless of their lineage;

---

* James Adair, c. 1709-83, was a highly educated Scot who had come
to America by 1735. From that date to his death he lived among, and
traded with, the Catawbas, Cherokees, Chickasaws, and Choctaws. His
History of the American Indians, published in 1775, is a rich source of
data on the Indians of the Southeast. See *DAB*. George Stiggins was
part Creek, part white. Around 1814 he wrote "A Historical Narration
of Genealogy, Traditions, and Downfall of the Ispocoga or Creek Tribe
of Indians, Writ by One of the Tribe." This manuscript, which was never
published, is in the Wisconsin Historical Society. Swanton relied on it
as a source for some of his knowledge of the Creeks.

but there is little evidence to show whether an oligarchy made the fateful decisions, or whether the rank and file of the warriors did so.

Among both the Creeks and the Seminoles a man was a member of his mother's clan, and home to him was where the women of this clan lived. The chiefs were chosen from a hereditary strain which ran through women. For example, the Cowkeeper was succeeded by "King" Payne, probably his sister's son, who in turn was succeeded by Bowlegs, probably Payne's brother, who gave place to Micanopy, probably the son of Bowlegs' sister.[24]

Aside from a few hereditary ones, most titles were awarded on the basis of prowess in war. Indeed the principal (but not the only) path to distinction in the Creek culture was warlike achievement. Naturally conflict with other tribes was essential to enable men to achieve status in their society. A man retained a "baby name" until he had earned a title through valor. More than that, he was obliged to undergo the humiliation of doing manual labor like a woman until he had proved himself in battle. But when proved in war, he might become the leader of a band and be entitled to the designation "emathla." Or he might by the same avenue be chosen a war leader and be called "tustenuggee." John R. Swanton says that the senior "tastanagi" in each town probably assumed authority in time of war but had no power in peace. The person who chose him, according to Benjamin Hawkins, was the appropriate mico. If the Confederation drew together to make common cause in a fight, superior war chiefs were created to direct the tustenuggees of the several towns. These received the title "tustenuggee thlacko." Among the Creeks, particularly in the eighteenth century, the number of functionaries in war was considerable, but the Seminoles seem to have reduced it. They preserved, however, essential leader positions and the practice of showing rank by painting face and body according to prescribed patterns.[25]

Reckless courage might bring a warrior the name "hadjo"; notably fearless conduct, the title "fixico." These and other earned designations were used, while given names were avoided. More often than not an Indian's title became his name in history. Micanopy, for example, is a title meaning "topmost king." Before being elevated to the post of head chief, he had been known as Sint Chakkee.[26]

The division of Creek and Seminole bands into clans governed nearly all aspects of social organization. It was absolutely forbidden to marry within one's own clan. A newly married man went to live with his wife's family and usually remained there. The father's clan was to be held in honor, and never referred to with disrespect. Although it was not against the mores, a warrior was not supposed to marry a girl of his father's clan. The clans were at the root of the rituals which made up daily life. Moreover, the punishment of most crimes lay within the clan's jurisdiction. When a wrong was done a Creek, his clan revenged it according to the primitive rule "an eye for an eye."[27]

Women benefited from being the transmitters of hereditary privileges. However, they did most of the heavy work and the drudgery, while their men concentrated on hunting and war. Some white observers saw them as ugly, squat, and held virtually in slavery; others saw them as nearly comely and in a better position relative to men than the women of most Indian cultures. The consensus favors the latter view. Personal property connected with housekeeping belonged to the women. It was easy to dissolve a marriage, and the woman kept the household things and the children. During the first month of an infant's life, the mother could kill the child if she chose, and the practice of infanticide was not uncommon when conditions for bringing up a child seemed unfavorable. But after the first thirty days, a mother who killed her child might be treated as a murderer.[28]

Taboos confined women far more than men. It was thought that females might bring sickness to those around them during menstruation and after childbirth, and they were subject at such times to temporary segregation. The basis for this was the belief that people were purified through bloodletting, that women were thus purified by menstruation, and that evil became a free agent, dangerous to be near, when it was being forced out. The punishment of a woman for infraction was severe. In general wives took good care of husbands, for the situation of a widow was gloomy. At the death of her husband a widow was put to bed blindfolded for four days. After that she was obliged to remain in a disheveled condition, and to have nothing to do with men for four years, unless the women of her husband's clan released her earlier.[29]

Sexual relations were not strictly confined to monogamous pairs. Intercourse before marriage was not regarded as evil. If children issued from it, in some cases the mother could destroy them, but in most cases they were accepted and nurtured by her relatives. Adultery, in contrast, was a crime subject to severe punishment, including cropping the nose and ears. This meant, in effect, that married women were confined to one sexual partner. Not so the men; they might take as many wives as they could support, but the first one held an ascendant position. Sexual intercourse, even within lawful bounds, resulted in impurity which was thought dangerous in war. Warriors about to take the field abstained from it. Persons who had copulated were not allowed to visit a sick person within twenty-four hours.[30]

The disciplining of children rested with their mothers and their mothers' brothers. White men recorded that Creek children were usually obedient, even though the whites had seldom seen physical punishment inflicted upon the children; but at least one case is recorded of whipping a boy who had become too effeminate. Aside from this, the severest punishment seems to have been to scratch the dry skin with a sharp object. The same ordeal was used as therapy and in rituals of purification, on the theory that scratching until blood flowed let evil out. The father did not do the disciplinary scratching. If the mother could not do it, one of her brothers or some other of her male relatives was summoned.[31]

As is always the case, the women were pillars of the mores. To begin with, they had much to do with forming the mores, because they molded the character of their sons. Seminole women could undergo fearful hardship in support of what they had helped build.

Seminoles, male and female, like their Creek forebears, habitually suppressed their feelings before outsiders. Mates seldom displayed affection in public. When a warrior had been gone for weeks at the peril of his life, his wife might greet him simply with "You are returned," and busy herself in serving him something to eat. Between parents and children there

was much more demonstration, but still some restraint. On the
other hand, intimate observers contended that in private the
Seminoles were as affectionate as the average of other cultures.[32]

Ritual loomed very large in day-by-day living. Although
modified somewhat, the principal ceremonies of the Seminoles
were Creek. The central one was called in English the "Green
Corn" dance or "busk." It might occur any time from late
April to early July, and might last from four to seven days.
During the ceremony, rituals vital to the continuance of the
Seminole culture went forward. It was not only a source of
great pleasure to the people, but more important it helped to
hold them together as a society. Here were displayed for the
only time during the year the symbolic objects, given by the
Great Spirit, which the Seminoles needed to carry on their
collective life. As new conditions arose, the Great Spirit sent
an emissary with added objects suitable to cope with them.
The total, old and new, were kept together in a "medicine
bundle," the Seminoles' ark of the covenant. This bundle contained all the medicine they needed to protect and preserve
them, if they handled it with proper ritual. The medicine bundle was a Seminole innovation, for the Creeks do not seem to
have had an equivalent.

The Green Corn dance gave cohesion and something more.
One of the days of the ritual was Court Day when the elders
judged the most serious infractions of tribal mores. Moreover,
at this time young men who had earned the right could drop
their baby names and receive more honorable ones. Finally, the
dance was a time of general cleansing. All males, from toddlers
to the oldest men, were ceremoniously scratched for purification.[33]

War ceremonies and customs were basically Creek. Individual leaders usually made the decision to open a conflict. If they
could not secure some sort of endorsement from the mico and
council, they had the right to set out to recruit followers without it. But the decision for war by a warrior was not ordinarily
lightly made; an unsuccessful leader, or one who brought about
heavy losses among his followers, was in danger of his life
from his own people. There was no organization which obliged
warriors to join a particular war party, but the status of a

man usually depended upon his performance in conflict. If he did not join one party, he would sooner or later have to take part in others. There was, accordingly, no problem in securing warriors and no loss from desertion. Even so, the decision to go to war was rarely unanimous within a band, and never unanimous within the Confederation.[34]

Once a leader had secured followers in a war party, tradition required that the party carry out certain rituals. Every man set out to purify himself, that is, to suppress the wants of the flesh and to eliminate the traces of those already gratified. He took part with the others in the ceremony of the black drink, a strong emetic which thoroughly cleansed the digestive tract. Sitting in a circle, the warriors received the potion from a medicine man and drank it in heavy draughts. Thereafter, from time to time, each warrior, hugging himself around the middle, belched out a spout to a distance of six to eight feet. After this ceremony, the party fasted and did not cohabit with their women. Purity, being synonymous with abstemiousness, was essential to victory. Even while on the expedition which followed, the warriors ate little, rested hardly at all, and otherwise deprived themselves. Vestiges of this association still persisted at the start of the Second Seminole War, but under the necessities of that conflict, which went far beyond typical Indian warfare, they faded out. Soon after the hostilities began, war parties ate and drank whenever they could; indeed, they drank themselves into a stupor when they could procure the liquor.[35]

Inseparable from ritual were religion and medicine, two branches from the same stem, both practiced by medicine men who were believed to be in communication with supernatural forces. As in most primitive societies, medicine men were important people. The principal medicine man in a community could use the title "hillis haya." He and others in the practice were expected to invoke the ubiquitous spirits. The Creeks and Seminoles frequently felt the presence of the spirits of their ancestors, and believed that those spirits would protect them. This belief was one pressing reason why they did not want to leave their native ground; their ancestors would remain behind. Visions were the stock in trade of the medicine men, but lay Indians sometimes had them too.[36]

A medicine man chanted, invoked, danced, and gesticulated to call the supernatural elements to aid a sick patient. In addition, he had at his command many useful drugs derived from the vegetable life around him. Indian cures for snakebite were so effective that few deaths from this cause are known among the Seminoles, although portions of arms and legs were often lost. Like the chiefs and the head men, the medicine men could display their specialties in symbols. A buzzard feather distinguished the doctor who could handle gunshot wounds, while a line from the corner of the mouth to the side of the torso indicated a general practitioner. The medicine men engaged in bloodletting; they were skillful in the use of splints, but never amputated. Whatever the level of their skill, they, like the head men, were held accountable. If a doctor failed to save his patient, he might be in danger from the members of the bereaved clan. But generally the lot of the medicine men as therapists was made easy because the Seminoles, at least according to William Bartram, were more free of ailments than whites.[37]

Creeks and Seminoles were inveterate game players and gamblers. Stick ball, the most significant of their games, was similar to modern lacrosse; it was violent and frequently bloody. When played by men only, it was regarded as a means of releasing tension between villages of the Confederacy. Thus it was a substitute for war. A version in which women and girls joined during the Green Corn dance had ritualistic significance. It played a minor role in courtship and marriage.[38]

Creeks and Seminoles were primarily farmers. It is true they lived in towns, but their sustenance came from the fields beyond, from pastures, and from the forests. Even though their agricultural tools were primitive, they were able to produce a wide variety of foods. In time they switched completely to iron axes and hoes bought from white traders. They owned horses that were descended from the original Spanish stock, but they developed no tools for farming which could be drawn by horses, and had not the advantage of horse power in their agriculture. Neither was their only other domestic creature, the dog, of use in farming. The dog was a fixture in the culture, for it was descended from strains which had followed the forebears of the Indian out of Asia thousands of years earlier.[39]

The Seminoles and Creeks were hunters as well as farmers. Their environment afforded them a wide variety of game, but deer were so numerous as to become the principal, even the commercial, source of meat and hides. For deer hunting the Indians had a far more efficient tool than any they used in agriculture. Using the white man's musket, they gradually reduced the deer herds. This destruction made it necessary for them to turn to a substitute after 1750, and they shifted more and more to cattle raising. To do so they had only to draw upon the herds of cattle which had been abandoned by Spanish rancheros and were running wild. In time they brought vast numbers of cattle under their control. It is important to note that these were not communally owned; individuals built up their own herds. In fact, the accumulation of cattle was an alternative to war honors in earning distinction within the culture.

What with game, fish, berries, fruits, coontie, cabbage palms, hickory nuts, acorns, and honey from the forest, combined with corn, beans, pumpkins, and beef from their own fields and pastures, the Seminoles enjoyed a richer diet than did most North American Indians. Nor were clothing and shelter difficult to acquire. Their clothes were usually made from cloth bought from white traders, supplemented by skins from the hunt. Their shelter could be easily drawn from the forest, especially after metal axes became available.

Their economy was a mixture of private and communal ownership. Cattle were owned by individuals, so were slaves; but no individual could possess land, for it belonged to the group. Men, women, and children worked the earth in common, yet the fruits of the land and labor were not as a rule communally held. Clans or families took them for private use, but left a portion to be put into a common store.[40]

Their mixed system produced wide distinctions in wealth and in social position. Bowlegs, Payne's successor, sold as many as 1,000 head of cattle a year from his own herds. Yet the habit of personal accumulation was probably a consequence of contact with the white men. Traditionally, wealth could not be transmitted to heirs. That which the deceased would need in the next world was put into the grave with him; the surplus was destroyed. As late as 1823 Horatio Dexter, an astute ob-

server, reported the continuation of this practice. He himself
had just looked upon the ruins of plantation houses and or-
chards, as fine as those of white men, lately the property of a
chief called Oponney, which had been destroyed in conformity
with the old custom. By this time the practice was an anach-
ronism. The break with the past probably began in the late
eighteenth century, partly as a result of the influence of Benjamin Hawkins, United States agent to the Creeks. He had
sought to break down the communal ways of the red natives,
and had been instrumental in opening up a sharp cleavage
among the Creeks. Some of them held to the old communal
ways, others adopted the capitalistic outlook of the white people. The Creek War had been to some extent a by-product of
this cleavage. Bit by bit the new ways triumphed over the old,
but never completely eliminated them.[41]

2

The First Seminole War

THROUGHOUT the eighteenth century various bands of migrating Indians established themselves in Florida and grew
attached to the land. Spain was nominally in control of the
peninsula during all but two decades of the century, but her
forces were too weak to interfere effectively with the red occupants. She confined herself to a few sparse settlements on
the coast. Some of the Florida Indians were hostile to Spain.
Cowkeeper, it is said, cherished the ambition to kill a hundred
Spaniards, and at his death he enjoined his successor to finish
off the fourteen he had fallen short.[1]

During the English Period in Florida (1763-83) the Indians
attained a high point in comfort and security. William Bartram, traveling in the 1770's, thought them a very gay people,
perfectly adjusted to their environment, and far more secure
than most societies. They were for the most part pro-British
during the American Revolution, but had few occasions, being
far removed from the rebels, to encounter the Americans as
enemies. Moreover, they existed upon the very fringes of
Alexander McGillivray's machinations, for the most part aloof
from the Creek Confederation. Thus, at the end of the eighteenth century, having found their way into a peninsula somewhat remote from interferers, where food was abundant and
the climate congenial, the Seminoles appeared to be on the
threshold of barbaric prosperity.[2]

But the American Revolution had already spawned a new political entity which was to be their nemesis. The citizens of that new polity, it developed, could not coexist peaceably with Indians on the Southern Border—or, for that matter, in any quarter. And then the eruption of another adventurer into the complicated web of affairs in Florida produced a confusion close to anarchy. During the late 1780's and into the 1790's, William Augustus Bowles of Maryland, a white man, undertook to establish himself as head of the Seminoles, including some Lower Creeks. He set out to found a new nation populated by Muskogeans, and he called it Muskogee. This policy thwarted McGillivray, and the new United States too, especially since Bowles maintained a close association with Great Britain. Styling himself Director General of the state of Muskogee, he persuaded some bands of Mikasukis to join him in forays. His fate, however, was not to be the founder of a nation, but to die in 1805 in a Spanish prison. Although he failed, his activities left repercussions. For one thing, they brought about a general movement of Lower Creeks to the St. Marks area of Florida. For another, they embittered relations between the Florida Indians and the American settlers on the Georgia and Alabama borders. Bowles' attempt at empire building thus prepared the way for Seminole decline.[3]

The turning point for the Seminoles came during the first two decades of the nineteenth century. Americans in the southern states coveted Spanish Florida. They felt that Florida belonged to the United States as a foot belongs to a leg. Moreover, the Spanish government was responsible for the Indians but lacked the power to control them. Since the United States government could not, or did not, restrain its settlers along the Florida border, there were numerous clashes between American whites and the Indians living in Spanish territory. Some of these clashes sprang from cattle raids which occurred steadily on both sides. Others stemmed from slavery.[4]

Beginning in the 1730's, the Spaniards had given refuge to runaway slaves from the Carolinas, but as late as 1774 Negroes do not appear to have been living among the Florida Indians. After that date enclaves of free Negroes began to arrive, mostly composed of runaways from American plantations. Around the Negro Fort on the Apalachicola River, for

example, there grew up a community of several hundred.
Sometimes they were on good terms with the Indians, sometimes not.[5] Other Negroes entered the Indian community as
slaves, but they served in a benign sort of bondage. The obligation to their masters was ended when the slaves had delivered to them each year about one-third of their crop. They
lived in villages separate from the Indians, but otherwise followed the Creek culture pattern. There was almost no mis-
cegenation between the two races.[6] When it came to fighting,
the Negroes, both slave and free, were armed, capable, and
willing, and they proved to be fiercer warriors against white
men than the Indians themselves. More significant in Indian-
white relations than their fighting ability was the Negroes'
knowledge of the languages on both sides. Through this knowledge they achieved an importance as interpreters and intelligence agents which cannot be overemphasized.

Whether slave or free, the Negroes among the Seminoles
constituted a threat to the institution of slavery north of the
Spanish border. The settlers in Georgia and in Mississippi
Territory knew this and constantly accused the Indians of
stealing their Negroes. The accusation was frequently reversed; the natives charged the American border dwellers
with raiding their region and forcibly taking their slaves. The
frictions thus generated along the Florida border heightened
those typical of race relations on all the borders of the United
States. To the Georgians and Mississippians, as to the majority of frontiersmen, the only good Indian was a dead one.[7]

The friction over slaves was triangular. The Florida Indians
and the whites made up two sides, the Creek Confederation
the third. In the Treaty of Colerain, 1796, some Creek chiefs
agreed to surrender all runaway slaves among them, and in
"among them" they included the Florida branch. Once having
unilaterally made themselves responsible for Negroes held by
the Florida Indians, the Creeks insisted that title to all slaves
owned in the Confederation rested with them. The southern
branch denied so preposterous a claim, and the dispute which
resulted helped make the Creeks willing to side with the Americans against their southern kin.[8] Border incidents occurred
and recurred. In retrospect it may be said that these incidents
formed a declining path, and down this the Seminoles went

unknowingly. Beginning in 1811, Georgians commenced an almost systematic attempt to take Florida from Spain. Much of
the time they thought they had the support of the United
States government, but the support was usually not open.
Finally, on the verge of conflict with England, President James
Madison drew back lest his government have to fight two foes
instead of one. In spite of this, the Georgians, with the aid of
a regiment of Tennessee volunteers, went ahead.[9]

Rubbed raw by the unending brutal border incidents, the
Indians allowed Spanish Governor Kindelán to induce them to
attack the Georgians. They commenced to do so late in July,
1812, with a measure of success.[10] In retaliation, Colonel Daniel Newnan led a body of Georgia militia a hundred miles
into Spanish territory to try to destroy the nucleus of Indian
power. In a running fight lasting from September 27 to October 11, 1812, the Seminoles pressed Newnan's force so hard
that it barely escaped annihilation. But the price for this early
success was high; their able chief, King Payne, worn out by
the struggle, soon died. Moreover, the Indian victory hardened
the determination of the border dwellers to wipe out the red
men, once and for all. In the matter of help, most of the Creeks
disavowed the Seminoles, but the Indian-Negroes fought beside them with unparalleled ferocity.[11]

After Newnan's retreat there was a lull, but active combat
resumed when a body of 250 mounted Tennessee volunteers,
commanded by Colonel John Williams, reached the border,
eager to fight Indians. Together with a detachment of United
States regulars, the Tennessee soldiers plunged into northern
Florida. In a three-week campaign, beginning February 7,
1813, the men of this force burned 386 Indian houses, destroyed 1,500 to 2,000 bushels of corn, and drove off several
hundred head of horses and cattle. As a result, the Seminoles
of north-central Florida faced starvation.[12] More than that,
their strength east of the Suwannee River was for all practical purposes broken. Obviously, their Spanish association, even
if only temporary, had speeded their ruin.

Border incidents continued, but there were no more military
expeditions like Newnan's and Williams' on either side. The
center of Indian conflict shifted westward to the Alabama
country. There, during the latter half of 1813 and the first half

of 1814, occurred the Creek War. It was as much a civil war among Creeks as between red and white, and it pointed up the separation of Creeks and Seminoles. The Seminoles gave the Creeks no aid, in retaliation for the failure of the Creeks to aid them against Daniel Newnan and John Williams.[13]

Andrew Jackson wrecked the fighting power of the Creeks, and on August 9, 1814, he exacted more than 20,000,000 acres from them. Although the Seminoles lost no territory, they too suffered, because defeat of the powerful Creek Confederation gave Southerners confidence that they could overrun any Indians standing in their path. Moreover, the implacable hatred of the whites which the Red Sticks carried into Florida helped to invite eventual doom upon all the Indians there. It is true that 1,000 Red Stick warriors migrated to Florida with their families, but the power they added did not offset, in the long run, what was lost.

During the War of 1812, the British regarded the Indians of the Gulf coast as important potential allies. In May, 1814, the admiral commanding the British North American station sent Brevet Captain George Woodbine ashore with 2 non-commissioned officers to aid and train the natives in the vicinity of the Apalachicola River. Three months later, Edward Nicolls, with local rank of lieutenant colonel of His Majesty's Marines, took 3 officers, a surgeon, 4 non-commissioned officers, and 97 enlisted men into the same area, and assumed command. Nicolls claimed that he rallied around him large numbers of Indians, but the Seminoles do not seem to have become involved in very much actual combat against the United States. There were, it is true, a few Mikasukis fighting on the British side at New Orleans from December 23, 1814, to January 8, 1815.[14]

One of Edward Nicolls' acts was to build a fort at Prospect Bluff, fifteen miles above the mouth of the Apalachicola and sixty miles below United States territory, and equip it with cannon, small arms, and large stores of ammunition. When Nicolls departed from American soil several months after the war ended, the fort was left intact for the use of the Indians. Instead, it came into the possession of a band of free renegade Negroes. By 1816 it was an effective stronghold, called the Negro Fort by the border folk.

This earthen fortress, sixty miles within Spanish territory, would not appear to be of importance. But in the spring of 1816, at the direction of Major General Andrew Jackson, United States Army commander for the southern district, Brigadier General Edmund Pendleton Gaines built a fort in Georgia upon the west bank of the Flint River, a few miles from the Spanish boundary. Called Fort Scott, it was to help guard the border.[15]

Supply for the new fort was a serious problem because it had to come overland through utter wilderness. How much simpler if it could be shipped up the Apalachicola River. Almost certainly the Negroes at the lower fort would resist the passage of supplies, and there would then arise an excuse to wipe out their stronghold, which was to the Americans a center of hostility and above all a threat to the security of their slaves. That this course meant violating Spanish territory did not perturb Jackson, who had done as much during the War of 1812. Accordingly, he ordered a supply vessel with a naval escort to move up the river in the summer of 1816. As anticipated, it was fired on, and some of its men were hit. Forthwith an order went to Gaines to wipe out the fort. He was able to carry out the directive with a minimum of expenditure when a hot cannon ball landed by chance in the powder magazine on July 27, 1816, and blew the whole installation to pieces, inflicting heavy casualties.[16*]

The American ground force accompanying the expedition against the Negro Fort was commanded by Lieutenant Colonel Duncan L. Clinch. Clinch had with him a body of Lower Creeks from Coweta to whom he had promised the loot of the fort for their help in its capture. They salvaged 2,500 muskets, 50 carbines, 400 pistols, and 500 swords from the ruins. Thus the Creeks gained power in weapons far beyond any they had enjoyed before. By the same token, the Seminoles were weakened in relation to them. What weakened the Seminoles even more, however, was the loss of 300 of their Negro allies, blown to bits with the fort. Acutely aware of the Creek participation against them, the Seminoles grew ever more bitter. Spain, of

---

* Giddings, *Exiles*, 38*n*, calls this the first slave-catching expedition in which the United States government ever engaged.

course, protested the violation of her soil, but lacked the power to do more.

A year passed, filled with still more border incidents. The Mikasukis across the Flint River from Fort Scott were angered by the destruction of the Negro Fort and by other aggravations. The chief of their village of Fowltown, not far from Fort Scott, in conjunction with other chiefs, warned General Gaines that if the Americans tried to cross the Flint they would be annihilated. The author of this threat was a remarkable chief named Neamathla. Not all the Mikasuki towns supported Neamathla's firm position, but at least part of the Alachua band did. The Alachuas, led by Bowlegs, had expanded to the banks of the Suwannee.* Virtually neighbors with the Mikasukis of Fowltown, they entered into a sort of semi-alliance with them. One contemporary even stated that Bowlegs had been made chief of all the hostiles and was accorded the deference due a king. Exact information concerning Indian leadership and alliances is nearly impossible, however, to come by.[17]

General Gaines bridled at what he regarded as sheer impertinence on Neamathla's part. Although it was said that 2,000 warriors were arrayed against him, he confidently sent 250 men under Major David E. Twiggs to arrest Neamathla and bring in the important men of his band. This could be done without violating Spanish territory, since Fowltown was on United States soil. There followed a gun fight near the village on November 21, 1817, the opening fusillade of the First Seminole War. Later the Indians struck back by attacking a party of forty under Lieutenant R. W. Scott coming up the Apalachicola River to Fort Scott. They wiped out all but six of them, and killed seven soldiers' wives.[18]

Jackson and Gaines now urged that a punitive expedition enter Florida to clean up the centers whence radiated border anarchy. The Madison administration, however, constantly involved with Spain in negotiations, did not think such action

* This Bowlegs was head chief of the Alachua branch of the Seminoles. He was the brother of Payne and probably the uncle of the Billy Bowlegs who rose to prominence in 1839 and after. See Kenneth W. Porter, "Billy Bowlegs (Holata Micco) in the Seminole Wars," *FHQ*, XLV (January, 1967), 219-42.

advisable. But as soon as knowledge of the annihilation of Lieutenant Scott's detachment reached Washington, the attitude there changed. Contradictory directives were issued from the War Department. On December 2, 1817, Gaines was told it was not politic to enter Spanish territory just to chastise the Seminoles. A week later he was allowed to do so or not at his discretion. Then, on the sixteenth, came permission to cross the line and carry retribution to the savages, with only one qualification: not to attack them should they take refuge beside a Spanish fortress. Finally, the War Department loosed its most lethal weapon. The day after Christmas the Secretary wrote the order directing Andrew Jackson to take command in person and bring the Seminoles under control.[19]

Even before Jackson arrived, the commanders at Fort Scott pushed the campaign forward. By this time it was reported that Capechimico, a Mikasuki chief, was directing the hostiles. If the report was true, it shows that the association of the Indians, whatever its nature, was dynamic. Bowlegs, of the Alachua band, had been in command only a few months earlier, whereas now the headship had shifted to a Mikasuki. Indifferent to the Indian leadership, the whites advanced to attack Fowltown on January 4, 1818, found it deserted, and burned it.[20]

Andrew Jackson received his orders on January 11. Two months later, less two days, he arrived at Fort Scott. Soon thereafter he began to move down the Apalachicola River with a force of 3,500, of which 2,000 were Creek warriors, now actively aligned against their southern kinsmen. Five hundred of the white troops were regulars, and the others, being militia, were mostly from Tennessee. Jackson's force overcame the Indian opposition rather easily, and soon destroyed the Mikasuki towns. The Seminoles had run short of arms and ammunition and were obliged to revert to bow and arrow. Probably the stiffest fight of the campaign was made by a band of two or three hundred Negroes who stayed west of the Suwannee River to delay the army's advance until the noncombatants could escape from Bowlegs' town. With muskets against rifles and one man against four, the Negroes fought a creditable rear-guard action. Thus, when Jackson reached the village, the principal center of the non-Mikasuki hostiles, he found it deserted. He gave the order to destroy it and to carry away all valuables.[21]

Once again, as in the campaigns of 1812 and 1813, the Indians of the central Florida area had borne the principal shock. But this time, unlike the earlier invasion, the Mikasukis, now in some manner of alliance or association with them, had borne it too. Just as the forays of 1812 and 1813 had broken Seminole power east of the Suwannee, this invasion wrecked it west of that river. The two campaigns so weakened the power of the Seminoles that they were not an effective obstacle when the United States procured Florida and began to occupy the territory.

Lest the advances into foreign territory seem like naked aggression, the United States government took care to drape its activity in rectitude. President James Monroe told Congress that the hostility of the Seminoles, altogether unprovoked, stemmed from long-standing antagonism to the United States. As for Spain, American invasion of the Floridas was justified on the ground of self-defense. General Jackson stated the case perfectly in his letter to the Spanish commander at St. Marks, dated April 6, 1818, demanding that he surrender the fort. "To chastise a savage foe, who, combined with a lawless band of Negro brigands, have for some time past been carrying on a cruel and unprovoked war against the citizens of the United States, has compelled the President to direct me to march my army into Florida."[22]

The American rationale put all parties but the United States and her border dwellers in the wrong. Hostilities by the Indians were wholly unprovoked. Yet even from the United States viewpoint the Seminoles were not solely at fault. Jackson's adjutant implicated another wrongdoer in an official report dated April 1, 1818. He described the destruction wrought by the army, "leaving a tract of fertile country in ruin, where these wretches [the Seminoles] might have lived in plenty, but for the infernal machinations of foreign traders, if not agents." Who were these traders, if not agents? Evidence of British collusion was plain in the towns overrun and burned. In Kenhadjo's town—one of the Mikasuki centers—letters implicating Englishmen were found, and even a British officer's uniform for the chief. What made this interference seem in-

excusable to Americans was the string of fifty fresh scalps in
the same village, many of them recognizable as having been
cut from particular Americans. It was unfortunate for all concerned that two British citizens, Alexander Arbuthnot and
Robert Ambrister, acknowledged Indian sympathizers, were
captured at this time. The appeals and descriptions they sent
to British officials throw some doubt on the official American
position that the cause of the trouble rested solely with the
Indians and their European abettors. It was not in Andrew
Jackson's nature to allow this sort of deviation from the viewpoint he had adopted; after a drumhead trial he caused both
men to be executed on April 29, 1818. This arbitrary action
produced vocal indignation in England, and caused Jackson
intermittent trouble ever afterward.[23]

Since destruction of the Indian centers west of the Suwannee proved easy and quick, Jackson became free by late April,
1818, to direct his force toward what in his eyes had always
been the main business of the expedition: to take Florida away
from Spain. The general believed that he had the tacit agreement of the Administration in this conquest. By May 28, a
little short of five months after his orders had reached him at
Nashville, he had taken St. Marks and Pensacola. Directing
General Gaines to capture St. Augustine, the last Spanish
stronghold in Florida, he began on May 30 his return to Tennessee. "I will assure you Cuba will be ours in a few days,"
he informed the Secretary of War.[24]

His rate of conquest was too swift for Monroe's administration. Within the President's cabinet a controversy raged over
whether or not the general should be punished for his arbitrary incursions at a time when negotiations with Spain were
in a delicate stage. Committees of the Senate and the House
offered resolutions—which failed—to censure him for his aggression, while minority members wrote opinions in his defense. The altercation was still vigorous when in January,
1819, Jackson himself turned up in the capital to defend his
reputation by forensics, influence, or dueling pistols if need be.
Even though President Monroe decided in August of 1818 to
give Jackson's conquests back to Spain, in the end they led
to the transfer of the territory to the United States. This in
turn brought about the eventual fall of the Seminoles.[25]

The invasion of 1818 initiated new migrations on the part of the Seminoles in its path. The Red Stick Creeks dropped down to the area of Tampa Bay, while the Alachua Indians moved south about 120 miles, where their principal town became Okihumpky in what is now Lake County. The Mikasukis, who had stood much of the shock, gave ground first into the area which had been occupied by the Alachuas and then moved northwest again to the vicinity of modern Greenville in Madison County.[26]

All the while that there was military activity in western Florida, the rest of the peninsula was relatively free of hostilities. The various bands of Seminoles were by no means unified against Jackson's army. On the Atlantic coast the Indians continued to come into St. Augustine to trade as if no conflict were in progress. One observer gave his impressions of them: wretched in general appearance, straight black hair reeking with bear grease, skin a dirty chocolate color, nose and ears pierced with rings of silver and brass. He was sure that they held white people in contempt and Negroes even lower, so low, in fact, that they were not even interested in Negro scalps. Unfortunately, their penchant for hard liquor was active, but not out of all reason. In town the men got drunk the first day, but on the second the women had their turn. In this way someone was always in possession of his faculties.[27]

3

Moultrie Creek

THE FOES OF Andrew Jackson and of his conquest of Florida fought a losing fight. Henry Clay tried by temporarily leaving his chair as Speaker of the House of Representatives to block Jackson, but all he achieved was the eternal enmity of the man. In the end, there was no official censure of the campaigns of 1817 and 1818.[1] In the end, too, Spain saw that she must dispose of the Floridas for some advantage before they slipped away from her without any consideration whatever. Accordingly, a treaty of cession was arranged in 1819. But because obstacles were many and tempers sensitive, it was not until two years later, February 22, 1821, that ratifications were exchanged. Article VI of the ratified treaty ran as follows: "The inhabitants of the territories which his Catholic Majesty cedes to the United States shall be incorporated in the Union of the United States, as soon as may be consistent with the principles of the Federal Constitution, and admitted to the enjoyment of all privileges, rights, and immunities of the citizens of the United States."[2] Literally interpreted, the clause seemed to mean that Negroes and Indians as well as white men would be admitted to the "privileges, rights and immunities of the citizens of the United States." In reality, however, the clause appears to have been a sop to the conscience of his Catholic Majesty, for there was little likelihood that members of either of the dark races would be speedily admitted to United States citizenship.

President Monroe looked for a man to govern the new acquisition. His eye fell upon the top command of the army, where there were two major generals, Andrew Jackson and Jacob Brown. Congress was known to be about to cut the service sharply, and when it did so, one general would have to go. Of the two, Jackson was the more troublesome, but he also enjoyed the larger popular following. It would be unwise to remove him without providing another position suitable to his prestige. The governorship of the new territory seemed ideal, especially since Jackson more than any other individual had been responsible for putting Spain in the mood to cede, and his appointment would vindicate his invasions of three years earlier, and so mollify him on a very sensitive point. At first Jackson declined the offer, but then yielded and received the commission on March 10, 1821. Thus began another stormy episode in the career of the border captain—stormy but short, for he did not assume authority in Florida until July, 1821, and left the territory early in October, never to return.[3]

Meanwhile the situation of the Seminole Indians remained gloomy. Their conflicts with the Americans, from 1811 to 1818, had already wrecked the abundant society Bartram had described. Whereas they had once been proud, numerous, and wealthy, possessing great numbers of cattle, horses, and slaves, Captain John R. Bell said in 1822, "they are now weak and poor, yet their native spirit is not so much broken as to humble them to the dust."* The following year Joseph M. Hernandez, a Spanish Floridian and a person of consequence in the peninsula, put it this way, "being thus broken up [they] have continued ever since, without the least Kind of Spirit of industry or enterprize,—they could at one time have been considered as having arrived at the first Stage Civilization." But it remained for one of their own to set their downfall in deeply touching

---

*John R. Bell went through the Military Academy and was commissioned a second lieutenant on January 3, 1812. Soon the War of 1812 broke out and he rose rapidly in rank. By 1814 he was colonel and inspector general. But in the drastic reduction of the army in 1821 he was cut back to captain in the artillery. This was his grade when he appeared in Florida soon after its transfer from Spain to the United States. He was brevetted major on October 10, 1824, but did not live much longer. He died on April 11, 1825. See Cullum, *Biographical Register*.

words. Chief Sitarky said, "When I walk about these woods,
now so desolate, and remember the numerous herds that once
ranged through them, and the former prosperity of our nation,
the tears come into my eyes."[4]

The territory was transferred from Spain to the United
States, but the Seminoles, who considered it theirs, had no
part in the negotiations. They went with the land, and as far
as the United States was concerned they were a nuisance upon
it. Rumors, not news, reached them. Recognizing that their
fighting power had deteriorated badly, the chiefs were gnawed
by uncertainty. White speculators, hoping to frighten them
away, whispered that Andrew Jackson was coming back with
a large army expressly to wipe them out. Some of the Indians,
believing this, sold their goods and cattle at disaster prices
and plunged into the interior of Florida.[5]

Since Jackson's recent campaign, the Indians had virtually
become wanderers. For the most part they did not put in crops
in the year of the transfer, for fear they would not be able to
harvest them. Hunger and misery overtook them. The warriors even went to work for white men—a desperate loss of
status for Indians—and, it is reported, showed skill in their
work. All the while it seemed that their population was declining; some observers reported that Indians were actually dis-
appearing from East Florida. In fact there were between 4,500
and 5,000 Indians in all of Florida.[6]

The appointment of their old conqueror was bad news for
the Seminoles. Could they have seen his correspondence, it
would have seemed worse. Jackson told John Quincy Adams,
Secretary of State, that in 1818 he had ordered many of the
Red Stick Creeks to go back north whence they had come.
"These Indians," he wrote, "can have no claim to lands in Florida, humanity and justice is sufficiently extended to them by . . .
permission to return, and live in peace with their own nation."
Either he did not realize the deep hatred existing between the
Florida migrants and the Creeks who had not moved, or he
did not care. If it was impossible to send the Seminoles back
among the Creeks, he wanted to see them concentrated along
the Apalachicola River near the boundaries of Georgia and
Alabama. There they could be sealed away from the coast and
from the trade with Cuba, and could be contained between

white settlements. There they could not break communications between St. Augustine and Pensacola.[7]

While the Seminoles waited apprehensively for more trouble, Congress, on March 2, 1821, cut the size of the army. The only rifle regiment was disbanded, as were the Eighth Infantry and the equivalent of one artillery regiment. The surviving companies of infantry were reduced in size from seventy-eight to fifty-one enlisted men. From the officer corps one major general, two brigadiers, and forty-four ordnance officers were cast out of the service without provision for their welfare. Some of them found situations. Andrew Jackson, for example, passed from the payroll of the army to that of the Territory of Florida (both, of course, were financed by the United States), and, as will be seen, several other displaced officers took the same path.[8]

If the government did nothing to ease the anxieties of the Seminoles, it was not because the men of the Administration had forgotten them. Even before Florida had officially changed hands, a subagent to the Florida Indians arrived on the ground. This was Jean A. Pénières, a Frenchman whose commission was dated March 31, 1821. He was appointed without the approval of Governor Jackson, who never met him then or later. The selection is hard to account for except that some persons in Washington believed Pénières to have had more practical experience with Indians than had other applicants. People closer to the situation thought otherwise.[9]

Until Jackson could reach his new post, he designated Captain John R. Bell to act for him in East Florida. Because by law the governor of a territory was also acting superintendent of Indian affairs, Bell filled that position, too. But the government failed to explain to him about Pénières. As a result he wrote, "I am informed that a French gentleman has been on the St. Johns River styling himself an authorized agent of the United States to explore the country and to hold talks with the Indians, him I shall take measures thro the Alcalde to have brought before me." Eighteen days later Secretary of War John C. Calhoun got around to posting a letter which straightened Bell out concerning Pénières. But even yet the acting superintendent saw little value in the subagent. To begin with, the Frenchman could not speak English, Muskogee, or Hit-

chiti. He had to have two interpreters instead of one to do
any business at all. Second, said Bell, he was unacquainted
with the Indian character; and, third, he did not understand
the liberal Indian policy followed by the United States. Certainly Pénières' selection did not stem from any predilection
on his part for the Seminoles, whom he described as dirtier
and lazier than other savages he had known.[10]

Even before an American government was formed for Florida, at least one speculator was gambling on the future United
States Florida. His enterprise rested on actions taken by the
Spanish before they transferred the territory. When his Catholic Majesty first began to see that his territory was slipping
away, he made grants of vast areas of land to certain gran-
dees, hoping that they could somehow prove their titles under
the American rule. One grant of 289,000 acres (lying in what
is now Alachua County) was to Ferdinando de la Maza Arredondo. It was from his assigns that Moses Levy, who had
made a fortune on the island of St. Thomas, bought a tract.
It lay squarely in the heart of the domain of the Alachua band
of Seminoles. The Alachuas acquiesced in Levy's plan to establish an inland settlement, provided that he would maintain
there a trading post for their use. This suited Levy, who forthwith enlisted two Floridians to found his colony. These two
were Edward M. Wanton and Horatio S. Dexter, both known
to, and popular with, the Alachua Indians. Accordingly, they
began in November, 1820, to establish a settlement, which they
named Micanopy for the head chief of the Alachua bands.
Thus was established the first town by white men in peninsular Florida not located near waterways. It lay in the center
of some of the finest limestone land in Florida.[11]

Meanwhile the suspense as to their status within the United
States was unbearable to the Seminoles. Several times some
chiefs went to St. Augustine to make inquiry, but they could
learn little. Micanopy arranged with the two trusted white
men, Dexter and Wanton, to negotiate a treaty for his people.
This was close to July 17, 1821, the date when Governor Jackson arrived and took formal possession of Pensacola. One of
Jackson's first acts was to issue orders to seize these "self
made" Indian agents; for, said Jackson, no white man had a
right to negotiate with the savages except an authorized agent

of the government. No harm came to Dexter and Wanton, but neither did any treaty result, for the governor refused to deal with them and stated his intention to be nevermore involved in a treaty with Indians. Inasmuch as Congress had both the authority and the power to handle Indian affairs, he said, there was no sense in treating the tribes as nations.[12]

On September 28, 1821, Secretary Calhoun appointed Captain Bell acting agent to the Seminoles. With Jackson superintendent, Bell acting agent, and Pénières subagent, the organization for handling the Indians was complete. With this full table of organization on the white side, it appeared likely that the Indians would soon know where they stood. Fate did not so dispose. On October 6 Andrew Jackson went off to the Hermitage, never to return to Florida. At about the same time Pénières died of yellow fever. Only a few weeks later Captain Bell was charged with conduct unbecoming an officer and was suspended from his duties. The organization was thus shattered, and the Indians were left still wondering.[13]

The government in Washington and the white leaders in the peninsula continued to ponder the problem of the Seminoles. They considered two possibilities: to concentrate the Indians somewhere in Florida, or to remove them altogether. Calhoun defined these alternatives as early as March, 1821. Most white men preferred to eliminate them from the peninsula, and the simplest way to do this, at least on the surface, was to send them off to rejoin the Creeks in Georgia and Alabama. This solution did not reckon with the will of the Seminoles. William Worthington, acting governor of East Florida, gave his estimate of their attitude, "It is said they never will consent to go up among the Creeks—They will assume no hostile attitude, against the United States, no matter, what Course they may adopt respecting them—But if they are ordered up amongst the Creeks, they will take to the bushes." Respecting the other alternative, Worthington said he thought they would willingly concentrate in Florida.[14]

Florida, being surrounded on three sides by water, was highly vulnerable to foreign attack, especially with the Indians in it. Yet late in 1821 the Secretary of War let it be known that the Administration would not try to force the natives out unless Congress authorized and paid for such action.[15]

While this debate went on, the white personnel for Indians affairs continued to alter. When Jackson departed, his duties were divided between two acting governors, William Worthington for East Florida and George Walton for West Florida. The Indian superintendency, so far as anybody knew, was split between them. The next change was the appointment on October 29, 1821, of Peter Pelham, a "riffed" officer,* to replace the late Pénières as subagent. Then on April 17, 1822, a commission was issued to William Pope DuVal, a judge in East Florida, to be governor of the Territory of Florida. Finally, three weeks later, Major Gad Humphreys of New York was appointed Indian Agent. He had served thirteen years in the army before being cast out by the reduction of 1821, and he was badly in need of a regular salary. Captain Bell—who had been cleared of the charges of misconduct—was assured that Humphreys had been chosen instead of him on the basis of need, not of ability. Now the table of organization was complete once more.[16]

DuVal, a descendant of Huguenots expelled from France by the revocation of the Edict of Nantes, left his home state of Virginia when very young, and became a hunter in Kentucky. Gradually dissatisfaction with his prospects needled him toward change, and he abandoned the free ways of the forest to begin the study of law. In spite of serious deficiencies in early education, he doggedly clung to his objective and in 1804 was licensed to practice. Five feet seven inches tall, with light brown hair, and a round humorous face, he had a gnomish look about him. He told funny stories well and loved to sing. There was much fun in him, but also some iron. It was DuVal's fortune sometime in life to have crossed the path of Washington Irving, and the author was so impressed with him as typical of the best in the frontier type that he wrote several stories in which DuVal, called Ralph Ringwood, was the central figure. President Monroe had appointed him judge for East Florida in May, 1821.[17]

Having assumed his duties, the new governor began to report that the Indians were hungry and restless. They would not improve their fields lest the white men take them. Their

---

* A riffed officer was one separated from the military service because of a reduction in force.

failure to put in crops, coupled with high water in West Florida, was forcing them to live on meat and the coontie root (*Zamia integrifolia*). The squaws pounded this root to break the fibers down and force out the poisonous juice. This produced a nourishing flour which kept them alive in more than one period of extremity. Unsettled as they were, the Indians committed a murder or two, but the governor did not lose his head over these. Instead he asked the War Department (which directed Indian affairs until 1849) to increase their allowance of food. This was only a temporary solution; the best permanent one, he agreed with Andrew Jackson, was to send them back to the Creeks. As early as 1818 some responsible officials had made the same recommendation. But as it seemed out of the question, the next best solution, said DuVal, was to ship them west of the Mississippi. Some eastern tribes had already made that excursion, but the government had not yet adopted the policy of sending all Indians west. DuVal was the first public official to suggest this course for the Seminoles.[18]

Even at the frontier itself people held different attitudes about the Florida Indians. Joseph M. White, an influential resident and the third Territorial delegate to Congress, saw little good in them. Since Jackson's campaign, he said, they seemed to be without abiding places, and they hung around towns, drunk and insolent. In White's view, they had no right to the land, and ought to be pushed off it. In contrast, DuVal seemed to have more regard for their rights, though he also thought they should be moved. Recognizing that they were easy prey for designing white men, he issued a proclamation on July 29, 1822, forbidding white people to purchase cattle, hogs, horses, and slaves from the Indians without a special license. He also forbade whites to settle near Indian towns. Such a policy made DuVal-extremely unpopular with the many persons who profited from dealings with the Seminoles, and his proclamation simply could not be enforced.[19]

The Monroe administration was now obliged to choose positively between alternative courses. At first it favored reuniting the Seminoles with the Creeks, but since this policy met opposition both from the Seminoles and from the people of Georgia, the President turned to Jackson's recommendation. He proposed to relocate the Seminoles near the Apalachicola

River by the fall of 1821. This relocation soon lost favor because the Administration realized that it might interfere with the Forbes Purchase,* which the United States was honoring pending final settlement of the case in the courts. All the while the Indians remained on tenterhooks, unable to find out what lay in store for them.[20]

The Seminoles were humble enough about it. Captain Bell had explained this while he was in Florida. "They appear sensible of their reduced situation; that they are too weak to make much resistance in war; and that the presumptive right to their land has passed into the hands of the American government. To that Government, they now look for that liberality, justice, and protection, which it has extended to other nations of Indians." It is noteworthy that his estimate added up to the same thing as Acting Governor Worthington's, that the Indians intended to keep the peace if at all possible. Nevertheless the pressure upon them was very great. Hunger, the thronging white men encroaching on their lands, and the inevitable frictions between the white and red cultures pushed them into a corner. There were many border incidents and several murders.[21]

A council with the Indians was set at St. Marks for November 20, 1822. This was expected to produce an agreement, but before it could take place, the organization in Florida broke down a second time. Peter Pelham, the subagent, fell ill and had to go north for his health. Late in September, 1822, Governor DuVal abruptly left for Kentucky to tend to his personal fortunes. Agent Humphreys did not appear in Florida at all, although he was supposed to organize and run the projected council. There was no one to negotiate for the government at the council. Acting Governor George Walton was in a state of panic. His nerves were near the snapping point anyway, because a terrible epidemic of yellow fever was rampant in Pensacola, carrying off his friends and loved ones. He had no knowledge of what the government intended to do at the talks

*The Forbes Purchase comprised about 1,250,000 acres along the west bank of the Apalachicola River. The litigation over it was finally settled in 1835 in favor of the assigns of Forbes. The brief concerning the case in printed in *Record in the Case of Colin Mitchell and Others v. the United States*, Washington, 1831. For the outline of the story see Cash, *Story of Florida* I, 328.

—DuVal had not posted him—nor had he any money to buy the necessary presents and food. The Indians had already been notified, and it was too late to head them off. Yet if they went to St. Marks and found no representative of the United States there, relations would be permanently damaged. Walton all but wrung his hands in his letters to Secretary Calhoun.[22]

Nonetheless, what the acting governor most feared did occur. A few chiefs went to the rendezvous on the twentieth and found no preparations to receive them. They waited three days, then left annoyed. It was not until a week later that the "crash" negotiator, Thomas Wright, a paymaster in the army, reached St. Marks. He called the nearby chiefs together and explained the government's embarrassment. The Indians were good-natured about it, for they apparently realized that they dared not ruffle the new lords of their peninsula. The head chief in that quarter, Neamathla, assured Wright that his people would remain quiet until a permanent arrangement was made for them.[23]

What a change was here revealed in Neamathla! In 1817, only five years before, he had sent word to General E. P. Gaines, commanding at Fort Scott, that if American troops so much as crossed to the Indian side of the Flint River, they would be attacked. Now in 1822, although goaded by uncertainty and suspense, he was meek and tractable while the United States, through carelessness and poor organization, appeared to trifle with the future of his people.[24]

At length the white personnel began to reassemble. Agent Humphreys made his appearance in Pensacola on Christmas Eve, 1822. A month later, Acting Governor Walton issued him instructions. Walton had delayed because in DuVal's absence he truly did not know what the policy of the government was. Naturally the orders he gave Humphreys were comfortably general. Try to get the Indians to give up the hunt and turn to agriculture, he said, and "prevent animosity and dissension among themselves, and suppress apprehension of severity or injustice from our Government, and of violence from the Creek Indians." General or not, this was a big order. Governor Du-Val returned to Florida in March, 1823, and bustled about condemning everyone but himself for the confusion which his absence had created.[25]

In Washington, meanwhile, the problem of the Florida Indians was still under discussion. In December, 1822, President Monroe referred to the issue in his annual message. Whatever Article VI of the treaty with Spain might say, he certainly did not appear to feel that the Indians were entitled to American citizenship. The Seminoles, he said, must either be moved out of Florida or be confined to a smaller area. Thereupon the House of Representatives established a temporary committee to report on that portion of the message. The head of this committee, Thomas Metcalfe of Kentucky, wrote to Florida for information, and then on February 21, 1823, gave his report to the House. His committee, marvelous to tell, took Article VI of the treaty with Spain seriously. The Indians, the report said, must be accorded the privileges of citizens of the United States. The thing to do, it continued, was to give each Seminole family a grant of land. This action would break up the tribal bond and introduce in its stead the energy of private enterprise. Thus stimulated, they would be prepared to amalgamate with the white society. Even though this report showed scant appreciation of the grip upon the Indians of their own culture, it was surprisingly humane. It was also largely ignored.[26]

Joseph M. Hernandez, Territorial delegate to Congress from Florida in 1823, helped lead the Administration toward action. In reply to his urging, Secretary Calhoun stated the new policy. Commissioners were appointed at once to hold a talk, and were instructed to insist upon a concentration of the natives south of "Charlotte's River."* If there should prove to be insufficient land for cultivation in that area, the commissioners were to be empowered to extend the reservation northward toward Tampa Bay. The documents do not show why the region along the Apalachicola was given up in favor of a southern reservation. They do, however, show that the Indians who

*"Charlotte's River" is a name which appears on several contemporary maps. Inasmuch as little was known of South Florida, its position does not correspond with any watercourse now known. Probably it was what later became known as Pease Creek, Peace Creek, and now the Peace River, which opens into Charlotte Harbor. This stream was also called Tolopchopka, or Talakchopko, Creek on some maps. See maps made by J. S. Tanner Company in 1823, by John Lee Williams in 1837, and by Captain John Mackey and Lieutenant J. E. Blake in 1840.

ranged east of the Suwannee favored the latter, while those to the west of that river were almost more willing to migrate to the West, beyond the Mississippi, than to such a place.[27]

In any case Secretary Calhoun meant what he said. On April 7 commissions went out of the War Office to James Gadsden of South Carolina and to Bernardo Segui of Florida, accompanied by the instructions to Hernandez. Both men accepted. Segui was a descendant of the Minorcans who had migrated to Dr. Andrew Turnbull's colony of New Smyrna and had moved on to St. Augustine when in 1777 they were driven out of that colony. In 1823 Bernardo Segui, like Hernandez, had become an American citizen and was a prominent man in St. Augustine. Gadsden's name is more widely recognized because of the purchase he made in 1853 which filled out the southern boundaries of the continental United States. He had been a lieutenant of engineers during the War of 1812 and an aide to General Jackson thereafter. He had accompanied the General in the 1818 invasion of Florida, and had remained on good terms with him. By 1820 he had attained the grade of colonel and had been appointed adjutant general, but he resigned in a huff when the Senate refused to confirm his appointment. This new assignment as commissioner to treat with the Indians brought about his migration to Florida.[28]

On June 30 Governor DuVal was instructed to make himself a part of the commission. He would have been appointed when the other two were, except that it had not been known then that he had returned from Kentucky. DuVal accepted on July 15, but much of his energy had to be devoted to being governor. Gadsden became the driving member of the commission. It did not seem feasible to meet with the red men until their summer agriculture was over, and the date set was September 5. Three months in advance of that day Micanopy and Jumper, a Red Stick Creek who had established himself as first counselor, committed the Alachua bands to appear at the time set. In an attempt to avoid incidents which might jeopardize the forthcoming critical negotiations, Governor DuVal revoked all trading licenses issued to white men prior to his administration.[29]

When he called the Indians to come to the talks, Gadsden took a hard tone. He gave them to understand that a treaty was to be concluded, and that "those tribes who neglect the invitation, or obstinately refuse to attend, will be considered as embraced within the compact formed, and forced to comply with its provisions." That this was obviously not the language of diplomacy but rather of the strong to the weak was perfectly clear to the Seminoles.

Gadsden's personal preference was to remove the natives from Florida altogether. Inasmuch as this was not included in his instructions, he undertook to sell the Secretary of War on the need. Florida "must ever be as internally weak as she is externally assailable. An Indian population, under these circumstances, connected with another class of population, which will inevitably predominate in Florida, must necessarily add to her natural weaknesses. . . . It is useless to enlarge on the policy of removing a class of savages from where they may prove dangerous to where they would be comparatively harmless. . . ." In this presentation the commissioner revealed a principal reason why many white men wished to get rid of the Florida Indians. That other "class of population" to which he referred was not secure as long as there existed Indian villages to which they could escape. Too many slaves had already disappeared to suit the masters, presumably in that direction.[30]

Calhoun needed no convincing. He agreed that it was important to move the Indians out of the peninsula, but he could do nothing to bring it about. There were no available lands west of the Mississippi which the government could assign to them, and no funds to purchase any. The policy of systematic Indian removal, although the Secretary could not know it, still lay seven years in the future.[31]

Andrew Jackson, living the life of a planter at the Hermitage, learned of the proposed negotiation and offered Secretary Calhoun his advice. He had already communicated his ideas to his friend Commissioner Gadsden, he said, and presumed to address the government unsolicited because he wished very much to see Gadsden succeed in his first Indian assignment. The thing to do, Jackson said, was to send half the Fourth Infantry Regiment from Pensacola to the vicinity of Tampa Bay. This show of force would hasten the concentration of the Indians, which was to be arranged in the forthcoming talks; indeed, without it they might refuse to comply.[32]

James Gadsden had already adopted his old chief's views. A month before Jackson's letter was sent to the Secretary, Gadsden had urged a show of strength, "a judicious location of an adequate force simultaneous with the concentration of the Indians cannot but have the happy effect of obtaining such a control as to render them perfectly Subservient to the views of Government." The use of the phrase "perfectly Subservient" once more indicates that the relationship between the two negotiating parties was hardly one of a balance of power.[33]

The movement of troops on the flanks of the proposed reservation was calculated to influence the Seminoles. But this was not the purpose of the detachment of soldiers present on the treaty grounds. A military detachment was a standard prop at Indian parleys; in truth the Indians would have felt deprived without the panoply and color which their presence added. Accordingly, Governor DuVal directed Captain John Erving, commandant of St. Francis Barracks in St. Augustine, to send one officer and twenty-five enlisted men to the site. The captain began by protesting that he could spare only half that number, but in the end produced the full complement under the command of Lieutenant James Wolfe Ripley.[34]

The detachment would not have far to go, since the spot selected for the council was the second landing place on the north bank of Moultrie Creek, about five miles south of St. Augustine. But the Indian bands west of the Suwannee River would have to travel 250 miles to get there. On the other hand, Micanopy's bands had been consulted and had no doubt favored the site because it was convenient for them. In judging the choice of the meeting place, one must remember that there were no inland white settlements at the time, no central points to which the supplies necessary for a council could be transported.[35]

During the summer Governor DuVal appointed Horatio S. Dexter, former negotiator for the Seminoles, to act as subagent in place of Peter Pelham, who was still ill and absent. Dexter, who knew the Indians of the peninsula quite well, estimated that 1,500 of them would attend the talk. They would consume three tons of rice. The other persons responsible for the success of the negotiation were not as optimistic as he. There was some anxiety among them that important chiefs might absent themselves in spite of Gadsden's dire warning. To insure the attendance of the trans-Suwannee bands, Agent Humphreys and interpreter Stephen Richards led a party of 350 the whole 250 miles. Their trek was conducted so skillfully that the Mikasukis and Tallahassees, the most important bands west of the Suwannee, did not feel themselves herded, and indeed were willing to see the two white men given a special reward (to be noted later). Actually the pessimists came closer to the truth than Dexter. Many Indian families were left home to tend the crops, so that only about 425 individuals, including a few women, attended the talks. If Dexter's estimate had been followed concerning provisions, those present would have had to wade through the rice.[36]

The Florida Indians, as has been related, did not constitute a cohesive society; about all they had in common was the Creek culture. For purposes of negotiation the diverse bands who arrived at Moultrie Creek needed a head chief. Accordingly, a mile and a half short of the treaty ground they gathered to reach an agreement among themselves. They chose as their leader Neamathla, head chief of the Mikasukis. He had the respect of his own people, and Governor DuVal called him the most remarkable red man he had ever seen. Fierce in bearing, he was the only chief able to exercise authority over the heterogeneous bands.[37]

Because of the Indians' organizational meeting, the council itself got under way one day later than agreed. The only known account of the opening day written by a person who was there, other than the official minutes, is the diary entry of the Reverend Joshua Nichols Glenn of St. Augustine. In company with numerous other townsfolk he took the day off to see the show at Moultrie Creek. These are his words: "Sat 6th, the Treaty with the Floriday Indians commenced to day in the morning Capt. Wm Levingston his wife and Daughter Mr. and Mrs. Streeter and my Self went up to Moultry the place of holding the Treaty in a very comfortable Boat—accompanied by many other gentlemen and Ladies in other Boats—a little after we landed the Indians came from their Camps to the Commissioners Camp to Salute the Commissioners & hold their first talk this was quite Novel—the Indians came in a body with a White Flag flying—beating a

little thing Similar to a Drum and Singing a kind of a Song
and at the end of every appearant verse one of them gave a
Shrill hoop—which was succeeded by a loud and universal
Scream from them all—in this way they marched up to the
Commissioners—when two of them in their birthday Suit and
painted all over white with white Sticks in their hands and
feathers tied on them—came up to them (viz the Commissioners) and made many marks on them—then their King
Nehlemathlas came forward and Shook hands and after him
all the chiefs in rotation—after which the King Smoked his
pipe and then observed that he considered us gentlemen as
Fathers and Brethren and the Ladies as Mothers and Sisters
the Commissioners then conducted the chiefs into the bark
house they had bilt to hold their talk in and after they had
all Smoked together they held their first Talk—in the evening
we returned to Town and the Governor was unwell he came
with us—"[38]

What was an outing for the curious townsfolk was the beginning of nearly two weeks of exacting negotiations for the
principals at Moultrie Creek. Seventy chiefs and warriors took
part in the deliberations conducted within the "bark house."
Here the show of immediate force played no part. The Indians
were not required to disarm at the treaty grounds, but it is
probable that they left their weapons at their camp farther
down the creek. As for the detachment of the Fourth Artillery,
they acted primarily as stage decoration, but had in addition
a policy function.[39] At least four officers who came along for
the spectacle added the color of their uniforms to the decor
and also added their signatures as witnesses to the document
finally completed.

James Gadsden opened the negotiating. As before, he followed a stern line. General Jackson, he reminded the Indians,
had subdued them twice, and might have driven them into the
ocean had he chosen. What the general had done had been
wholly just, inasmuch as they alone were the cause of the
quarrel which had brought him upon them. Nevertheless,
Gadsden continued, the President, their "Great Father," was
willing to forget the past. But in return they would have to
concentrate their bands in the assigned territory; he would
not permit them to remain scattered all over Florida. "The

hatchet is buried; the muskets, the white men's arms, are stacked in peace. Do you wish them to remain so?" The implication was plain enough: the Seminoles had better agree to the terms offered them or they would take the consequences. The silken glove here poorly concealed the iron fist.[40]

Two days elapsed before Neamathla replied. The records do not chronicle what took place in the interval. From the fragments of his talk, which Gadsden reported, it is clear that the chief's tone was surprisingly defiant. He let the commissioners know, for instance, that the Florida Indians regarded the Red Stick Creeks in their midst as incorporated in their tribes. They would not drive them out. This attitude brought a rejoinder from Gadsden the following day. Again the mailed fist shone through the thin covering. "Brave warriors, though they despise death, do not madly contend with the strong." The events of that day, September 10, seem to have broken the Indians' resistance. Neamathla's next speech showed the change. His people did not want, he said, to go onto the reservation to the south. It was a bad place because the soil was too poor to sustain them and because it was too close to the big water across which evil influences could waft to corrupt the young men. The rest of what he said can best be told in his own words. "We are poor and needy; we do not come here to murmur or complain . . . we rely on your justice and humanity; we hope you will not send us south, to a country where neither the hickory nut, the acorn, nor the persimmon grows. . . . For me, I am old and poor; too poor to move from my village to the south. I am attached to the spot improved by my own labor, and cannot believe that my friends will drive me from it."[41]

The allusion to the acorn and the hickory nut was not mere caprice. Like most primitive peoples, the Seminoles needed oils and they derived them from nuts. Concerning the tenor of the whole address, its abject humbleness is striking. Was this genuine or was it deceitful? In the light of the additional clause finally appended to the completed treaty, it is possible that Neamathla humbled himself to impress his own people rather than the white men. It is also possible that the pity he induced in the white negotiators may have influenced them to modify the instructions of the authorities in Washington.

The minutes of the talks kept by the commissioners include nothing about activities on September 12, 13, or 14. They tersely report that on the fifteenth the outline of a treaty was read to the Indians. How the provisions in it were shaped is not known. Nor is it known how the red negotiators reacted to it, for September 16 and 17 are also slurred over. Indeed there is only one other entry of consequence, except the bald statement that on September 18 the chiefs signed the treaty. But the event recorded for September 19 is of unusual interest. On that day an additional article was drawn and signed by the interested parties. It allotted reservations in the valley of the Apalachicola River of from two to eight square miles each to Neamathla, Blunt, Tuskihadjo, Mulatto King, Emathlochee, and Econchatomico. These chiefs and their followers did not have to move south after all, the move they had so much detested; in fact, they scarcely had to change position. The commissioners frankly told the Secretary of War that the assent of these six powerful western headmen could not have been secured without this "equitable provision." Using balder terms, it would be possible to call this article a bribe.[42]

On September 20 presents were distributed by the whites. And then on September 21, seventeen days after their first arrival, the Seminoles left the treaty grounds.

The first paragraph of the new treaty stated that the Florida Indians appealed to the humanity of the United States, and threw themselves upon its protection. They surrendered all claim to the "whole territory of Florida" except for the district shown on the fold-out map. Their reservation as it was finally enlarged covered 4,032,940 acres. The commissioners had exercised the discretion, given them in their instructions, to move the reservation northward if there was not enough good land in the preferred area to support the Indians. The latter had said that they would not go south of Charlotte's River unless forced. On these two counts, the entire tract lay north of that stream, not south of it. In addition, it was provided that the boundaries could be extended to the north if the reservation did not include enough tillable land. (Two extensions were made, one in February, the other in December, 1825). All in all, if the Seminoles had title to the "whole territory of Florida" they were ceding roughly 28,253,820 acres of ground. In return for this concession the United States obligated itself to (1) protect the Indians as long as they obeyed the law; (2) supply them with $6,000 worth of agricultural equipment and livestock on the reservation; (3) pay them an annuity of $5,000 a year for twenty years; (4) keep white men off the reservation except those authorized to be there; (5) provide the Indians who had to move with meat, corn, and salt for one year; (6) pay up to $4,500 for the improvements which the Indians were obliged to abandon outside the reservation; (7) provide up to $2,000 for transportation to the reservation; (8) maintain an agent, a subagent, and an interpreter on the reservation; (9) pay $1,000 a year for twenty years to maintain a school on the reservation; and (10) pay $1,000 a year to maintain a blacksmith and a gunsmith on the reservation. The cash considerations, and those in kind converted to cash, add up to $221,000. Expressed in payment per acre, this amount comes to roughly three-quarters of a cent (78/100 of a cent, to be precise).[43]*

Three other points in the treaty are worth highlighting. First, the Indians agreed to try to prevent the concentration of runaway slaves in their midst. Inasmuch as the presence of fugitives among them was one reason the white men were determined to force them out, this provision was very important. Second, the boundaries of the reservation were nowhere closer to the coast than twenty miles. Thus it was intended to cut the natives off from intercourse with Cuba and their customary supply of powder, ammunition, and arms, and, Commissioner Gadsden believed, their market for stolen slaves and cattle. Being cut off from outside influence and the chance of expansion, the Indians would be forced to take up agriculture, the commissioners believed. This in turn would eventually soften their barbarism. Finally, the document made no mention of duration, that is, it did not guarantee the reservation to the Seminoles for any specified span of time. Later, the red men claimed that the duration was clearly twenty years, because the annuities and other payments ran for that period.[44]

* The consideration paid to the Indians was calculated from the provisions of the treaty itself, with some added data. For example, rations were on the basis of 12.5 cents each for 1,500 Indians fed daily, making a total of $68,439.55. The number of Indians fed and the cost per ration were taken from DuVal to SW, July 12, 1824, *TP: Florida*, XXIII, 15.

Buried in the body of the treaty, in Article X, was a grant of land one mile square each to Gad Humphreys and Stephen Richards. Like so much of the rest of the document, it is impossible to say how this provision found its way in. But the Senate of the United States thought it improper and struck it out before ratifying the treaty.[45]

The marks of thirty-two Indian chiefs are on the Treaty of Moultrie Creek. Were they representative of a majority of the bands in Florida? The answer is at best incomplete. Neamathla submitted, during the talks, a list of thirty-seven Florida towns with their chiefs. Seventeen of those chiefs can be positively identified as markers of the treaty. But what of the other twenty towns and chiefs? Either they were not represented, or refused to sign, or were considered to be represented by the mark of some higher chief. To offset the twenty missing chiefs, we find on the document fifteen additional names whose bearers do not appear on Neamathla's list. It is not known whom they represented. It is possible that the names on the treaty do not coincide with those Neamathla gave, since white scribes put down the Indian names as they heard them; it was uncommon for the same chief to be recorded the same by any two white men. Only this much is certain—here was a more representative group of Seminoles than the white men ever again gathered into a Florida council.[46]

In spite of the inequality of the power of the two negotiating parties, there was some give on the part of the stronger. The principal point yielded was the shifting of the reservation from the south side of Charlotte's River to the north of it. In addition there was the special article which bought the support of six influential trans-Suwannee chiefs. The commissioners at least implied that these six would not have knuckled under without it. When one ponders the abject plea of Neamathla, therefore, he cannot help wondering what part of it was sincere and what part window dressing.

The effect of the inequality of the two parties nevertheless looms large. Each side recognized the imbalance and shaped its conduct accordingly. In a personal letter to Secretary Calhoun, written ten days after the signing, James Gadsden said as much. "It is not necessary," he wrote, "to disguise the fact to you, that the treaty effected was in a degree a treaty of imposition—The Indians would never have voluntarily assented to the terms had they not believed that we had both the power and disposition to compel obedience." Yet the commissioners felt they had exercised no more coercion than any powerful party would have done in a similar situation.[47]

The taint of coercion did not fade away. Two years after the signing, the newly appointed Superintendent of Indian Affairs wrote a letter to each of the three commissioners. Each was directed to respond to the charge that the Indians had been forced into the agreement at Moultrie Creek. It is hard to say what the superintendent expected to get in answer, and I have seen but one of the responses. Governor DuVal reacted with indignation. "Who is my accuser?" he demanded. Not until he was confronted by him, and also accused of specific sorts of duress, would he reply. Since the proceedings were public, he added, anyone could have attended and checked what went on. Coercion, it seems clear, stemmed altogether from the discrepancy between the power of the two parties. James Gadsden did not scruple to remind the Indians over and over of the engulfing power almost certain to be unleashed against them if they refused to reach an agreement satisfactory to the United States. On the other hand, no Indian was abused or manhandled on the treaty grounds. Would any government, having the same margin of power on its side, have shown greater forbearance in the 1830's?[48]

The Senate found the treaty legitimate enough to ratify on December 23, 1823. Thereupon, since the Indians had no such formality to go through, the provisions were presumed to be in effect.[49]

John C. Calhoun seemed to regard the arrangement made in the treaty as enduring. He wrote to the President on January 24, 1825, "it is probable that no inconvenience will be felt, for many years, either by the inhabitants of Florida, or the Indians, under the present arrangement . . . there ought to be the strongest and most solemn assurances that the country given them should be theirs, as a permanent home for themselves and their posterity."[50]

In contrast, James Gadsden wrote to Andrew Jackson in 1829 that the idea behind the treaty had been to get the Indians concentrated in order to eventually move them west. It is probable that he was here expressing the views of the commissioners rather than those of the government. The three negotiators had stated in their report that it would have been much better to get the Seminoles out of Florida. As for the Seminoles, the other party to the treaty, the chiefs claimed when pressed later to leave Florida that they were allowed by the Treaty of Moultrie Creek to remain there twenty years.[51]

Writers have more often than not condemned the Treaty of Moultrie Creek. Annie Abel, a competent scholar, called it one of the worst Indian treaties ever made by the United States.[52] It does not seem to me to warrant quite so strong a criticism. Whatever the moral judgment passed on it, no one can deny that this treaty was the first in a series of disasters to befall the Indians of Florida.

At about the time that the treaty was signed, the United States Supreme Court pronounced a decision which fixed the nature of Indian rights to the land in American law. Chief Justice John Marshall read the opinion in the case of *Johnson & Graham's Lessee* v. *McIntosh* in 1823.[53] Title to the land in the United States, Marshall said, rested upon discovery, which "gave an exclusive right to extinguish Indian title of occupancy, either by purchase or by conquest." The original occupants had no true title, but they did have an inalienable right to occupancy "with a legal as well as a just claim to retain possession of it, and to use it according to their own discretion. . . ." The decision was based quite frankly on expediency, as the following quotation demonstrates. "However this restriction may be opposed to natural right, and to the usages of civilized nations, yet, if it be indispensable to that system under which the country has been settled, and be adapted to the actual condition of the two people, it may, perhaps, be supported by reason, and certainly cannot be rejected by courts of justice." Thus, although the Seminoles did not know it, and would not have understood the distinction, they had by the Treaty of Moultrie Creek given up their right of occupancy to 28,253,820 acres, and had confirmed the same right to themselves within the 4,032,940 acres of the reservation. They had not transferred title according to the white law, because they did not have it to transfer.

4

The 1820's

THE SEMINOLES were slow to move onto the reservation, but
this tardiness did not relieve the white agents in Florida
from the responsibility of feeding those who did move. In the
spring of 1824 Governor DuVal advertised for bids to furnish
the corn, beef, and salt stipulated in the treaty. His idea of a
sensible cost per ration was twelve to fourteen cents, but the
lowest of the first bids was eighteen cents. Rejecting all bids
as too high, he later secured a contractor willing to supply the
required food for eleven and a half cents per ration delivered
on Tampa Bay and fourteen cents delivered on the St. Johns
River. It soon appeared that Benjamin Chaires, the successful
contractor, had agreed in writing to pay another would-be bidder $500 to withhold his proposal. When Chaires refused to
pay this fee on some technicality, the suppressed bidder indignantly turned the note over to the government. DuVal, who
had awarded the contract, defended the way in which Chaires
carried it out, and the matter was not pressed.[1]

By July, 1824, 1,500 Indians were being fed daily at the two
points of issue, Tampa Bay and the St. Johns River at or near
the mouth of the Oklawaha. The governor protested that the
$65,700 appropriated for the Florida Indians (from which the
price of rations had to come) was not enough.[2]

DuVal traveled about among the dilatory Indians, urging
them to get ready to move onto the reservation. Reluctantly

he came to the conclusion that they would not do it without a show of military force from the United States. It was to be regretted, he said, that there was no regular force under his own command. He did not mean that the area was bereft of soldiers. On the contrary, in response to repeated requests from the commissioners who had negotiated the Treaty of Moultrie Creek, the War Department sent Lieutenant Colonel George M. Brooke in 1824 with four companies of the Fourth Infantry Regiment to the vicinity of Tampa Bay to establish a military post on the flank of the reservation. Selection of the site was entrusted to James Gadsden, who picked the head of Hillsborough Bay. There, in a beautiful grove of live oaks and orange trees, Brooke erected a post named by Gadsden in the beginning Cantonment Brooke. Governor DuVal's complaint was that he could only request from Brooke the use of his troops, he could not order it. Before long the War Department gave the governor control of a company stationed at St. Marks.[3]

From Neamathla contumacy radiated out among the red men. The chief's influence stretched back to the era of Jackson's invasion in 1818 and earlier. DuVal had great respect for the man, at the same time that he saw in him a menace. "Uncommonly capable, bold, violent, restless, unable to submit to a superior or to endure an equal," ran the governor's estimate of him. His men were the most "lawless and vile" in Florida. It was absolutely necessary to overawe them.[4]

The time to do it arrived late in July, 1824. An uprising seemed inevitable. DuVal spared no effort to avoid it. Hearing that there was a large gathering of armed warriors at Neamathla's town, he hurried there with only an interpreter. He found three hundred warriors in an ugly mood. Striding into their square, trailed by the interpreter, he faced them all and delivered a stern talk. They must meet him at St. Marks on July 26, he ordered, or face destruction. In reporting this episode, the governor himself omitted all the dramatic details, but Washington Irving in "The Conspiracy of Neamathla" asserted that DuVal struck Neamathla and seized him by the throat. If so, his boldness had turned into rashness, for it was an act of great courage even to face the Seminoles in their inflamed state. Recognizing this, six hundred warriors came to the parley on the twenty-sixth. At that meeting Neamathla was displaced as head chief of the bands west of the Suwannee River. Governor DuVal proudly claimed that he had been responsible for the ouster and the elevation of a successor. But all he got for his audacity was the sharp censure of Secretary Calhoun. Such interference in the internal affairs of the Indians, said Calhoun, was not warranted. Nevertheless, Neamathla's displacement proved permanent, and he dropped out of the front rank of leadership.[5]

The new chief was Tuckose Emathla (mole or ant leader), called by the white men John Hicks, a fit man for the post. About fifty years old, he appeared to Lieutenant George A. McCall, then on duty in Florida, to be one of nature's noblemen.* His height was six feet two inches, his proportions classical.[6] Hicks was a Mikasuki, and one can assume that he was descended from chiefs through the female line. His principal counselor was the son of Kenhadjo, the hereditary leader of the Mikasuki bands. It would appear that the bands west of the Suwannee were drawing closer together than ever before.

Whoever was chief of the group of bands, and whatever the growing concentration of the tribes, the plain fact is that the Seminoles did not want to move onto the reservation. In the beginning Governor DuVal did not blame them. He recognized the appeal of their "delightful" country, and he said, "There are no people more attached to their native soil than Indians, or who are more averse to emigration." As he observed events from Hillsborough Bay, Lieutenant Colonel Brooke also recognized the Indian reluctance. They were dissatisfied with the treaty, he wrote, and with the running of the boundary line. He requested more cannon for his stockade because there was a steady series of incidents between Indians and white Floridians. Seminoles now and again killed white men's cattle, and the rumor reached the governor that they had threatened to drive the whites away. One thing led to another. DuVal found

---

*George A. McCall, a Pennsylvania boy, was graduated from the United States Military Academy and commissioned a second lieutenant in the First Infantry on July 1, 1822. He was to have extensive experience with the Florida Indians, first serving in Florida from 1823 to 1826. He returned in 1829, 1836, 1838, 1839, 1841, and 1842. He reached the grade of major general of volunteers during the Civil War, and died in 1868, aged sixty-five.

it necessary to call out some volunteers. This threat may have had a softening effect upon the red men; then, too, the Indians in West Florida were influenced by the Apalachicolas who were more tractable than the rest, and more civilized. Their houses and fields were as good as the white men's in the same area. Under persuasion by the Apalachicolas, the Tallahassees and Mikasukis grew less belligerent. Finally, all Indians west of the Suwannee agreed to be within the reservation by October 1, 1824.[7]

Unfortunately, just when the details of negotiation and preparation were myriad, Agent Gad Humphreys was of little help. During the first half of 1824 he mostly found fault with the plans. It was not wise or humane, he pointed out, to move the Indians too hastily, even though some of their "unfeeling" white neighbors insisted upon it. He criticized the handling of Neamathla. It was not sensible to have given him a separate reservation, for he was the only chief who could control all the bands. Then at the moment when DuVal was bearding Neamathla in his own village, Humphreys set out for the North on leave. For some time the governor did not even know he had gone, and he complained to the War Office of the agent's inaccessibility.[8]

As if Indian-white trouble was not enough, Governor DuVal, working practically alone, had to try to keep peace among the Seminoles themselves. Two towns fought each other with clubs and knives, and several men were terribly maimed. Perhaps whiskey set them upon each other; for, like most red men, the Seminoles were addicted to alcohol. They would ruin themselves to get it, and drink themselves stupid after they had it. True, federal law forbade its sale to them, and the War Department ordered the superintendent to carry out that law (as well as the other trading provisions of the Indian Intercourse Act), but it goes without saying that he could not do it. White panderers set up small grog shops close to the reservation and urged the Indians to demand their annuities in cash. Cash could be converted into whiskey, to the great profit of the shopkeepers.[9]

Under the terms of the treaty, up to $4,500 was available to compensate the natives for the improvements they were to abandon outside the reservation. DuVal appointed John Bellamy, a wealthy planter, to appraise this property, and Bellamy set its maximum value at $4,500. This doubtless was far from enough. Both compensation and annuity were payable in cash, but conscientious officials on the spot pled for commutation of the cash payments into goods because they knew the natives would be defrauded of hard money by liquor dealers and other sharpers. The Seminoles themselves refused paper currency. At last DuVal paid out cash through the micos of the towns, upon whom rested the responsibility for a just division. He paid promptly because the Seminoles were by this time devoid of such absolute necessities as blankets.[10]

The mere physical movement of the Indians to the reservation required much administering. Since horses were hard to acquire, DuVal offered to allow from five to ten dollars per canoe to migrants willing to travel by water. Somehow, too, cattle had to be procured because the plan was for the natives to sell off the herds they had, and to replace them with new ones once they had entered the reservation. But in spite of the governor's energy, the October 1 deadline came and went without notable success. There still were more Indians off the reservation than on it.[11]

Seminoles, both on and off, asserted that their 4,000,000 acres could not sustain them. Gad Humphreys agreed. He and DuVal favored extending the northern boundary to include Big Hammock. In contrast, Gadsden was in favor of moving the line only a few miles to include the towns where Chiefs Sitarky and Micanopy lived. In July, 1824, the President approved the inclusion of Big Hammock, but the change was not officially made until ten days before the Monroe administration ended. Meanwhile, Indians and some white men were already calling for an additional enlargement. Among the latter was Benjamin Chaires, the ration contractor, who said the land the Seminoles had received was the poorest in Florida. The boundary ought to be extended this time, he said, to include Big Swamp, which contained 5,000 to 6,000 acres of good land. The terms employed were meaningful to Chaires and to other knowledgeable persons on the ground, but in Washington officials sometimes thought Big Hammock and Big Swamp one and the same.[12]

Modern writers have occasionally contended that the Semi-

noles were purposely forced onto a reservation which would
not sustain them, so that they would in a short time be willing
to leave Florida altogether. If this contention is true, there is
nowhere in writing any direct acknowledgment of it. It is true
that James Gadsden flatly admitted that the purpose in placing them on a reservation was to concentrate them so that they
might be moved later. Yet, he insisted that four times their
number could live in the area assigned them if they would farm
it sensibly. Nor did the Secretary of War John C. Calhoun
think that the land was unable to support them. The truth
would appear to be as follows: if the land would not sustain
them—this is by no means certain—such was not the intent
of the white men; the fact was that no one knew very much
of the region, least of all whether it would support 3,000 to
5,000 Indians.[13]

Toward the end of its two terms, the Monroe administration
brought about an important change in its organization relating to the Indians. As a result of intensive attacks by private
fur interests, notably John Jacob Astor's company, the government factory system was finally done away with in 1822. The
government factories had been trading posts operated by the
War Department since the 1790's, under the theory that red-
white relations could not be controlled unless the United States
also controlled much of the interracial trade. In 1824, after two
years of organizational confusion, an Office of Indian Affairs
was established in the War Department, and Thomas L. Mc-
Kenney, erstwhile director of the government factories, was
put at its head. As McKenney was devoted to John C. Calhoun,
and also dependent on government pay for a living, the Secretary chose him for the new post. Apparently McKenney genu-
inely sought to promote the well-being of the Indians. In time
he came to consider their removal as the most humane policy,
and labored to bring public opinion behind it. After his own
dismissal in 1830, partly on political grounds, he wrote books
about the red natives which earned him more renown than all
but a few of his successors were ever to enjoy.[14]

John C. Calhoun, the cabinet member responsible for administering Indian affairs, was now concluding eight years of
service as one of the ablest of all the secretaries of war. But
his reputation did not rest on any special tenderness for the

Indians. For several years he had hoped to move them westward out of the white heartland. Up to that point the removal of individual tribes had heightened sectional controversy because the Indians were generally moved into the path of Southern expansion westward. What is more, the individual moves had proved unduly expensive. They highlighted the need for a general policy. Accordingly, late in 1824 President Monroe came around to Calhoun's removal policy, and on January 27, 1825, sent a plan to the Senate in a special message. Its essence was that the area west of Arkansas should be made into Indian territory. Land there would be given to tribes in exchange for that which they would surrender in the east. A cardinal point in the policy was that removal must be voluntary. Naturally Monroe asked for an appropriation to carry the scheme out. In response the Senate accepted the plan at once and asked Calhoun to draft a bill. When he complied, the Senate promptly passed his bill on February 23, 1825. The Georgia delegation in the House of Representatives killed it, however, lest it interfere with the special problem of their state.[15]

Georgia's problem carried over into John Quincy Adams' administration. Adams picked up the Monroe-Calhoun policy toward the Indians and continued it, but he was even more determined than his predecessor that there should be no forcible removal of the tribes. Georgia did not agree. During the years when tension was mounting in Florida, the government of Georgia and that of the United States reached a dangerous impasse over the rights of Creeks and Cherokees within the state. President Adams forbade Georgia to survey the Indian lands, but the state successfully defied him. The best the President could do was to make a new treaty with the Creeks, extracting from them precisely what the Georgians wanted.[16]

It was becoming painfully clear that the Treaty of Moultrie Creek had not resolved Indian-white relations in Florida. The red men had simply not entered the reservation. At the start of the Adams regime in 1825, Indians had entered the special reservations along the Apalachicola, assigned to Blunt, Neamathla, and the four other chiefs. There are no statistics for the main reservation. Its northern boundary, not yet run, was in an area that both Indians and whites were already settling. Here a later point of tension would surely develop.

Agitation continued over the addition of Big Swamp to the Indian land. James Gadsden and Joseph M. White, recently elected delegate to Congress, opposed the extension as contrary to the treaty. Some citizens fought it because it would bring the Indian border too near to the rich Alachua prairie and the white settlements there. On the other hand, George Walton, Territorial secretary, and Governor DuVal held the position that the reservation would not sustain the bands. In February, 1826, DuVal rode over it for thirteen days and did not see 300 acres of good land. "Nineteen-twentieths of their whole country within the present boundary," he said, "is by far the poorest and most miserable region I ever beheld." After due deliberation, the Adams administration granted the use of Big Swamp to the Seminoles on the day after Christmas, 1825, but it was not given as permanent Indian property. Tenure was not guaranteed; the natives were to have the use of that 6,000 acres of rich land only as long as the government wished.[17]

Nothing the Administration did could stop the hunger of the Seminoles. Spring had been for many years their time of hunger: from April 1 until the new crop of corn was ripe they had often been forced to live on roots and other forest foods. But in 1825 their shortage was rendered more acute by a severe drought during the growing season. It was as hard upon those who had moved onto the reservation as upon the recalcitrants, for the government ration, Acting Governor George Walton testified, was too scanty to sustain life. Agent Humphreys and Colonel Brooke both requested additional rations for them. Brooke pointed out that the issue had officially terminated on October 10, 1825, and that some Indians had actually starved to death. The government, heeding these pleas, allotted an additional $2,000 for rations, and later another $5,000.[18]

The famished Indians wandered outside the reservation, searching for food. They preyed upon the cattle of white men. Some bands who had entered the boundaries found they could not live there, and turned back across the Suwannee. Their movement caused alarm among white settlers flowing into the Tallahassee area; indeed Middle Florida, between the Apalachicola and the Suwannee, was the most heavily populated portion of the territory. Gad Humphreys claimed the Alachua citizen-soldiers ought to have been able to drive them back. The settlers countered by accusing Humphreys of condoning the wanderings of the Seminoles. They assumed that he could use the regular force at Tampa to stop the movement; but their assumption was wrong.[19]

In truth, the militia was scarcely organized anywhere in the territory. Calls upon it had met with ragged responses. Frequently it had proved more of a troublemaker than a fighting force. Governor DuVal took pains in December, 1825, to order the Alachua militia not to attack Indians for killing cattle. But the only recompense he could offer to frontiersmen whose cattle had been killed by hungry Indians was the information that the government of the United States might—just might—compensate them for their losses.[20]

If in 1824 Gad Humphreys had been inattentive to duty, in 1825 he began to make up for it. DuVal left the territory to visit in the North, leaving George Walton to act as governor. Walton and Humphreys did not work well together, and the load upon the agent was increased. Bit by bit he began to emerge as a champion of the Indians. They badly needed a champion. There was a sharp fight in Cabbage Swamp near St. Augustine in July, 1825. The agent claimed that an Indian-hater named Solano had instigated it, while certain local leaders, notably Joseph M. Hernandez, recently Territorial delegate to Congress, sided with Solano. All that came of the incident was a dangerous honing of already razor-edged relations.[21]

Wherever the white officials looked, they saw cause for worry. Through the fisheries along the Gulf coast, especially those around Charlotte Harbor, the natives had access to Cuba. There, it was said, they received royal treatment. Even Gad Humphreys complained of this intercourse, while Colonel Brooke in August, 1825, asked permission to break it up by force. Yet in 1827 and 1828 when hunger still tormented the red men, DuVal permitted them to go to the coast to fish in spite of the boundaries designated by the treaty expressly to keep them away from the water's edge. The trade with Cuba continued.[22]

Slavery was of course another source of friction between whites and Indians. Many fugitive slaves continued to dwell among the Seminoles. Naturally their presence was an ever-rankling annoyance to white slaveholders. Three years after the transfer of Florida to the United States, the Legislative Council had passed a slave code, but it seemed constantly jeopardized by the presence in the territory of the Indian-Negroes. Even when calling the Seminoles to meet in 1823, Governor DuVal had directed Horatio Dexter to pry away from them as many runaways as possible. To repossess those thus secured, the owners would have to pay the territorial government fifty dollars per head. Similar instructions were issued to Gad Humphreys when he became agent. He was to have the chiefs understand that they might not harbor runaways, and was to see that white claimants had every chance to identify Negroes they claimed had escaped from them. With the passage of time there were mutterings against Humphreys on the grounds that he did not aid the owners enough. These rumors, combined with charges that the agent allowed the natives to roam, caused DuVal, when he returned from his leave, to inquire whether or not Humphreys' conduct deserved impeachment. No one was willing to carry the charges that far. The governor himself recognized that the restrictions imposed on the trade of local whites with the Indians made the whites peevish toward all officials.[23]

Reacting to the runaway slave problem, Governor DuVal urged that white people be permitted to purchase Negroes from the Indians. The Indian-Negroes were a bad influence on their Seminole masters, he said, and this influence might be eliminated that way. Here was one of the rare points on which the agent agreed with him. When permission was refused, DuVal asked for more specific directives about the determination of ownership. Were slaves taken by the Indians during the "late war"—presumably the War of 1812—to be surrendered to owners who could identify them? If so, were the Indians to receive compensation for property they lost in that conflict? Must he try to check title to slaves and other chattels back to Spanish times? Finally, what about slaves and other property sold by the Indians to unscrupulous traders who had represented to them that the Americans intended to take everything from them? These traders had virtually stolen valuable property, they had bought it so cheap. "I cannot consent," DuVal told the Secretary of War, "to that sort of left-handed justice which gives all that is demanded to our citizens and which withholds justice from this cheated, abused, and persecuted race."[24]

Meanwhile he had given a talk to some chiefs on February 23, 1826, admonishing them to bring in runaways. In response they had surrendered large numbers. He was ashamed, he added, to demand the runaways among them since the whites held many slaves belonging to the Seminoles.[25]

Relations between whites and Indians approached a crisis in the summer of 1826. Although most of the Indians had entered the reservation by this time, hunger again drove them outside in search of food. Petitions came in from white communities in Florida asking their removal to the West. At first the governor was irritated at the white complainers, and demanded legal evidence of the depredations perpetually charged against the Indians. To that end he conducted full-scale hearings in Alachua County, and found that many of the complaints lacked solid basis. Nevertheless, his tolerance of the Seminoles was for some reason eroding away. Writing to Thomas L. McKenney on July 27, 1826, he displayed a change of tone. The best hunting, he said, was in the Indian reservation, yet the red men neglected it, preferring instead to maraud upon the cattle and provisions of white people. The whites had been good to them, he continued; they had set out food at any house where the natives asked for it. Apparently this practice had spoiled the Indians.[26]

The documents contain no direct clues to the reason why DuVal's attitude changed so drastically in six months. One can infer that the double burden of governorship and superintendency had frayed his nerves. After all, he was under steady attack from all quarters. The tender-minded assailed him for having used force at Moultrie Creek (which he denied); the economy-minded criticized him for spending money to feed the Indians (yet if he had not done so, they would have starved); while day in and day out the slaveholders carped at him for every move. As if this were not enough, he brooded over being badly underpaid. More than once he hinted that he might resign if not given a raise, and late in 1826 he asked to be relieved as superintendent because the job cost him heavily.[27]

The governor agreed with the Administration that it would be a good policy to send a few influential chiefs to Washington, primarily to impress them with the power of the United States. In 1824 Neamathla and John Hicks had refused to make the trip, but May, 1826, found them and five others in the capital. There, John Hicks, interpreted by Abraham—a Negro of whom we shall see much more later—spoke for the others. First, he asked that Big Swamp be transferred outright to the Seminoles. Under the existing arrangement it might be necessary to move any day, but his people could not face this as they had suffered so much from the trek onto the reservation. It had torn up their roots. Nor did they want to go West. It was on this occasion that Hicks described their attachment: "Here our navel strings were first cut, and the blood from them sunk into the earth and made the country dear to us." He bluntly stated that the Seminoles wanted the white men to return their slaves. Finally, the chief said, let the endless talk of schools come to an end. The Great Spirit did not intend that Indians should learn to read and write. In the beginning the Great Spirit had placed a book in the hands of a blind old man. The old one summoned red and white men before him, and announced that the book, and the learning it represented, should go to the first people to kill a deer and bring it to him. All sped out. Because deer were scarce the Indians ranged widely. Not so the white men. Happening upon a sheep close by they killed it and brought it in. Since the old one could not see, he gave the book to them. Thus, book learning came first to the white man by deceit, and was withheld from the red men forever.[28]

Those who signed the talk, signifying their agreement with its contents, were: Tuckose Emathla (John Hicks), Neamathla, and Itcho Tustenuggee representing the Tallahassees and Mikasukis, Micanopy for the Alachua band, Holata Mico for the Pease Creek Tallahassees (this was not the Alachua Holata Mico, who was called Billy Bowlegs), and Tulce Emathla and Fuche Luste Hadjo for the towns around Chocachatti, which were off-shoots from the Alachua band. The major segments of the Seminoles were thus represented.[29]

Not long after the visit to Washington, the white officials in Florida brought off a *coup de main*. They had perennially sought to draw all or most of the Florida Indian bands into some sort of centralized organization. This time they achieved it. Most of the credit probably belongs to Gad Humphreys. An election was scheduled for late July, 1826, to be held near the Indian Agency, which Agent Humphreys had established in 1825, about two miles west of Silver Springs. The Alachua band and their affiliates backed Micanopy, while the Mikasukis and Tallahassees supported John Hicks. So intense was the rivalry that violence was feared, and this fear prompted Humphreys to ask Colonel Brooke to send a detachment of soldiers to keep the peace. Brooke designated two companies, and the units were on hand through all the critical moments. When the count was made, John Hicks was the winner. Now began large-scale preparations for an induction ceremony. Half a mile from the Agency the Indians erected a circular arbor two hundred feet in diameter. Choice seats were reserved for the agent and the troops. Lieutenant George A. McCall, a witness, believed three thousand persons were present. At dusk a hundred picked warriors, led by a Mikasuki, performed a rattlesnake dance. Hand in hand, single file, they made loops and coils around the huge fire while the last man rattled a gourd. At the same time, all present chanted the merits of the chief. When this was ended, a herald advanced into the center of the circle and called three times for Tuckose Emathla. Solemnly Hicks came forward, naked except for a breech clout hanging knee-length fore and aft. The herald attached a miniature war club to Hicks' forelock and proclaimed him Supreme Chief of the Seminole Nation. With that Hicks launched into an oration which the white listeners, even though they heard it through an illiterate interpreter, thought very grand. By 10:00 P.M., at the end of three hours, the ceremony was over. Thus was inducted the first chief of all the bands of Florida Indians. His power was doubtless limited, but it suited the white men well to have one responsible person with whom to deal.[30]

The two companies detached for service at the Seminole election returned to Cantonment Brooke late in September, 1826. By that time there had been so many requests to place soldiers closer to the reservation that the War Office issued the order to establish a second post. At first Colonel Duncan L. Clinch, commander of the Fourth Infantry Regiment stationed at Cantonment Clinch near Pensacola, was ordered to send a company to erect a temporary post on the Suwannee River. But Humphreys, the governor, and others lost no time in protesting that this was too remote from the reservation. In the end the War Department left it up to DuVal to establish the new post where it was most needed. He placed it within a quarter of a mile of the Indian Agency near Silver Springs, where Gad Humphreys conducted his business.[31]

In spite of everything, efforts to keep the peace failed, and the year 1826 drew to a close with relations worse than before. In an attempt to improve them, Congress appropriated another $20,000 to relieve Indian suffering. Its action prompted Superintendent McKenney to write DuVal that he feared the Seminoles would be pauperized. Perhaps so, the governor replied acidly, but on the other hand something had to be done for them. Drought had destroyed their crops again, and if not fed they would certainly overrun the country. Meanwhile the number of atrocities mounted, including murders, mostly committed by the Mikasukis. Governor DuVal called on Lieutenant Colonel Brooke at Hillsborough Bay and upon Colonel Clinch at Pensacola for a force, and he also felt obliged to call out the militia of Jackson, Gadsden, Alachua, Duval, and Nassau Counties to form detachments to scour the country and arrest any Indians found out of bounds. But the call for militia was not productive. Most of the men dared not leave their homes unprotected to answer the summons. It was not surprising, therefore, that there was vehement protest when General Winfield Scott, commander of the eastern district of the army, ordered the withdrawal of the solitary company of regulars from St. Augustine. This order was not executed. Neither is it surprising that a few citizens stood to their own defense. One of them wrote the governor that he had armed two of his Negroes and had given them positive orders to shoot any Indian they found plundering his fields.[32]

Early in 1827 the Legislative Council of Florida passed an act to restrain its own citizens. They might not trade with the Indians except at licensed places, nor trespass on Seminole land. The penalties for infractions were heavy. One clause was aimed at the Indians. It made aiding a slave to escape a crime punishable by death. Next, on January 15, 1827, the Council passed "An Act to Prevent the Indians from Roaming at Large through the Territory." Under its provisions, any citizen finding an Indian outside the reservation might personally drag him to the closest justice where the judge could inflict thirty-nine lashes and confiscate the Indian's gun. When word of this reached the Indian Office in Washington there was consternation, for McKenney and others believed that white men would not bother to go through the justices, but would take the punishment into their own hands. Governor DuVal, however, assured them that no one had tried, or would try, to enforce this provision.[33]

As for the government in Washington, it reacted to the growing tension by centering military responsibility in Florida in one officer, Colonel Clinch, on January 4, 1827. To discharge this responsibility, he had his own regiment at Pensacola, and, if needed, a battalion of the First Infantry Regiment also at Pensacola, besides one company of the Fourth Artillery at St. Augustine. In investing Clinch with this responsibility Jacob Brown, the Commanding General of the Army, cautioned him that the public mind was inflamed, and that he must not be swayed by it to deal harshly. "With our power," he wrote, "I hope also that [the Seminoles] may be made to feel our justice."[34]

Duncan Lamont Clinch had been born in North Carolina in 1787, and had entered the army as a lieutenant, direct from civil life, when the establishment was enlarged in 1808.* Although his service during the War of 1812 was undistinguished, by the spring of 1819 he had risen to be colonel of the Eighth Infantry Regiment. If we may look beyond the moment of his elevation to command in Florida, he advanced by brevet, ten years after being made colonel, into the roster of general officers. But in 1836—under circumstances to be developed below—he resigned his commission. All the while he was rising in the army, he was prospering as a planter, with plantations in both Georgia and Florida. One orderly who admired him described him as "fat and lusty, gray and muscular." Fat and muscle combined, he weighed in the neighborhood of 250

---

*The increase of the military establishment in 1808 was precipitated by an attack of HMS *Leopard* upon the USS *Chesapeake*, June 22, 1807. The issue was impressment, and the outcome a war fever in America.

pounds. His face was fine and open, his manners and dress not ostentatious. He was kind to his soldiers, and especially tender with the sick and wounded. If he was not quite so gentle with his slaves, it was because of the culture in which he was born and bred. Finally, he had deep religious convictions.[35]

About a month after receiving his orders, Colonel Clinch reported the disposition of his troops. One company was stationed near the Aucilla River to keep order west of the Suwannee, two companies were stationed at Cantonment Brooke, and the colonel kept four companies with him at Cantonment Clinch, ready to move wherever needed. It was up to the commanding officer at St. Augustine and his one artillery company, which had remained in spite of General Scott's desire to move it, to maintain order east of the St. Johns. Clinch believed that this arrangement, and the number of troops he had, was adequate for the job, for he was convinced that a few outlaws were committing the atrocities, and that the majority of the Seminoles were not hostile.[36]

Clinch now sent the two companies at Cantonment Brooke under the direction of Lieutenant J. M. Glassell to the site selected for the new post near Humphreys' agency, which they reached on March 25, 1827. Here they began at once to erect a log fort on a high knoll overlooking a dense forest of fine old trees. The stockade around the work, when completed, stood twenty feet tall and was made of logs split in half, with the flat surface turned to the inside. A platform about three feet from the ground ran all the way around, to be manned by musketeers when there was need. Within each of the angles of the stockade a blockhouse was built, while at the center of the enclosure stood a two-story building with a cupola on top. Here a sentry kept watch at all times and clanged a raucous cowbell when someone approached. At first this post was designated Cantonment King, after Colonel William King who had commanded the Fourth Infantry before Clinch.[37]

The defense posture in Florida looked fairly adequate to the colonel commanding at the close of 1827. But in 1828 Brevet Major General Scott came near upsetting it.* He issued an

* A brevet was an honorary commission by which the United States could promote an officer in recognition of his bravery and distinction without having to pay for it. The brevet carried no additional pay.

order to withdraw four companies of regulars and send them to New Orleans. Worse yet, he directed that Cantonment King, not yet a year old, be closed. It was too costly, he said, to supply it overland from Tampa Bay. Many Floridians protested, and Colonel Clinch took the liberty of suspending the order until his own objections should be heard. In time the War Department informed Scott that he could neither withdraw the companies nor abandon Cantonment King. But that was not the last of the story. In 1828 General Jacob Brown died, and the position of commanding general passed to Alexander Macomb. Since he agreed with Scott, Cantonment King was abandoned in 1829. Hardly had this been done than D. L. Clinch, newly appointed brevet brigadier general as of April 20, 1829, urged that the post be reopened. Macomb overruled him. It was too expensive, he said, to maintain small units in so isolated a place. Moreover, if proper vigilance was exercised, "I cannot see that any danger can be apprehended from the miserable Indians who inhabit the peninsula of Florida." This view of the Seminoles was the common one, but not among officers on the ground. The officers finally somehow prevailed, for during the last half of 1832 the post was once more activated. This time the captain in command referred to it in his reports as Fort King.[38]

In the year 1828 Lieutenant Colonel Brooke was transferred out of Florida. Subordinates mourned his leaving. Although they may not have been aware of it, the Indians, too, had lost a friend when he departed. With his second in command gone, Colonel Clinch felt it necessary to move closer to the reservation. Accordingly, he transferred the headquarters of the Fourth Infantry to Cantonment Brooke and brought the companies from Pensacola with him to that place.[39]

Everyone connected with Florida knew that communications were vital to the success of American rule. They had persuaded Congress as far back as 1824 to appropriate $20,000 to construct a road from St. Augustine to Pensacola. Two years later the job was finished. The eastern portion of it became known as the Bellamy Road because it was built under contract by John Bellamy, the same rich planter who had served as the appraiser of abandoned Indian improvements. In addition, 125 miles of road were opened by the army between Can-

tonment Brooke and King early in 1828. These roads were
far from being highways. They were just wide enough for a
wagon to pass, and there often were stumps between the
tracks. Yet they were openings cut through the heavy forest,
with crude bridges over waterways and corduroy over the bog-
giest places, in every way easier to traverse than the forest
tracks which they supplanted.[40]

The government in Washington had reacted to the gathering tension by centralizing military control in Florida. It had
also reacted by trying to persuade the Seminoles to move west.
Numerous petitions out of the territory, from individuals, communities, and even the Legislative Council itself, to remove
the Indians altogether carried conviction. Joseph M. White,
the Territorial delegate, undertook to sell the Indians themselves on migration. He assembled a group of chiefs on May
20, 1827, for that purpose. Basically his technique was the
iron-fist-in-velvet-glove type which Gadsden had used four
years earlier. The President, he told them, "now offers you a
good country and a great deal of money and provisions, do not
therefore listen to bad counsel but take them for this sickly
country where you now are. If you do not in a dozen moons
your bad men may do wrong again, and your Great Father
will send soldiers and destroy their town." His audience listened impassively and then refused to consider moving at all.
They were not yet sufficiently reduced or intimidated to come
to that. Nevertheless the situation was satisfactory to no
one. In October, 1828, five important chiefs signified to Gad
Humphreys that they were willing to send a delegation to look
at the western country. But nothing came of it.[41]

5

Payne's Landing and Fort Gibson

THE TWO PRINCIPAL MEN grappling with the Indian problem in Florida seemed to be developing opposite attitudes
toward their native charges. Gad Humphreys spoke so strongly in their defense that a grand jury issued a presentment
against him in February, 1827. Writing to DuVal to defend
himself against it, he vowed that the Indians were not solely
at fault. The country, he said, "was filled with reckless adventurers from all quarters of the globe." To give them freedom
of action against the natives, as the Legislative Council had
done with its act to prevent the roaming of the Indians, was
to apply sparks to tinder.[1]

Governor DuVal, who seemed to show less and less sympathy
for the Seminoles, did not agree. In his view Floridians were
not the reckless adventurers the agent said they were. Actually, he insisted, they had shown great forbearance. Had they
not provided food whenever hungry Indians asked for it? Yet
their recompense had been the growth of a "wanton and insolent" attitude among the recipients. His shift in mood may
have been induced not by the Indians so much as by Washington. In expending money to keep the Seminoles from starving
he had exceeded appropriations. In March, 1827, Superintendent McKenney informed him that the excesses would have to
come out of the contingent fund. Inasmuch as this fund was
always lean, DuVal and his employees would have to skimp,

for their pay came out of it too. Unwilling to take a cut in pay, the blacksmith for the Indian reservation, the subagent, and the interpreter all quit. Small wonder that the governor's outlook was somewhat jaundiced.[2]

Not everything, fortunately, went wrong at once. Neamathla, on his own reservation on the Apalachicola, was no longer the center of contumacy he had been earlier. He was apparently satisfied with the arrangement. When murders were committed by some of his tribesmen, he took a party and pursued the murderers. For two months he trailed them before success came; then, marvelous to tell, instead of visiting Indian justice on them he turned them over to white courts. Still more remarkable, those courts acquitted them. Nor was this the only sort of cooperation given by the bands along the Apalachicola. Governor DuVal was able to use some of them to help round up hostiles west of the Suwannee.[3]

Gad Humphreys' story, although it extended to 1830, can now be told to the end. Championing the Indians, he made bitter enemies among the white Floridians. The Seminoles delivered more and more runaway slaves to former owners, but the Floridians insisted that they held back others. Finally, the Indians came to the conclusion that it was intended to deprive them of all Negroes. Agent Humphreys was supposed to turn redeemed slaves over to the white men who claimed them as runaway property, yet there was no assurance that the Indians would get them back, even if the courts ordered their return. Local owners regarded Humphreys as too slow in restoring their property to them. DuVal, in his capacity as superintendent, refused after an altercation over the alleged delay to communicate with Humphreys further, until the War Department stepped in. Humphreys denied that he was failing to follow orders, but admitted that he did not approve of the policy. His detractors further accused him of profiteering from deals with the Indians in slaves and cattle. He was even charged with keeping Negroes whom the Indians had turned over to him, and working them on his own property instead of returning them to their owners.[4]

The Adams administration sent Alexander Adair to investigate the charges against Humphreys. Holding hearings in St. Augustine, he found that the persons loudest in complaint were

unwilling to testify. DuVal claimed that Humphreys had persuaded these people not to appear, but this seems unlikely,
considering how little they cared for the agent. The principal
charges against Humphreys related to slaves, and Adair repeated that he could find scant foundation for them. His report, however, was not the decisive factor in determining Gad
Humphreys' future. During the controversy Andrew Jackson
became President. Governor DuVal wrote him congratulations
on the reforms he had begun, and asked that they be extended
to Florida. The President's friends there had been overlooked
for a long time! He demanded that Humphreys and Judge
Joseph L. Smith should be relieved. On the grounds that the
Indians had failed to give up all runaway slaves, he had withheld part of the annuity during 1828. Humphreys protested
this on behalf of the Indians. Somehow the matter came before
Judge Smith, who ruled that the annuity could not be withheld.[5]

Joseph M. White and James Gadsden, both influential citizens, joined the chorus for getting rid of Humphreys. In
response to the pressure, the President made the removal in
1830, and filled the vacancy with John Phagan, who had been
subagent since January, 1826.

A committee of Congress turned down Humphreys' request
for a land grant in 1832 because he had placed government
buildings worth $2,000 on his own land. The location of those
buildings might have been accidental rather than intentional,
for land boundaries were vague at best. More important than
this in the committee's refusal was the political atmosphere at
the time of the committee's report, a product of Jackson's assault on the second United States Bank. Humphreys was not a
Jackson man in politics, and that to many Jacksonians was a
higher crime than speculation.

The Seminoles lost a friend when Humphreys, guilty or innocent, was forced out because of his views on Negro policy.
If they gained an ally in Phagan, they certainly did not get a
more honest man. As for Humphreys, he settled close to the
reservation and ran a small trading post. During the years
that followed, some white men accused him of urging the Indians not to migrate.[6]

John Hicks voiced the sense of injustice building up among

his people at a talk on January 14, 1829. The Seminoles had delivered over all Negroes "with no masters," yet the white men demanded more. Often a white man sold a Negro to an Indian, only to claim him later as a runaway. Apart from the slave question, where were the promised corn and presents? Hicks admitted the theft of $1,500 worth of goods from a trader named Marsh, but insisted that the whole sum would be repaid as soon as the withheld annuity was turned over to them. Finally, why had the government paid John Bellamy $1,600 for damages alleged to have been suffered through Indian action? The Seminoles owed him nothing, the chief said wrathfully; on the contrary, Bellamy had stolen their hogs, and he owed the Seminoles.[7]

Even as Hicks voiced his lament, the outgoing Adams administration decided that the Seminoles must be removed. This was one of the few Adams policies which Andrew Jackson, the incoming President, could heartily endorse. From the earliest times Jackson had been in favor of clearing the Indians out of the path of civilization, and may even have been the instigator of the removal policy sponsored by President Monroe. In any case, in his first annual message President Jackson recommended that land west of the Mississippi be set apart, and that the Indians in the East be encouraged, but not forced, to trade eastern for western land. If they failed to do so, they would be obliged to come under the harsh jurisdiction of the states. His recommendation triggered, four months later, one of the bitterest of debates in Congress. Certain members who no longer had an Indian problem in their states sternly opposed the measures proposed by the President. What honesty was there, they asked, in prattling about benefiting fairly civilized tribes, who had homes and farms, by moving them to a wild country where they would have to start all over again, and in the presence of really savage plains Indians? Nevertheless, the Administration's bill passed the House, with the dangerously slim margin of 101 to 97. Passing through the Senate with less opposition, it became the "Indian Removal Act" on May 28, 1830. Its provisions were at once momentous and simple. The government might trade land in the West for Indian land in the East, and might do what was necessary to remove the Indians to the new land. For these purposes Congress appropriated half a million dollars. Superintendent of Indian Affairs Thomas L. McKenney at least professed to believe that the removal policy was the only humane one. His position within the Jackson administration was precarious, and he pushed the act perhaps partly to render himself more secure. But he barely survived the passage of the new law, being dismissed on August 16, 1830. His seat in the Bureau of Indian Affairs was filled by clerks for the next two crucial years.[8]

The year 1831 brought the affairs of the Florida Indians to another crisis. Many starving bands were preying upon the whites' herds and provisions. Inasmuch as DuVal was on one of his numerous junkets to Kentucky, Acting Governor James D. Westcott summarized their condition. Those Indians on the Apalachicola, he said, were better off than the others, but even they, when their corn ran out in February or March, became dependent until the new crop ripened. The annuity paid under the Treaty of Moultrie Creek did not help them much because they wasted their share. The chiefs received from twenty to seventy dollars per year as their part, while a common warrior drew three to four dollars. Westcott called the common Indians "drunken, lazy, worthless" vagabonds. In the past they had been high spirited and noble, he said, but now there was no hope for them except to move west. Only about half the men had guns, and in other ways their strength, and consequently their bargaining power, dwindled with every passing moon.[9]

A steady flow of petitions from white communities kept before the federal government the urgent need to get the Indians out of Florida. At the same time the Indians' cost to the government ran high, for Congress continued to appropriate money to keep them from starving. The true situation of the red men was probably well summarized by the Florida Legislative Council in a petition to Congress begging for removal. "The Treaty of 1823 deprived them of their cultivated fields and of a region of country fruitful of game, and has placed them in a wilderness where the earth yields no corn, and where even the precarious advantages of the chase are in a great measure denied them. . . . They are thus left the wretched alternative of Starving within their limits, or roaming among the whites, to prey upon their cattle. Many in the Nation, it seems, annually die of Starvation; but as might be expected, the much greater proportion of those who are threatened with want, leave their boundaries in pursuit of the means of subsistence, and between these and the white settlers is kept up an unceasing contest."[10]

In spite of the pressure and of his own inclinations, it was not until the last year of his first term that Andrew Jackson reached the point of taking action. When his government did move, it was of course not primarily because of the plight of the Indians, but rather because of the indignation of the white Floridians who found the Indians in their way. On January 30, 1832, instructions were issued from the War Department to appoint a special agent to negotiate with the Seminoles. The agent was none other than James Gadsden, the moving spirit nine years earlier in the Treaty of Moultrie Creek. That he was a friend of the President was enough to secure him this appointment, but in addition his selection was an endorsement of his earlier negotiations. His reward was eight dollars a day and eight dollars for every twenty miles traveled; he also got five dollars a day for a secretary and five dollars for every twenty miles the secretary traveled. These were good wages in the 1830's.[11]

The government's instructions to Gadsden exuded lofty motives. The Indians, they said, unable to provide food for themselves, were suffering desperately. To relieve their distress, Gadsden was to persuade them to move west. This purpose was the core of his mission. Now appeared an extremely startling stipulation: the Seminoles were to become a constituent part of the Creek nation and share with it an allotment of land west of the Mississippi. This was almost a calculated affront to the Seminoles, for whenever the Florida Indians had fought white men, they had had to fight the Creeks as well. During the War of 1812 and again in Jackson's invasion of 1818, the Creeks had joined the whites to battle their southern cousins. What is more, there was unremitting bad blood between them about the ownership of slaves. Seeking slaves, the Creeks had frequently raided Seminole settlements. The only sentiment the Seminoles felt toward the Creeks was hatred. Despite this hostility, Andrew Jackson and other statesmen had as early as the acquisition of Florida by the United States set the amalgamation of Creeks and Seminoles as a goal, but they had been obliged to give it up. Now in 1832 the moment to achieve it had come because the Florida Indians were in so sad a plight they could not resist.[12]

This time Gadsden was to handle the negotiations alone. He began preparations at once. It was not necessary to consider the Apalachicola Indians in his plans, for he was later to deal with them separately. It is curious that he set the treaty grounds farther west than Moultrie Creek. In conference with Micanopy, he appears to have selected Payne's Landing on the Oklawaha River, a few miles from the modern town of Eureka. Whatever the reason for the choice, the spot was easy of access and well known to all bands. But not until three months after receiving his commission was Gadsden able to assemble enough chiefs to hold a talk. Finally, the meeting began at Payne's Landing at the close of the first week in May, 1832.[13]

It is unfortunate that Gadsden never submitted any minutes of the talks held with the Indians at Payne's Landing. This failure laid him open to endless charges that the treaty signed there was obtained by force and fraud. Without such a record, we know little of what did occur. Later Gadsden reported two of the things he told the Seminoles: first, that the government could not continue to feed them year after year; and, second, that their situation would be more wretched when they came under the laws of the Territory, as they must do if they refused to move. We know nothing more except that a treaty was signed May 9, 1832. The marks of seven chiefs and eight subchiefs appear on it. These fifteen probably pretty well represented most of the Mikasuki bands and the Alachua band with its numerous offshoots. But certainly they were fewer and less representative than the signers at Moultrie Creek nine years before.[14]

Twenty-nine months later Micanopy declared that he had not marked the Treaty of Payne's Landing. Even though his name appeared on the document, he insisted that he did not touch the pen. Of course the white men denied this, but in the last analysis it was their word against his. The rumor circulated that none of the senior chiefs had made their marks; the young bucks, disguised as their elders, had done it. Worse yet, Charley Emathla claimed that all the signers were coerced.

This allegation, uttered on October 25, 1834, made Indian Agent Wiley Thompson, successor to John Phagan, furious; "it is said by Charley Emarthla [sic], that the white people forced you into the treaty of Payne's Landing. If you were so cowardly as to be forced by anybody to do what you ought not ... you are unfit to be chiefs." His argument, though lofty in tone, was not very strong in reasoning, for overwhelming force has obliged many people to do what they thought wrong. Moreover, the Indians did not nurture a tradition of martyrdom in their culture.[15] It appears unlikely that we shall ever know who actually marked the treaty and whether or not they did so because of force or the threat of it.

The Preamble of the Treaty of Payne's Landing contained the crucial words. They stipulated that the Seminoles were willing for seven of "their confidential chiefs" to travel west to inspect the Creek lands, and "should they be satisfied with the character of that country, and of the favorable disposition of the Creeks to reunite with the Seminoles as one people," then the articles of the agreement were to be considered binding. To whom does "they" refer? Since the first sentence was long and involved, the reference is not at all clear. Did it point to the delegation of seven chiefs or to the Seminole nation? In this matter, Indians and white men took opposite views. Charley Emathla said in October, 1834, that his people were not bound to emigrate "because the question was not submitted to the Seminole nation, after their delegation returned, whether they were willing to go." Other Indians agreed with him. White men, on the contrary, contended that "they" referred to the delegation of chiefs, who had full power to bind the group. This much can be said for the white position: the various bands, which made up the loose association referred to as the Seminole Nation, seldom had any sort of national council except at such times as the United States government obliged them to do so. The Indian contention that important decisions had to be decided by council seems shaky. Yet only six years before, in 1826, the diverse bands had elected a supreme chief to head them all; and this new departure may itself have altered their traditional ways of operating.[16]

Major Ethan Allen Hitchcock, although he was not there, contended as "simple, unquestionable truth," that Abraham,

the Negro interpreter at the treaty meetings (and a powerful
leader among the Seminoles) misrepresented the treaty's opening sentence to the chiefs. Abraham knew, Hitchcock said,
that the Seminoles had no intention of leaving Florida before
the twenty years had passed which they considered to be the
limit of the Treaty of Moultrie Creek. It follows that they
would not have signed the treaty had the pitfalls in its words
been apparent to them. Gadsden, he added, bribed Abraham
to conceal the truth—but more of that later.[17]

The articles of the treaty were to go into effect only when
the stipulation in the Preamble was satisfied: the Seminoles
would be out of Florida within three years after the ratification of the treaty, one-third of them leaving every year. The
Indians were, of course, to surrender all claims to their Florida land in return for various considerations. Estimated, these
grants added up to around $80,000. If the Seminoles were sur-
rendering the 4,032,940 acres assigned them at Moultrie
Creek, their return equaled about two cents per acre.

In addition—and startling to see in print—the treaty stipulated that the Seminoles would become a part of the Creek
Nation, occupy land assigned to the Creeks in the West, and
draw their annuities from the lump sum appropriated by Congress for the Creeks. They were thereby, in effect, surrender-
ing their separate entity. To make so radical a departure, they
had to be hard pressed indeed. It is not unreasonable to suggest that nothing but coercion could have obliged them to be
swallowed up by their enemies.[18]

The people of Florida praised the Treaty of Payne's Landing because it freed them of the "savages," but they stood almost alone in its support. Thomas L. McKenney later wrote of
it as an open fraud, "a foul blot upon the escutcheon of the
nation." Officers of the regular army who served in Florida
nearly to a man took the same view. Finally, latter-day writers
have been all but unanimously condemnatory. Yet interpretation of the scanty evidence left by those who were there offers
little direct substantiation for so strong a condemnation. On
the other hand, there is not much which flatly rejects it.[19]

It seems plain that there was no force at the treaty grounds
sufficient to coerce the Indians. I have not seen any record describing the military detachment that was present. But it was

almost certainly smaller than the twenty-five soldiers at Moultrie Creek. It is reasonable to presume that at this time a less immediate and subtler type of pressure was applied. One cannot explain the agreement of the Seminoles to merge with the Creeks without such a presumption. Gadsden had not hesitated in 1823 to flex a mailed fist, and inasmuch as the government had ratified his handiwork then, it would be likely that he used the same tactics at Payne's Landing. Finally, the Seminoles were even weaker in 1832 than in 1823, and they knew well that they were.[20]

Contemporary evidence is characteristically scarce concerning the charge of fraud. The most damning statement comes from Ethan Allen Hitchcock, who was not present but who claimed that he had interviewed those who were. He put in his private diary his conviction that the treaty was drawn up in Washington and sent to Gadsden with instructions to get the concurrence of the Seminoles. Nor was it possible to make headway, Hitchcock wrote, until Gadsden had bribed Abraham with two hundred dollars, to be paid after ratification. Hitchcock's authority concerning the bribe was Captain Charles M. Thruston, who claimed to have been present when James Gadsden told President Jackson in person that he could not have procured a treaty without it. Thruston was a graduate of the United States Military Academy, with an honorable record as a commissioned officer. There is no reason to suspect him of inventing an incident, or to suspect Hitchcock of perpetuating a fictitious one. Yet neither is impossible. This much is certain: Article II of the Treaty provided that two hundred dollars each should go to Abraham and Cudjo, Phagan's interpreter, "in full remuneration for the improvements to be abandoned on the lands now cultivated by them."[21]

Few white men could handle Hitchiti and Muskogee; few Indians, English. Thus, the interpreters were the channels through which communication had to flow. In most cases they were Indian-Negroes devoid of education, yet what they reported as being said was perforce the basis for all official action. It follows, naturally, that the interpreters, whether bribed or not, and even though they were usually slaves, were as important in any negotiation as the most exalted person present.[22]

The Preamble of the Treaty of Payne's Landing requires additional scrutiny. The Indian position about "they" in the Preamble has already been stated. It remained consistent. Even the seven chiefs who went to Arkansas, and in 1833 signed an agreement which the white men contended bound the Seminoles to move, never pretended that they had authority to bind their people. In contrast, the white stand was not as consistent. Gadsden, when reporting the treaty to the Secretary of War, wrote, "with the condition that a deputation of seven confidential chiefs . . . should previously visit the Creek country west of the Mississippi, and should it correspond with the representations made of it, then the agreement made is to be binding on the respective parties." Who was to judge whether or not the new land corresponded "with the representations made of it?" But seven years later, when the Second Seminole War was raging, Gadsden, in reply to criticisms of his treaty, flatly labeled as a fatal mistake the attempt to get the nation to move on the grounds that the seven chiefs had bound it to do so. Had the matter been submitted to the people in council, he insisted, they would have agreed to move.[23]

Lewis Cass, who had become President Jackson's Secretary of War, seems to have had but one view of the subject. This was expressed in December, 1832, in his annual report to the President. "The treaty, however, is not obligatory on their part until a deputation sent by them shall have examined the country proposed for their residence, and until the tribe, upon their report, shall have signified their desire to embrace the terms of the treaty." It would be hard to be more explicit; but, when the matter came to a head, Cass did not enforce this interpretation of the treaty.[24]

The exploratory party of seven was supposed to leave for the West after the Green Corn Dance in July, but did not get away until about October 10, 1832. Jumper, Charley Emathla, Coa Hadjo, Holata Emathla, and Yahadjo, named in the treaty, were present. John Hicks took the place of Sam Jones, who was an old man, and Nehathoclo went in the stead of Fuche Luste Hadjo, who for some reason could not go. With the seven Indians went the agent John Phagan and their "faithful interpreter, Abraham."[25]

The attention of the government turned now to the small

reservations along the Apalachicola. James Gadsden returned from Washington in the fall of 1832 to open negotiations with their chiefs. He estimated that the land within those reservations would bring $30,720, and that it would cost $38,000 to buy the occupants out, move them, and issue them rations for one year.[26] If the estimate was correct, here was a fair bargain. Nor was it difficult to persuade the chiefs. Three of them, Blunt, Davy Elliot, and Cochrane, agreed on October 11, 1832, to migrate, taking 256 people with them. Most of the rest acquiesced the following spring. But when it came to the actual moving, there was much delay. Lawless Alabama Indians, accompanied by white men, moved onto Blunt's reservation, did violence to him and his family, and defied the United States. The government invoked an elaborate set of legal processes to rescue the chief. Another cause of delay was the decision that the Apalachicolas were to take up land not in Arkansas Territory, but in Texas. Presumably this was done by agreement with Mexico, but there was a lobbyist on hand to try to prevent it. He represented a land company which claimed title to the ground marked out for the migrants.[27]

To compensate Blunt for the depredations he had suffered, James Gadsden proposed to the Indian Office that a small sailing vessel be given the chief. He had been on the white side, Gadsden pointed out, as far back as Jackson's campaign of 1818. "He rendered most essential personal services to the commissioners in concluding the Treaties of Camp Moultrie and Payne's Landing." Considering that the chief was not present at Payne's Landing, it would be useful to know what Gadsden had in mind. Be that as it may, Blunt received the boat. One more thing was to be done for him. Some time earlier he had allowed his son to go to the Choctaw Academy in Kentucky run by Richard Mentor Johnson (Vice President of the United States a few years later under Martin Van Buren). Now, as the time to leave Florida approached, the chief asked that his son be returned to him. No one at the academy could identify the son. Indeed, they were afraid that he might have died of cholera a few months before. In time the youth was located and sent back to Florida in December, 1833, along with five or six other Seminole boys. Thus it was 1834 before Blunt and Davy, another influential Apalachicola chief, left Florida and settled on land along the Trinity River in the northeastern part of Texas.[28]

As of November 9, 1833, 605 Indians were still along the Apalachicola River: 241 men, 143 women, 167 children, 34 slaves, 15 free Negroes, and 15 persons merely labeled as "others." Many of these Apalachicolas lingered on in Florida for six more years, siding all the while with the white men. If in so doing they were playing policy, the outcome was not satisfactory, for they found themselves the victims of attacks by both Indians and border whites. Nor did they receive adequate compensation or even recognition for the scouting and actual fighting they undertook for the white cause. In the end their fate was the same as that of all the other Seminoles who were not intransigents, for on October 28, 1838, the last of the Apalachicolas were shipped off to the West.[29]

Meanwhile the national government was trying to perfect the policy of Indian removal. On July 14, 1832, Congress created a committee of three to gather information about the country west of the Mississippi and the Indians there. After encountering several refusals to serve, Secretary Cass at length appointed Governor Monfort Stokes of North Carolina, Henry L. Ellsworth of Connecticut, and the Reverend John F. Schermerhorn of New York. These men bore the title "Commissioners of Indian Affairs, West."* Also, during July the organization of the War Department was made more efficient. The head of Indian Affairs was designated Commissioner, to be appointed by the President with the advice and consent of the Senate. At the same time, greater powers were assigned to him than the head of the old bureau had held. Now finally the regime of clerks as acting heads ended, and on July 10, 1832, Elbert Herring was appointed Commissioner. The next step was to make a formal agreement with the Creek Indians concerning their removal and their relationship to the Seminoles,

---

*A total of five men turned down the job of commissioner before three were found who would agree to serve. Stokes resigned as governor of North Carolina in order to accept the position, and he remained in Indian country afterward on various assignments. Least is known of Schermerhorn. All three men seem to have been conscientious in the discharge of their duties. All appeared to believe that the policy of removal was best for the Indians. See McDermott, *Western Journals*, 9 ff.; Foreman, *Pioneer Days*; Ellsworth, *Washington Irving*.

once both peoples were in the West. This was accomplished in a treaty signed at Fort Gibson (on the Grand, or Neosho, River a little above its confluence with the Arkansas) on February 14, 1833. The Seminoles, that treaty stipulated, should become a part of the Creek nation, but should occupy a separate portion of the Creek reservation.[30]

The lack of evidence shrouds in a fog the fateful events which occurred in Arkansas Territory. The delegation of seven Seminole chiefs, at the end of a long, hard trip reached the "promised land," and after waiting and waiting for the three commissioners, made a reconnaissance of the country. They returned to Fort Gibson in March, 1833. Later Jumper said they found bad Indians on the borders of the land proposed for them, and this is the only bit of positive evidence of their reaction to what they saw. All we know is that, beginning on March 25, 1833, the seven entered into meetings with the white authorities at Gibson. Those authorities, besides the three special commissioners, were General Matthew Arbuckle, commanding officer of Fort Gibson, and John Phagan, the Seminole agent. Among these, the prime mover seems to have been Phagan. According to the scanty white record, the chiefs expressed willingness to leave Florida, provided the Seminoles receive a tract of land to themselves, and an annuity separate from that of the Creeks. They also stipulated that Agent Phagan must be the removal agent. John Hicks told the three commissioners, "We have been kept here a long time while you were making treaties with other Nations. . . . " Whatever the Indian delegation thought, the principal reason for the delay was that the three Commissioners of Indian Affairs, West did not all reach the Fort until early in February. Once there, they had several special problems to address before they could properly turn to the Seminoles. The only other fragment to be drawn from the uninformative record of the talks is the portentous one that on March 28 the delegation signed what has come to be called the Treaty of Fort Gibson. This fateful document was simple and direct. The delegation of seven, it read, were satisfied with the land allotted to their people. It delineated the boundaries of that land. The Seminoles, it continued, "shall commence the removal to their new home as soon as the Government will make arrangements for their emigration satisfactory to the Seminole nation." That was all. The marks of the seven chiefs appear on it, together with the signatures of the three commissioners and of some witnesses.[31]

Holata Emathla, Coa Hadjo, and Jumper later claimed they did not sign the treaty. Whether they said this to justify themselves before their own people, to whom the treaty proved to be anathema, or whether they spoke the truth, we cannot know. Charley Emathla, himself a signer, in October, 1834, asserted that he and the other six had not the power to bind the Seminoles. Why then did he sign? Why did the others? We have no evidence from the participants, but once again Major Hitchcock recorded in his diary some information received from "the officer at the post." His version ran thus: Major Phagan submitted papers to the chiefs, which they refused to sign because they had not the authority. Their duty, they contended, was to submit their findings to "their king" who, with his chiefs, would make the final decision. It is by no means clear who this king was; about the only person coming anywhere near the station was Hicks, who was present. Phagan became angry, and warned that if the chiefs refused to sign he would not "proceed with them on their journey home." Fearful that they might never get back to Florida, they signed; but not, Hitchcock continued, in the presence of the commissioners. The latter accepted the document uncritically as Agent Phagan presented it.[32]

Captain George A. McCall, who was at Fort Gibson, alleged that it was General Arbuckle, not Major Phagan, who cajoled the seven into signing. But the only evidence from the signers themselves was the muddy statement made in council by Charley Emathla nineteen months later: "When I was there, the agent, Phagan, was a passionate man. He quarreled with us after we got there—had Major Phagan done his duty it would all have been settled, and there would have been no difficulty."[33]

There is one other piece of evidence which does indeed cast doubt upon the integrity of the white men who made this treaty. In the Treaty of Payne's Landing the crucial clause read, "should they be satisfied with the character of that country," then the articles of the treaty were to be binding upon the nation. But who were "they," the nation in council or the delegation of seven? Seeing the weakness in the original document, whoever drew up the Fort Gibson treaty misquoted the older treaty. The altered clause read "should this delegation be satisfied," instead of "should they be satisfied." One cannot know whether the seven chiefs were apprised of this vital alteration or not; but if their later arguments were in good faith, they were not informed.[34]

In their official report the three commissioners said that, "The Seminoles, who were referred to the commissioners for advice and assistance . . . have been well accommodated. This nation is, by the late treaty, happily united with its kindred friends (the Creeks) and forms with them one nation; but is secured the privilege of a separate location. . . . This tribe, it is expected, will remove immediately to the lands assigned them." The reference to happy reunion with "kindred friends" indicates either hypocrisy or ignorance of the true state of affairs. I conclude that the commissioners acted out of ignorance, not dissimulation. Indeed, although it cannot be proved by specific documents, I believe that Agent John Phagan prepared the treaty, forced it upon the Indians, and then secured the acquiescence of the commissioners without their bothering to inquire into it. Part of his game was the stipulation in the document that he himself should be agent for the Seminole removal. This the Indians swallowed with the rest. He had also, when quoting from the Treaty of Payne's Landing, altered the words. Considering that Phagan was soon removed from his post for malfeasance, the presumption of questionable conduct on his part seems justified.[35]

An investigation of Phagan's stewardship began about the time he finally shepherded the ill-starred Seminole delegation back from the West. The investigator found that vouchers, after being certified by merchants, had been altered upwards, the difference going to the major. Acting Governor James D. Westcott felt that the evidence showed fraud and improper conduct. Forthwith part of Phagan's pay was stopped to reimburse the government for losses. But in justice to the disgraced agent, it must be noted that there was a political undertone to certain of the charges against him. Delegate White submitted affidavits to prove that the agent had said he would not employ anyone at the Agency who voted for White.

In retaliation, White countercharged that there was no parallel to the fraud, oppression, and inhumanity practiced by Phagan on the Florida Indians. Whatever the measure of his guilt, Phagan was dismissed and his successor appointed.[36]

The United States did not act on the two treaties with the Seminoles for months and months. President Jackson finally submitted them to the Senate on Christmas Eve, 1833, nineteen months after the signing at Payne's Landing and nine months after that at Fort Gibson. Such delay itself seems suspicious, but the explanation for it is simple, even though it has to be based on presumption. The President withheld the Payne's Landing treaty from the Senate until the Seminoles had accepted the land in the West. This they did to Jackson's satisfaction on March 28, 1833, after the session of Congress had already ended on March 3. Submission was necessarily delayed until the next session commenced. From that point on, the handling of the document was perfectly routine in the Senate. After the regular number of reports and readings it reached a vote on April 8, 1834, and was unanimously accepted. The President proclaimed the treaty four days later.[37]

Pressure for removal of the Seminoles became intense in the fall of 1834. The text of the treaty called for complete removal three years after ratification; the deadline should have been April 12, 1837, but it was clear that the United States meant to move the Indians much earlier. To that end the Indian Agent held a series of talks in October, 1834. The Seminoles claimed then that they did not have to move because the Treaty of Moultrie Creek ran for twenty years. This was the duration of the annuities and other payments, and they construed it to be also the time limit. By this line of reasoning they still had several years to remain in Florida.[38]

Agent Wiley Thompson replied angrily and illogically to the Indians' excuses on October 25, 1834. "You solemnly bound yourselves to remove within three years from the ratification of that treaty, and the whole delegation that went west confirmed that promise by entering into a final agreement to do so, by which the whole nation is bound. You know you were not forced to do it. You know that Colonel Gadsden told you at Payne's Landing that it was the wish of your father . . . to

remove you west of the Mississippi River." But his vehemence
could not possibly have been very persuasive to the red men,
for his version of what had been agreed upon differed altogether from theirs.[39]

The three treaties between the United States and the Semi-
noles became the legal framework underpinning the decline of
the Florida Indians. From Moultrie Creek though Payne's
Landing to Fort Gibson there was a path toward destruction.
These three treaties were no more nor less just than the other
treaties drawn up at the same time to implement the policy of
Indian removal. If the policy was just, so were the treaties.
Obviously the Seminoles themselves did not regard them as
just, nor did they expect to be able to obtain justice from the
United States. In the end they refused to abide by the docu-
ments, and war came.

6

Conflict

ONCE JOHN PHAGAN was dismissed, Captain William M. Graham, in command at Fort King, was ordered to act as agent until a regular successor could be named. As the winter of 1833 approached, the Seminoles were without blankets. In addition, they had not been inoculated for smallpox as directed by the government for the simple reason that the hundred dollars offered by the War Department to do the job was insufficient. No medic in his right mind, said Graham, would vaccinate 3,000 to 5,000 bodies for such a fee.[1] Naturally, not all white men saw the plight of the Indians as wholly evil; some felt it would render them more willing to migrate.[2]

Very shortly a replacement for Phagan was chosen. This was Wiley Thompson, a tall, powerful man, usually called General Thompson. He had served with Andrew Jackson during the Creek War, but owed the title to service as major general of the Georgia militia from 1817 to 1824. During the twelve years prior to his appointment as agent he had represented Georgia in the House of Representatives. Could he have known what lay ahead, many times his salary of $1,500 per year would not have lured him to Florida. Not being prescient, he gratefully accepted the commission bearing the date of August 29, 1833. His first duties were in the Apalachicola area, where he assisted in corralling and shipping the Seminoles west. From that task he was directed to make his way to the

Agency near Fort King, where he arrived and took charge on December 1, 1833. It was his misfortune that John Hicks had recently died, removing a powerful restraining force which would have helped him, especially among the belligerent Mikasukis.[3]

The new agent at once became immersed in the problems of Seminole removal under the provisions of the disputed Treaty of Fort Gibson. Unscrupulous white men had been trying in every way to seize the Negroes of the remaining Apalachicola Indians, and Thompson could see no security except for the natives to leave their reservations and come closer to the Agency for protection. Farther east he found that the Indians on the large reservation were reluctant to leave Florida for a number of reasons. They were dissatisfied with the treaties which had placed them under the necessity of moving. They were afraid that once they had gone west of the Mississippi, the more powerful Creeks would take their Negroes from them by force. Many white men who traded with the Indians urged them not to go. But the most influential group bringing steady pressure upon the Seminoles were the Indian-Negroes. They had everything to lose and nothing to gain by a change, and their influence over their "masters" was decisive.[4]

Early in 1834 few white men seemed to appreciate the strength of the forces holding the Seminoles within Florida. Far off at Fort Gibson the three commissioners thought of Seminole migration as all but accomplished. Much closer to home, and in the same vein, the Legislative Council of Florida stated in February, 1834, that "the portion of the Territory hitherto occupied by the Seminole Indians is about to invite a numerous population," as if the red men were already removed. Even as late as April, 1835, the *Florida Herald* at St. Augustine stated in print that there was nothing to be feared from the Seminoles because they had been reduced to a condition of utter dependence.[5]

All the while, affairs in Florida churned and changed. The turbulent politics of the time now brought about the appointment on April 24, 1834, of John H. Eaton to replace William P. DuVal as governor. Perhaps Eaton's surest claims to fame were his longstanding friendship with the President—the two had been neighbors back in Tennessee—and his marriage to

Peggy O'Neale Timberlake, which had kept the Jackson administration in a turmoil during its first two years. The new governor was certainly no conformist, a fact revealed anew when he faced the Indian problem. About one year after his induction, he wrote to Washington desiring to know if the delay of the Senate in ratifying the Seminole treaties of removal had not in fact abrogated those documents. He was of the opinion that it had. Such a perverse view of the nature of Indian treaties was not welcome to President Jackson, even from an old friend, and the Attorney General lost no time in informing the governor that the treaties were still in full force and effect.[6]

At the national level a law was enacted on June 30, 1834, reorganizing the Indian Department in the War Office. It gave legal status to the posts of superintendents and agents, which they had not had before. Regarding Florida, it removed the superintendency from the governor, under the assumption, apparently, that there would soon be no Indians in Florida. This change seems not to have affected the conduct of affairs to any appreciable degree.[7]

Meanwhile, the national government was moving to close out Seminole affairs in Florida. To that end the agent received $7,000 to pay claims against the bands, most of them for slaves supposed to have been stolen by the Indians. Thompson advertised in newspapers that he had the money and that claims should be made to him before December 31, 1834, when the Seminole Agency in Florida was to be closed. The several authorities had decided that the most practicable time for final removal would be the spring of 1835.[8]

Agent Thompson convened the chiefs on October 21, 1834, to distribute to them in specie what was supposed to be the last annuity payable in Florida. In spite of the fact that Territorial laws forbade the sale of liquor to the Indians, here was a chance for the "avaricious, unfeeling human vultures" (as Thompson characterized them) who supplied alcohol to feed ravenously on their willing prey. But all the annuity did not go for drink. The Indians bought more powder and ball than usual. Two days later, at the agent's insistence, they reconvened to talk about removal. For this occasion Thompson tried an approach which he thought would have appeal. The Creeks, he said, wanted very much for the Seminoles to settle among

Osceola
Portrait by George Catlin

them in the West so that the two branches could reunite. Once again a single nation, the Muskogees would doubtless become a great people as they had been before. Supposing that he had thus softened them, he turned to grimmer business. The question was not whether they wanted to remove or stay, but how removal was to be achieved. With this, the first day's session adjourned.[9]

That night the Seminoles gathered in their own council. Osceola, whom the white men called Powell, here for the first time came to the white men's attention. Thompson had spies present, and they reported that Osceola favored proscribing every Indian who advised migration. Osceola had no hereditary claim to leadership, but was an example of the fact that the Creek system left room at the top. Thompson referred to him as "bold and dashing." About thirty-five at the time, he sat close to Micanopy during the councils, prompting the chief to be firm. At the end he stated defiantly that his associates had no intention of moving. He had begun life in the Creek country of Alabama. At the time of his birth his mother was married to a white man named Powell, but there is no evidence that Osceola was Powell's son. Yet he did have white blood in his veins, that of his great-grandfather, the redoubtable Scotsman, James McQueen. At the time of the Creek War, after the Battle of Tohopeka, his mother took him with her when she migrated to Florida, accompanying a Red Stick band led by a half-breed relative, Peter McQueen. White men dogged the boy's youth. They drove him out of Alabama, and they captured him during Andrew Jackson's invasion in 1818. Finally settled among the Tallahassees, he grew to young manhood known as Tallahassee Tustenuggee.[10]

Contemporaries said that he was a little below common height, elegantly formed, with small hands and feet, and that he displayed great skill in all physical games. His face was variously described as thoughtful and cunning, with piercing eyes, chiseled lips, and having a mild, sweet expression. One observer recorded that "a continuous smile played over his face, particularly when shaking hands with the officers." His address was easy and affable, his manners courtly, his handshake firm. The military officers gave him special attention. He was one of the only two persons to whom the struggle, soon to ensue in Florida, brought a national reputation. The name by which he came to be immortalized was derived from the Creek words Asi Yaholo, meaning "black-drink singer," easily corrupted into Osceola or some variation of it.[11]

On that portentous day not all of Osceola's hearers agreed with his intransigent proposal. Holata Emathla insisted that the bands must migrate, but in the end Osceola's policy prevailed, and Jumper was selected to present the Indian objections to the whites on the morrow.[12]

In spite of the selection of Jumper, other Indians carried as much of the discussion as he did on the second day. Micanopy said that the Treaty of Moultrie Creek ran for twenty years, of which nine remained. Jumper added that as a member of the exploratory party he had seen the Pawnees who were to be their neighbors in the West. They were bad Indians and his people did not want to settle near them. Charley Emathla, also one of the seven who had seen the western land, declared that Major Phagan had been guilty of passionate action while they were at Fort Gibson, and had caused much of the trouble. In response the agent told them that he could not accept such evasions. They were not there, he repeated, to discuss whether to remove, but how to do it. Thus ended the second session.[13]

The third session was very stormy. Holata Mico flatly stated that he did not consent to go.* Now the validity of both the Payne's Landing and Fort Gibson treaties came under attack from the chiefs. Micanopy, as already recorded, asserted that he had not signed the first document, while Charley Emathla insisted that all the signers had been coerced. The chiefs generally took the position that they could not be forced to go until the twenty-year period implied in the Treaty of Moultrie Creek had expired. The agent's responses were irate, but Osceola had the last word. "There remains nothing *worth words*!" he said. "If the hail rattles, let the flowers be crushed—the stately oak of the forest will lift its head to the sky and the storm, towering and unscathed." Out of spite Thompson refused to distribute the customary presents, and the chasm opening between the two parties continued to widen.[14]

---

*It cannot be determined whether this recalcitrant was Billy Bowlegs of the Alachua branch or Holata Mico of the Pease Creek Tallahassees.

In reporting this fateful council to Commissioner Elbert Herring, Thompson said that the chiefs frequently interrupted him as he spoke. Such rudeness was so rare as to require an explanation; Thompson thought that the radical chiefs were afraid he would sway some of their people. After all, four influential chiefs had steadily favored migration, although they had sometimes talked against it. These four were Fuche Luste Hadjo (Black Dirt), Charley Emathla, his brother Holata Emathla, and Otulkechala, called Big Warrior by the white men. Their opposition to resistance put them in danger from the fire-eater faction led by Osceola. Indeed, Fuche Luste Hadjo and Holata Emathla asked permission to migrate to the Apalachicola until time for departure from Florida, in order to be far removed from assassins.[15]

Thompson said that the white men who kept urging the Seminoles to remain in Florida were actuated by greed. They wanted the Indians to stay until the laws of the Territory should be placed over them, and then the whites could obtain Indian slaves, which they coveted, by fair means or foul.[16]

When President Jackson read Wiley Thompson's report of the October conferences he scrawled across the back, "Let a sufficient military force be forthwith ordered to protect our citizens and remove and protect the Indians agreeable to the Stipulations of the Treaty."[17]

As time passed, the mood of those involved in the controversy seemed to fluctuate. Thompson thought in December, 1834, that Osceola was more willing to move than before. But when early 1835 arrived, the Indians showed no disposition to modify their stand, and swore injury to anyone who consented to migrate. Upon one issue particularly peace seemed to hang: the ownership of the Indian-Negroes. Citizens estimated that a hundred runaway Negroes had found sanctuary with the Seminoles since Moultrie Creek. How could human property be safe as long as the red men remained in the peninsula? The white men who lusted to own some of the splendid Negroes known to belong to the Seminoles sided with the aggrieved owners of fugitives. Among them were influential friends of President Jackson who sought permission directly from the President to purchase the Negro leaders from the Indians. This purchase would at once solve two problems: it would remove the dangerous influence of these men over their owners, and it would, at the same time, eliminate the species of property which might cause Creeks and Seminoles to fall out in the West. The *Florida Herald* favored this stratagem, but Agent Thompson let it be known that, unless restrained by government, he meant to resist any attempt to take the Seminole's Negroes from them.[18]

It was in February, 1835, at the time when Seminole-white relations were most strained, that one of the severest cold waves in history smote Florida. On the night of February 7 the temperature at St. Augustine dropped to seven degrees above zero, and many days of low temperature followed. The result was the utter ruin of the flourishing citrus industry around St. Augustine. Modest fortunes were wiped out in a few days. The Seminoles were also affected, for the cold reduced their food supply and rendered them more desperate than ever. It could as well have made them more tractable, but cornered as they felt themselves to be, and stiffened by such intransigents as Osceola, they grew more hostile.[19]

White leaders were aware of stiffened resistance among the Indians, and Governor Eaton warned that if force was used against them they would fight. Should the government decide on violence, he recommended a "strong imposing regular force," not volunteers. General Clinch, who would have to direct the violence if it came, requested additional strength. The War Department replied that ten regular companies would soon be in Florida, stationed six at Fort King, three at Fort Brooke, and one at Key West. It also left the timing of removal up to the officers on the ground. Previous plans for removal had gone awry so often that the agent and the general were authorized to delay it as late as the spring of 1836.[20]

Considering the Indian-white tension, which ever since Moultrie Creek had increased year by year, the provisions made by the government for the defense of Florida in the late 1820's and early 1830's seem all but inexplicable. The details of the defense posture are themselves hazy. But it is clear that the centralized responsibility for the military force—established in 1827 with D. L. Clinch as commander—had been allowed to lapse in the ensuing years. It is also clear, as noted earlier, that Fort King had been closed down and not reopened until

1832. At some time, too, Fort Brooke was left without a garrison. It was necessary during the troubled three years from 1832 through 1834, in consequence, to do much redeveloping of forces and forts which ought never to have been allowed to deteriorate. On November 24, 1834, Clinch was once more given central command in Florida, and at about the same time Fort Brooke was reactivated.[21]

Whatever the target date for removal, the officers close to the problem thought it necessary to hold more talks with the Seminoles, and the chiefs for once were of the same mind. A meeting was arranged for March 27, 1835 at Fort King. Meanwhile an address from the Great White Father himself came to the Agency, and Thompson determined to read it at this council. One hundred and fifty chiefs and warriors listened on that date to Andrew Jackson's admonition that they must migrate as they had promised. Both white and red dignitaries were impressively seated upon a platform about ten feet from the ground. Suddenly, with a rending of green boughs, the platform caved in. Red and white men became one tangled knot. Some Indians, suspecting a trap, ran howling from the tangle, while others, once they had taken in the situation, laughed. This unexpected development had no effect on the negotiations. Jumper, speaking for the assemblage of Seminoles, on March 29, asked for thirty days in which to consider the President's weighty directive, and to bring together, "a fair representation of the whole nation." Agent Thompson and General Clinch agreed to a postponement until April 20.[22]

Because of delays the April council did not commence until the twenty-second. Some 1,500 Indians were then gathered in camps around the Agency. One thing that had drawn so many there was the expectation of the payment of an annuity, for the stipend of 1834 had not proved to be the last after all, nor had the Agency closed down as planned. The first order of business was food, because the bitter winter had killed the Indians' cattle. The chiefs asked help, without seeming to feel that to do so weakened their bargaining position. Some stormy sessions followed, out of which the white men finally gained more by far than the Seminoles. On April 23, 1835, sixteen headmen signed a paper acknowledging that the Treaty of Payne's Landing was valid. Five refused to sign, or were not present to do so, and Agent Thompson wrathfully struck their names from the list of chiefs. One of those absent was Mica-nopy, who pled illness. We cannot be sure whether or not he had been on hand for the opening meeting on April 22, but certain it is that he was not there for the crucial signing. Thompson belittled the excuse of sickness and ascribed the chief's truancy to a "shuffling disposition to shun responsibility." Also stricken by the agent were Jumper, who spoke two hours against moving, Holata Mico, Arpeika (Sam Jones), and Coa Hadjo. All the chiefs were doubtless angered by the meetings, but Arpeika could not conceal his rage. He stamped his feet in anger and literally gnashed his teeth. General Clinch also became angry, and in the heat of the exchange bluntly stated that he would expel the Seminoles by force if they would not go any other way. After that there was open talk of warfare. But Thompson, Clinch, and Lieutenant Joseph W. Harris, special disbursing agent for the expected migration of the Seminoles, decided to defer removal at least until January, 1836. In the meantime, they agreed, the military force had to be increased.[23]

As relations deteriorated, the role of the military enlarged. During the spring of 1835 General Clinch took an ever increasing part in the negotiations. He did so under a heavy burden of grief, for his wife died in Mobile, Alabama, while he was on duty in Florida, leaving his eight children motherless. But knowledge of his sorrows did not deter the War Department from criticizing the high-handed way in which the five headmen had been deposed. He should, the Secretary informed him, have induced the tribe to ratify the action.[24]

With Indian-white tension at an explosive level, Osceola was almost certain to get into trouble. Early in June Thompson seized him and put him in irons. For several hours the prisoner raged like a wild animal, and then his cunning began to reassert itself. The following day he agreed to sign the document which certified the validity of the Treaty of Payne's Landing. This was not enough, said the agent, whereupon Osceola offered to bring in a band of followers converted to migration. When this was agreed upon, runners went out, and seventy-nine loyal supporters turned themselves in. Now Osceola was free, but more dangerous than before, for to chain an Indian

Duncan L. Clinch

was to degrade him to the utmost. It is to be supposed that the agent knew this, and that he had had extreme provocation before resorting to so desperate a measure. No document reveals for sure what had provoked him. Thompson said that Osceola had insulted him in his own office. Whatever the truth, it was a fateful thing to do, one for which Osceola never forgave him. As far as the Indian was concerned, revenge must follow. The agent, for his part, seems to have believed that Osceola's mark on the document recorded a true change of heart, whereas it actually signified nothing but cunning.[25]

At one of the conferences described above, Osceola is supposed to have driven his knife through a document lying on the table before General Clinch. Although it is true that the original of the Treaty of Fort Gibson has a slashed place in it, no observer on the spot left any record of this moment of drama. It may have occurred, or it may be purely legend.[26]

Violence was not far below the surface. To keep it suppressed after the April talks, the agent forbade the sale of ammunition to the Seminoles. During the next three months they resentfully stayed away from Fort King. More to their liking, Thompson also requested that Negro-seekers and traders be kept out of Seminole territory. Heeding his request, the government ruled that no persons could enter the Indian reservation except with passes either from the War Department or the agent. On July 7 President Jackson gave this policy his personal endorsement.[27]

These measures did not achieve their purpose. There was an explosive flare-up in mid-June in Alachua County. Seven white men, coming upon five Indians hunting outside their reservation, overpowered and beat them with cowhide lashes. While the beating was in progress, two other Indians appeared on the flanks and opened fire, wounding three of the white men. In the scuffle that followed, one Indian was killed, another wounded. When news of this affair reached him, the agent called the chiefs together and demanded the surrender of the warriors involved. The headmen turned the offenders over for white justice. What followed had a comic touch. Thompson offered the prisoners to the judge of the court in Alachua County, but in thirty days his Honor did not even reply to the letter. The culprits were remanded to their own chiefs for punishment. This incident brewed bitterness on both sides.[28]

Early in August Private Kinsley H. Dalton of the Third Artillery (after whom Dalton, Georgia, was named) was murdered while carrying mail from Fort Brooke to Fort King. The Indians did this, the reports said, to avenge the death of the warrior who had been killed in the Alachua fracas in June. This and many similar incidents prompted the agent to hint to his superiors that bribery of some of the chiefs might save much money and woe; but the Secretary of War repudiated out of hand that approach. About the time that Cass said no to bribes, General Clinch began to urge an enlargement of his force. His immediate need, he said on October 8, was for 150 mounted volunteers to range along the frontier lines and prevent the continuous and dangerous intercourse between the Seminole-Negroes and the slaves on plantations. The War Department denied this request, but stated that four more regular companies would be added to the general's command in lieu of the mounted volunteers. Clinch was not satisfied. He needed staff, he said, for he lacked even a confidential secretary to copy his letters.[29]

Really serious trouble between the races commenced in October. Such prominent men in the territory as Joseph M. Hernandez felt the need for mounted volunteers to move quickly to curb disorder. Hernandez was a Spanish Floridian, born at St. Augustine, who had transferred his allegiance to the United States when Florida was ceded. On September 30, 1822, he became the first congressional delegate from the Territory and sat until March 31, 1823. He served as a militia general throughout the conflict with the Seminoles and earned some opprobrium among humanitarians as the captor of Osceola. Later his public career was ended when he failed to be elected to the United States Senate as a Whig in 1845. Thereafter, he removed to Cuba, where he died in 1857. When the War Department refused to take militia onto the federal payroll, Hernandez as brigadier general of the East Florida militia called some of his command out on his own authority. Part of them were later accepted into federal service.[30]

All the while one chief undeviatingly prepared to migrate. Notwithstanding that he had denounced the removal treaties at the October councils, Charley Emathla had made up his

Joseph M. Hernandez

mind to go. In accordance with this decision, he sold his cattle and was returning homeward with a small party on November 26, 1835, when a larger band under Osceola surrounded him. After a bitter colloquy, Osceola shot him dead on the trail, leaving his carcass for the wolves and vultures. Contemptuously Osceola threw the money from the sale of his herd in all directions. Near panic seized the Territory after this so that General Clinch had to keep moving constantly from one strong point to another to buoy up the courage of the white people. As for the other headmen who thought as Charley Emathla had, they sought protection close to Fort Brooke. Holata Emathla, Fuche Luste Hadjo, Conhatkee Mico, Otulkechala, Econchatomico, and Fushutchee Mico, with five hundred of their people, made a camp near Brooke. They came destitute, but Captain Francis S. Belton, the post commander, subsisted them on government rations. Meanwhile, communication between Fort Brooke and Fort King was broken.[31]

At the governor's orders five hundred horsemen enlisted for a tour of four weeks under the command of Major General Richard K. Call. There was no appropriation to support these volunteers in federal service, but General Clinch, who needed all the men he could get, accepted them anyway; and President Jackson ultimately sanctioned the $3,000 of expenses incurred by the year's end.[32] The presence of this militia force in the vicinity of the Indians brought on an action which might be termed the first battle of the Second Seminole War. The militia was in motion to try to prevent some of the many attacks on isolated houses. Colonel John Warren of Jacksonville detached his baggage train at Kanapaha to go by way of Micanopy to Wetumpka. Once it was separated from the main body, about eighty Indians led by Osceola ambushed and captured the train. Just as they had secured this prize, Doctor (later Major) McLemore galloped up with thirty horsemen. He immediately ordered a charge, but when only twelve men responded he was forced to retreat with six of his command killed and eight wounded. This action occurred on December 18, 1835 along the rim of the Alachua Savannah and was dubbed the Battle of Black Point. Only a few days later scouts located the hostile band in a hammock. Six companies were dismounted and ordered to charge the band. When they did so, the Indians fled, and the whites recovered some of the papers lost in the wagon train and even their own cooking utensils. A part of the men engaged their foes waist deep in the water of a pond at "half pistol-shot" distance (about five yards). This small action was the first of an almost unending series of desperate fights to be waged under cruelly adverse conditions.[33]

The heaviest Indian depredations began around Christmas-time, 1835, in the sugar-growing district east of the St. Johns River and south of St. Augustine. Here was a cluster of some of the most valuable plantations in Florida, where cultivation of the soil was carried on at a higher level of efficiency than the Florida average. Naturally, Brigadier General Hernandez, the militia commander in the area, tried to dispose his force in such a way as to minimize spoilation of these valuable properties. But curiously enough several of the planters would not cooperate with the general. They chose instead to try to defend themselves without the aid of militia, fearing that the presence of such a force might bring the Indians upon them. John von Bulow, one of the wealthiest planters, went so far as to forcibly resist the occupation of his plantation by the militia, precipitating a contest which he lost. Neither planters nor militia proved able to defend the sugar plantations. The Seminoles, under the direction of a Mikasuki chief named Philip, wrecked five of them on Christmas and the day following. Within a week or two, the whole industry was destroyed. By this time nearly all the Indians had deserted the reservation and were roaming freely. In fear of them, white folks crowded into the settled areas. Richard K. Call reported that the area from the Suwannee to the St. Johns for fifty miles north of the Indian boundary was virtually deserted by the whites. Normal life in the peninsula came for a time to a standstill. The *Florida Herald* issued no numbers from October 22, 1835, to January 6, 1836, and when it resumed publication, the editor explained that he had been away on military duty.[34]

There was not enough regular military force on hand to stem the rising fury. As of December 9 the total number of men was 536, only 26 of them officers. Accordingly, the War Department allowed General Clinch to take into federal service the 150 mounted volunteers he had before requested unsuccessfully. President Jackson, surprised by the turn of events and never very patient when it came to Indian actions, endorsed the report of developments, "Referred to the Secretary of War for his report of what Col Clinch is about, what is his force, & why it is that he is permitting such outrageous depredations by the Indians without inflicting just punishment for outrages so unpunished—Let order be forthwith given to him to act with promptness & call upon the Governor of Georgia for a force."[35] Of course General Clinch was not idle. He had even bethought himself of the need for a revenue cutter to gain command of the coastal waters. Although his request was not honored, a naval vessel was dispatched to cruise from Charlotte Harbor to Tampa Bay.[36]

Insofar as the Indians were capable of acting upon a concerted plan, they did so now. Halpatter Tustenuggee (Alligator) later said they had been formulating their plan for a year. Part of the plan was the violent wave of depredations referred to above, but the core of it was something else: to kill Agent Thompson and at the same time strike an effective blow at the meager American military force. Behind this central plan stood Osceola, lusting for revenge. The first step after the murder of Charley Emathla was to keep Indian strength clear of possible white retaliation. To that end the bands disappeared from their usual haunts. Safe from attack themselves, they watched for their opportunity. It came late in December, 1835. The garrison at Fort King had been mostly drawn away to General Clinch's plantation, about twenty miles west and north, where a picket work was thrown up and the place given the name Fort Drane. Whatever the purpose of this move, only one company was left at Fort King. Even though almost everything had been drawn within the stockade there, the time now seemed to the Indians favorable for eliminating the agent. It happened also that at this time two companies started from Fort Brooke along the 100-mile road to Fort King. Part of the Indian plan was to ambush these troops. Osceola intended to be present both at Thompson's liquidation and at the ambush of the relieving force, but the destruction of his humiliator held the higher priority for him. His party lay in ambush around the agency on the afternoon of December 28, 1835. Between three and four o'clock in the afternoon the agent and his dinner companion, Lieutenant

Constantine Smith, took a postprandial stroll outside the palisade. They never returned. Shot poured in on them from all quarters, riddling Thompson with fourteen balls and killing him instantly. His scalp was taken and cut into tiny pieces so that each participant might have a trophy. Smith was also killed. At the same moment another party surprised the sutler Erastus Rogers and his two clerks, eating their meal at Rogers' home outside the pickets, and shot them through the windows. Thus ended a long association with the Seminoles on the part of the sutler, who had been one of the witnesses of the signing at Payne's Landing. The officer commanding the fort, hearing the shots and not realizing that the agent was outside, closed the stockade gates and awaited developments. He had but forty-six men at his disposal, and some time elapsed before he sent out a force.[37]

Fifty miles to the south, the second front of the concerted attack was already, at the time of Thompson's fall, just about over. It was the end of the road for the relief column marching toward Fort King under the command of Major Francis L. Dade. The detachment consisted of eight officers, including a surgeon, and a hundred enlisted men from Captain George Washington Gardiner's Company C, Second Artillery, and Captain Upton S. Fraser's Company B, Third Artillery. All were redlegged infantrymen (artillery soldiers trained to fight as infantry), but they had one six-pounder with them, dragged at first by four oxen and later by two teams of horses. Their route was the stretch of road built in 1828 between Forts Brooke and King. It was a perfectly plain gash in the otherwise heavy wilderness where there was no other road and few trails. Nevertheless the column had a guide, a slave named Louis Pacheco. There was no need for anyone to betray the route, for that was obvious, but it is a reasonable presumption that Pacheco notified the Indians of the time of departure and the strength of the column.[38]

Major Dade was not to have conducted this march at all, but fate seemed to have him marked for destruction. He arrived at Fort Brooke from Key West on December 21, at which time the orders were already issued for the relieving column. Captain Gardiner was to lead it. Because Gardiner's wife was gravely ill, Dade offered to take over the assignment. Accordingly, on December 23, two days after his arrival, he led the column out of Fort Brooke, heading northward. Gardiner too, it would appear, bore the mark of doom. A chance arose for him to send his wife back to Key West where she would receive better care. He took it eagerly and then bolted out to catch up with the expedition. His only companion on the bolt was a small dog.[39]

The Indians scouted every step of the detachment's march. When Dade sluggishly took two days to cross the Hillsborough River, the watchers might have struck him at a particularly vulnerable time, but they were then waiting for Osceola to join them. On the morning of December 28 conditions were too favorable to wait any longer. Dade's column, advancing with little preparation for an attack, inched in two files out into thin, open pine woods. So little was hostility expected that the men, because the day was sharp, wore their overcoats over their cartridge boxes. Escape in this barren terrain would be difficult. The Wahoo Swamp lay just to the northwest, and the Indians counted on it to shelter them if something went wrong. Even so, Micanopy, who had just arrived, was reluctant and doubtful, but Alligator, Jumper, and other head men insisted on an immediate attack. Entirely unknown to the white marchers, the warriors silently lined the west side of the road opposite a pond. Now the column, divided into advance party, main body, and rear guard—but with no flankers out—picked its way forward until the advance was opposite the pond. According to Ransome Clarke, Major Dade had just promised the men that they could hold a late celebration of Christmas at Fort King when a sheet of fire beat them down. Dade and half the command dropped with the first volley.[40]

The sky-blue uniforms of the soldiers made easy targets, but there was no panic among them. One officer, who had survived the first blast, especially helped maintain good order. Alligator described his activity thus, "There was a little man, a great brave, who shook his sword at the soldiers and said, 'God-dam!' no rifle ball could hit him." This was probably Captain Gardiner who had come so near missing the show. Barely five feet in height, he was nearly as thick as he was tall. Probably under his direction the troops fell back slowly, firing from behind trees, while the six-pounder helped keep the Indians at bay. The fire so chastened the attackers that they drew off for three-quarters of an hour, an interval which the defenders used to construct a triangular log breastwork, about two hundred yards from the spot where Dade had fallen. Into this they carried their wounded, for Gardiner was determined that no man would be left to the possibility of torture. Apparently, he was not aware that the Seminoles rarely applied it.[41]

One hundred and eighty Indians kept up so heavy a fire that the trunks of the trees were later found to be full of lead, and the logs of the breastworks solid with rifle bullets of small caliber. Under this hot blast, the defenders dropped one by one, shot in the forehead or neck. The living stood in blood. In time the cannon ran out of ammunition, and when the red men saw this they charged once with tomahawks and clubs, but were repulsed. Finally, by four o'clock, not a white man was left standing.

The Indians did not scalp or loot. They took food, and some clothes and ammunition, but nothing else. Only when they had withdrawn did a swarm of Negroes come to kill the wounded and loot the dead. Lieutenant William E. Bassinger, it is said, rose from the ground to offer his sword and beg for his life, but they shot him down. Three wounded men, however, remained alive. The Negroes saw the life in Ransome Clarke and chose to let him continue to suffer. Later, when night fell, he crawled out from the charnel heap and staggered off in the direction of Fort Brooke. Days later, in a deplorable condition, he reached the fort. What he told there is the only account of the massacre by a white witness. Two other white men also escaped from the site of the battle, but one was discovered by the Indians and dispatched as he fumbled toward Fort Brooke, while the other reached the fort but died a few months later without having left any narrative. No other living thing ever returned from the white side except Captain Gardiner's little dog. Louis Pacheco, it developed, had slipped over to the Indians after the first fire.[42]

During the ensuing days the garrison at Brooke lived in daily expectation of attack. Not so the Indians. From their limited perspective, it seemed they had achieved a great objective. The night of the massacre they held a drunken celebration in Wahoo Swamp. Osceola was present to tell of the coup carried out at Fort King. Their revel was ill-timed because they had not achieved any valuable end at all, but on the contrary had precipitated a long, hopeless war.[43]

Meanwhile the troops at Fort Drane on General Clinch's plantation were far from being in an exhilarated state. Clinch's property, called "Auld Lang Syne," was about four miles square, with the cultivated part planted in sugar cane. The move there certainly had not enhanced the comfort of the troops. Even the room where the general slept was only one cut above a pigsty, while the slave quarters, where the troops had to find shelter, without windows, thatched with reeds, were wretched. A diminutive Englishman named John Bemrose, a hospital orderly, recorded that he slept with his clothes on and his forage cap buckled over his ears to fend off insects.[44]

The general had a picket work twelve feet high, thrown up around the buildings, enclosing an area 150 yards long and 80 yards wide. At the east end was a block-house mounting one cannon. Bemrose was dumbfounded to see a crew of axe-men build this two-story structure in three days. The officer supervising the entire fortification was Captain Augustus Drane, commanding the Second Artillery, and when it was completed, General Clinch gave the fort its builder's name. Drane, who was a little on the swashbuckling order, bragged that he could take 60 men and march from one end of the Seminole country to the other without harm. The pioneer folk in the vicinity did not see things his way. Once the stockade was completed, 150 pioneers deserted their homesteads and crowded into the fort without food or enough clothing.[45]

Fort Drane was no closer than Fort King to the Seminole stronghold in the Cove of the Withlacoochee. Lieutenant Joseph W. Harris claimed that the purpose of the transfer was to concentrate the force for a blow against the Indian families in their hideaway along the Withlacoochee River. Drane was fifteen miles closer to Micanopy, a natural supply point, and the most logical interpretation of this move is that Clinch made it for logistical reasons.[46]

On Christmas Eve, 1835, Richard Keith Call arrived with 560 mounted territorial volunteers at Fort Drane. Since the term of these volunteers was to end on New Year's Day, it was necessary to use them soon or not at all. Call later claimed that he persuaded General Clinch to move against Indian concentrations not thirty-five miles from Fort Drane, but he stressed that the movement must be swift to achieve surprise. If this was true, it was on Call's advice that Clinch depleted Fort King. Once the force was collected at Drane, the general ordered an expedition against the Indians at the Cove. Six companies of regulars, about 250 men in all, formed into a battalion under Lieutenant Colonel Alexander Fanning, started the march with 500 of the Florida volunteers on December 29. Clinch had not yet learned of the fate of Thompson and Dade. Some of the volunteers afterwards claimed they could hear Dade's cannon, but supposed it to be thunder. A company of regulars and about 100 sick men were left at Fort Drane.[47]

Acrimonious disputes later arose over the size of the general's command. He himself accused the War Department of sending 890 fewer men than he had urgently requested during the past year. Secretary of War Lewis Cass, he said, had wakened from his dreams of political preferment too late to do his duty properly. Cass retorted that he had sent all the men Clinch requested, and countercharged that Clinch had failed to estimate the true gravity of the situation. There seems to be more fact to support Clinch than Cass, for all the companies sent were below the full strength of 51 enlisted men.[48]

Be that as it may, Clinch, encumbered by an unnecessarily heavy baggage train, made his way southward much more slowly than Call could have approved. On the night of December 30 the column halted about three miles short of the Withlacoochee River. No fires were allowed and quiet was enjoined in order to improve the chance of surprise on the morrow. Cheerless as the camp was, there were all sorts of jokes about the coming contest. Typical was the quip of a little Irishman who had served in the British army against Napoleon. "Begorra," he said, "the Battle of Waterloo will be a cockfight to it." Before dawn the stillness and the chance of surprise were shattered by the morning call, blown by an irresponsible militia bugler.[49]

The army reached the Withlacoochee on the third day after leaving Drane, instead of the twenty-four hours Call had anticipated. Surprise was thus lost, Call claimed. This does not seem to be wholly true, for the Seminoles were lying in wait at the most likely fording place, but the white force did not go there. For whatever reason—certainly not by design—Clinch's force avoided this ambush. About dawn it reached the north bank, expecting to find a ford, but encountered instead swift, deep water fifty yards wide. The objective of the expedition, the native settlements, lay on the other side, but the only vehicle for crossing was an old leaky Indian canoe on the far bank (in *Seminoles* McReynolds has claimed that the Indians planted it there). As this was the last day of 1835, and as the volunteers had been promised that they could go home on the morrow, Clinch ordered the crossing to begin by means of the canoe. The regulars went first, seven or eight at a time, bailing frantically. The general was not deterred by the report of scouts that they saw Indian signs on the southwestern bank.[50]

In time, by this flimsy vessel, the whole force of regulars reached the southern bank. They then marched away from it about 400 yards by means of a "sinuous path" and found themselves in a horseshoe-shaped opening surrounded on all sides by a thick hammock, which afforded good concealment for hostile riflemen. Here they rested—and so did the force on the other bank—with sentinels out and arms stacked. This was the moment the red men picked to open fire upon the regulars, aiming especially at the officers. General Clinch, a large target on horseback, lost no time in dismounting.[51] After some moments of anarchy, officers formed the men into ranks, improving cohesion but at the same time making easier targets for the concealed foe. Lieutenant Colonel Fanning, a small, fiery man with one arm, twice begged Clinch to allow a charge as the only way to escape the hidden, galling fire. Finally the general agreed, whereupon three successive bayonet charges went forward. The general's admirers later claimed that he led them, but it seems more likely that Fanning did. Even though one-third of the white men dropped in the assaults, the tactics were correct, for they followed the lessons so hard-learned from Braddock's disaster in 1755 and Henry Bouquet's classic victory at Bushy Run in 1763. Still, the situation of the regulars on the southern bank, cut off from the rest of the expedition by the river, was critical.[52]

Reinforcement proved to be all but impossible. General Clinch later declared that most of the volunteers on the north bank refused to cross to the aid of the beleaguered regulars, even though Call and other volunteer officers did their best to get them over. As time passed after the battle, Clinch came to believe that General Call had given them a positive order not to cross, because he feared an attack on the north bank. Since their tour of duty expired the next day, the natural inference was that most of them did not care to risk their lives. But somewhere between thirty and sixty did cross, and (so their commanders claimed) formed in two lines, one above, one below the crossing place. In that posture they occupied a vital position, for later, at Call's suggestion, the regulars fell back in a half circle until their flanks rested on the two volunteer lines. Now for the first time, Call said, they held a defensible position. The action of this choice group of volunteers, their commander contended, prevented the Indians from getting between the regulars and the river.

Although General Clinch praised in it the exertions of Richard K. Call, Call took violent exception to the report Clinch made to the War Department. "The fictitious reputation and vainglorious boasting of this individual," he said, referring to Clinch, "has long excited my mirth." He sharply criticized Clinch for trying to pass the army over the river in one canoe. The lack of transport, and not unwillingness, he asserted, was the reason most of the volunteers stayed on the wrong bank. Perhaps it was not the wrong bank, for there was every reason to expect an attack on the north side; so much so, indeed, that Call had faced his men away from the river. General Clinch, he insisted, ought to have built a log bridge, or at least a raft. The volunteers finally did so, and it was on this span that the regulars at last crossed to safety. From Call's point of view, the general hardly made one correct move. Nevertheless, he became terribly fatigued, and at last adopting Call's plan for extricating the regulars, he turned the execution of it over to Call. As the regulars fell back slowly, until they had formed a half circle anchored on the two lines of volunteers as described above, General Call deployed the volunteers on the north side up and down the bank for 200 yards and ordered them to keep up a fire. Although the volunteers could not see the action from their positions, Call said their fire expedited the recrossing of the regulars.[53]

About 250 warriors, including 30 Negroes, had gone to oppose Clinch's crossing. They had prepared an ambush at the fording place, but had not had an opportunity to use it. The presumption is that more warriors joined as Clinch's force drew near, but the correct number is not known. One contemporary writer, John Lee Williams, claimed that the Indian line extended for half a mile in a half circle. Such a line could have been manned by 250 men at wide intervals. Osceola commanded the attackers, wearing a United States Army coat, and it is alleged that he also served as a rifleman, stepping out from behind a tree for each shot, taking careful aim and firing with great effect. According to one story, he put a ball through Clinch's clothes. Alligator stated that in the course of the fight, lasting about an hour and a quarter, Osceola was wounded slightly in the arm.[54] Because of their better use of cover, the Indians held their casualties far below the whites, 3 killed and 5 wounded against 4 whites killed and 59 wounded.[55]

Once the white force was safe again on the north side of the river, there seemed to be nothing for it to do but to backtrack to Fort Drane. It appeared to be necessary to blame someone for this retrograde movement. The volunteers blamed General Clinch because, they said, he had purposely restricted their supplies to four days (the balance left of their tour of duty), and made it necessary to return to revictual. Clinch, on the other hand, blamed the volunteers because they would not stay beyond their "hitch." Shamelessly, they left him with no force but the dangerously weakened regulars. The casualties of the battle had fallen mostly on the latter. The four killed were regulars, as were fifty-two of the fifty-nine wounded.

Wherever the fault lay, the destination of the diminutive army was Fort Drane, and since the Indians did not harass its withdrawal, the return was accomplished on the third day. It was filled with agony for the wounded. Hospital orderly Bemrose reported severe wounds in lungs, head, face, and abdomen. This indicates accurate shooting by the hostiles, but the caliber of the bullets was so small that few of the wounds caused death. Even so, those injuries were so hideous that six attendants who should have aided Bemrose shirked their duty by hiding out. In contrast, the general himself was all kindness to the wounded.[56]

Evidence regarding the Battle of the Withlacoochee is hard to weigh because it stemmed from two types of soldiers, regular and citizen. Each type sought to justify its own kind and to impugn the other. As a result, Call's testimony simply cannot be reconciled with Clinch's. Nor can the charges of the regulars that the volunteers malingered be reconciled with volunteer explanations as to why so few of them crossed the river to enter the fight. Certain aspects of the generalship are easier to judge. It seems hard to find justification for Clinch's dividing his force in the presence of the enemy, with nothing more than a canoe to connect the two parts. It is equally hard to excuse the relaxation of the army just at the time when it was divided by the river.[57]

This battle probably did more harm than good. First, it created in the army the erroneous impression that the Indians could be brought to fight in large groups, more or less whitestyle. Second, it gave the savages confidence in the leadership of Osceola. Finally, when the column withdrew without trying to strike at Seminole settlements, the Indians reached the conclusion that they could stop any white force.

The Second Seminole War suddenly became a serious affair with the Battle of the Withlacoochee on December 31, 1835. Activities throughout Florida were disrupted, particularly in the plantation area east of the St. Johns River. There, Brigadier General Hernandez had established a strong point at Bulow's plantation and hoped to hold it. His citizen soldiers in that region were involved in some hard skirmishes, the severest of which occurred on January 17, 1836, at Anderson's Plantation. There the St. Augustine Guards, a volunteer unit under Benjamin A. Putnam, were forced to retreat after suffering nearly 50 per cent casualties. But in the melee some of the white combatants became infected by the savagery of their foes. One stated proudly that he had scalped an Indian and taken his ears for trophies.[58]

Not all citizens were as available as the St. Augustine Guards. Many would not turn out to militia calls because they were not willing to leave home and family unguarded. Hernandez was hard pressed to find enough men to hold his strong point. He could not even reach Picolata, eighteen miles away, to pick up desperately needed stores. Meanwhile the defense of St. Augustine rested upon two companies of about fifty men each, one of regulars, the other militia. Hernandez could not get either of them to move, but their intransigence stemmed from different motives. The militia company would not leave their homes undefended. Captain Giles Porter of the regulars, on the other hand, flatly stated that he was subject only to the orders of his superiors in the regular service. Until one of them ordered him out, he would not go. The fact that orders from General Clinch could not reach him did not move the captain. He was revealing the gap between regulars and citizen soldiers which was to hamper operations many times during the coming war.[59]

7

The Antagonists

THERE WAS no need for the United States to declare war
against Indians. Congress merely recognized a belligerent
situation by appropriating money from time to time to conduct
hostilities. Even though this Seminole conflict took place in one
of the least known parts of the United States, it received notice
in most of the American newspapers. Nevertheless it could
not loom very large in the whole spectrum of American affairs,
since Jacksonian Democracy was in full career. Although Jackson himself was old and ailing, with only fifteen more months
in office, the heady interest in public affairs and the greedy ex-
ploitation of the riches of the continent now known as Jacksonian Democracy were young and lusty.

During 1835, for the only time in its history, the government of the United States paid off its bonded indebtedness. In
conseqence, there was a vigorous debate in political circles concerning what to do with the surplus accruing each year in the
treasury. The excess of intake over output was greatly augmented by a near frenzy in the purchase of public land. During
1836 purchases mounted to the crazy figure of $24,900,000,
which at $1.25 per acre meant heavy volume. And the specula-
tion in public lands was but one facet of what seemed to be an
unparalleled boom. In all sections business was good, but the
Cotton Kingdom was rising in the Gulf states and the cotton
market was especially prosperous. New enterprise was trying

its strength in a thousand ways with promise of unheard of profits. Jackson had only recently killed the Second United States Bank, thereby throwing the field of moneylending open to hundreds of local banks. And the local bankers, without much scruple as to method, sought to feed the insatiable demand of a rising people for credit upon which to build a new economy.

An intricate web of transportation had to be spun over the land if the new economy was to mature. Building it was more than a job for private capital, but since the federal government withdrew from the support of internal improvements and poured its resources into the liquidation of its debts, it was the state and local authorities who pledged their public money to build turnpikes and canals. Thus, while the debt at the center was erased, that of the parts rose about fifteen and one-half times in two decades. In the prosperity of the end of 1835 this sharp rise scarcely alarmed anyone; indeed, since there was no science of statistics, it was not realized that the multifarious local and state public debts added up to an ominous total.

Besides the preoccupation with profits, other distractions in the nation seemed to reduce the importance of the conflict in remote Florida. Ohio and the Territory of Michigan were all but at war over a strip of territory that both coveted. More exciting than this was the Texas fight for liberty against Mexico. The birth of the Republic of Texas under Sam Houston, a former distinguished citizen of the United States, attracted much attention and caused an almost hysterical excitement. The question of Texas was intimately related to the growing problem of slavery. Although the Missouri Compromise of 1820 had supposedly settled the boundaries of slavery extension, the possibility of annexing the Republic of Texas reopened that sore issue. In 1832 South Carolina's Ordinance of Nullification had demonstrated that slavery was becoming a sensitive matter and that moral forces were aligning themselves for and against it. William Lloyd Garrison's antislavery society was in full and strenuous operation, helping to make partisans on both sides more and more touchy. In time, slavery was also to draw public attention to the war in Florida, but at the start the connection between the two was not apparent.

There were nearly 15,000,000 people in the United States

at the end of 1835. How could a few thousand Indians expect
to make any headway against such numbers? The disparity in
strength was not as great as it seemed. The brunt of the
fight would fall upon the military services, and these were by
no means commensurate in organized power with the society
which they represented. The land army consisted of 603 officers and 6,595 enlisted men: one regiment of dragoons totaling
749, four regiments of artillery counting 2,180 men, and seven
regiments of infantry with 3,829 men. The soldiers were scattered the length and breadth of the country in 53 posts, with
usually no more than a company to a post, and with ten companies as the highest number concentrated anywhere. The balance of 440 personnel were engineers and staff. The latter
consisted of a quartermaster general, an adjutant general, an
inspector general, a commissary general of purchases, and a
commissary general of subsistence. Not listed as staff, but in
the same category, were the paymaster general, the surgeon
general, the chief of engineers, and the chief of ordnance. In
addition, there was one commanding general (an office which
had existed since 1821), but his duties were so ill-defined as to
be almost embarrassing. The commanding general was supposed to be field commander when the nation was at war, but
the various Indian wars seemed too unimportant for him to
take over. Yet no other war occurred. In peacetime he had little
control over the staff, nor was his advice often sought by his
civilian superiors, the Secretary of War and the Commander
in Chief (the President). It is true that orders went out subscribed, "By order of the Commanding General," but they were
actually processed by the adjutant general, and the commanding general had to make a special effort to see most of them.
The incumbent in 1835 was Major General Alexander Macomb,
and his efforts to integrate himself into the real chain of command were almost pitiful. Having seen orders to General
Clinch from the Secretary of War as they passed over his
desk, Macomb jumped in. He directed Clinch not to divide his
force, and to attack. He added, "I desire you to cause to be
kept a journal in detail of your operations. Transmit it to this
Headquarters at the end of the war . . . and besides keep me
constantly informed of your operations. Write at least once a
week."[1]

The war was obviously to be directed by the Secretary of War with such supervision as the President wished to give him. Lewis Cass, Secretary of War, was fifty-three, with a long record of public service behind him. He had been an officer himself in the War of 1812 and had witnessed in person one of the worst disasters in American arms, the surrender of Detroit by General William Hull in 1812. Cass had advanced to the rank of major general in the Ohio militia and of brigadier general in the regular army. Before the end of the war he had become governor of Michigan Territory, a post he held for eighteen years with great credit. Serving in this post, he had much to do with the Indians and enough to do with the British to make of him a lifelong Anglophobe. In the growing controversy over slavery he showed sympathy for the claims of the slaveholders. Portly in frame, with a morose mouth, pendulous cheeks, and cold eyes, he was past his greatest days of personal magnetism. He possessed mental power, but by 1835, having suffered considerable ill health, he was stirred to use his mind only by some powerful appeal to self-interest, vanity, or resentment.[2]

At the outbreak of the Seminole War, Cass was preoccupied with defense against European powers. His concern stemmed from the "brinkmanship" practiced then by Andrew Jackson. The President kept letting it be known that if France did not settle the claims of Americans upon her for spoliation—settlement had been long promised and long withheld—he would be willing to use force. This prompted the Secretary to issue a lengthy report in which he represented the navy as America's first line of defense. As for the Seminoles, they seemed to him to offer but a feeble threat. The proper response to such paltry danger was to get them into that portion of the West allotted to them. This done, a string of forts could be erected to hem them in, and a good road built to connect the forts. Patrols would then be kept in motion upon that road.[3]

Beneath Alexander Macomb there were only three commissioned general officers; Brigadier General Winfield Scott, Brigadier General Edmund Pendleton Gaines (each also a major general by brevet), and Brigadier General Thomas S. Jesup, the Quartermaster General. The first two were bitter personal enemies and professional rivals. In fact, it was because of the rivalry between them that the post of major general had fallen to Macomb in 1828. The other generals, fourteen in all, held their grades by brevet only. None of them, whether by commission or by brevet, was a graduate of the Military Academy, but most of the rest of the officer corps were. Almost the only way to obtain a commission in 1835 was through the Academy, a limitation which created loud complaint. One of the facets of Jacksonian Democracy was a deep mistrust of professional soldiers and a consequent desire to get rid of the Academy, where, Jacksonians were sure, an aristocratic tradition was being bred. Foes contended that Academy-trained regulars were incompetent as Indian fighters, and that their monopoly cost lives in fights with the red men. They were not, however, able to do away with that institution which, after all, had been founded by Thomas Jefferson.[4]

West Point, stressing "Duty, Honor, Country," indoctrinated its graduates with an outlook which set them apart from John Q. Citizen. To the officers glory and honor had great value. Jacob Rhett Motte when he had enrolled felt himself to be "among the elite few, the brave and the honorable spirits of our small but unsurpassed army." Even so, there was a tension in the officers' attitudes created by the conflict between the values with which they had been indoctrinated and those they saw in the society around them. One officer on duty in Florida wrote his wife, "If Henry could help me to anything, by which with application I could support us—I would willingly quit a profession for which I think there is no longer a feeling of respect entertained by the country." Another remarked that "Love of glory . . . which alone gives dignity to the profession of arms, and distinguishes the soldier from the cutthroat," had been dangerously diluted by the love of money. The truth is, glory had declined so far in value in American society that even a man with a soldier's ideals could hardly afford to pursue it. For instance, a major general earned $4,590 a year, a brigadier $3,000, a colonel $1,776, a lieutenant colonel $1,328, and a major $1,038. Participants in the commercial world commanded many times these sums.[5]

But in their own realm the officers were kings. They considered themselves to be, and were, a class apart from the enlisted soldiers. They were carefully educated and drawn from

well-placed families, whereas the enlisted men were usually
ignorant, dredged up from the outcast elements of society.
Most of them, indeed, were foreigners who enlisted because
the transition from the culture of the Old World to the New
was too hard. Bemrose, himself an Englishman, listed the following national strains around Fort Drane: German, French,
Irish, Scot, Minorcan, Polish, Swedish, Canadian, and Nova
Scotian. Out of the 104 killed with Major Dade, 43 were foreign born. Talk at the post sounded to Bemrose like the chatter
of Babel, and seemed equally Godless. He recorded gaping
stab wounds among the men, the result of the "irascibility and
licentiousness of southern troops." It may have been that
southern soldiers were more brutal than others, but all enlisted
men were bent in that direction by heavy drinking. Drunken-
ness was the army's most serious problem. The government
sought to combat it in 1833 by substituting coffee and sugar
for liquor in the ration, but there was no noticeable improve-
ment. Almost on a level with alcohol as a problem was desertion. This, too, is easy to understand; a laborer with any skill
at all could make a dollar a day outside, but only five dollars a
month in the service.[6]

A soldier's duty in Florida was especially ill-compensated.
In the main it was laborious, sweaty foot-service. The infantry, even then known as "dough-boys"—although the origin of
the term is lost—had no monopoly of service on foot. The redlegged infantry and the dragoons shared it with them. None of
the arms of the service, however, was trained for the sort of
war which had to be fought in Florida. All arms drilled according to the stipulations of the new manual, *Infantry Tactics,* by Winfield Scott. Issued in 1835, this manual actually
was a translation of the best French drill guides, and so was
suited to European rather than American conditions. Scott's
Tactics, it is true, included a section on light infantry not
drawn from French texts, but close students of warfare criticized even this because the light infantry drill was dependent
upon regular line drill. Soldiers, they said, ought to be able to
learn light drill without having to pass through line tactics
first.

The uniform reflected both the European tradition and the
demands of harsh service. The dress outfit for infantry was

sky-blue with white crossbelts and gleaming black patent-leather caps. It was wholly out of place in the field and was not expected to be worn there. When caught in a campaign with this on, the soldiers hastened to blacken the white crossbelts. But in the field, if not taken by surprise, they wore a fatigue uniform of sky-blue kersey (a rough woolen material) for winter, and of white linen for summer. Naturally dirt soon altered the color of both. At their inception, the Second Dragoons were weighed down with sabers, pistols, and carbines, but before long had "streamlined" their load and adapted it to the rugged conditions.[7]

With service on foot the chief reliance, the shoulder arm became the key weapon. Generally speaking it was a flintlock muzzleloading musket, of a standard .69 caliber. This means that it was fired by a flint and steel mechanism, was loaded downward through the muzzle, and had no rifling in the bore. It was by no means the latest in firearms, for percussion firing mechanisms, breechloading, and rifling already existed. The army had some rifles, but the ratio was one to twenty-two muskets. Not so with the Seminoles. Every warrior seemed to have a rifle, and a superior one at that. No Seminole rifle of the period has been preserved, but it is known that they were effective small-bore Spanish weapons made in Cuba.[8]

Even though the Indians had better shoulder arms, the consensus after the Battle of the Withlacoochee seems to have been that they used them carelessly. They took pains with the first shot, but after that, more often than not, loaded carelessly. From a cluster of balls carried in his mouth, the warrior spat one into the barrel on top of a powder charge he had not troubled to measure. Some shots, thus loaded, fired off with no more force than a popgun; indeed, some were known to strike soldiers and drop harmlessly to the ground. One direct hit on a volunteer's forehead only knocked the man out. A participant claimed that Seminole fire was not dangerous beyond twenty yards, that he had even seen it miss at four. Another observer reported that sometimes their bullets cut branches twenty and thirty feet overhead. In any case, the Indian habit was to fire, whoop, and then drop to the ground on the left side to free the right for loading. White soldiers, after observing this pattern, began to shoot to the right of the muzzle blasts.[9]

Army Ordnance, conscious of the advantage of rifles, had been building an improved type in its arsenals since 1811. Known as Hall's rifle, it incorporated two advances, rifling and breechloading, over the standard musket. It was also of much smaller caliber than the standard musket, .52 as contrasted with .69 (thirty-two of its bullets could be made from a pound of lead instead of sixteen for the musket). By 1835 the principal model was that of 1819, but limited numbers of several others were in use. Like any rifle, the Hall's could strike hard at 400 yards compared to 100 for the musket. Moreover, because of the breechloading, a marksman could fire it four times as fast, at least under garrison conditions. But troops in the field complained of the weapon because its mule-like kick often broke the stock, its breechblock leaked vital powder and gas, and it fouled so badly after a few shots as to become nearly frozen into position. Finally, some soldiers objected that the rifle's small bullets were not big enough to produce casualties. But this last applied to Indian rifles even more, for theirs were of smaller caliber yet.[10]

Even though the army was the preponderant service, the navy now was to play its biggest role in an Indian war. It was a lean service, made up of 746 officers and 4,801 enlisted men, with a Marine Corps of 68 officers and 1,349 enlisted men. These personnel manned nineteen ships on active duty, the ships divided into five squadrons, and shore installations. Of the five, the West Indies Squadron was to be intimately involved in what lay ahead. Commanded by Captain Alexander J. Dallas (who bore the honorary title of Commodore, though the rank did not exist in the navy), it comprised a frigate (used as flagship) and four sloops of war. In addition to the nineteen ships on active service, there were as many "in ordinary," that is, out of commission for repairs or as being irreparable. Finally, thirteen vessels were building. One of these was a steamer, and there was another steamer on the navy's roster, carried as beyond repair. In the course of the war both sailors and marines often fought as foot soldiers.[11]

The Seminoles, of course, had no such organization for war as the one that confronted them. Their power did not come from organization, but from desperation. The wisest of them knew that they were heavily outweighed. There were about

4,000 of them, but opinion differed as to the number of warriors. The highest estimate was 1,400, but old President Jackson was sure the figure was 900 too high. From the President on down, the tendency was to underestimate the foe. *Niles' Register* predicted that "the miserable creatures will be speedily swept from the face of the earth." Later it added, "It is confidently hoped . . . that ten years intercourse with the whites has so far corrupted and demoralized the Seminoles as to make them incapable of protracted resistance."[12]

Certainly in Washington the Seminoles appeared to be only a minute portion of the Indian problem. It was estimated that 31,348 Indians had migrated west of the Mississippi River under the policy of Indian removal (including 265 Florida Indians from the Apalachicola region). There remained about 72,000 still east of the river, of which the 4,000 Seminoles were only a tiny fraction. Counting those who had migrated, the estimates of the Indians in the country west of the Mississippi ranged from 150,000 to 230,000.[13]

If the situation seemed easy to control on paper, it looked otherwise to the President's old friend John H. Eaton, the Governor of Florida Territory. Eaton warned Jackson that the Seminoles would not give up easily. There is but one sound course, he added, to send against them an overwhelming force of 4,000 to 5,000 regulars. Only by this means could the conflict be brought to a speedy end. He was probably right, but he might as well have asked for a force of flying machines. To ship most of the United States Army to fight a handful of savages seemed silly to the old Indian fighter in the White House. Moreover, people on the east coast north of Florida already felt that their shore was dangerously denuded of military force. The President's brinkmanship with France made coastline protection more than usually essential. So, as Lieutenant Colonel Alexander Fanning complained from the midst of the trouble, the time-honored and foolish method of coping with the Indians was to be exercised again—to start with too little to do the job and have to pour in more and more at great cost.[14]

The Seminoles' principal weapons were firearms, but they also employed knives and hatchets bought from white traders. The warriors had to rely upon white men for all their weapons save one, because they had not reached a level of culture in which metal was worked. They could neither make nor repair the guns they fired, but with the native bow and arrow they needed no white assistance. They could use them well when necessary, and did so frequently before the war was over. Their arrows, about four feet long, were made of a straight cane stalk which grew in a few places in Florida. They pointed the fiber tips and hardened them in fire, or they put on a metal tip, made occasionally of silver.[15]

Several of the Indians' fighting techniques were calculated to strike terror. Some warriors entered battle naked except for a loin cloth, but their bodies were streaked with bizarre symbols in red and black paint. Other fighters wore battle costumes ranging from captured military uniforms to their traditional finery of feathers and medallions beaten from silver coins. Especially effective was the war cry, shrieked each time a shot was fired, which began like a growl and ended with a shrill yelp. The best rendition of it that any contemporaries could give in print was "Yohoehee," which does not recreate the crawling of the skin that the soldiers felt who heard it first hand. To Bemrose it smacked of Gaelic war cries, but to us it savors more of the later Rebel yell.[16]

Observers did not think the Seminoles as strong man for man, as either the whites or the Seminole-Negroes. Yet the Indian men were often six feet tall or more, and were well built. Legs and feet showed beautiful development, probably because the Indians hunted on foot, but chests and arms were not proportionate, possibly because the men did very little manual labor. Aside from physical powers, the persuasive capacity of the Seminoles was very high, white men thought. Though they usually could follow an oration only by means of the gestures and the interpretation of a Negro who knew nothing but coarse English, they frequently called the speakers eloquent. In council the ceremonial dress of the chiefs heightened the impact of their language. Hair was worn in two strips an inch wide, one running from temple to temple, the other at right angles to it from the center of the forehead to the base of the skull, with a small braid at each end. They worked feathers into this coiffure and dyed their hair and eyebrows black, sometimes with shoe polish. There might be a half circle of red paint under each eye and silver rings in the nose. A few famous braves had their ears slit and elongated. If a tunic was worn, it was spangled with ornaments hammered from silver coins.[17]

Seminole women showed a constancy uncommon in the history of Indian warfare. Often in the conflict of red and white in America Indian women betrayed war plans to white husbands or consorts. But this sort of treachery did not occur during the Seminole War, largely because Seminole women had little to do with white men, and nothing to do with them as sexual partners. Indeed, the Seminole squaws would have killed one of their number who cohabited with a white man.[18]

The injunction which kept Seminole women aloof from white men did not, of course, apply to their warriors. When not actually at war the warriors spent a good deal of time at white camps, and in a few cases some of them developed strong attachments for certain white men. Osceola was for a time a constant companion of Lieutenant John Graham. It is said that he directed the warriors at the Battle of the Withlacoochee to spare his friend. In the same manner Blue Snake attached himself to Surgeon Motte. Even though they could not communicate, Blue Snake insisted on sleeping in the tent with the surgeon, and there, Motte reported, lay upon his back, looking at the tent roof, drumming with his fingers on his chest, and humming a wild, soft chant. Certain white men like John Lee Williams lived throughout the war in exposed places, free of harm from the natives. Of course the Indian mood could easily change. The relationship of Osceola with Wiley Thompson was an illustration of this. The belief was that the two were rather good friends, but after the agent put the Indian in chains the need for revenge crowded out friendship.[19]

William Bartram had spoken of the Seminoles as notably gay, but if his observation was correct, gaiety had been slowly squeezed out of them during the troubled decades after 1811. Yet the men had retained a sense of humor, although their laughter seemed unnatural to white listeners. Grim or smiling, they gave a hearty greeting. One method was to grip the elbow of the visitor and shake the entire forearm; but if a handshake sufficed, it was carried out with a violent downward jerk. In all communication they were quiet. Talk was soft, and even the children played without making loud noises.[20]

Those individuals within the nation who violated the customs could expect ruthless treatment. For example, nose and
ears were cropped for adultery. Children, though, were never
harshly disciplined, and prisoners of war were more humanely
treated by the Seminoles than by most Indians. The heritage
of torture from eighteenth-century Creek culture had disappeared by the early nineteenth. To be sure, there were scores
of undeniable atrocities committed during the war, but there
was no authenticated record of the systematic use of torture,
and none of rape.[21]

One asset with which the Seminoles seem to have entered
the war was good health. They themselves would have ascribed
this in part to what they ate and how they prepared it. Raw
foods were in disfavor, everything had to be cooked; they even
roasted oranges. All ages and both sexes used tobacco if they
could get it. As for drugs, they could find many of these growing wild, for example quinine. Their method of combating
fatigue was to scratch themselves with a sharp object until
the blood flowed. Infection from this, and from other causes,
does not seem to have been very much of a problem with them;
nor did they lose people due to snake bites. White men noted
among them a few persons with parts of feet gone due to
venom, but nothing worse.[22]

After John Hicks' death, Micanopy because of his ancestors
had the best claim to central authority. He was a descendant
of Cowkeeper of the original Alachua band, and as splinters
from that band scattered throughout the peninsula, his authority to some degree expanded with them. One of Micanopy's
sisters had married King Philip, whose band was responsible
for the destruction of the sugar plantations east of the St.
Johns. Philip's group was probably Mikasuki, and this marriage widened the web of cooperation possible among the several bands. Just what authority Micanopy could in fact exercise
is in no wise clear. At an important council in 1837 Alligator,
a war chief from the Alachuas but associated with Philip's
band, asserted in the presence of the white men that when
Micanopy spoke all must obey. But this may have been window
dressing. This much is certain: except for the authority in-
herent in his position there was little leadership in Micanopy.
General Clinch described him as, "a man of but little talent or

Micanopy
Portrait by George Catlin

energy of character, but from his age and wealth [he] has much influence in the nation." He was between thirty-five and forty at the outbreak of the war, and he had a rather stupid, fat, dull face set on a short neck. About five feet six in height, he weighed 250 pounds and kept his weight up by heavy indulgence. One diarist noted that he downed enough breakfast for three people and then wanted wine. He was used to command, but other more talented Indians habitually manipulated him to their ends, as Osceola had done at the fateful councils of 1834 and 1835.[23]

Close at hand and active in the manipulation of Micanopy's power was Jumper (Ote Emathla), who was married to another of the chief's sisters. Although a Red Stick Creek who had fought against Jackson in 1818, he had risen in his adopted band to become the chief's sensebearer, that is, his lawyer or advocate. White estimates put his age anywhere from forty to fifty-five. Contemporary white men applied many adjectives to his appearance and personality: small, deadly eyes, contracted forehead, protruding nose; cunning, intelligent, deceitful, active, brave, and eloquent. All of them knew he was a force to be reckoned with.[24]

Halpatter Tustenuggee, called Alligator by the white men, was another important influence on Micanopy. Around forty years old, well proportioned, he seems to have been only five feet tall. He was a natural comedian, evoking a laugh even in solemn councils. Yet in dealing with white men he acted as if born to the purple. His manners, in all respects, were as fine as theirs. Behind his open face and Roman nose was a stock of shrewdness, craft, and intelligence second to none.[25]

The warrior marked to succeed Micanopy appears to have been Holatoochee, the chief's brother or nephew. He was around thirty years old, five feet ten, and well built. Observers ascribed to him a thoughtful, melancholy look coupled with good judgment and integrity.[26]

Little is known concerning the person of Philip. He was a "good natured, sensible Indian," about sixty years old, who sought rather to avoid the white men than to resist them. His greatest fame came through being the father of Coacoochee (Wildcat), who will later intrude violently into the narrative.[27]

One of the important leaders of the Mikasukis was Arpeika,

Bon,
≈ 1765

called Sam Jones by the whites. He was not a war leader but a medicine man. Because of his age (near seventy at the war's outbreak), his medicine was powerful and inasmuch as he was adamant against moving, he had great influence. His role was to hold his people in the determination to fight, plan the actions, start them, and then retire to tend the wounded and make medicine to insure victory. Regarded by Bemrose as ferocious looking, he was, we have seen, unable to suppress his rage against the white men. In person he was small and white-haired; in spirit he was inflexible.[28]

Even though the Seminoles regarded the Negro race as inferior, everyone knew that Negro influence with the natives was great. At the start of the war certain Negroes were among the top war leaders. In 1822 William Simmons called the Indian-Negroes the finest looking people he had ever seen. It is certainly true that they came from some of the very fiercest fighting tribes of Africa: Ibo, Egba, Senegal, and Ashanti. It is also true that they were armed and willing, for they had everything to lose if the Seminoles agreed to leave the peninsula.[29]

Among the important war leaders was Abraham, whom Major Hitchcock believed to have been bribed to help push through the Treaty of Payne's Landing. Described as being tall and having a courtly manner, Abraham's most distinguishing feature was his squinted right eye. He knew both Indian and English, and rose in influence as an interpreter. His first notable service to the Seminoles was rendered in 1826 when he accompanied the delegation of chiefs to Washington. This service earned him freedom. Abraham stood close to Micanopy and was one of those who exerted great influence through him. It would appear that both sides thought he was working for them on the eve of the war. All the while the whites believed him to be doing everything he could to induce removal, he was secretly visiting the slaves on the plantations east of the St. Johns and urging them to join the Indians. He was also accumulating ammunition. It is said that he once persuaded Osceola not to kill Charley Emathla, but failed in the end. There is no doubt that until he was finally shipped out of the territory in February, 1839, he was one of the key Indian leaders.[30]

No other Negro attained Abraham's status, but several became important. There was John Caesar who stood in about the same relationship to Philip as Abraham did to Micanopy, and John Cavalo who escaped with Coacoochee. Others too will come and go.[31]

The theater of conflict, the Territory of Florida, was itself a mystery in 1835. Aside from a few points along the coast and fewer still in the interior, it was scarcely better known than Africa. No white man had seen the greater part of its 58,560 square miles, nor did anyone then know its area. Maps accurately showed the outlines of the peninsula, but the interior, south of the little town of Micanopy, was either incorrectly shown or else left blank. Mapmakers filled in the blanks with vague descriptions: "High pine lands, rich open savannahs, undulating and fertile country, and hilly land." All maps, however, included one of the wonders of the world, even though they had no idea of its extent: the great swamp called by the Indians Paihokee and by the white men the Everglades. This dominated the southern one-quarter of the peninsula. Swamp land was one of the terrain features which gave peculiar and strenuous character to the Seminole War. There were large swamps in all quarters of the territory where the Seminoles were at home, and where the white man could not go without an Indian or a Negro guide. The other types of terrain encountered in Florida were hammock land and pine barrens. The former was high enough to escape inundation and grown over with a splendid stand of live oaks, deciduous trees, and magnolias. Bartram had been all but poetic in his description of the forests of Florida. Stands of pine covered the areas where the soil was little but sand.

Equal with the terrain in impact upon the course of the war was the climate. Because it was semi-tropical in nature, operations during the summer were at first thought to be impossible. Heavy rains fell, humidity rose, and temperatures soared. Inasmuch as these conditions produced disease, summer was often described as the "sickly season." It was possible to operate in the field during other seasons of the year, but not often with comfort. In the winter there was cold, which in the northern parts of the Territory sometimes dropped down close to zero, while at other times there were clouds of insects. Nothing about the weather was certain except that it would not snow. There could be drought so severe that it was hard to find drinking water on a march, and there could be violent fluctuations in temperature from day to day and from day to night.

Florida Territory was usually thought of as being divided into three natural parts. West Florida extended from the Perdido River to the Apalachicola, and was by many considered certain to become in time a part of the state of Alabama. Similar in geography, Middle Florida comprised the area from the Apalachicola to the Suwannee. Out of a total population (in round figures) of 34,000 people in all the Territory, Middle Florida contained 16,000. Nearly 16,000 Negro slaves were scattered throughout the three sections. East Florida had a very small population.[32]

The 18,000 white people (as is their wont in all eras) bustled around in the little-disciplined corners of this wilderness like lords of creations. They erected the apparatus of civilization, including towns and government. Beginning in 1824 they raised up a capital from nothing in Middle Florida. It stood on high ground where a Tallahassee village had once been, and on that account was denominated Tallahassee. By 1835 about 1,500 people lived there. There was a vigorous, if small, society in the village, and it enjoyed typical frontier diversions, the chief of which was horseracing. Volunteer soldiers from older states thought it a pretty town. But then, a rare distinction set Tallahassee apart: about twenty-six miles of railroad ran from it to St. Marks. Begun in 1834, it was one of the early stretches of track built in the United States, and, according to the Comte de Castelnau, one of the worst. The rails would not support the weight of a locomotive (even supposing there had been enough traffic to pay for one), and mules pulled the trains. Good or bad, this was one of two railroads then in Florida.[33]

The executive officer of the territorial government seated at Tallahassee was the governor, appointed by the President with the consent of the Senate. For a salary of $2,500.00 per year he was at once governor and superintendent of Indian affairs in his Territory. The legislature was a unicameral affair, called the Legislative Council, which beginning in 1826 was elected by the people. It consisted of twenty-five members, one from each of the nineteen counties, with six extras apportioned to the large ones. Federal judges were of course appointed in Washington, but the governor and the legislative council appointed the judges of the nineteen county courts, as they did the justices of the peace and in some cases sheriffs and other county officers. A few were elected by the voters. The Territory was represented at the national level by one delegate, elected by the people, who sat in the House of Representatives and took part in the debates, but could not vote. That seat had been filled since 1825 by Joseph M. White. White had been born in Kentucky in 1781, had there been admitted to the bar, and at the age of thirty, the very year Florida was transferred to the United States (1821), had migrated to Pensacola. In 1822 he was appointed one of the commissioners who under an act of Congress undertook to ascertain the validity, or lack of it, of the innumerable claims to land in Florida. He subsequently published a book on the law of land titles.[34]

There were besides Tallahassee other growing towns in Florida: Pensacola, St. Augustine, Apalachicola, St. Joseph, and Key West, to mention the most important ones. Of these we have occasion to notice only the two oldest. Pensacola had a beautiful harbor and a naval station built upon the harbor in 1830. The station became the base for naval operations in the impending war, and had been the main station also for the army in West Florida until the establishment of Fort Brooke on Tampa Bay. St. Augustine was closer to the theater of violence and more intimately involved in the Indian troubles. It housed 1,700 people proportioned thus: 488 white men, 519 white women, 151 free Negroes, and 571 slaves. Ten lawyers resided there and presumably earned a living. They may have been helped by the fact that the climate made of the town a health resort where scores of frail sufferers from the North clung to life. St. Augustine had preserved the Spanish flavor, seasoned also by a cluster of Minorcans from New Smyrna. These "old Floridians" held many balls, open houses, and other fetes which the officers of the United States Army found delightful. The Spanish and Minorcan girls were so pretty and the officers so lonesome that marriage caught several of them, even though commanding officers warned against it.[35]

The center of the town was the old Castillo de San Marcos,

renamed Fort Marion by the Americans, but it had fallen into a state of dilapidation. The citizens seemed to crave some of the cultural refinements; the grand jury gave a concert at the courthouse, and the repertoire included some Haydn. If it seems strange to us that the art of music depended on the grand jury, the military officers were glad that any agency at all was there to keep it alive on the rim of the wilderness. There was also a reading room and a small circulating library. The leisure elements in that society even recognized the beauty of the wild country at their very thresholds. From time to time sightseeing cruises took paying customers up the St. Johns River (fifteen miles west of the town) to the farthest reaches of settlement.[36]

According to modern standards you could live cheaply in "urban" Florida. The Picolata House, just west of St. Augustine and on the St. Johns, a fashionable hostelry insofar as there was one, advertised board and lodging for seven dollars a week or twenty-five dollars per month.[37]

Some of the attributes of an intricate society came rapidly to Florida after its acquisition by the United States. By 1835 there were six newspapers in the Territory, one each in Apalachicola, St. Augustine, Jacksonville, Key West, Pensacola, and St. Joseph. At the same time thirteen banks had been chartered, although not all thirteen were in operation at the end of 1835. At least one of these served as a link between the Jacksonian Era outside Florida and the Indian conflict within. Early in February, 1835, the president of the Union Bank in Tallahassee received notice that his bank had been chosen as a repository for public funds. It was, in other words, to be one of Jackson's "pet banks." The formal grounds given was that this transfer of funds would facilitate payments necessary to carry out Indian policy in Florida.[38]

When the United States took the territory over from Spain, there was but one road in all of East Florida, and it ran from the St. Marys River to St. Augustine. Then from 1824 to 1826 a track was cut from St. Augustine to Pensacola. As most of this ran through wilderness, some portions of it were soon overgrown. In the 1820's another road was built in the peninsula from Fort Brooke to the Indian Agency near what is now Ocala. This was the extent of the road system in East Florida.

The mails were slow. It took twelve hours to move mail from St. Augustine to the dozen houses which made up Jacksonville. And even though there was a better road network in West and Middle Florida, mail leaving Tallahassee on Monday at 6:00 A.M. did not reach Micanopy until the following Thursday at 7:00 P.M. The residents of Florida were keenly alive to their deep need for better communications, and they looked to one primary source to provide it. Many, many petitions requesting funds for roads flowed from Florida to the Congress of the United States.[39]

Newcomers who entered Florida to aid in the fight against the Indians were not without misgivings. Henry Hollingsworth, a Tennessee volunteer, stated that he and his associates expected it to be "swampy, hammocky, low, excessively hot, sickly and repulsive in all its features." He did find some of his fears realized, but he was also surprised to find Middle Florida a beautiful country with pretty towns, rich land, fine farms, and happy people. Most entrants dreaded the gators, the fevers, and the rattlesnakes. The first of these fears was not justified, for the gators seldom hurt anybody; but the last two were indeed menaces. Yellow-fever plagues had struck the Florida settlements more than once, and remained an enduring menace in the hot weather. As for the rattlesnakes, certain areas were so infested with them that even the Indians could not live there; yet the records of the Seminole War contain no reference to snake bites. One dismal effect of nature which the newcomers found without having expected it was the clamorous howling of the wolves at night. With the roaring of the gators, the screaming of panthers, and the hooting of owls, the wolf howls made many a volunteer soldier feel he had offered to do duty in Hades.[40]

Visitors contradicted one another in their appraisals of the whites in Florida and of the environment. The Comte de Castelnau, who observed Middle Florida, declared that Floridians were a hard-bitten, violent lot. They drank and fought incessantly and abused their slaves with indifference. The Englishman Bemrose recorded that John von Bulow, the wealthy Prussian planter, casually shot and killed one of his Negroes when the slave mishandled some targets at which Bulow and his friends were shooting. But John Lee Williams, who lived in

Florida, flatly asserted that Floridians were gentle with their slaves.[41]

Even in 1835 the country-dwelling whites were known as "crackers." Indians and crackers were enemies long before the war began. Each mistrusted the other and would allow no quarter. Their antagonism gave the war its most vicious characteristics. Jacob Rhett Motte, whose background was genteel, said of some of the whites, "They were mostly small farmers who had emigrated from different States and settled in Alachua County to plant corn, hoe potatoes, and beget ugly little whiteheaded responsibilities."[42]

Reactions to the environment were as varied as those to the people. Motte said of the terrain, "The poorest country two people ever quarreled over. . . . It is a most hideous region to live in, a perfect paradise for Indians, alligators, serpents, frogs, and every other kind of loathsome reptile." It seemed to him the wildest stupidity to try to wrest it from the Indians. In contrast, Captain George McCall loved the climate and the hunting; James Barr, a Louisiana volunteer, said it was no wonder the Indians refused to leave because their peninsula was a paradise; and Lieutenant John Pickell liked the climate so well that he intended to migrate to Florida when the war ended.[43]

8

Winfield Scott

AT THE START OF 1836 the settled areas of Florida were in
desperate danger. Sixteen additional plantations were destroyed near the east coast during the month of January.
Across the peninsula at Fort Brooke, Captain Francis S. Belton braced for an expected onslaught. Governor Eaton had
given him permission to abandon the fort if he deemed it in-
defensible, but Belton's decision was to hold on at all cost.
Cannon came to him from Key West and Baton Rouge but being short of defenders, he called upon the navy to strengthen
the garrison. In response, fifty marines commanded by Lieutenant Waldron moved in. Not yet satisfied, Belton ordered all
the houses close to the fort to be torn down in order to open up
his field of fire and at the same time to eliminate lurking places
for the hostiles. He also dug wolf pits around the stockade, put
sharp stakes at the bottom, and covered them with straw.[1]

St. Augustine was in equally grave danger. Most of its able-
bodied men were in the field; indeed, only seventy citizen soldiers remained in town, and these had but one serviceable
firearm for each two of them. There was also a powder shortage because the Indians had previously bought most of the
supply. Even food was scarce, for numbers of refugees from
the countryside crowded into the town. The crisis in St. Augustine remained acute until two companies of volunteers from
Charleston arrived on January 30, 1836.[2]

Cries for help from the jittery peninsula penetrated to all parts of the Southeast and beyond. Some of them touched raw nerves. Lieutenant John C. Casey aroused the brother of Lieutenant William E. Bassinger (killed with Dade) with well-chosen words: "We expect your Georgia volunteers . . . and let them know that your brother and my best friend after fighting til the last . . . was butchered by the Indian Negroes." Emphasis on the evil character of the Indian-Negroes was well calculated to produce a response throughout the South. And it did. By the end of January 997 militia and volunteers had entered service in Florida, at least half of them from outside the Territory. Not all of them, of course, volunteered because of the Negro issue. Some had started without waiting for an official invitation. Offers to serve in Florida came from volunteer units as far away as Pennsylvania and New York. With these offers came others of a different sort; a few southern banks proffered funds for operations if there was a lag in appropriations. But the War Department courteously declined all these offers.[3]

The Romantics in the arriving volunteer companies were full of zeal to free the white citizens from the clutches of savages and Negroes, and they thought well of their qualifications to do so. A Charleston officer wrote, "Never did Rome or Greece in days of yore—nor France, nor England in modern times—pour forth a nobler soldiery than the Volunteers from Georgia, Alabama, Louisiana, and South Carolina." The officers were proud young men almost entirely from the gentry, the enlisted men came from the elite of small farmers and laborers. Some of the volunteers wore resplendent uniforms, but most of them were dressed in ordinary clothes for roughing it. In the main, they were well armed. They were also addicted to prose writing. No less than four of them rapidly produced small books on their experiences in the field, books written in a turgid, fulsome style saturated with the fashionable Romanticism. Witness, "the dark demons of ruin were rioting, not 'mid barren wastes, where no grateful verdure quickens, and no generous plant takes root . . . but on the cultivated lands, the valuable mills, and mansions . . . the planter could only flee for succour and for safety (as flee he must) to the garrisoned city, guided by the conflagration of his own dwelling . . . where the sun was wont to shine most brightly, there rolled dark clouds of war . . . where man once dwelt in peace 'neath his umbrageous and wide-spreading oak, or by the flower-enamelled margin of some limpid brook, there . . . the trees were fired, the flowers trampled, and above all, human blood poured out like water. Yes! where the lark had carolled its matin hymn most gaily, thence it fled affrighted from the shrieking bird of prey. . . ." Style aside, their volumes rank now as documents, containing useful information not to be found elsewhere. They were also full of much introspection on how it felt to go to war, to leave home, and to plunge into a savage wilderness. When the authors first encountered campaign conditions, the rosy hue before their minds' eyes somewhat faded. Yells and howls in the night caused more than one sentry to desert his post and run into camp; but when two stood watch together, it was not quite so lonesome.[4]

These volunteer companies who came to Florida's rescue were backed by communities eager to "do their bit." Charleston sent supplies which St. Augustine could not have done without. Augusta, Georgia, furnished blankets and knapsacks for its own company of volunteers. More impressive yet, the legislature of Louisiana subscribed $85,000 to equip volunteers for Florida. All these benefactors later petitioned Congress to reimburse them for their generosity, and Congress did so, but not until a good deal of time had passed.[5]

Many of the volunteers received their baptism of fire in January, 1836. This experience came in a series of small actions which contained every mode, from the comic to the tragic, typical of green troops. For some the initiation took place when their company and another from their own troops blasted at each other by mistake. For others there was more fun than danger. Certain of the citizen soldiers loaded themselves down so heavily with sugar cane and pumpkins from an abandoned plantation that they could not even march. One action out of the many very nearly deserved the designation "battle." On January 17 Major Benjamin Putnam of the Florida Volunteers led the St. Augustine Guards and a company from Mosquito Inlet to Dunlawton on the Halifax River to bring away abandoned stores. A sharp fight developed around the ruins of buildings which had belonged to a Mr. Anderson.

About 120 Indians were involved, and the casualties they inflicted—4 killed and 13 wounded—wakened many volunteers
to the fact that they were playing with death. Perhaps to
hearten themselves, the volunteers claimed that Indian casualties were much higher than their own. Whatever the truth, by
February 1 the Seminoles had forced the white men to abandon most of the country south of St. Augustine.[6]

Before news of the tragedies of December 28 and of Clinch's
battle had reached Washington, Congress took its first notice
of the state of conflict clearly existing in Florida. On January
6 Churchill C. Cambreleng, a Jacksonian from New York and
chairman of the House Committee on Military Affairs, acting
for the Administration, proposed that $80,000 be appropriated
to suppress the hostilities in Florida. Just at this time rumors
of the events of December began to arrive at the capital, and
the appropriation rose to $120,000. On January 17 official
notice of Clinch's battle reached the government, and triggered
a second act, dated January 29, allotting $500,000 more to de-
feat the Seminoles.[7]

With affairs in this state, Congress called upon the War Department for detailed information. In supplying it, the Adjutant General revealed that the Department, perhaps under the
influence of the President, was determined to protect the property of slaveholders. No terms would be offered to the hostiles,
he said, as long as one slave belonging to a white man remained among the Seminoles.[8]

The Secretary of War was forced to turn more and more of
his attention to the Florida imbroglio. He gave Clinch permission to call for all the militia needed, and arranged for three
revenue cutters to cooperate with the general. On the day when
word of the Battle of the Withlacoochee arrived, Secretary
Cass directed Brevet Brigadier General Abraham Eustis, stationed at Charleston, to gather all the troops that could be
spared and lead them to St. Augustine. Eustis was to report to
Clinch, but a higher ranking officer was to supersede the latter
in command. Five days later an order was issued to Brevet
Major General Winfield Scott, commanding the Eastern Department of the Army, to assume command in Florida. Scott
was empowered to call upon the governors of South Carolina,
Georgia, Alabama, and Florida for as many citizen soldiers as

might be needed, and the governors were so notified. He could draw equipment from arsenals in Augusta, Georgia, and Mt. Vernon, Alabama, and the depot at Charleston would supply arms. He was warned that the Seminoles and the Creeks might unite but the most important item in his instructions concerned the sensitive issue of slavery. He was forbidden to adopt any pacific measures as long as one white man's slave remained among the Seminoles. If this clause was inflexible, the next one was even more so: he might not open negotiations with the Indians until he had first reduced them to unconditional surrender.[9]

It happened that the line dividing the Eastern from the Western Department ran through the zone of combat. The Secretary therefore directed General Scott to disregard that ill-defined boundary. This was easier in theory than in practice because it involved the old feud between Scott and Major General Edmund Pendleton Gaines who commanded the Western Department and would resent Scott's operations on his side of any line, however vague. He was especially sensitive because the War Department had sent Scott into his command area to direct the Black Hawk War only three years before. Andrew Jackson had scant use for Gaines, and Gaines knew it, but he was not one to be intimidated by even so towering a personality as Jackson, or to submit quietly to an affront.

Nor were Gaines' feelings the only ones hurt by the designation of Winfield Scott to the field command. Duncan L. Clinch revealed to Cass that this selection seemed to be a disapproval of his own operations, especially of the Battle of the Withlacoochee. The Secretary hastened to send a mollifying reply. The purpose had not been, said Cass, to supersede him. It had been thought necessary to employ a major general, lest the federal commander be outranked by some state officer certain to accompany the inevitable swarms of militia. In addition, it was easier to give instructions to a fresh general and send him forth from Washington than to try to get them through to Clinch. All this made sense, but it did not mollify the superseded officer. He served for three months and then submitted his resignation.[10]

Meanwhile the Territorial government also found it necessary to take action. This was not easy, for the Legislative

Council was prevented by the hostilities from meeting at its scheduled time. When it could finally convene, it had to deal with appeals from the militia commanders for reinforcements and supplies. The Florida militia was in no condition to cope with such an upheaval. Knowing this full well, the council passed an act on January 15 to expand the militia. Among other stipulations, it provided for a draft in counties where the number of volunteers was insufficient and gave the governor power to borrow $20,000 for defense of the Territory.[11]

The projection of Winfield Scott into the Florida action was sure to give it color. No West Pointer, Scott had entered the service before the War of 1812 and had in that war proved himself to be a skilled and determined leader of men. As early as 1814 he had become a brigadier in the line and a major general by brevet. Afterwards he had remained at the top of the military hierarchy and had been kept from the number one position only by the feud between him and Gaines. The little Englishman Bemrose thought Scott, when he appeared at Fort Drane, "one of nature's finest specimens of the genus homo." Then fifty years old, the general stood six feet four, although one shoulder drooped a little from a wound acquired in the War of 1812. He was fond of fine uniforms and the other panoply of rank. Even in Florida he traveled with a band, "marquees of furniture," wines, and other luxuries. Bemrose said it was easy to imagine that his train belonged to some Indian nabob rather than to a republican general. Yet Scott was not all fuss and feathers. He was ubiquitous where duty was concerned. A South Carolina officer, lying undressed in his tent, nearly prostrated by the heat, was taken aback when none other than the general himself poked his head inside. Clad in his heavy military coat, Scott was inspecting in the broiling sun, and had just returned from visiting the sick. The general's greatest weakness was indiscretion whenever he put pen to paper. Yet under the pomp and ill-considered writing lay a real military ability. Unfortunately he was neither trained for nor amenable to Indian warfare. Scott did not favor the rough dress of the woods fighters, nor did he approve of taking to trees as the natives did. He had after all copied from the French the drill manuals then used by the United States Army, and was thoroughly steeped in European methods of warfare.

Winfield Scott

He had no experience with any other kind.[12] (Although Scott had been given command of one Indian war—the Black Hawk, 1831-32—hostilities were over before he arrived.)

Scott was inclined to prepare carefully, even slowly, but knowing that he had to please Andrew Jackson, whose fetish was celerity, he left Washington on January 21, the same evening that his directive was published. As he passed southward, he issued orders calling for 3,700 citizen soldiers: one mounted regiment and one of foot from South Carolina, two mounted regiments from Georgia, and one infantry regiment from Alabama. He desired to arm these volunteers with rifles. At first all were to have the Hall's, but when it developed that these were not in the arsenal at Augusta in the quantities expected, he called for common rifles as well, the citizen soldiers to be given their choice. He ordered 320,000 rations to be laid down during the next three months on the St. Johns River and 250,000 on Tampa Bay. He requisitioned knapsacks and camp equipment for the volunteers, only to be told by the War Department that there was no appropriation to provide such things for citizen soldiers.[13]

Because of this flurry of preparation, all of which Scott believed to be necessary, he occupied a month passing from Washington to Picolata on the St. Johns, the starting point to the interior. Naturally, when he arrived there he expected to find most of the 3,700 volunteers on hand. Actually, only the regiment of South Carolina infantry and seven companies of Georgia mounted men had arrived by the end of February. Inasmuch as the general estimated that he needed 5,000 men to carry on a successful campaign, there was no choice but to wait. From March 1 to March 10, Alabama and Florida volunteers crowded into Tampa. All were enrolled for three months, which meant that by the time there were enough troops on hand to begin operations, they had but sixty days left to serve. Their presence put heavy pressure on consumable goods. A biscuit brought three dollars at Fort King and a cup of coffee twenty-five cents.[14]

While waiting for troops, Scott did his best to hurry the accumulation of supplies. At first he hoped to use the Oklawaha River as a supply route, but such use proved impossible on two counts: the weather turned unfavorable and the Indians destroyed the necessary special boats, causing seventy tons of supplies to be hauled overland on abominable trails.[15]

The primary objective of Scott's campaign plan was to drive the hostiles into the northern part of the Territory where white troops could get at them. It was based on the assumption that the main body of warriors was in the Cove of the Withlacoochee, a natural stronghold (now known as Lake Tsala Apopka). Accordingly, three grand columns were to converge on that point, taking care as they advanced to see that no large body of Indians slipped by them. The strongest column, known as the right wing, commanded by General Clinch, was to move toward the objective from Fort Drane. The left wing, under Brigadier General Abraham Eustis, was to ascend the St. Johns River from St. Augustine, cross it at Volusia, and make its way across the whole width of the peninsula. The center wing was to move from Fort Brooke under the direction of Colonel William Lindsay. All were to reach points near the fringe of the Seminole stronghold according to a coordinated schedule—Clinch across the Withlacoochee, Eustis at Peliklakaha, Lindsay at Chocachatti—and while in motion were to try to keep track of each other by firing cannon morning and evening.[16]

The general had to prepare his plan on the basis of flimsy geographical information. The territory he was to operate in— particularly that to be traversed by the left wing—had not been mapped with any accuracy. Lines of communication altered from month to month according to rainfall and high or low water. It was doubtless a good idea to converge upon the Cove of the Withlacoochee, but it was not so clear that the convergence could be achieved quite as neatly as Scott's plan envisaged. Afterwards Secretary of War Cass asserted that neither he nor the President thought very highly of the plan, but approved it because the general was in Florida and they were not. The commanders of the three wings, on the other hand, labeled the strategy good. But one officer of high rank, who might have expected to be consulted, had no chance to pass upon it at all! Alexander Macomb as usual was virtually bypassed. Scott did not even report to him, but sent his letters to Adjutant General Roger Jones for channeling.[17]

At this moment another strong figure projected himself into

the Florida campaign. Brevet Major General Edmund Pendleton Gaines was a man of action. He heard of the trouble in Florida on January 15 while at New Orleans. His duty, in his view, was to face it without delay. He at once issued orders to Lieutenant Colonel David Twiggs, stationed in New Orleans, and called upon the governor of Louisiana for volunteers. For the next two months Gaines kept things astir in his vicinity. He was, like Scott, ever a quantity to be reckoned with.

Fifty-nine years old at the time, Gaines had also earned his position at the top of the army hierarchy during the War of 1812. Since 1821 he had alternated with Scott in command of the Eastern and Western Departments, but he preferred the frontier and contrived to keep the Western Department much of the time. Of middle height, he had a stiff shock of bristly hair, already gray, and a gaunt face with deep furrows running down the cheeks. There was no spare flesh anywhere on him. But more remarkable than his appearance by far was his candor. Not likely to spare criticism of anyone, he bordered most of the time on the choleric. This trait had turned Andrew Jackson against him, and was a prime reason why Jackson picked Scott instead of Gaines to go to Florida. Another obvious reason was that Gaines' rival was in Washington where the government could give him instructions without delay.[18]

Gaines and the troops he had been able to assemble put to sea from New Orleans on February 4, 1836. When he reached Pensacola on February 6, a letter from the War Department advised him of Scott's appointment, but a careless clerk had forgotten to include a copy of the official order. It happened that Secretary Cass had written on January 23 directing him to go to the borders of Texas to take command there. This order reached him on February 9 at Fort Brooke. Should he turn back or go ahead? Members of his party strongly urged him to proceed, for, they said, Scott might be a long time reaching the peninsula. Meanwhile the rapine continued. Also, the Louisiana volunteers, with Colonel Persifor F. Smith in command and Thomas Lawson (soon to become surgeon general of the army) as lieutenant colonel, intimated that if Gaines turned back, they would do the same. Swayed by these persuasions, and possibly by bitterness toward Scott, Gaines decided to plunge ahead.[19]

Edmund Pendleton Gaines

He and his command had reached Tampa on February 9, and were joined by a body of Florida volunteers under a swashbuckling Floridian, Major Leigh Read. Gaines organized his own troops into a brigade, and took command of the Floridians as well. With about 980 men (out of 1,100 at his disposal) and one six-pounder, he began to advance toward the interior on February 13. Major Ethan Allen Hitchcock, who was present as his inspector general, confided to his diary that he sought to persuade the general to remain in the Tampa area because Scott would need a force there. Gaines seemed to agree to this proposal, but once on the move he headed for Fort King. After all, as far as he knew, General Clinch might be beleaguered there, as no communication had come through from him. Besides, Gaines learned that Scott had ordered 120,000 rations to be laid down at Fort King and his own force was in real need of supplies. The column took the regular wagon road from Fort Brooke to Fort King, retracing the path of Dade's ill-fated column. Gaines' men, therefore, became the first whites to visit that grisly site. They found the carcasses of men and animals lying just where they had fallen but unrecognizable because of decomposition and scavengers. The bodies of officers, however, could all be identified by means of rings, gold teeth, and other imperishables. Gaines had the remains gathered and interred, while the command stood in mournful ranks and the band, playing a funeral march, marched in a circle around the pitiable breastworks. Overhead the cheated buzzards wheeled in ugly flocks. If the general had ever entertained any idea of stopping short of Fort King, he now gave it up, for it was five days' march back to Brooke and only two to King.[20]

When he arrived at Fort King on February 22, Gaines suffered a shock. Not the smallest part of the huge store of supplies ordered by Scott had come. (Afterwards there was a bitter altercation over who was to blame for the shortcoming. Hitchcock claimed that the supplies were in Florida at Picolata and that they had lain there since January 28, awaiting transportation over the ninety-two miles to Fort King. The lack of transport was said to be chargeable to the quartermaster, but Quartermaster General Jesup refuted this with equally convincing figures.) Since Gaines could not move without rations, he sent off a train of packhorses to borrow some from Clinch at Fort Drane. Clinch, it developed, could spare only 12,000, not enough but better than starvation. With these in his possession, Gaines decided to move back to Fort Brooke, this time by way of Clinch's battleground. This route was one day shorter, and besides he might get a chance to strike at the Indians in the Cove of the Withlacoochee.[21]

Marching in three columns about a hundred yards apart, the troops cleared Fort King on February 26, 1836. They reached the Withlacoochee the next day at three different points, all of them close to Clinch's battleground. While probing for a crossing, the force received fire from the southern bank. Confronted by hostiles and with the day far spent, it camped for the night. Early the next morning it inched its way down the stream for two or three miles until it came upon the ford. So far the pattern resembled that of Clinch's column two months before, but now a telling difference developed. The Indians attacked before Gaines could put even one man across the river. They shot Lieutenant James F. Izard as he stood in the water preparing to lead over an advance party. The fatal ball entered Izard's nose, passed behind his left eye, and came out his left temple; yet he lived five days. Indian fire lashed the force from 9:00 A.M. to 4:00 P.M. and was so punishing that the general gave the order to erect a log breastwork. Enclosing an area about 250 yards square, it was designated Camp Izard. Within its none-too-secure ramparts that evening Gaines wrote to Clinch, urging him to strike the Indians while they were concentrated around him.[22]

All the next day bullets spanged into Camp Izard from three sides. When they could not produce a second Dade-type massacre, the Indians set fire to the grass and brush. A change of wind foiled them. It was apparent to General Gaines that nearly the whole force of Seminole warriors was around him in the forest. Afterwards one of the chiefs told Hitchcock that they totaled 1,100. The second day, being February 29, 1836, Gaines sent off another letter urging Clinch to come at once. Already one of his men had been killed and thirty-two wounded. He did not admit to being trapped. He chose to remain in position, his argument ran, to hold the Indians together until Clinch could take them in the flank. The important thing was to keep them from scattering until that moment, whatever the cost.[23]

The cost was high. Apparently there was enough ammunition but far from sufficient food. Days dragged by and Clinch did not come. Gaines butchered his horses and mules and rationed the meat, yet his men grew daily more emaciated. The general undertook no sortie. When censured for this later by a board of inquiry, he insisted that he purposely avoided a sortie, lest he scatter the foe and spoil Clinch's chance to deliver a really destructive blow. He could not know why a flank attack, and incidentally help, had not come from Fort Drane.[24]

The reason was Winfield Scott. He had reached Picolata the same day that Gaines arrived at Fort King, February 22, and remained there until March 9. Gaines, who never minced words, least of all where Scott was concerned, later asserted that Scott purposely delayed there "beyond all doubt hoping daily to hear of my disgrace, and not of the defeat of the Indians." Had Scott heard this he would have been furious. As it was, he was enraged that this old enemy had intruded into his command. Gaines, as Scott saw it, had spoiled the chance to strike the Indians by surprise, and had eaten up vital rations. Scott was a careful planner, and the impetuous entrance of an erratic man like Gaines seemed to him to ruin nearly everything. More could be salvaged from the wreckage, he said, if the Indians drove Gaines than if he drove them, because in pursuing him they would at least remain concentrated. So, on March 1 he gave Clinch a direct order not to aid the beleaguered general or to join him.[25]

Clinch now had to make a command decision of the most delicate nature. Gaines' requests (or orders) had gotten through to him, and each day he could hear the faint thud of the cannon thirty miles away. Both generals issuing orders, be it remembered, had legitimate command over him; Gaines as commander of the Western Department, and Scott as special commander assigned to duty by the President. Doubtless after a good deal of torment of soul, Clinch reached a humane, and probably a sound, decision to go to Gaines' assistance. Enjoined by Scott's direct order not to carry government supplies to the besieged, he took food from his own stores on the plantation. As it happened, Scott had, in the interval, relented, and on March 4 had written permission for Clinch to give aid if he deemed it necessary. But on March 5, before this message could reach him, Clinch started from Drane toward Camp Izard.[26]

By now Gaines' force had been besieged for eight days, and had lost five men killed, and forty-six wounded. Such an attrition rate could not be borne much longer. If help did not come soon, it would be necessary to try to fight a way out. Even when his troops were fresh this might have been too big an undertaking. Through it all the general himself displayed the composure which had marked him for two decades as a splendid field commander. When a bullet knocked out two of his teeth, he spat them out and said, "It's mean of the redskins to knock out my teeth when I have so few." In spite of his spirit, the prospects for his command seemed dim if it tried to fight its way out. The men were too weak from malnutrition.[27]

Fortunately the Seminoles were also finding the operation burdensome. Like others of their race, they were not accustomed to prolonged siege-type operations. Thus, out of the darkness on the night of March 5, like the voice of a delivering angel, came a clear call from the Indian quarter, asking for a parley on the following day. The listeners inside Camp Izard could not know that the speaker was John Caesar, an influential Indian Negro, and that he had offered a parley on his own initiative without consulting the chiefs. Certain of the chiefs in fact prepared to kill him for his presumption, but Osceola is said to have saved John's life and to have argued for the council. Inasmuch as General Gaines had nothing to lose, the talks began as requested on March 6. Gaines would not condescend to be present himself. The Seminoles, represented by Jumper, Alligator, and Osceola, offered to lift the siege and retire across the Withlacoochee if the General would guarantee that they might remain there despite the offensive treaties. Through emissaries Gaines replied that he had not the authority to grant this, but would present it to the proper officers. This was the point at which matters stood when Clinch's column marched into view. Surely the red men knew it was on the way, but contemporary accounts give the impression that they were surprised. Clinch's men, not realizing that a talk was in progress, fired a volley, whereupon the Indians melted away into the surrounding forest. Gaines' mobility was once more restored, and two days later the two generals and their commands reached Fort Drane. Gaines' men were skeletons.[28]

The Secretary of War, thoroughly upset at finding Gaines and Scott in the same theater and unable to prevent Gaines from remaining in Florida, now at last found a job for Alexander Macomb. Go to Florida, Cass ordered, and solve the command impasse developing there. Let Scott, however, proceed with his plans. This directive was issued on March 11, 1836, before the authorities in Washington knew that Gaines was about to take himself out of the peninsula. Before Macomb could depart, that news arrived and the commanding general was left, as in the past, with no part in the conduct of the Seminole War.[29]

At Camp Izard on March 9 Gaines turned over the command to Clinch. In doing so, he took credit for ending the war. Lavish in his praise of those who had served with him to achieve the "victory," he thrust one parting jibe at Scott. Clinch, his order read, was to be in command until the arrival of "the officer charged with the diplomatic arrangements of the War Department." As matters fell out, that officer put in his appearance before Gaines got away. He arrived on March 13 at Fort Drane, four days out from Picolata—weather had held him up. For one long day the two antagonists were confined within the stockade of the same fort. John Bemrose also was there. "I noticed a cold salutation passed between them. There was no companionship and evidently there existed a distaste, a repelling power proving that when interests clash two of a trade seldom agree." *Niles' Register* later said that they showed as much courtesy to each other as any two can who take no notice of each other. Scott beyond doubt was in full dress, all 200-pounds-plus of him. Gaines, on the other hand, probably had nothing but field clothes, worn and stained, and doubtless wanted no other. In any case, subordinates must have breathed easier when Gaines departed on the following day, March 14. This left Scott, fuming over the dislocation that Gaines' interference had caused him, to make final arrangements to put his elaborate plan into motion.[30]

He could not bring himself to begin operations until supplies were available for his army. To handle them in the quantities deemed necessary, he created a special supply base at Garey's Ferry on Black Creek. This was no farther from Forts Drane and King than Picolata, but had a better landing and lay on a better road. The main depot on the east coast for the Army of Florida as a whole remained at Picolata. Early in March the general put a baggage train in motion toward Drane, and then himself started there. But he informed the Adjutant General that his movement was merely a rescue mission—to extricate Gaines—rather than the opening of the offensive he had planned.[31]

On the thirteenth and fourteenth of March at Fort Drane he directed the commanders of the left and center to be at the designated points of departure on the twenty-fifth. By the time those orders were delivered there were no moments to waste, for any delay might upset the precise timetable necessary to trap the Indians. The right wing had a smaller problem than the others, because it was concentrated at Drane, and Scott himself was with it. There was thus no need for it to start to move until March 26, one day after the others were supposed to have reached their points of departure. Commanded by Duncan L. Clinch, it was the heaviest wing, containing 1,968 men of whom 720 were regulars, the rest Louisiana and Georgia volunteers. The men from Louisiana and 270 of the regulars had been transferred from General Gaines' force when he left it. Scott always claimed that their addition obliged him to delay the start of the operation because the emaciated men had to be rested after the ordeal at Camp Izard. But even had they been able, he could hardly have commenced earlier, since the left wing could not have gotten into position. The right wing was supposed to drive the hostiles out of the Cove and into the clutches of the other two, poised at Peliklakaha and Chocachatti.[32]

This was very neat, too neat to work well. Because the going was harder than expected, the right wing did not reach Camp Izard until March 28. It had marched to that place from Drane in three days, exactly the time required by Clinch three months earlier. If R. K. Call had been correct in calling Clinch slow then, the same criticism applied to the right wing now. Late or not, it became necessary to cross the Withlacoochee and flush the quarry out of the Cove. To give heart to his tired men the general ordered the band to play during the evening meal. Cheerful as the music was, Bemrose claimed it brought enemy fire into the camp and caused the death of two men. Nothing illustrates Scott's shortcomings as an Indian fighter better than this. The kind of war he understood was that in which one did not fire at the enemy except when he had offered himself in battle. In short, Scott was a practitioner of the "limited" war of eighteenth-century Europe.

For the army crossing-day began at 4:00 A.M. Two flatboats had been made at Drane and hauled on a huge pair of wheels over twenty-five miles of rough trails to the river. They were now brought into position. Cannon and sharpshooters took their posts to cover the crossing. The Indians let the van cross unopposed, but opened fire upon the rear as it came over. There was also firing from an island in midstream. Scott ordered bayonet charges in extended order, and so dislodged the hostiles from the south bank. There was one more sharp gunfight on March 31 in which two additional men were killed and thirteen wounded. Reassuring to the regular officers was the conduct of the Louisiana volunteers. Lieutenant Colonel William S. Foster, a hard-bitten regular not much given to praise of citizen soldiers, said they cheered so loudly that they drowned out the terrifying yells of the Indians.[33]

In spite of good conduct on the part of the soldiers, Scott's plan was not working out well. His right wing now stood on the Indian side of the Withlacoochee, but the Indians were not concentrated before it. Obviously the crossing had not been opposed by the main strength of the Seminoles. Nor was the commander in communication with the other two wings. Now and again, when the wind was right, Clinch's men claimed they could hear the morning and evening guns of some other wing, but although the three wings were for a time only thirty miles apart, they never made contact. The wilderness wrapped each one around like cotton batting. This being the case, it was up to Scott to decide the next course of the right wing. Should it search the Cove of the Withlacoochee or head for a resupply point? With a gesture toward searching the Cove, Scott ordered the march toward Fort Brooke, and the column reached that place on April 5. The center had already gotten back there, having come in the previous day.

The center wing was filled out by the arrival of Alabama volunteers on March 13, the very day that Scott had written his instructions for its conduct. Under the command of Colonel William Lindsay, Second Artillery, who had served with Jackson in Florida in 1818, it was dominated by the regiment of volunteers from Alabama under the command of Colonel William Chisolm. The regiment had 750 of the wing's total of 1,250. Hopelessly romantic about their mission, proud and touchy, the Alabamans conceived a violent dislike for Colonel Lindsay. When he would not let the sutlers sell them liquor, they docked the mane and tail of his horse. When they had to carry their duffle, they argued insubordinately with him about it, and blamed him for the absence of transport. They criticized him for issuing them only four rounds of ammunition, yet proved how right he was when on the march they blazed away, contrary to orders, at a herd of cattle and again at some deer, wounding one man. As if this were not enough, Lieutenant Colonel Crabbe of the Alabama regiment chose to lay the blame for the wounding on one of the friendly Seminole scouts. He ordered that all the scouts be taken into custody. Because these Seminoles were indispensable, Crabbe's action sent Lindsay into a rage. The Alabamans were equally irascible, and when he released the scouts they came close to mutiny. Thereafter, at least so the volunteers claimed, Lindsay dared not show himself around the volunteer camp except when guarded by a detachment of marines from the *Constellation.*[34]

Relations between regulars and citizen soldiers were not smoothed by the presence of Major Leigh Read of the Florida militia. His 260 militiamen were amalgamated into the center wing, but they took no pleasure in the connection. Major Read habitually dwelt in a medium of violence. Not long before joining the center, he had engaged in a duel, which began with pistols and ended in a hand-to-hand fight with knives. During the campaign he accused Colonel Lindsay of every sort of misconduct from stupid delay to outright cowardice. In the end Read would not associate with the colonel. His volunteers thought of him as a brilliant leader, and following his line regarded Lindsay as a clod. But the opinions of Read at the higher levels of authority were by no means unanimous. The friends of Andrew Jackson in Florida took opposite sides of the question and sought to sway the old President to their side. John H. Eaton reported that Read was a nullifier and an anti-Jackson man, but R. K. Call denied these charges and urged that he be made a brigadier.[35]

In spite of all this internal dissension, the center was able to function as a military unit. Lindsay saw the need for a supply base closer than Fort Brooke to the Cove of the Withlacoochee, and his command built a fort where the road from Fort Brooke to Fort King crossed the Hillsborough River. Perhaps as a gesture to obtain more harmony he named it Fort Alabama. When this stockade was completed on March 20, a small garrison was installed and the balance of the command returned to Brooke. The following day, March 21, Scott's orders arrived. They directed Lindsay to move his wing to Chocachatti, its point of departure, on March 25. He started his column at once, but made slow progress, for the Seminoles harassed it every foot of the way. On March 26, while still two days away from Chocachatti, the center fought what almost amounted to a battle. Stinging fire struck the column from a thick hammock, and the colonel applied the approved solution. He brought up cannon to play upon the hammock, then ordered a bayonet charge. Often in the Seminole War this maneuver was successful. The right wing used it to cross the Withlacoochee and it was to bring results on many future occasions. Naturally, there were casualties, in this case two soldiers killed and two wounded.[36]

On March 28, three days late, the center reached its point of departure at Chocachatti. It remained there three days, firing cannon, sending out scouts, and in other ways futilely trying to establish contact with the two other wings. Finally, with supplies dwindling, Colonel Lindsay decided on March 31 that he must return to Fort Brooke. The march back fortunately passed by Fort Alabama, where the approach of the column frightened away a large body of Indians who had been investing the fort for some time. Minus the garrison for Fort Alabama, the center returned to Brooke on April 4, having been in the field fourteen days on ten days' rations.[37]

The longest and hardest march fell upon the left wing commanded by Brevet Brigadier General Abraham Eustis. Pursuant to orders, he had reached St. Augustine on February 15

Abraham Eustis

and had for the next thirty days found it necessary to establish small posts every twenty miles from there to Mosquito Inlet. He was obliged to use the South Carolina volunteers for this, and they soon developed a dislike for him, similar, but by no means equal, to that which the Alabamans felt for Colonel Lindsay. The citizen soldiers recognized that Eustis was a good soldier, but they were repelled by his cold manner. He was a strict disciplinarian and perfectly just. Bemrose dryly remarked that the volunteers did not like him because he played no favorites. He did nothing to win their loyalty, indeed he punctured the romantic dream in which they had gone off to war. They wanted an officer who looked like one, but Eustis wore civilian dress and did not even bother to carry a sword.[38]

On March 15 he began to move his column toward Volusia, where he intended to cross the St. Johns River, but it was a full week before the wing had gotten ready to cross the broad river. The movement began early on March 22, and when two companies of South Carolina volunteers had crossed, the Indians peppered them with a heavy concentration of fire. There was a smart skirmish before another portion of the white force could come to the aid of the advance guard. Three white men were killed and six wounded. Crossing and reorganization consumed four more days. Eustis had with him 1,400 men: four companies of the First Artillery, commanded by Major Reynold Kirby; a regiment of mounted South Carolina volunteers, Colonel Goodwyn commanding; a South Carolina infantry regiment, Colonel Abbot H. Brisbane in command; and Captain Elmore's company of Columbia volunteers. Leaving two companies under Major William Gates, First Artillery, to hold the position at Volusia, General Eustis on March 26 got his column in motion across what amounted to a trackless wilderness. The first two days the troops traveled but seven miles; the going was so heavy that horses died of exhaustion. Then it was necessary to bridge the Oklawaha. The objective was Peliklakaha, an important Indian or Negro village, and the date set by Scott for arrival there was March 25. The deadline date came and passed with the left wing still hacking its way through the wilderness. On March 30 there was another smart skirmish near Okihumpky (which had for some time been the seat of Micanopy). The wing arrived at Peliklakaha that same day, and found it abandoned. They were then five days late for the start of General Scott's ambitious converging movement. On March 31 Eustis ordered the village to be burned; then, seeing no other course open to him, he also turned south on the Fort King road and headed for Fort Brooke. When his wing reached that haven, it found the other two wings already there.[39]

The left wing never knew how many red men it had dispatched in its skirmishes, but two notable kills were reported. One was identified as Yuchi Billy, chief of the tiny band of Yuchis who were part of the Seminole tribe. The identification proved to be wrong, though, for Billy was captured alive a year later. The second was Yahahadjo, apparently one and the same with Yahadjo. Yahadjo is mentioned in the text of the Treaty of Payne's Landing but the name beside the signature X at the end is Yahahadjo, and the same name is also beside the mark on the Treaty of Fort Gibson. One articulate South Carolina volunteer, pensively gazing at the cadavers, remarked in both cases the superb development of legs and feet and the amazingly small hands these chiefs had. Sadly he recorded that the body, thought to be that of Yuchi Billy, was scalped and otherwise mutilated, then trussed up on a framework of poles like a dead wolf, and carried triumphantly into camp.[40]

Making no effort to conceal the truth, General Scott ruefully reported to the Adjutant General that his three wings had converged on Fort Brooke not because of instructions but because they had run out of supplies. The grand campaign had not resulted in the death of as many as sixty Indians, he admitted, and now the hostiles were split up into bands, none larger than two hundred persons. As for his command, the horses were broken down by weather and hard use, measles and mumps were rampant among the volunteers. There was nothing to do but pick up the loose ends and try to achieve some measure of victory. To that end the commander sent his three wings out on missions before the volunteers would be entitled to go home. Certain Indians had told Scott that many bands of Seminoles had moved south to Pease Creek, and he directed two volunteer regiments to scour that area. Colonel Smith with his Louisiana regiment and a navy party was to go south by boat, disembark, and scout the south bank of the creek, while Colonel Goodwyn with the South Carolina mounted regiment was to advance overland to the north bank and follow it. The infantry of the left wing were to follow Goodwyn by a day or two. Then after scouring the north bank, the whole left wing was to face east, cross the peninsula, and return to Volusia. Once again General Scott was directing Eustis to lead his command into a trackless wilderness. He apparently had no true conception of the difficulty of crossing the peninsula from Pease Creek to Volusia, since no map accurately depicted that region. Clinch and Lindsay were directed to use their wings to scour the country drained by the Withlacoochee, the former to end up at Drane and the latter back at Brooke. General Scott frankly admitted that he did not know what these movements would accomplish, if anything; he hoped they might uncover the hiding places of the Seminole women and children. Whatever the accomplishment, when these orders were executed, the volunteers would be entitled to go home. There would then be only 789 regulars in the trouble zone, too few to prosecute the war.[41]

If it can be said that the Indians ever operated upon a plan of campaign, now for the second time they appeared to be doing so. Unwilling to strike in strength at one of the main wings, they hit all three around the edges. This strategy involved them in a few investments, a rare operation for Indians. For example, from April 5 to April 17, they closely surrounded Camp Cooper, a picket work built in the heart of the Cove of the Withlacoochee and manned by a battalion of Georgia troops and a few regulars. About the same time, they tried to overpower the garrison of Louisiana volunteers left at Fort Alabama. They failed, but killed one soldier and wounded two. On April 14 a band attacked a burial party sent out from Fort Barnwell at Volusia across the peninsula.[42]

The last-named foray produced a celebrated court-martial. The officer tried was Major William Gates who had graduated with the first class at West Point. The charge against him was that he had left two bodies lying outside the works of Fort Barnwell after the Indians had driven the burying party inside, and had made no effort to recover them for a full twenty-four hours. During the trial General Scott himself testified, and what he said pretty well sealed Gates' doom. Commanders in Florida, he offered as an obiter dictum, had been bemused by defensive works, and had stayed inside them when they ought to have been aggressive. Small matter that Scott had aimed this barb at General Gaines; it lodged instead in Gates. He was convicted by the court, and his name stricken from the rolls of the army on June 11, 1836. The disgraced major, however, had defenders who never rested until they got him reinstated. In time they convinced the high command that under the circumstances it would have been imprudent to risk living men to rescue two dead bodies. In consequence, Gates was restored to the service with the rank of major on January 7, 1837. Thereafter he put in nearly another thirty years in the service, and finally was brevetted a brigadier general.[43]

Returning to the peripheral strategy of the Seminoles, in this full flush of power they did more unusual things for Indians. From 1:00 A.M. to 3:00 A.M. on the night of April 20 they rushed the pickets at Fort Drane, hoping to overpower that stronghold before General Clinch, who was then marching toward it, should return. This was remarkable because Indians rarely chose to fight at night. The garrison held them off, and on April 24 Clinch led the right wing back into the stockade. He had found no Indian hideaways and fought no more than minor skirmishes, but his men were exhausted. Detractors criticized both him and Colonel Lindsay for failing to probe thoroughly into the Cove of the Withlacoochee. The critics claimed that the Indians were still there and could have been brought to bay.[44]

There was yet another small garrison upon which the Seminoles might concentrate. It was in a blockhouse that had been established twelve miles from the mouth of the Withlacoochee on April 4 by Major John McLemore (whom we met earlier as Dr. McLemore), and then apparently forgotten. McLemore left Captain Holleman and fifty Florida militiamen as garrison. Beginning on April 12, the Indians kept the blockhouse surrounded for forty-eight days. In time the roof was burned off and the provisions reduced to nothing but parched corn. Shelterless and hungry, the fifty, minus a few, held out against five hundred or so. Captain Holleman died and Lieutenant L. B. Walker took command. Now some daring soul made his way through the ring of Indians and reminded the outside world of the plight of his nameless blockhouse. Inasmuch as there was ill-will just then against him, General Scott was at once charged with having criminally left the heroic band to its fate. The general, who probably did not even know the place existed, countered by accusing some of the militia commanders of negligence. On May 1 his order went to General Clinch to send relief. The latter now held a council of officers, and on its recommendation decided he had not sufficient force to comply. All he could do was call upon adjacent counties to raise a rescue party. None materialized. Another month passed and the plight of the men in the blockhouse grew extreme. This was a situation suited to Leigh Read. It was he who at last led a volunteer detachment to lift the siege. With deep feeling the liberated officers wrote to Read thanking him for their deliverance. They charged Scott with having abandoned them.[45]

Besides the investments described above, there were many skirmishes in the last phase of Scott's campaign. One of these might be rated as a battle. Since the campaign for which it had been built was terminating, Colonel Lindsay decided to break up Fort Alabama. To that end he placed Colonel Chisolm in command of a column of about six hundred men, made up of Chisolm's own Alabama regiment and a detachment of regulars led by Lieutenant Colonel William S. Foster of the Fourth Infantry. It was hard for a veteran regular like Foster to serve under a citizen soldier, but Foster did his duty and, more than that, spoke well in his reports of his irregular associates. As Chisolm's command neared Fort Alabama, at 3:00 P.M., April 27, 1836, Indian fire swept them at close range. Once the momentary anarchy was overcome, the cannon was turned on the source of the bullets, while Foster put his regulars into a single rank with one-pace intervals between the men. Now came the ever effective charge with bayonets. Both regulars and citizen soldiers splashed across Thlonotosassa Creek to prick out the concealed foe. As usual the maneuver stopped the galling fire, and as usual it exacted some casualties. Five soldiers were killed, and twenty-four wounded.[46]

After the battle Colonel Chisolm took the garrison away from the short-lived fort, but left the work standing. His men had made it into what we would now call a booby-trap. Two strings ran from one of the doors to the trigger of a loaded musket with its muzzle buried in a barrel of gunpowder. Twenty-one minutes away from the place, the withdrawing column heard the explosion. Later examination showed that the charge had thrown the heavy logs of the fort far and wide. But how many Indians were killed could not be determined.[47]

There was no doubt that Scott's campaign was a failure, but the inevitable discussion about why it failed exacerbated the already bad relations between citizen soldiers and regulars. In such a situation Scott could be counted on to utter some ill-chosen words. Writing to the Adjutant General on April 30, he asserted that 3,000 troops would be necessary to end the fight; these should be "good troops (not volunteers)." Even though addressed to Roger Jones, Adjutant General of the army, this report soon became known to the people in Florida. They emitted a roar heard as far away as Washington. But Scott had not yet done his worst. On May 17 he issued his famous Order Number 48 which deplored the panic into which Floridians had let themselves drift. "The inhabitants," he said, "could see nothing but an Indian in every bush." He also referred to "the planters in the recent case near Tallahassee, who fled without knowledge whether they ran from squaws or warriors." This was too much for the proud Floridians. Even if it were true, they would have denied it, and they castigated their own Richard K. Call for agreeing with Scott. They burned Scott in effigy and darted sharp invective at him in the newspapers. Leigh Read wrote that Scott had tried to apply "the shreds and patches of the obsolete system of European tactics where they could not possibly work." Other writers were less restrained. One referred to Scott's "incapacity, presumption, and ignorance."[48]

This billingsgate stung the general, but he did not have to remain long in the theater to face it. War with the Creeks in Alabama had again flared up, and the government at Washington was worried that Creeks and Seminoles might pool their effort. Since Scott's usefulness was patently over in Florida, Secretary Cass informed him on April 15 that he could go to the Creek area as soon as the situation in Florida permitted. It would have been simpler for him to get away if the succession to the Florida command had been plain. The logical successor was Duncan Clinch, but he had not gotten over the sting of being superseded by Scott. Accordingly, on April 26 he offered his resignation. The President turned it down. A couple of weeks later the command in Florida was offered to him, but he had already left the theater for his plantation in Georgia. He declined it. He had intended, he said, to resign even before Scott had superseded him; after all he had served twenty-eight years in the army and his eight motherless children badly needed his presence at home. His resignation, to be effective as of September 21, 1836, was finally accepted.[49]

One man who badly wanted the Florida job was writing his old friend Andrew Jackson to that effect. This was Richard K. Call. Adversity and good fortune both had struck him during Scott's campaign. Summoned from the field because of the serious illness of his wife, he had killed a horse riding to reach her, but had arrived too late. Meanwhile President Jackson in February had sent Call's name to the Senate as his nominee to be governor of Florida Territory. John Eaton had long sought to be relieved, and the President now made him minister to Spain.

The Senate confirmed Call as governor on March 16, 1836. In spite of his personal grief, the new executive plunged into his duties. As early as April 30 he wrote to the Secretary of War protesting Scott's disbandment of the volunteers. At that time, he suggested, if the government would support him, he himself could carry on a summer campaign which would destroy the Indians' crops and end the war. Twelve days later he addressed Jackson himself. Scott's campaign was a failure; he had only exhausted resources and had given the foe additional confidence. But, said Call, if allowed to assemble 2,500 men, he could carry the war to the enemy and end it. Washington replied promptly on May 14 that the President favored a summer campaign if Call would conduct one, but the President did not officially appoint him to the command.[50]

Meanwhile Scott remained reluctantly at his post. He was soured on the citizens and citizen soldiers of Florida as much as they were soured on him. But for the regulars, he told the Adjutant General, sixty Indians would depopulate the area in one season. He spoke disparagingly of the "bad dispositions" of the Alabama regiment, which had had so much trouble with regular Colonel Lindsay, and he excoriated Major Leigh Read for uttering falsehoods concerning the forgotten blockhouse on the Withlacoochee. Read was a favorite of Governor Call and would work hard to turn the tables against Scott in Washington. "Associated with such officers and men," he concluded gloomily, "no man's honor is safe." Reflecting on some of this later, he relented a little, and one day before he left the theater for the Creek area, he wrote the Secretary that he had been ill, and had indited some of his most misunderstood statements when very weak. "If I can be convicted," he added, "of having committed one blunder in theory or practice since I left Washington to conduct the War in Florida, let me be shot."[51]

Delegate Joseph M. White implored President Jackson not to accept Clinch's resignation until White could reach Washington. Clinch was the only man "who had the confidence of the southern militia, and his being *driven* from service . . . will be disastrous." Another Floridian wrote that Clinch's supersession had been achieved by the same influence "that has constantly poisoned the ears of the present administration." On May 16 Cass notified Call that Scott was authorized to turn the command over to Clinch, but that if Clinch declined it, then Call should take charge. On May 18 the President himself wrote a letter which Call interpreted to be a directive to take command. To this the governor returned a grateful reply. He would assuredly put a speedy end to the war or perish in the attempt. But in the days that followed, Call fretted over the un-Jackson-like ambiguity which marked his military position. When orders came from the Adjutant General, one week after the date of Jackson's letter, they contained qualifications. Only if Clinch had resigned and Scott had left Florida was Call to take over. Then in a letter dated May 26 came still another qualification. "If General Jesup, in the course of the campaign, shall move into Florida, and General Scott shall be absent, he will, of course, be entitled to, and will assume the command." All this left Call much perplexed as to his situation. Was he governor and commander in the field, or only governor?[52]

General Scott, like every other high-ranking officer of that day, had staunch political friends and enemies. One of the enemies, Florida Delegate White, was but voicing the wishes of his constituents when on May 28 he wrote the Secretary of War bluntly asking for Scott's removal. Scott, he said, had lost the confidence of all local officers, and could not hope to operate effectively without it. White obviously was unaware that the General had departed the Florida command on May 21, a week before his letter was written. Since Scott did not know then what the Administration had decided concerning his successor, he turned the command over to the senior regular officer in the theater, who was Abraham Eustis. Far from seeing glory for himself in this elevation, Eustis notified the Adjutant General that he desired to remain in charge only as long as he had to. Apparently he was one of the few general officers to see that scant honor was to be won in the war against the Seminoles.[53]

The second front of the Seminole War was, one might say, all the while in Washington. There Delegate White insisted that the people of Florida had had nothing to do with the coming of the war, and demanded that the government indemnify them for the losses they had borne. He chided the Administration for being cold and indifferent to their pleas. Others supported his position. One argument ran thus: the government would gain by the war about 20,000 head of Indian cattle and many slaves. Besides, removal of the Indians would enhance the value of 20,000,000 acres of land. From these profits, help for sufferers ought cheerfully to be drawn. The best that Congress would do in response was to authorize the field commanders to issue rations to refugees. Yet when it came to the conduct of the war itself, Congress was not niggardly. In mid-March it passed an act giving volunteers and militia in federal service the same pay and disability benefits as regulars. During April alone the legislators appropriated $1,500,000 to suppress the hostilities in Florida. Next they opened a lively debate about the length of volunteer service. This resulted on May 23, 1836, in an act authorizing volunteers to enlist for six or twelve months instead of the traditional three. At the same time they added a second regiment of dragoons to the army, and appropriated $300,000 to bring it into being. The Second Dragoons was not activated, however, without a struggle. Jacksonians in Congress used the opportunity to attack the United States Military Academy. Do away with it, the Jacksonians said, for its graduates do not learn how to fight Indians, yet they engross all the commissions in the service. Despairing of the elimination of West Point, Mr. Hawes of Kentucky proposed that two-thirds of the officers of the new unit be taken from non-Academy applicants. This was defeated. The Second Dragoons, staffed by West Point graduates, became a permanent and celebrated unit in the army.[54]

Late in November, 1836, a court of inquiry met at Frederick, Maryland, to investigate the charges and countercharges which Gaines and Scott had hurled at each other. Scott charged Gaines with having disrupted his plan, indeed with having been the most important cause of the failure of his campaign. Gaines blasted back. He had moved forward after learning of Scott's designation to command, he said, because he expected Scott to be slow. Had not that officer proved himself dilatory in the Black Hawk War? Operating beyond steam power, Scott was immobilized. Meanwhile depredations multiplied in Florida. It was Gaines' duty to stop them if he could, and this could not be done at a distance. Far from weakening Scott's plan, the forces he brought greatly strengthened him. Nor did he deprive Scott of critical transport or supplies; he brought more than he used. (Here it seems that Gaines was closer to the truth than Scott, for his action did little to handicap his rival's complicated plan.) General Gaines next taxed his rich vocabulary of vituperation, which had made him many enemies, to berate Scott's order to Clinch not to help him. Scott's "starving scheme" he called the order, and he applied to its author the words "folly," "malice," "evil genius." Then he soared to his highest invective. This order marked its author as "the second United States general officer who has ever dared to aid and assist the open enemy. . . . The first great offender was Major General Benedict Arnold; the second, as your finding must show, is Major General Winfield Scott."[55]

This court of inquiry afforded various dissidents a chance to air old grudges. Duncan Clinch took the opportunity to lash out at the recent Secretary of War, Lewis Cass. "When at last the late honorable Secretary woke from his dreams of political preferment . . . it was too late. . . ." To Clinch, Cass was one of the prime causes of failure. Scott had a different grievance. "Unable, as I am," he said, "to remember one blunder in my recent operations or a single duty neglected," he could see no grounds for the court except that he lay under the displeasure of Andrew Jackson. As has been shown, General Gaines found sufficient release for his feelings in blasts at Scott. His violent attacks make amusing reading today. "I had reason to apprehend," he said, "from the tardiness of his movement, that a disease which General Scott contracted towards me, in August, 1814, had not been completely cured. It was, probably, that sickness of the spleen, which the best doctors say finds ease only in the misery of others."[56]

The court censured Gaines for the malice of his utterances. It also censured him for failure to make a sortie from Camp Izard. Otherwise the verdict held him blameless, and General Scott as well. Any other verdict would have been surprising, for however viciously the regular officers might quarrel among themselves, they were professionals with the army's reputation to defend before the rest of the world. They would not convict two of their ablest practitioners of incompetence. Thus, the Court served primarily as a healthy purge for pent-up grievances, and secondarily it provided the historian with much necessary source material.

Assuming that the verdict of the court was not an accurate estimate, what judgment must we pass upon Winfield Scott's campagn? It was almost certain to fail because the Indians were too mobile and too vigilant to be caught between the slow-moving, noisy columns trying to converge upon them. To have ended the war in one campaign would have required the invention of a new method of using soldiers against Indians on a large scale. It would have been necessary to undo all the training of both regulars and volunteers. Small parties of rangers, equipped to live off the land, to operate separately yet keep in touch with each other, were probably the only solution. And they were all but out of the question at that day and time. Considering the novelty of the problem, the lack of knowledge of the terrain, the unprepared state of the military, the need to gather large quantities of supplies in a hurry, the terrible conditions of transport, the foul weather, and the determined nature of the foe, it is surprising that Scott got his three wings into the wilderness and back again at all. But that is the only praise that can be offered him, for the campaign was by no means a work of genius.

As for Gaines, he did what he believed was necessary. He

probably decided to go inland because he thought Clinch was surrounded and in serious danger. Once there, the series of events which befell his command were not the result of plan but of circumstance. Whether he was helpless at Camp Izard and in need of rescue, as his detractors claimed, or holding his force for the hostiles to concentrate around at great cost of suffering to his troops, as he asserted, will never be known for sure. Probably he refrained the first few days from a sortie because he did not want to scatter the foe, and after that was indeed hopelessly hemmed in.[57]

9

Richard Keith Call

T HE COMMAND IN Florida remained ill-defined for so long
that at last, on May 30, Governor Call again wrote directly
to the President. He was sharply critical of Scott's campaign,
and boldly sanguine about what he himself could do if officially
given the task. Here was his proposal: use the Withlacoochee
as a supply line, for by means of the river supplies could be
brought within twenty miles of the hostile villages in the
Cove; feint an attack with horsemen while supplies and men
were being pushed up the river in fortified boats at night;
when prepared and in position, beat Osceola once and the
Seminole war spirit would wither. Jackson liked this proposal.
It was the only way, he scrawled on the letter, to put a speedy
end to the war. It "will redeem us from that disgrace which
now hangs over us." Where was General Clinch? the President
continued; if Call had not received the supreme command he
should have it. In spite of Presidential nudging, it was June 18
before Secretary Cass finally determined that Scott was out
of Florida, that Clinch had resigned, and that the way was
open for Call to take over. On June 21, 1836, Call at length
received from the Secretary of War the sanction he had so
avidly sought.[1]

Rarely before had a civil governor been given command of a
field army made up, not only of his own militia, but of militia
from other states and of units of the regular army. At this

time Call had no army rank. He had been a regular officer for eight years, but in 1822 had resigned his commission to take up the practice of law in Pensacola. Consequently, his only military title in 1836 was that of commander in chief of the militia of the Territory of Florida. He had been a brigadier general in the Territorial militia since 1823.[2]

Richard Keith Call was born near Petersburg, Virginia, in 1792. While he was still very young, his father had died. His mother, a woman of strong character, took her four boys and five slaves and migrated to Kentucky to be near her brothers. Until Call was twenty-one, she was the most influential force in his life. Most of his education came from her, for he had little formal schooling. But the decisive event in his career occurred in 1813 during the Creek War. Serving as a volunteer officer with a Kentucky unit, he suddenly found himself without anybody to command. His men, insisting that their enlistment was up, summarily went home. Lieutenant Call presented himself at the general's tent, denounced the action of his erstwhile associates as mutinous, and offered to remain on duty in any capacity. The general was none other than Andrew Jackson of the Tennessee militia, and men of Call's stripe were the kind he liked. Thereafter Call was with Jackson at many vital moments: in Washington in 1819 while the General sought to fend off hostile criticism of his Florida campaign of 1818; in Florida in 1821 when Jackson became the first governor of that Territory; and in Washington again when Call, Jackson, and John Eaton served together in the Eighteenth Congress, and roomed together as well. It was Jackson who urged him to wed Mary Kirkman in 1824, even though her parents objected. When his mentor became President of the United States, it was not surprising that Richard Keith Call should be one of the group of Jackson's old cronies who made up what was called the "nucleus" in Florida politics. To this nucleus went the spoils.[3]

It may be that the dominant note in the character of the new commander was ambition. In an age very fussy about honor he was known by friend and foe as especially touchy about it. He could not forgive those who by his sensitive standards had affronted him. Dynamic and commanding in manner, he had a powerful, melodious voice with which to win

Richard Keith Call

people. Even friends called his manner imperious and feared his fierce temper, while the unfriendly labeled him selfish, lofty, and arrogant.[4]

Commodore Alexander Dallas, who commanded the naval detachment in Florida and remained at all times watchful lest a ground officer take liberties with the navy, found his imperiousness hard to bear. "I beg that your suggestions," he wrote the general, "may have less the character of an order than those heretofore received." Call, for his part, was quick to criticize the navy's methods in Florida. He sent letter after letter to Secretary Cass complaining of its failure to do what he thought necessary. The navy was not cutting off the foreign trade with the Indians, he said. The naval view, in contrast, was that this trade did not exist. The War Office replied to Call that it had no control whatever over the naval service. But if Call had to work with Commodore Dallas he saw no way to harness the navy into his immediate operations. Instead, he urged Dallas to send an expedition into the area south of Charlotte Harbor. This region was all but unknown, except that it was too watery for land operations, but some bands of Indians were believed to be there. Meanwhile, detachments of marines and sailors served ashore as garrison for such posts as Fort Brooke. When, for some reason, the naval garrison was withdrawn from Fort Brooke in August, the army officers remaining there reported to their superiors how burdensome guard duty had become.[5]

Farther down the chain of command, regulars and citizen soldiers chafed over their association. Lieutenant Colonel William Foster, Fourth Infantry, unbosomed himself in a letter to General Scott concerning the action at Thlonotosassa Creek. "I spoke well, and perhaps too well, of the Alabama Regiment . . . my motives will be only appreciated by you." If he had to serve again under a militia colonel, he vowed that he would resign. "It appears to be determined by Congress to adhere to Militia." Naturally the citizen-soldier viewpoint was the exact reverse of Foster's. To many a militiaman the standing army constituted a threat to the very life of the republic. Service under the regular officers was irksome to sturdy republicans. One Tennessee volunteer recorded in his diary that he was unwilling to act as "laquey boy to little upstart foppish lieutenants of the regular army who thought it a great condescension to speak to or notice a common person."[6]

Hard though it might be, Call had to try to yoke citizen soldiers and regulars together into an effective force. When he assumed command, there were only about 1,000 regulars in Florida and 230 citizen soldiers. He could not start his promised campaign until he had somehow doubled this force. It happened that at this time militia and volunteers from Georgia and Alabama were becoming harder and harder to recruit for duty in Florida, especially after fighting against the Creeks broke out in their own states. Few wanted to serve in the peninsula during the "sickly season." Some said they would run away if drafted, others threatened bodily harm to anyone who undertook to conscript them.[7]

This resistance made it necessary to go beyond the states bordering Florida to secure citizen soldiers. Since the traditional recruiting ground was Tennessee, General Scott, then in the Creek country, called for 2,500 Tennessee volunteers, 1,000 to be used against the Creeks and 1,500 to go to Florida. But Call waited in vain all summer for the detachment assigned to Florida. They had started on schedule in June, only to be held in Alabama to fight against the Creeks. Call was not informed of the change in plans. It was September before they were released from Alabama. To make matters worse, it appeared that they might then refuse to go on to complete their term in Florida. But one of their influential officers made the peninsular service a point of honor. Death in Florida, he said, was better than dishonor at home. Few Tennesseans could resist such an appeal, and most of them agreed to continue until the end of their six-months enlistment.[8]

Call's forces needed further strengthening, and friendly Indians were recruited for that purpose. Some of them were the Seminoles who had from the start agreed to the course the white men wanted them to follow. After the murder of Charley Emathla late in 1835 many of these docile Indians sought American protection, and now 450 of them were gathered around Fort Brooke. Thirteen transports were in the harbor waiting to carry them west in April. Seventy-five of these friendlies served as guides in the early actions.[9] It was a simple matter also to enlist a regiment of Creeks to fight the Seminoles, even though Seminoles and Creeks had been scheduled by the government to unite soon in brotherly love west of the Mississippi. There was competition among white officers for commissions in the Creek regiment, but the colonelcy fell to a flamboyant character in the frontier style who had first attracted Andrew Jackson's attention by flogging Representative John Ewing of Indiana on the streets of Washington. The new colonel was John F. Lane who only a month or two before had been a lowly captain in the Second Dragoons.[10]

The summer of 1836 was a time of frustrations for the new commander in Florida. It was an uncommonly sickly season, and Call himself was from time to time severely indisposed. Fever, coupled with Indian aggressiveness, brought about the gradual abandonment of the interior of the peninsula. Out of six companies at Fort King only 166 men were fit for duty. The fort had another disadvantage in that it could be supplied only from Volusia, and it was becoming harder and harder to convoy trains from that place. Finally, Fort King was no better situated in relation to the Cove of the Withlacoochee than was Fort Drane. On these grounds, the nine-year-old fort was evacuated between May 17 and June 9. The adverse effects of this move were felt at Drane almost at once.[11]

Overall commander in the area was Major Julius F. Heilman stationed at Micanopy. Captain Lemuel Gates arrived at Drane on May 29 and took command there. In the days that followed, the Seminoles pressed his log works relentlessly until he was tired of unrelieved defensive action. Gates took the offensive in an unusual way. A howitzer was hauled out in front of the fort and fired, whereupon the Indians raised a yell which disclosed their location. Gates ordered a charge with bayonets. This scattered the natives, but he could detect where the main body of them went, and the howitzer was directed to shell that spot. Cannon fire from the lone gun, unprotected by any works, continued until the Indians went away.[12]

Heilman himself conducted an interesting action on June 9, 1836. Concluding that Osceola was seeking to draw him out from behind the pickets of Fort Defiance (a work erected near Micanopy), he decided to accept the offer, and to try at the same time for a double envelopment. One foot artillery company was sent around the Indian right flank and a detachment of the Second Dragoons around the left. Another element advanced in the center to hold the Indians in position. Reaching the left flank, Lieutenant Thompson B. Wheelock gave the order to the dragoons to charge. Abandoning the usual dragoon pattern, they made their charge on horseback, and fired and reloaded without dismounting. Meanwhile, the foot artillery had gotten themselves in a vantage point on the right where they could watch the Indians from behind. When the firing of the dragoons began, they charged upon the Indian rear. The most bizarre part of a bizarre action then took place. Heilman had nothing in reserve but one six-pounder and its crew, yet seeing the right moment to commit his reserves, he advanced with the howitzer, firing as he went. Before this unusual reserve could tell on the action, word reached him that the picket was in danger, and he took the reserve back to protect it.[13]

Even though the odds—if white reports can be believed—were 70 soldiers versus 250 Indians, had this remarkable engagement occurred in an open area, European style, it would surely have brought the annihilation of the Indian fighting force. But in the woods the Seminoles seemed to melt away, until there was no one left to surround and annihilate. The woods into which they vanished were once called by William Bartram Cuscawilla Hammock (since altered to Tuscawilla), the very hammock where Cowkeeper presumably had founded the earliest Seminole village one hundred years before.

Two days later Major Heilman transferred his headquarters to Fort Drane. His command now consisted of 307 men, of whom 121 were sick and all were low on ammunition. What a time for him to receive a letter from General Call directing the establishment of a new post between Drane and Suwannee Old Town in the Wacahoota Hammock. The new post was part of Call's plan to start an offensive which must at least drive the natives beyond the Withlacoochee. But the new fort was not established, and the Indians were not driven. On the contrary, aided by disease, the Indians did the driving.[14]

Weather and fever continued to take their toll. Lieutenant Wheelock committed suicide on June 15, 1836. The living suffered terribly. Heilman urged the War Department to send mounted troops because the intense heat and burning sands rendered foot soldiers useless after one day's march. Even with mounted men it would be hard to accomplish much in the fiery summer. He began to think of substitutes for arms carried by men; Congreve rockets might be useful thrown into the hammocks. Then the fever struck Heilman too, and by June 27 he was dead. Like Wheelock, he was to receive no other memorial than to have a short-lived log fort on Black Creek named for him.[15]

Call planned to take the field early in August, but fate was working against him. Now the garrison surgeon recommended that Fort Drane too be evacuated because of the sickness. Since 99 out of 289 men were ill there, Call accepted the recommmendation. Before dawn on July 19, 1836, twenty-two wagons of stores escorted by 62 men, 26 of them mounted, commanded by Captain William S. Maitland, started from Drane toward Fort Defiance near Micanopy, less than ten miles distant. A quarter of a mile from Micanopy about 200 Seminoles under Osceola opened fire on the whole 500-yard length of the column. Badly outnumbered, the soldiers were hard pressed until 31 men joined them from Fort Defiance. All now made a charge to push the Indians back to where the cannon could play on them, and the column was able to reach the fort. In this action, known as the Battle of Welika Pond, five white men were killed and six wounded. Indian casualties are not known.[16]

Captain Charles S. Merchant meanwhile remained at Fort Drane in command of the sick. He could bring them out only under a strong escort, and he appealed to General Call for 250 men. Not until August 7 was it possible to evacuate the invalids and completely abandon the fort. With it were lost 12,000 bushels of corn standing in the fields ready to harvest, which General Clinch had planted on his plantation before the war had gotten out of hand. Now, except for Micanopy, Garey's Ferry, and Newnansville, white settlers had deserted the interior.[17]

About 650 persons crowded into Newnansville. From 700 to 800 thronged Garey's Ferry, where they felt some security because of the army depot there. At all three concentration points the refugees lived in leaky, drafty shacks. There were frequently four makeshift beds in a 10 by 10 hovel. Fifty-two persons died of measles and diarrhea at Garey's Ferry during the month of July. Captain Thomas Childs, Third Artillery, recorded in his diary the case of five children, the oldest thirteen, trying to fend for themselves because the mother and father had died of measles. Under orders to leave for Micanopy, Childs was helpless to do anything for them except to leave them a religious tract.[18]

If John Bemrose complained that he found mostly godless men in Florida, there was a large number of deeply religious soldiers whom he overlooked. Captain Childs, for example, was so religious that he even hated to evacuate the distressed garrison of invalids at Fort Drane on a Sunday. He was comforted to learn that his friends at home prayed for him. "My Christian armor, I would fain hope, grows brighter and brighter . . . I would not be a prayerless man for worlds."[19]

Just at this time the war penetrated farther south than ever before. On Cape Florida, at the southern tip of Key Biscayne, white John Thompson and his Negro helper stood to their duty, tending the lighthouse, when a body of Indians attacked them on July 23, 1836. At first the two defenders held the ground floor until the shooting ignited the kegs of oil stored there for the light. With flames licking behind them, they climbed the ninety feet to the top of the tower. For a time they kept the fire out of the light chamber, but when it did burst in they had to lie down on the narrow plank which made the only platform. Nearly being roasted alive, and wounded by the incessant gunfire of the Indians below, Thompson dropped a keg of powder down the shaft, half hoping that it would end his own misery. Except for the loud explosion, it accomplished little. Soon the Negro was killed by a bullet. Outside the Indians danced, whooped, and fired. Finally, believing they had killed both men, they gathered up their plunder and departed. Wounded in both feet so that he could not move, Thompson lay all night on the plank. On July 24 help arrived. The men on the United States schooner *Motto,* on duty in the vicinity, had heard the powder explosion and had seen the flames. Crowding on sail, the *Motto* reached the Cape and put a rescue party ashore. A ramrod, with string attached, was fired from a gun into the beacon chamber, and with great difficulty Thompson reached it. With this he could pull up a rope and a block. Two sailors were then hoisted up to bring him down.[20]

Four days later Lieutenant Alfred Herbert led a foray by boat into the ruins of the Travers Plantation east of the St. Johns. Finding the Indians there in force without having been discovered himself, he directed his men to load with buckshot and lie in wait. They opened fire at forty paces. Several Indians went down, but at the end of an hour and twenty minutes the white ammunition was running out while the Indian fire continued unabated. It became necessary for Herbert and his party to escape to their boat and leave.[21]

On July 24 Lieutenant Colonel Ichabod Crane assumed command of northeastern Florida. The bounds of his command were not sharply defined, but they extended at least to Micanopy. He sent Major B. K. Pierce from St. Augustine on August 15 to close out Fort Defiance. Drane had been evacuated a week before. Pierce marched with a force of 125 men and 27 wagons to carry away the stores. It took him six days to reach Micanopy, going by way of Garey's Ferry to escort a wagon train. An express rider could cover the same fifty-five miles in one night. Pierce reached Micanopy on August 20 and found 147 men on the sick list. Even so, he could not resist a stroke at the Indians. Learning that Osceola's warriors had taken over abandoned Fort Drane, he started a column of 110 men and one cannon from Defiance at 2:00 A.M., August 21, on the ten-mile march to Drane. To increase his mobility, Pierce mounted half his men on wagon horses. This draft-horse cavalry rode at the gallop into the surprised Indians. Being inexperienced, many a man charged hanging onto his horse's mane. The Seminoles, caught in the open, scurried into the edge of a hammock, there formed as much of a line as they ever did, and commenced to return a heavy fire. In reply, the white cannon rattled canister into the palmettos. After about an hour of this, Major Pierce, concluding that he had not enough force to charge the hammock, pulled his men back and returned to Micanopy. His losses were one killed and sixteen wounded; Indian losses were unknown.[22]

Floridians very much admired Pierce. Their admiration in itself was no small compliment, for they were usually suspicious of the regular army. General Call wrote confidentially to the President that except for Pierce his field officers were inefficient. Accordingly, he wished a brevet colonelcy given Pierce so that he might outrank the lieutenant colonels who would otherwise command him. The *Florida Herald* admiringly noted that in order to expedite Call's campaign Pierce had cut fifty miles of new wagon road in five days with a battalion of 200 artillerymen.[23]

Carrying out his orders, Pierce began to evacuate Fort Defiance on August 24. Once this was done, all of the peninsula south of Black Creek and Newnansville and west of the St. Johns had been abandoned to the Indians. The latter must have risen for a time above the mood of desperation with which they had started the war. Perhaps, after all, they had a chance. But when General Call heard of the breaking up of Fort Defiance, he was furious. This move, he said, disrupted his plans, and Colonel Crane had made it contrary to his order.[24]

Frustrated as he was, Call yet continued optimistically to plan for his summer campaign, now pushed into the fall. His basic idea was to hem the Seminoles in by means of four supply points, all accessible by steamboat. Two of them, one at Tampa and the other at Volusia, were already in operation. A third was to be established at the shoals of the Withlacoochee River twenty miles from its mouth, a fourth at Suwannee Old Town. As of September 8 he had not been able to establish the last two because of the lack of manpower. But he had ordered forage and rations from New Orleans.

Supply by steamer was effective, though expensive. The rent of one steamer for such use ranged from $3,500 to $4,000 per month. One trip of a vessel from New Orleans to Fort Brooke cost the government $10,000. Call suggested that it would be much cheaper to purchase a steamer than to rent it. No comparable figures on the cost of land transport are at hand, but it too was high in the rough country. Call's solution of the land-transport problem was to buy pack horses, but it was difficult to obtain them at any price. He was thrown back, therefore, on the forty wagons then concentrated at Garey's Ferry.[25]

General Call could not begin his operations until the Tennessee volunteer brigade arrived. Its progress toward the fight is easy to trace because of a revealing diary kept by Lieutenant Henry Hollingsworth. When they first entered Florida, the Tennesseans came to believe that their misgivings had been

chimerical, for they found West Florida inhabited by happy
people and dotted with fine farms. Encouraged by what they
saw, and mindful of their state, they spruced up to enter Tallahassee. Down the main street they went, 1,200 strong, on September 11, 1836, but they created no more stir in the capital
than if they had been a procession of farm wagons.

One resident of Tallahassee, however, was so delighted to
see them that he dragged himself up from the sick bed where
he had lain for a week sweating out a burning fever. This was
R. K. Call, and the next day, he led them, plus 140 Florida
militia, toward the Suwannee River. The Tennesseans commenced to meet the Florida they had dreaded, "swampy, hammocky, low, excessively hot," Hollingsworth complained, "sickly
and repulsive in all its features." They were not encouraged
when they reached the famous river on September 24 and
found only one small boat provided to ferry the whole brigade
across. They paused here five days for provisioning and preparation.[26]

Getting this brigade across the Suwannee was the least of
General Call's worries. What if General Jesup should turn up
in Florida before he got a chance to show his mettle as commander? Unable to stand the suspense, he wrote Jesup tender-
ing him the command. Even though that officer was nearly
finished with his assignment in the Creek country, he declined
to assume control until Call had had an opportunity to carry
out his planned campaign. He even offered to serve in a subordinate capacity. This response confirmed Call's earlier estimate of the man. "He is a soldier of the first merit and is
worth a battalion of your other generals."[27]

The same day that the Tennessee brigade reached Tallahassee (September 18, 1836), the opening action of Call's campaign took place. Colonel John Warren of the Florida militia,
who had fought earlier in the Battle of Black Point (December
18, 1835), led one hundred men with one cannon out on a reconnaissance. In the timber called the San Felasco Hammock
(west of modern Gainesville) Indians attacked the party. They
must have had Warren outnumbered to have undertaken the
assault. They tried to turn one of his flanks and then the other,
only to be foiled by mounted charges. But the artillery tipped
the scale in favor of the white party, for it played upon the

Indians with what Colonel Warren called "fine effect." Surprisingly, the Seminoles charged the cannon twice. This opening fight ended after an hour and a half with unrecorded losses.[28]

A series of small operations took place on the fringes of Call's main thrust. The earliest of them was a skirmish on the last day of September between the hostiles and Colonel Lane's regiment of Creeks as it marched into Florida. The next day, farther to the east, Major Pierce reached Newnansville with supplies and ammunition. With these, and the protection of the log fort and picket works called Fort Gilliland, the 650 refugees could probably hold out. Southward at Tavernier Key, a band of warriors surprised and captured the schooner *Mary* on October 8. They burned her and escaped before a pursuit party of marines from the *Vandalia* could punish them for their boldness.[29]

September 29 was the pivotal day for the main column. All the troops were then across the Suwannee River, provisioned as well as they could be and ready to strike into Indian country. The general deemed it advisable to split his force. He ordered Leigh Read to take the Florida troops with a small detachment of regulars and travel to the mouth of the Withlacoochee River on the steamboat *Izard*. This vessel was then to tow two special barges twenty miles upstream, and establish a crucial supply depot. Naval officers operated the steamboat and sailors manned the barges. The new base was necessary because Call had been forced to give up plans to use Micanopy for a depot and point of departure, since the fort there had been abandoned against his wishes. On the same day the main body loaded ten days' rations on a train of pack mules and started hastily for abandoned Fort Drane. On October 1 it spurred up its horses to a gallop and covered the last thirty miles to the objective. Call expected to find the foe in force there, but the Indians had fled. The general believed they had been forewarned by escaped prisoners. Except for this leak, he wrote dejectedly, he would have eliminated nearly all the Mikasukis.[30]

For nine or ten days thereafter this portion of the army had to remain amidst the charred ruins of Fort Drane, abandoned in July and burned later by the Indians. When supplies ran low, the volunteers blamed Call. On October 8 Major B. K. Pierce reached the ruins with a few days' supplies and 200 regulars, and the inactivity ended. The reinforcements raised Call's strength to about 1,350, and he turned toward the Cove of the Withlacoochee.

On the twelfth the advance guard came upon forty or fifty Indians, and killed fourteen of them. The next day it emerged upon the bank of the Withlacoochee nearly opposite the Cove. Protected by cannon, the scouts and advance guard began to cross. A withering fire which was too hot to bear lashed them from the west bank while they were trying to swim their horses. Perhaps they could have made it on rafts, but there were not enough axes to build them. In the interest of mobility, Call had left the axes behind. He now had to rely on a party of Tennesseans he had sent downstream a few miles to attempt a crossing. That party overran an Indian village on the east side but could not reach the west bank because the river was badly swollen by rain.[31]

The general apparently accepted the fact that he was temporarily restricted to the east bank of the Withlacoochee. A council of officers agreed with him that the best course was to advance northward along the river's edge. With this movement they could reach Read's depot. The new course was held for a day or two, and then it was discovered that the army was nearly out of food. Horses were dying by the score for lack of forage; at least 600 perished during the campaign. Every morning the volunteers burned a dozen or so saddles rather than carry them on foot. And their grumbling rose as high as the smoke, for they had come to fight, they said, not to hike. When advance scouts could not locate Read's depot, resupply became the decisive factor in command decisions. Call reluctantly turned the column back to Drane, where it arrived hungry and disaffected on October 17. The much vaunted offensive had not provoked even one major engagement.[32]

Read in the meantime had after numerous frustrations reached the mouth of the Withlacoochee and had pointed the bow of the *Izard* upstream. The steamer soon ran aground squarely across the channel so that no large vessel could pass her, and there she broke up. Read blamed the naval officers who were handling her, but they denied preventable error.

(One of them was none other than Raphael Semmes, of later Confederate navy fame.) Read manfully continued to struggle with his problem, and at last, on October 22, succeeded in establishing a depot where Call had ordered it. By that time the force that was to use it had been back at Drane for five days. Call was obliged to send the Tennessee mounted men 105 miles northeastward all the way to Garey's Ferry where they could be subsisted. When these starving men reached the abundance of the depot, they ate until they vomited, and then filled up again.[33]

Call held the foot troops with him at Drane where they were augmented on October 19 by the Creek regiment, 750 strong. That unit had reached Fort Brooke at the end of September and had at once started for the interior. On the last day of the month it had had the mentioned sanguinary encounter with the Seminoles on the margin of the Cove. Afterwards the regiment had crossed the Withlacoochee (although Call had not been able to do it because of opposition and high water), and continued to Fort Drane. There it was arranged that the Creeks should wear white turbans in combat lest their friends mistake them for the enemy. Their progress must have been difficult, for the day of their arrival at Drane, their commander, Colonel John F. Lane, retired to his tent and ran a sword into his brain through his right eye. The official explanation was that he was deranged by fever and fatigue. Whatever the reason, thus passed a versatile man, at once street fighter and the inventor of a pontoon bridge which was successfully used during the war.[34]

Lane's death left Lieutenant Colonel Harvey Brown in command of the Indian regiment. Call, with this unit at his disposal, now began to formulate fresh plans to end the war. Elsewhere more powerful persons than he were making contrary dispositions. Rumors of Call's campaign reached Washington, and so did Lieutenant Alexander M. Mitchell from the combat zone. Since the general's own report never arrived at the capital, the Administration took action on the basis of such information as it had. Rumor and Mitchell both said that Call had been battling ill health. President Jackson was astounded and angry that his long-time friend should have come to the very edge of the Seminole heartland, and then turned back.

There were no reasons which in Jackson's eyes could justify such retrogression. Accordingly, under his orders, Acting Secretary of War Benjamin F. Butler wrote a harsh letter on November 4 to the Florida commander. The President, it read, was regretful and surprised that Call had not attacked. He was also disappointed that the general had started a campaign without adequate supplies. Call's retrograde movement had given heart to the Indians. Next came the high explosive: due to his ill health, said Butler, Call was relieved of the command, and ordered to turn it over to General Jesup as soon as the latter should arrive. Jesup, who had reached Apalachicola on October 13, received there the order to take over.[35]

Fortunately for Call's peace of mind, he did not receive Butler's letter for nearly a month. In the meantime, he launched in happy ignorance the grand attack he had designed from the first. With his diverse force of Tennessee volunteers, Florida militia, regulars, and Creek Indians, numbering close to 2,500 effectives, he sallied out of Fort Drane. On November 13, one month to the day after the previous failure, Call's army stood again on the banks of the Withlacoochee. The main body crossed without opposition at a point where the river was 220 yards wide. The only casualties were four men who drowned. In order to develop a pincers movement, the general sent the Tennessee brigade to make the crossing at the place which had been so hotly contested thirty days before. When both wings were over, the entire force made for the heart of the Cove. It was abandoned. The army had come thirty days too late. All Call could accomplish was to burn three large deserted log villages.[36]

Frantic to find the new Indian stronghold, the general divided his force in order to sweep more territory. He himself took the Tennessee brigade, some regulars, and the Florida militia back to the east side of the river. The balance under Colonel Pierce began to work its way southward. The two wings were to meet at Dade's battleground. For the next several days the fighting fell to the northern wing. It discovered a large Indian encampment on November 17, whereupon the Tennesseans rode rapidly ahead of the column, dismounted, and made a gallant charge. As usual, this broke the Indian position, and the Tennesseans pursued. The pursuit led them sometimes waist deep into mud and water. In half an hour the fight was over at a cost of one soldier killed and ten wounded. The Indians left twenty bodies where they had fallen and lost their horses and baggage to the pursuers. General Call was lavish in his praise of the Tennessee brigade.[37]

The next day the scouts located a Seminole fighting force on the edge of a hammock; the warriors were facing a cleared area and were apparently inviting attack. Call put a detachment of horsemen on each flank, and ordered a charge of the line. Forward it went with spirit, but soon was clearly in danger of envelopment. It was to counter this that the general had posted his horsemen. He ordered them to dismount and charge straight to the flanks at right angles to the line. This charge broke the envelopment. The entire action was over in thirty minutes, except for burying the dead: three soldiers and twenty-five of the enemy. There were twelve white men wounded and an unknown number of Indians, but Call estimated the hostile force at six to seven hundred.[38]

Now Call's division marched to Dade's battleground. Since Pierce did not reach the rendezvous until a day later, it was November 21 before a concerted action could be launched. The objective was the fighting force of the Indians which, according to all signs, was concentrated in Wahoo Swamp across the Withlacoochee from the Cove. So far the Tennesseans had born the brunt of the fighting, but for what lay ahead the entire army had to be committed. On the same day scouts located the body of the warriors apparently determined to make a stand in the edge of a dense woods bordering an open field. When Call arranged his line to oppose them it extended for a mile: the Tennessee brigade on the right, the regulars and Florida militia in the center, and the Creek Indians on the left. At the general's command, the line moved forward in extended order across the open field. The Tennessee line was only one rank deep, whereas Lieutenant Colonel Pierce (he had been breveted for the action on August 21 at Fort Drane) advanced the regulars and the Florida militia in two lines of two ranks each, with a distance of twenty yards between lines. All held their fire until within fifty yards of the well-protected Seminole position, then they blasted and charged on the run. The fire was returned, but the Indians soon began to give ground.

The entire attacking line, now badly disorganized, floundered through the dense swamp growth in search of the foe. Wading through mud and water for a mile and a half, the Creek wing at length reached a running stream about ten yards wide which looked deep because the water was black (as is usually the case with Florida swamp water). From the far bank the Seminoles opened a destructive fire, indicating that they had made another stand. The white men recognized the voice of Yaholoochee (Cloud) haranguing the warriors. They could distinguish Osuchee (Cooper), too, as one of the leaders. But what sent a chill through the Floridians was the recognition of an ex-plantation-slave serving as a conspicuous leader in this fight.[39] If former slaves could control arms and men, what atrocities might not the future hold?

Major David Moniac now boldly sought a place to ford the narrow stream. A bullet dropped him, and his body sank in the opaque water. Moniac was no ordinary officer; he was a full-blooded Creek and a graduate of the United States Military Academy. Unit by unit, man by man, the rest of Call's army floundered to the bank of the branch and added its fire-power. A heavy gunbattle continued across the ribbon of water until around 3:30 P.M. When the hostile fire seemed to slacken, the white commanders had to decide what they should do next. They decided not to try to force a crossing, but rather to withdraw and seek a supply point. The army had been on half rations for two days and was weak, and the short winter day was drawing to a close.[40]

John T. Sprague criticized this command decision in his history of the Seminole War. Later investigation revealed that the narrow branch could easily have been forded. The blackness of the water concealed the fact that it was only three feet deep. Had someone had the courage to repeat Moniac's try, he would have discovered this, and a crossing would have been decisive, for it would have laid open to the white army a settlement where 200 Negro men and 420 Indian warriors with their women, children, and gear had lived since the start of the war. Moreover, said Sprague, the fact that the decision was based in part on the need to find a supply point revealed this basic truth: so large a force as Call's ought never to have been operating in wild country without a base of operations.[41]

The fog of war hung over the Battle of Wahoo Swamp. Captain Thomas Gardner protested that he had been slighted in the official reports. Lieutenant Colonel Pierce, Gardner said, had failed to give him credit for the critical place he had occupied during the engagement because to do so would have revealed that Pierce had missed a trail which Gardner had found, the use of which by Pierce would have altered the action in favor of Call's army. Since the way to promotion and pay for the regulars could only be opened by favorable notices in official reports, Gardner expended twenty-three longhand pages to develop his case.[42]

Either Call did not know that Leigh Read had established a depot on the Withlacoochee, or he did not believe it big enough to furnish the needs of his column, for he decided to strike across the peninsula fifty to sixty-five miles to Volusia, a few miles south of Lake George. The strenuous march began on November 22, and took five days. Henry Hollingsworth, the Tennessee diarist, met the column there; he had scarcely been with his brigade since Call had sent it to Black Creek in mid-October. Most of its men had returned on foot to take part in the November campaign, but Hollingsworth, because he had declared he meant to ride and would not walk, was given assignments carrying dispatches and other similar tasks. "Welcome November," he wrote in his diary. "We hail thee as next to the last link in the chain of our bondage." At Black Creek he had seen 500 horses with which to remount his outfit, but the outfit had only two more months of service. "That is Callism," he observed. About 1,500 pieces of mail awaited the Tennessee body at Volusia; but they had been forwarded through so many hands that the postage was as much as ninety cents on one letter. Hollingsworth reported how ragged, dirty, and worn his fellow Tennesseans appeared, but he wrote wistfully that, "as there had been fighting, I would feel much better if I had staid with the army."[43]

A few days after his arrival at Volusia General Call received Secretary Butler's harsh letter. Stunned, dumbfounded, and enraged, he sat down on December 2 and wrote a long and bitter defense of his campaign. What hurt most was that his old friend, the President, had judged him on hearsay evidence. In addition, of course, he felt that he had done all he could with what he had. As for the euphemism about relief because of ill-health, it was plain that Jesup was to supersede him because he was judged to have failed.[44]

The Secretary of War replied that the appointment of Jesup was in no wise meant as censure, "but it was originally designed, and so made known to you at an early day, that the command should be taken by General Jesup on his arrival in Florida. Knowing as we did that General Jesup had arrived in Florida, with what propriety could the campaign have been left, at a juncture so critical, to the contingencies of your recovery?" Jackson was not convinced that Call had made the best of his opportunities. He agreed that the general had had a right to expect the depot on the Withlacoochee to be where he had ordered it; still it was a mistake to have marched from Drane without knowing for sure whether it had been established. Regarding the failure to cross the Withlacoochee on October 13, Jackson never ceased to believe that Call could have done it had he been properly supplied. To all this Call reacted by demanding a court of inquiry, but one was never granted, ostensibly, at least, because he was not at the time the holder of a United States commission. Here began the estrangement of R. K. Call from the man who had been his benefactor for twenty-three years. Call never forgave Andrew Jackson, and from that time forward slowly moved out of his party and into the Whig camp.[45]

What is to be said on balance of Call as commander? He cannot be blamed for the lateness of the start. On the other hand, the supply problems which undoubtedly hamstrung his efforts were partly his fault. He had, after all, never commanded large bodies of men, and had had none of what we would call logistical experience. To his credit, no other commander came as close as he did to bringing the main body of the Seminole warriors to bay. In two cases a stream of water stood between him and important Indian camps. Both times the Seminoles undertook to make a fight to protect their settlements. Call never got his armies across the two streams. In both cases it would have been difficult, for his men were hungry and consequently disgruntled. Yet a commander like Andrew Jackson would have gotten across and into those camps, one way or another.

The service in Florida was deservedly unpopular with the men because the incidence of disease was high, the chances of glory were small. As a result, 103 company officers resigned during 1836. To add to the pinch, many men were on detached service, helping to build the new railroads and to carry out other assignments in which their knowledge of engineering was valuable. (The West Point graduates were the only trained engineers in the United States at that time.) Lieutenant Colonel Pierce reported he had six officers on duty where the tables of organization called for fifty-five. The situation was aggravated by the fact that the whole number of regulars slowly rose in Florida. At the start of Call's term there had been 1,007 of them; at the end there were 1,890. These men were in forty companies from the First and Second Dragoon Regiments, the First through the Fourth Artillery, and the Fourth Infantry.[46]

The Adjutant General reported to the Secretary of War how costly the Indian wars in the southeast had been. During 1835 and 1836, 23,530 citizen soldiers had been mustered into United States service, some of them only for short periods. These all came from the southeastern states except for one company, 67 strong, from the District of Columbia. It would appear that 13,000 of the total saw some service in Florida. For many of them, the romantic luster associated with war disappeared in the swamps of Florida. Henry Hollingsworth recorded his impression. "So little demand has one for mind here—helter skelter, rough and tumble, march all day, eat if you have it, then fall down on the earth and sleep like a beast soundly until day, or until the drum beats for the men to rise, which on a march is generally about 4 am, and go through the same routine. This is a picture of the soldier's life! A life of dirt and toil, privation and vexation, and the poorest pay in the world $6 per month."[47]

It was said that Osceola used his authority to prevent making war on women and children. Yet some hostiles had not received the message, or did not care for his authority. A Mrs. Johns was struck by a rifle bullet in the arm and neck and was scalped when she fell. Although conscious, she lay as if dead until the marauders departed. Fire raged in the house, and she put out with her own blood the flames burning her clothing. A Mrs. Jackson was scalped that same year, and like Mrs. Johns she lived to be very old.[48]

In the late fall a dinner was given in St. Augustine to honor General Clinch who had temporarily returned to Florida from his Georgia plantation. A judge proposed that the surplus in the federal treasury should not be distributed until Florida had been compensated for her losses in 1812 and 1835. Closer to home, some intrepid diner offered a toast to Osceola, "the great untaken and still unconquered red man," who was fighting for his home. It was a visitor from New York who replied. He toasted the white suffering which made such sympathy for "the poor Indian" so badly misguided.[49]

10

Thomas Sidney Jesup

WHEN Brevet Major General Thomas Sidney Jesup took over the command in Florida on December 9, 1836, from his deeply disgruntled predecessor, Richard K. Call, he was tranferring from one to another Indian war. A flare-up among the Creeks in Alabama in the spring of 1836 had produced a near panic in Washington, lest Seminoles reinforce Creeks or vice versa. Accordingly, commanders in the Creek country were ordered to seal off the routes from Alabama to Florida. As early as May, Jesup had been sent to take command against the recalcitrant Creeks, but hardly had he reached Alabama when Winfield Scott arrived from Florida and superseded him. Scott's brevet as major general dated from 1814, Jesup's from 1828, giving the former fourteen years seniority.[1]

Using Georgia as a staging area, Scott, with his usual thoroughness, began rather deliberately to try to assemble enough men and material to crush the Creeks. On June 1 he directed General Jesup to pass on into Alabama, assume command of the Alabama troops, and be prepared to join later in a converging movement against the foe. Jesup followed these instructions so far, at least, as to gallop with a tiny escort right through the heart of the hostile country and make contact with the Alabamans. These militiamen did not want to serve under a regular officer, but in two or three days their governor persuaded them to do so. Once Jesup had taken command, he moved his troops into the field and began operations without notifying Scott. Unofficial reports reached Scott that Jesup was on the move, but nine days passed with no word from the field. Here, in Scott's eyes, was a premature action such as Gaines had set off in Florida. On June 16 the commander wrote Jesup, "I desire you instantly to stop all offensive movements . . . on the part of the Alabamans until the Georgians are ready to act." This went out by Indian runner through hostile country and reached its destination the next day. Jesup later claimed that he had not kept Scott informed because of the press of responsibilities; he had not averaged three hours sleep out of twenty-four in two weeks. But he replied to Scott that he had acted because the situation demanded it. "I have none of that courage," he wrote, "that would enable me to remain inactive when women and children are daily falling beneath the blows of the savage." Right or wrong, Scott chose to doubt that Jesup's motive was really to stop depredations, because, Scott contended, all the white population in that area had long since fled out of it. As he saw it, Jesup was trying to take credit for subduing the Creeks. "Who gave you authority," he wrote, "to roam at pleasure through the Creek nation?"[2]

Jesup was obliged, as Clinch had been and with the same commander, to make a difficult command decision. He had 1,500 Indian warriors with him (Creeks as usual fighting other Creeks) who would defect if he paused and waited as Scott had ordered; he also had to keep moving to retain the Alabama militiamen. He decided to advance in spite of Scott's order, and by doing so he secured a good many prisoners. A second peremptory order came from Scott. Not daring to disobey twice, Jesup halted his force and hurried off to Fort Mitchell to try to find Scott. Failing in this effort, he returned to his camp on the banks of Hatchacubby Creek, where he wrote Scott again. "If you will move today, general, we can end the war before tomorrow night. I am not ambitious of the honors of Indian warfare. I can prevent the escape of the enemy on this side of the country; and if you attack them in front they are yours. . . . By my former friendship, let me entreat you again to act promptly." That note went off on June 19, and on the following day, seeing what he believed to be a priceless opportunity irretrievably slipping away, Jesup wrote in irritation to Francis Preston Blair, editor of the Washington *Globe* and political crony of President Jackson. "We have had the Florida scenes enacted over again. This war ought to have been ended a week ago. . . . I was in full march with a force sufficient to have terminated the war in five days, when my progress was arrested by an order from General Scott. He has censured me in the most unmeasured and unwarrantable manner. . . . Let the President see this letter; he, I am sure, will approve the promptness with which I have acted, when he shall be sensible that I have tranquilized the whole Alabama frontier."[3]

Eight days later, on June 28, a terse order issued from the Secretary of War directing Scott, with no explanation, to turn over the command in the Creek country to Jesup and repair to Washington. Scott immediately complied. By that time he was convinced that Jesup had acted in good faith, even though he did not agree with Jesup's judgment. But upon arriving in Washington he learned of the letter to Blair. His gorge rose, and he referred to the Blair letter as "the treacherous instrument which had stabbed me in the dark." From that moment on it was war to the hilt between the two brevet major generals. Later that year their squabble was ajudicated at the same court of inquiry which weighed the controversy between Scott and the third brevet major general, Edmund Pendleton Gaines. As might have been expected, all were exonerated.[4]

The evidence presented at the hearing does not afford an explanation of Jesup's intention when he wrote to Blair about what Scott had done. Apparently Jesup wrote the letter in anger, only half aware of the events it might bring in its train. We cannot know what his deepest motives were when he acted contrary to Scott's orders. The presumption is that he saw a rare opportunity opening before him and seized it. The results confirmed his judgment, because soon thereafter the main resistance of the Creeks subsided. For his failure to keep his chief informed there can be no excuse except that he could not find enough hours in the day. As for Scott, he was probably too slow and thorough in his preparations. As shown by his Seminole campaign, he was not well suited to Indian warfare; he could not, indeed, adjust to the improvisations that such campaigning required.

When the Administration summarily removed Scott, it could have had no clear knowledge of the situation in Alabama. Jesup's assertion that he had tranquilized the frontier could not be accepted without reservations. But President Jackson was already predisposed against Scott on account of the failure of his campaign in Florida, and was ready to believe him to be dilatory. After all, Scott was no Jacksonian and Jesup was; although Jesup told Blair in a later letter that he did not meddle in politics and "would not consent to be defended on party grounds," politics could not be factored out so easily. When General Jesup took over in Florida, Scott's partisans in Washington accused him of derogating his predecessor to gain glory for himself, while good Jacksonians as staunchly took his part.[5]

Jesup's military career was already long and distinguished. It had begun at the time of the expansion of the Army in 1808. Only twenty years old in that year, Jesup had received a second lieutenant's commission without prior military experience. He fought with credit in the War of 1812, and his rise afterward was so swift that by 1818 he was quartermaster general, with the rank of brigadier. He continued in that capacity for forty-two years until his death on June 10, 1860. No other United States officer has ever held a staff position for so long. It is generally conceded that Jesup showed far above average competence as quartermaster, and that the organization which he created in that department persisted after him. In 1828 he was given his brevet as a major general for long and faithful service.[6]

Unfortunately General Jesup did not leave a sharp image to posterity. Though he served in the army for fifty-two years and contributed much to our military history, little has been written about him and not a great deal is known. Such is the usual lot of the quartermaster. It may be asserted, however, that Jesup was the most important white individual in the Seminole War. Reactions to his policies were violent then, and they still are. Even now there are persons, not all of them with red skin, who detest the man. They charge him with shiftiness and bad faith. Jesup was forty-eight when he took command. His portrait shows a steady intelligent eye and a prominent, square jaw. He looked anything but shifty.

Thomas Sidney Jesup

Whatever Jesup's true character, the President and the Secretary of War judged him to be the man to run the Florida war; and from the time he took over, they began to regard this conflict with more determination than formerly. His opening instructions were to achieve what Call had failed to do: attack the Seminoles in their strongholds and drive them from the area between Tampa Bay and the Withlacoochee River. Beyond that, he was to use his own discretion. The new commander naturally had certain preconceptions about how to run this war. It was impossible, he said, to coordinate the movements of several columns because of insuperable difficulties in communication. A united force was the proper tool. This could be used to push depots ever closer to enemy strongholds and to harass the Indians without surcease. While crossing the peninsula on the way to relieve Call at Volusia, he concluded that both Fort King and Volusia were poorly situated to serve as depots.[7]

Surprising as it may seem, he did not criticize Call's generalship. He reported to Secretary Butler that Call had done as well as a man could under the circumstances. To do any better, he, Jesup, must have more force. Speed was essential because most of the mobile force, taken over from Call, consisted of citizen soldiers whose terms had not much longer to run. It was necessary to use the Tennessee brigade and the Creek regiment while they were still available. The second cause for haste was the situation of certain of the Seminole bands. Jesup's scouts told him that Osceola, Micanopy, Philip, and Cooper, each with from 100 to 200 warriors, were about one day's march apart. His strategy was to strike them before they could unite.[8]

On December 12, 1836, the Tennessee brigade happily started its march across the peninsula from Volusia to Tampa Bay, there to board a ship and go home. Even though the weather was wintry, Henry Hollingsworth thought he saw in the country, dotted with small lakes, a future dwelling place for large numbers of people. How right he was! General Jesup, with the rest of his mobile force, accompanied the brigade in order to utilize the services of the Tennesseans to the last moment. His objective was to swing out to attack Osceola or Micanopy, or if this did not prove feasible, to continue on to the area of the Withlacoochee and seize opportunities as they came up. On the march to Volusia to assume the command, his force had overrun and burned a Negro village at the head of the Oklawaha, capturing forty-one Negroes. But on the westward swing no such opportunity arose. Upon arriving at Dade's battleground, the general set one last mission for the Tennesseans. A fort was needed there and they were told that they would be free to go home sooner if they helped. Before midnight of the first day all the picketing was up, and soon the whole layout was constructed. The new fort was named for Robert Armstrong, the commander of the Tennessee brigade. Once it was completed, Jesup left in it a garrison of 150 men, and minus the Tennesseans advanced toward the Withlacoochee to scour Wahoo Swamp and the Cove.[9]

He was now reduced to the following mobile force: 350 Alabama volunteers, led by Colonel Benjamin Snodgrass; 250 marines from the Creek fighting in Alabama; 450 regulars; and the Creek regiment. Letters went off to the governors of the adjacent states calling for regiments of twelve-months volunteers. In stressing his great need, Jesup did not hesitate to mention a fact harrowing to his correspondents. "This is a negro not an Indian war," he said.[10]

By that time Commodore Dallas had assembled under his command the largest naval squadron in the American service: one frigate, six sloops, one schooner, three steamers, and four revenue cutters. To help General Jesup overcome his acute manpower problem, Dallas operated his ships with skeleton crews and sent the surplus men ashore. Sailors thus garrisoned Forts Brooke, Drane, Clinch, and Foster. (Drane had been reoccupied, Clinch had been built near the mouth of the Withlacoochee, and Foster was Fort Alabama rebuilt.) The marine battalion also helped, under the immediate command of none other than Colonel Archibald Henderson, the commandant of the Corps. Determined to be where the fighting was, he had hung out a sign at his Washington office "Gone to Florida," had gathered up a battalion, and had headed south.[11]

Now Jesup divided his area into two zones. The northern one, more or less a "zone of interior," was put under Walker K. Armistead, brevet brigadier general. Armistead was directed to try to garrison all posts with sailors and Florida

militiamen in order to free the regulars to follow the Seminoles southward. General Jesup theorized that the bands who
had been around the Withlacoochee were moving south to link
up with Philip, Micanopy, and Jumper. This exodus made it
safe to try to hold the valley of the Withlacoochee with the
chain of forts then built, namely, Foster on the Hillsborough
River twenty-five miles from Brooke, Dade on the Withlacoochee twenty-nine miles beyond Foster, and Armstrong on
Dade's battleground. These, with Fort Clinch near the mouth
of the Withlacoochee and Fort Barnwell at Volusia across the
peninsula, were enough for the time being.[12]

The Withlacoochee area, it developed, was not entirely deserted. The column captured fifty-two Negroes there, and then
on or about January 10, 1837, flushed out and pursued a small
party commanded by Osceola himself. Nothing came of the
pursuit except information from captives that Osceola had
made his escape in company with but three warriors, and that
he was ill. If he had not seen it before, General Jesup now
began to realize that it was entirely possible to chase small
parties endlessly through the palmetto scrub without decisive
results.[13]

On the Atlantic side the usual depredations continued. At
Hanson's plantation the local militia overtook the marauders
on January 17, and in the resulting fight killed John Caesar,
one of the important Negro leaders. This event was equivalent
to a victory, but it was not so received because white men
were startled to find enemies willing to operate within two
miles of St. Augustine. They were also alarmed to see that
most of the raiding party was composed of Negroes who only
a short time before had been slaves. Worse yet, the captured
provisions, it was discovered, had been procured right in the
city. Inasmuch as there were a hundred or more Negro refugees within the town, the white people were fearful of a black
insurrection in conjunction with Negro attacks. A few months
later two free Negroes were indicted by the grand jury for
having supplied the Seminoles. Yet General Jesup could not
spare any appreciable force to help the citizens protect themselves.[14]

He was bent upon proceeding with his offensive plans, especially since four companies of Georgia mounted men had joined

him, raising his mounted arm to about five hundred. The Sixth
Infantry of regulars also arrived. In spite of orders from
Washington to send it west at once, Jesup determined to keep
the Sixth until he had completed a thrust toward the Oklawaha
River. To that end he put his army in motion from the vicinity
of Fort Armstrong on January 22. Right away it began to
show accomplishments. One section surprised Chief Osuchee
(Cooper) near Lake Apopka on January 23, 1837, killed him
and four others, and captured eight Indians and eight Negroes.
Osuchee had been one of the leaders at the Battle of Wahoo
Swamp and was the most important Indian killed thus far.
Thomas Childs, now brevet major, Third Artillery, watched
the chief's widow curiously at the burial, and reported that she
showed not a trace of emotion, but that one Indian boy of
fifteen cried briefly.[15]

The next exploit was led by Colonel Archibald Henderson
acting as commander of the Second Brigade, Army of the
South. Temporarily detached from the main body, his command scrambled over the highest ground in Florida. General
Jesup referred to it as the White Mountain, called by the Indians "Thlawhathee," and noted that it did not show on any of
the maps. Beyond this the Second Brigade tracked down a body
of Indians in the vicinity of Hatcheelustee Creek, draining into
Lake Tohopekaliga, and on January 27 engaged it. The volume
of fire which ensued was battle-size, but otherwise the action
was formless. The soldiers overran an Indian camp where they
captured one hundred ponies, half of them loaded with packs.
Pursuit then led into Big Cypress Swamp (not to be confused
with the much larger one of the same name south of Lake
Okeechobee). There, for a time, the troops faced the foe across
a stream twenty-five yards wide. Colonel Henderson ordered
that a crossfire be brought upon the opposite bank, whereupon
several officers ran across the stream on a log. For this gallant
conduct Henderson recommended that they receive special recognition. Although five Indian noncombatants and twenty-
three Negroes were bagged, as usual the warriors got away.
This and other inconclusive engagements apparently gave General Jesup a twinge of conscience. "If I have at any time said
aught in disparagement of the operations of others in Florida,"
he wrote to Roger Jones, "either verbally or in writing, offi-

cially or unofficially, knowing the country as I know it, I consider myself bound, as a man of honor, solemnly to retract it."[16]

Nor was the general's measure of others the only portion of his thought which had altered. Gone too was his early idea that the military force in Florida should be held intact at all times. In its place was a policy of sending off a detachment in any direction where his scouts indicated there might a vulnerable Seminole band. Thus he had these expeditions in motion all at the same time: Lieutenant Colonel Foster with five hundred men was searching for bands of Tallahassees said to have remained in the swamps south of the mouth of the Withlacoochee; a force hovered near the Oklawaha where prisoners said Alligator and Micanopy headed substantial bands; Lieutenant Colonel Fanning was moving up the St. Johns in search of Philip; a body of dragoons was aiding in the defense of Newnansville; another was operating around Orange Lake; and a militia force, under General Hernandez, patrolled the region east of the St. Johns. Obviously, his strategy had become one of opportunity.[17]

Henderson's Battle of Hatcheelustee on January 27 produced some negotiations with important enemies. Prisoners brought in Jumper, Micanopy, and Abraham on February 3 for a talk. Both sides agreed to a suspension of hostilities until February 18. At that time there should be another meeting with the same leaders at Fort Dade. But this truce did not prevent bloodshed. On February 8 Colonel Fanning's detachment had a sharp fight with five or six hundred of Philip's warriors led by Philip himself and his son Coacoochee (Wildcat). This fight began two hours before dawn, and lasted until 8:00 A.M. If the white men had not slept on their arms behind a low log breastwork, the attack of such superior numbers would probably have finished them. Then too they were aided by the guns of a steamer in the lake, which beat the hostile position heavily with grape and canister. Captain Charles Mellon was killed in this action at the head of Lake Monroe, and when a fort was erected on the site soon thereafter, it was named for him.[18]

Next day Colonel Foster's command came upon a large Seminole encampment on the Crystal River about sixty miles due west from Lake Monroe across the peninsula. While Foster's men assailed it, a detachment of sailors, near enough to hear the firing, rowed to the sound and joined in the fray. Much Indian equipment was destroyed, but the natives themselves again got away.[19]

The day agreed upon for a second meeting, February 18, drew near. Waiting at Fort Dade, General Jesup reviewed the situation for the authorities in Washington. In the numerous actions not a single first-rate warrior had been captured, indeed only two Indian men had surrendered. From this he concluded that the Seminoles and their Negro allies would fight until killed rather than leave Florida. With their knowledge of the terrain, if they had skill, they could hold off five hundred times their number. He took pride in pointing out that through prodigious efforts by the commissary and quartermaster departments, he had been able to keep his army in the field continuously for two months, and would continue to keep it there.[20]

February 18 came, but no chiefs. A few appeared a day or two later, but were not of high enough rank to suit the general. Until Micanopy would come, only a tentative agreement to extend the truce could be reached. It was early March before the next council met at Fort Dade, but Micanopy was not there. This time his absence did not halt the negotiations, for the chiefs present convinced Jesup that they had full power to act for him. In the council, therefore, they agreed to a document entitled "Capitulation of the Seminole nation of Indians and their allies by Jumper, Holatoochee, or Davy, and Yaholoochee, representing the principal chief Micanopy." Marked on March 6, 1837, this extraordinary instrument contained the following important provisions: (1) hostilities were ended, once and for all; (2) the Seminoles agreed to migrate immediately west of the Mississippi, give hostages to insure their living up to the terms, withdraw south of the Hillsborough River until they were shipped west, present themselves at a concentration point no later than April 10, 1837; and (3) the white men agreed to subsist the Seminoles from the time they turned themselves in at Fort Brooke until they reached their new homes, and thereafter for one year. Certain of the most important wording ran (italics added) "the Seminoles, *and their allies,* who come in and emigrate west, shall be secure in their lives and property . . . *their negroes, their bona fide property,* shall accompany them to the West."[21]

General Jesup really thought this agreement would end the war "if a firm and prudent course be pursued." Events seemed to support him. Yaholoochee with two hundred of his people turned in at Fort Brooke. Word reached Jesup that the principal chiefs on the St. Johns, Philip and Tuskinia, his brother, had indicated that they would obey Micanopy's order to observe the capitulation. Philip, it was said, had required Sam Jones to do the same. No white man knew whether Micanopy's order to Philip or Philip's to Sam Jones carried any authority.[22]

The persons upon whom success or failure really depended were the Indian-Negroes. General Jesup knew this and had framed the capitulation to gain their support. Abraham had also seen to that. The free Negroes with the Seminoles were the "allies" stipulated in the document. They were to be safe in their life and property. The capitulation also provided that those Negroes who were the bona fide property of the Indians were to accompany their masters west. Should these stipulations be carried out, Negroes, whatever their status, would no longer be an obstacle to the westward migration of the Florida Indians.[23]

At this time Jesup's idea of a "firm and prudent course" was to honor these stipulations. But the pressures to prevent it were heavy. Everything depended on the deportment of the slave hunters. These men, indeed Floridians in general, could not protest the capitulation fast enough. One meeting published the basic position of this interest: "The regaining of our slaves constitutes an object of scarcely less moment than that of the peace of the country." They objected that the document contained no provision to indemnify them for slaves taken by the Seminoles. They objected also to allowing so many Negroes to leave Florida, for every one of them belonged rightfully to some white owner or other. They knew that many Negroes had entered into agreements with Seminoles, by which the Seminoles would certify that the Negroes were their bona fide property whether they were or not. The Florida press vilified Jesup. He responded that had the newspapers approved of his program, he would have begun to doubt the rightness of it.[24]

The policy concerning Negroes of the general commanding in Florida was crucial to the entire country. Jesup's first expression of it was hard to misunderstand: the Negroes were to go with the Indians. The man was Virginia-born, and this position sprang, not from a humanitarian view of black persons, but from his determination to carry out his orders to remove the Indians from Florida. After this phase was spelled out in the capitulation, intense pressure bore upon him. Under it he bent toward a modification: to distinguish between Negroes who had lived with the Seminoles before the outbreak of the war and those who had fled to them, or had been taken by them during the war. Now he began to urge the Indians to deliver up all wartime runaway slaves. Probably April 8, 1837, can be taken as the pivotal date, for on that day he extracted from certain chiefs a secret agreement that they would deliver all Negroes "captured" during the war. This arrangement opened the way for much sharp practice, for in the absence of any formal system of recording ownership among the Indians, how could a Seminole prove the date of his title to a Negro? The agreement, nevertheless, resulted in the surrender of many Negroes by the Indians, and Jesup was accused by anti-slavery men in Congress of making it easy for white men to claim them.[25]

On April 5 he had issued Order No. 79 forbidding white persons to enter the territory south of a line drawn from Fort Foster on the Hillsborough River due east to the Atlantic. Floridians answered with a snarl of vituperation. The result was a modification on May 1 that allowed people with land and cattle in the out-of-bounds area to cross the line. This amounted to abrogation of the order, since in practice it was impossible to prove who had a right to be south of the line and who had not.[26]

General Jesup was teetering along a course as precarious as a dance on a tightrope. On the one hand he sent out threats to the chiefs that they would be in danger if they did not turn in every slave belonging to a white man. On the other he reminded white claimants that the Seminoles were not really bound to surrender fugitives. By the Treaty of Moultrie Creek in 1823, his reasoning went, they were obligated to turn over runaways, but when they surrendered their Florida land under the terms of the Treaty of Fort Gibson, the obligation was vacated. Moreover, the United States had appropriated $7,000

to settle all claims against the Seminoles, and that fact had
been widely advertised by the late agent Wiley Thompson. Persons who had not filed their claims then had lost the opportunity. "I will not," he said, "make negro-catchers of the army."
Yet antislavery men claimed that once he had modified his
original firm policy concerning Negroes with the Indians, he
had in fact made slave-catchers of the army.[27]

The capitulation seemed to be working out satisfactorily. On
April 18 Yaholoochee and his people were at Tampa ready to
migrate. Across the peninsula at Fort Mellon other important
leaders were gathering, ostensibly for the same purpose; among
them were Osceola, Sam Jones, Coa Hadjo, Philip, Tuskinia
and Philip's son Coacoochee. These had indicated that they
would start for Tampa by March 20, but as of April 18 they
had not done it. More than one officer was convinced they were
stalling and securing free food and liquor at the same time.
The total of red men on hand to migrate six weeks after the
capitulation did not exceed three hundred, and few of these
were women and children. To force them along, Jesup directed
General Armistead to drive all of their cattle out of the area
north of the agreed line. This would at least prevent them
from staying there.[28]

It is difficult to determine whether General Jesup really had
hope for the peace by this time or merely talked as if he did
in order to hearten subordinates. He wrote General Hernandez on April 29 that he considered the war over, even if
emigration was slower than promised. Yet about the same time
he indicated to some associates that he felt the Indians did not
intend, after all, to turn themselves in. He grew suspicious of
just about everybody. Here he displayed a turn of the American mind which seems to have been characteristic throughout
our history whenever things go badly. White traitors, he was
sure, were at work. Could he but unmask them, they would
soon have "iron ornaments" for arms and legs. Nor were all
the traitors white. Over on Mullet Key was a band of Indians
who worked for Captain William Bunce in the fishing trade.
Jesup suspected these of being the bridge between sinister
foreign influences and the hostile Indians. Although they were
not known as Seminoles, they must go west too.[29]

Measles broke out in the detention camps and slowed the inflow down to almost nothing. Exasperated by the delay, Jesup sent word to Osceola that bloodhounds were coming from Cuba to be loosed upon the holdouts, and that the captured would be hanged. Meanwhile the numbers in the detention camp at Tampa slowly increased. At the end of May such notables as Micanopy, Jumper, Cloud, and Alligator were there.[30]

A report from spies that a band of Mikasukis meant to raid the detention camp now reached the Florida commander. The alert was given, and Captain William M. Graham sent Creek spies into the Indian camp to give him warning at the proper moment. Jesup also gave Lieutenant Colonel William S. Harney an order to seize all Indians outside the camp who might fall into his hands. None of these precautions availed. On the night of June 2 Osceola and Sam Jones with two hundred warriors stealthily surrounded the camp and cleaned it out. The number who departed—some of them later asserted they were forced to go—has been set as high as seven hundred.[31]

This abduction brought General Jesup's peace plans crashing down. Fearfully bitter, the general blamed various agents: the Creek spies who were supposed to give warning, Captain Graham who had been in charge, and the greedy slaveholders who had pressed too hard for the return of their property. In contrast, many people, especially antislavery advocates, blamed Jesup himself. Had he scrupulously lived up to the capitulation of March 6, had he left it unmodified, there would have been no abduction. What enraged Osceola and Sam Jones was the unwillingness of the white side to honor Seminole relations with the Negroes. But considering the intransigence of the two abductors, this argument does not seem sound. Regardless of the white policy concerning Negroes, Osceola and Sam Jones and their followers would doubtless have kept up the fight.[32]

One of the ineradicable consequences of the abduction of June 2, 1837, was its impact upon General Jesup. At first he was cast into deep gloom. "This campaign so far as relates to Indian migration," he wrote the Adjutant General, "has entirely failed." Now the only way to eliminate the Seminoles from Florida was by extermination. Not being interested in that course, he asked to be relieved from the command. With the passage of time he grew more cynical, more willing to employ treachery to carry out his orders. And since he no longer

had confidence in the promises made by Seminoles, he felt little
compunction about violating his to them. The war now entered
a new phase.[33]

On June 22 General Macomb offered Jesup the chance to
withdraw from the Florida campaign if he still desired to do
so. By that time, though, the criticism of his conduct had so
piqued Jesup that he decided he must stay to justify himself.
There were at least two attempts to dislodge him. In August,
General Gaines claimed his right as senior to resume the direction of Florida affairs, and in October, Scott made the same
demand. But to both the Secretary responded that no officer
had a vested right in any command, and Jesup stayed for another eighteen months.[34] Sometime between July 1 and July 11,
1837, the name of his command was changed to the Army of
the South.

The strategy which now seemed most likely to be rewarding
was the old one of divide and conquer. Jesup's first effort was
to split the milder Alachua bands away from the intransigent
Mikasukis and Tallahassees. If the Alachuas could be induced
to fight the others, he asked Governor Call, would Floridians
be willing to allow them to remain in Florida? Call's answer
is not of record. The policy worked poorly upon the Indians. If
it gained a few Alachuas to the white cause, it stiffened the
resistance of others. Micanopy, a moderate, was degraded, and
Sam Jones, one of the intractables, put in his place.[35]

In September, 1837, a break began to develop in the manpower of the hostiles. Privation—and, it may be, dislike for
the Seminoles upon close contact with them—drove some erstwhile slaves back into their bondage. Some of them told tales
of dreadful hardship, even of abuse at the hands of the Seminoles. This was what slaveholders wanted to hear; they were
sure that Negroes were better off in slavery than in any other
condition. In this situation General Jesup saw a chance to
apply the divide-and-conquer strategy to Indians and Negroes.
Early in 1838 he began to offer Negroes freedom and protection if they would split away from the hostiles and come in.
There followed a marked increase in the number of Negro de-
fections from the Seminoles.[36]

With more and more of them coming in, General Jesup had
to decide what to do with the captured or surrendered Ne-

groes. One type of solution had already been developed in connection with the Creek regiment. To lure Creek warriors into
the white service, recruiters had promised them possession of
the plunder they took from the Seminoles. The most valuable
booty was of course Negro slaves. The general extended the
same offer on June 11 to units of citizen soldiers. Field officers
were to get three shares of all plunder, company officers two
shares, and enlisted men one. In August, Jesup enlarged the
offer of booty to include the whole of his force. Before long,
though, the policy began to defeat itself. Obviously it worked
at cross-purposes to the one which promised Negroes freedom
if they would leave the hostiles. They would never reach an
installation to give themselves up before some predatory Creek,
volunteer, or regular seized them as booty. The booty policy,
in short, began to choke off the inflow of Negroes from the
Seminole side. It was soon replaced.[37]

On September 6, 1837, a new order directed that all Negroes
captured by the army were to be held by the commander, pending orders from the Secretary of War. To placate the Creeks,
Jesup offered them $8,000 for the Negroes they had taken
under the rule of plunder. They were also to receive $20 for
every Negro who had once been the property of a white man.
Each shift Jesup made seemed to involve him in more compli-
cations than before. Now the government itself was to become
the owner of a body of slaves. There was no precedent for this,
and vital decisions were therefore required from authorities
higher than the field commander. Meanwhile the latter worked
out a way to handle the Negroes who had surrendered in response to his promise of freedom and safety. In reality he had
no power to give many of them the freedom he had promised.
Any who could be legally proved to have been slaves of white
men might not be freed, whatever Jesup's promise to them.
Nevertheless he came close to keeping his word, for he treated
them all, at this stage, as the bona fide property of Seminoles.
As such, under the capitulation of March 6, he could ship them
west with the Indians, and that is what he did. To round out
the story of the Negroes, the inducements offered them to split
away from the Indians worked so well that by the spring of
1838 they had ceased to be an important factor in Seminole
resistance. Thereafter they worked for negotiated removal.[38]

By this time General Jesup had become convinced that the
United States was wrong in trying to remove the Seminoles
before their land was needed for settlement. In all previous
cases Indians had been left alone until settlement pressed upon
them. Accordingly, he proposed to the Secretary of War to
leave them where they were.

His proposal went to Joel Roberts Poinsett (for whom the
poinsettia was named), picked by President Van Buren to be
Secretary of War partly because he, a South Carolinian, had
stood with Jackson against nullification. Poinsett was fifty-
eight at the time, and his biographer feels he was better qualified than any other man for the cabinet post. His deepest
interest was military, he had acquired some military education
of a formal sort, he had observed the armies of Napoleon at
close range, and he had himself been involved in the liberation
of Chile. Handsome, intense, and capable, Poinsett rates as one
of the most efficient secretaries of war.[39]

Communication had now been so much improved that a message could pass from Florida to Washington and an answer
could get back within ten days. The Secretary fired back a response reflecting the government's position. It was out of the
question to allow the Seminoles to remain. To do so would
betray weakness and invite trouble from all the tribes who
were expected to move west of the Mississippi. As an alternative, the government would strengthen Jesup's force, and he
could round up the Indians in the fall. Speaking from knowledge of the "hot, sickly" climate, Poinsett recommended that
Jesup delay the start of his operations until November 1.[40]

Meanwhile, the general made his estimates of necessary
force: 1,680 men would be required to garrison the essential
posts, 750 would be needed for escort service, and four mobile
columns, 3,750 men, would be required as a striking force, in
all an army of 6,180 men. One of the mobile columns would
move up the St. Johns; the second would operate from Mosquito Inlet and the Indian River; the third would start from
Tampa, cross the peninsula to the Kissimmee River and move
down it; and the fourth would ascend the Caloosahatchee.
Those Indians in the north had been scattered very widely by
his command, and less than 200, he estimated, remained above
the latitude of Lake Monroe.[41]

Quite naturally General Jesup was concerned over the quality as well as the quantity of troops available. It troubled the commander that the enlisted men were mostly either foreigners or broken-down laborers and mechanics from commercial cities. These city boys, he felt, had lost the traditional American military characteristics. This loss made it essential to work hard at recruiting in the agricultural districts where the martial spirit yet lived. Nor was the loss of these characteristics confined to enlisted men only. "It may be truly said the spirit of the service is gone," he wrote the Adjutant General, "when officers abandon the high and honorable duties of their profession to become *schoolmasters* at West Point." Many had done just that.[42]

It was also essential, the general instructed his superiors, to offer incentives to men to enlist in the regular service. As things stood, there was no reason why any regular should re-enlist. In the army he had nothing to look forward to in the end but to be turned out to starve when his usefulness as a soldier was over. And the Florida service broke men rapidly. There ought to be a life pension for any man who re-enlisted three times.[43]

Jesup would rather have done without citizen soldiers altogether, but since there never were enough regulars to make this possible, the mounted variety was the only acceptable kind. Poinsett objected to them because they cost four times as much as regulars. Their use would bankrupt the country. What resulted from the disagreement was a compromise; not as many mounted volunteers as Jesup wanted, but more than Poinsett thought could be afforded.[44]

Poinsett directed Jesup to use citizen soldiers to carry out his plan. Their employment perpetuated the old problem of relations with the regulars. Jesup placed Brevet Brigadier Walker K. Armistead in command in his northern zone partly because he had enough rank to handle the squabbles over precedence which inevitably arose. Governor Call, commanding in West Florida, also had sufficient prestige to resolve the same sort of bickering. As for the most active zone of combat—the southern part of the peninsula—Colonel Archibald Henderson of the Marine Corps commanded there, but Jesup himself was close by to take care of precedence and the like.[45]

General Jesup threw himself into the task of preparing for a fall campaign. Although he had privately called the policy of the government toward the Seminoles unholy, he had no intention of substituting his judgment for that of the Administration. He carried out his duties with less humanity than before. When still under the shock of the escape of June 2, he directed that Negroes found in opposition be summarily hanged; but this order was modified in a cooler moment. To Lieutenant Colonel William S. Harney, already known as being heartless toward Indians, he wrote, "I will sanction all you may find it necessary to do in relation to the Indians." No quarter should be shown the Mikasukis and Tallahassees, for they, with the Indian Negroes, were keeping the war alive. There was a need for more Indian allies, the General thought, but not Creeks because he had slight regard for them. (The Creeks, for their part, had a similar feeling toward army service. While they were away their families were gathered into detention camps under the protection of the federal government. This "protection" did not prevent citizens of Georgia and Alabama from attacking, killing, looting, and raping them.) Jesup wanted, instead, Miamis, Delawares, Shawnees, and Sioux, who would ruthlessly kill the Seminole men and enslave the women and children. In response the government authorized him to employ 400 Shawnees, 200 Delawares, 100 Kickapoos, 100 Sacs and Foxes, and 200 Choctaws; but only a band of Delawares and one of Shawnees ever served.[46]

Jesup's ruthless policy toward captured Seminoles kept him pretty well informed concerning the whereabouts of the foe. He threatened captives with hanging if they did not reveal what they knew. Holata Mico, captured on July 7, 1837, was so threatened, but neither he nor any other warrior carried this threat to the final test, and none was ever hanged.[47]

Billy Bowlegs

The immediate problem was to keep the troops as healthy as possible during the feverish summer. Some of the "sickly posts" were shut down for the season, but this action did not stop the ravages of disease. Jesup declared he had never seen a service in which soldier's energies were so completely used up, "and the mental energies seem to be equally affected by the baleful influence of climate." One company of regulars once had but eight men in it fit for duty. The Alabama and Georgian volunteers were little better off. Under Governor Call they were responsible for the peace in West Florida, but heat and disease rendered them all but ineffective. Out of five battalions not one hundred men and less than fifty horses were fit for duty. Discussing this sad story with General Call, Jesup urged secrecy lest the weakness of the posts cause alarm among white people. Moreover, any data not protected was known at once by the enemy.[48]

In the hope that Floridians were already acclimated and therefore immune to disease, the General called for mounted Florida militiamen to guard the settled areas. As usual, their use raised problems. He had to stop the pay of some of them because they refused to obey orders to operate beyond a certain limited area. He told the remainder that if they were enterprising enough they might even strike an offensive blow. To get their mettle up he praised the services of Georgia and Alabama citizen soldiers. These had clung to Indian trails the previous summer until they had found the quarry. "I am sure the Florida troops may be equally efficient if they think proper themselves to act like men." Such writing from General Scott would have brought forth a forensic blast, but when Jesup uttered it, the insult did not go beyond the Florida lieutenant colonel to whom it was addressed.[49]

Apparently impervious to the climate, the general himself labored on to provide men and supplies for the fall campaign. The only time he was incapacitated was when he fell through a rotten board and wrenched his ankle on the veranda of an old house serving as his headquarters.

"The consumption of horses by this service exceeds anything I have ever witnessed before," he wrote. He had spent $1,300 of his own money for mounts and was not done yet. Now glanders broke out, and it was necessary to reduce the supply further by shooting the poor infected brutes. For heavy drayage mules were superior to horses, but it was difficult to buy them. Then there was the matter of special wagons suitable for this strenuous service. What the general wanted were Dearborn wagons, valuable because they had large wheels, wide tires, watertight bodies, and were drawn by two horses. They could even be used as boats when needed. His request was granted and the wagons were on hand when the fall campaign began.

Horses, mules and wagons, packsaddles, steamers for the rivers, and hundreds of other necessities were the subject matter for an unending correspondence between Jesup and the supply departments of the army. He pled for efficient quartermaster officers and for a representative of the commissary department to centralize procurement of food in his command. There was mention of India rubber pontoons and boats, and of the gum necessary to repair them.[50]

He was willing to try new firearms, such as Colt's revolvers and Cochran's repeater. But the mountain howitzers sent him were of no use whatever under Florida conditions. They showed the slavish emulation of French weapons and methods, too common then in the American establishment. (This was probably Jesup's thrust at that erstwhile friend, now enemy, General Scott.) Shotguns were needed for use by the light companies. More Mackinaw boats were needed, flat-bottomed, with a double set of oars, each capable of carrying twenty men. Barricades should be prepared to fit the sides of three small steamers. Haversacks, wall tents, common tents, hospital tents, camp kettles, mess kits, canteens, axes, spades, and hatchets— all must be provided in time. Large-size sheets of rubber cloth, sheepskins for saddle blankets, halters, hobbles, wagon harness, whips, sadler's tools, and a few thousand horseshoes must be on hand for the mounted men. Parched corn meal would be useful, as would "portable" soup. Three ounces of soup, a little rice, and half a pound of bread would make a day's rations weighing no more than three quarters of a pound. Light astringent wines would be good in this climate, so would garlic and onions; but the present ration was wholly unsuited to Florida.[51]

When early in September certain of the ex-plantation Negroes returned to the white fold in the vicinity of St. Augustine, they brought with them John Philip, a slave of Chief Philip. The slave had deserted the Seminoles because his wife was tired of the hardship of life in the scrub. He agreed to guide the white men to an Indian encampment south of the Tomoka River. Whether he did so voluntarily or under duress is not recorded, but whatever his reason, he guided a detachment of 170 men (three companies of regulars and two of Florida citizen soldiers) under the command of General Joseph M.

Hernandez toward the ruined plantation area thirty miles south of St. Augustine. On the night of September 8 they bivouacked quietly among the ruins of Dunlawton Plantation, while scouts guided by John reconnoitered the Indian camp. Finding it feasible to attack, they moved about midnight into positions. The Florida volunteers dismounted and enclosed three sides of the Seminole location, while the regulars remained on their mounts to attack at first light. The red men reposed blissfully unaware of all this, for like other Indians, they did not post a guard at night. It is remarkable that no horse neighed, no dog barked. When first light came, the mounted men closed the ring around the camp with a charge. All hostiles save one were captured, and none was injured. Jacob Motte, surgeon to the attacking force, recorded the haul. "We soon found ourselves unexpectedly in the presence of royalty, for there stood King Philip . . . naked as he was born, except the breech-cloth; and covered with most unkingly dirt." (He had been knocked down and begrimed by a charging horseman.) Here was the most important capture since the war had begun. Motte continued, "There were also a number of women and children captured; the former miserable, blackened, haggard, shrivelled (smoke-dried and half-clad) devils; the latter, ugly little nudities."[52]

Among the captives was an Indian called Tomoka John. He offered to guide the party to another camp, this one of Yuchis, five or six miles away. The same technique was followed at the new camp, except that the terrain was too difficult for the horses, and they had to be left with seventy men to guard them. One hundred men advanced during the night, crawled at the last until they had ringed the sleeping camp. Single file, ten paces apart, they could do nothing but lie on the ground, facing the unsuspecting Indians, and wait for dawn. Just before daylight the Yuchis' dogs began to bark. But the encirclement was complete, and at a signal all the hundred men jumped up and sprinted the hundred yards into the tent area. Completely surprised, the naked or half-clad Indians fired some random shots. Lieutenant John Winfield Scott McNeil fell dead, the only white casualty. One Indian was killed and several wounded. The bag this time included Yuchi Billy (who had been reported killed the year before) and his brother Jack. Their complete surprise is easier to excuse than Philip's, for

King Philip
Portrait by George Catlin

they were on a pine barren placed like an island in the midst
of a swamp, inaccessible except to those who knew the trails.
Tomoka John was foremost in gathering plunder for his own
use. This was the reason, Motte said, that he had betrayed his
recent associates.[53]

These captures made a serious breach in the Seminole leadership. Those that followed hurt even more. Philip sent runners
out with a call to his son Coacoochee (Wildcat), who later in
the month came in, accompanied by Blue Snake. Apparently at
this moment General Jesup decided to ignore one of the most
respected rules of war. In spite of their white flag, he detained
Coacoochee and Blue Snake. If he liberated Coacoochee to go
out to bring in more of his followers, it was because he held
Philip as an hostage. The general made it clear that, should
the son fail to return, the father would pay.[54]

Philip, the Yuchi leaders, Blue Snake, and Coacoochee were
all captured in the vicinity of St. Augustine. Why they were
there instead of farther south is not known. Other important
leaders and their bands were also in the area. Two very influential men, Osceola and Coa Hadjo, sent word on October
27, 1837, that they were willing to meet the white officers in a
parley. General Jesup now reached the decision which was to
make him more infamous than famous in the eyes of many
generations. He decided to persist in his new policy of ignoring flags of truce. Orders went to General Hernandez to agree
to the conference and to seize the two leaders while they attended it. Hernandez arranged the council near Fort Peyton, a
log work which Jesup had erected recently on Moultrie Creek
and had garrisoned with a detachment from the Second Dragoons. General Hernandez started from St. Augustine on October 21, paused at Peyton to pick up some of the dragoons
there, and proceeded about a mile farther to the place where
Osceola was camped. His force consisted of two companies
of Florida mounted men and some dragoons, a force of about
250 men. These, under the direction of Brevet Major James A.
Ashby, Second Dragoons, were to close in when a prearranged
signal was given. Not present himself, General Jesup was so
nervous over the parley that he awaited the outcome close by
at Fort Peyton. Meanwhile Hernandez had no trouble locating
the Indian camp because of the white flag flying over it. Some

time before, Jesup had thoughtfully provided the Indians with many yards of white cloth so that they could come in without fear of injury.[55]

At the sight of the white men Osceola is said to have choked up, and to have asked Coa Hadjo to do the talking for the Seminoles. Surgeon Nathan Jarvis, who had accompanied the white party, recorded the conversation (of which only the crucial parts are here reproduced):

General: I speak to you as a friend—what induced you to come?

Coa Hadjo: We come for good.

General: At whose request did you come?

Coa Hadjo: Philip sent a message by Coacoochee.

General: What do you expect from me? Have you come to give up to me as your friend?

Coa Hadjo: No, we did not understand so. . . . We have done nothing all summer and want to make peace.

General: Are you ready to give up all the property you have captured?

Coa Hadjo: We intend to do so . . . we have brought a good many negroes in now.

General: Why have you not given up the negroes before as Coahajo promised at Ft. King? [Note the emphasis placed on surrender of the Negroes.] Why did not Micanopy, Jumper, and Cloud come instead of sending a messenger?

Coa Hadjo: They all got the measles.

General: I am an old friend of Philip's and I wish you all well, but we have been deceived so often that it is necessary for you to come with me. . . . You will all see the good treatment that you experience—You will be glad that you fell into my hands.

Coa Hadjo: We will see about it.[56]

After further exchanges, Hernandez called on Blue Snake, whom he had brought with him, to support the white position. But Blue Snake flatly stated that he thought the Indian negotiators were to have been allowed to go free. At this time Hernandez gave the prearranged signal for the troops to close in. Although the Seminoles carried loaded guns, there was no resistance, for Major Ashby's encirclement was so expeditious that no warrior had a chance to shoot. Dr. Jarvis closely watched the faces of Coa Hadjo and Osceola and saw no trace of surprise.[57]

Thus was the most notorious treachery of the Second Seminole War carried out. The haul from it was truly impressive. Osceola himself was of course a great catch, but in addition there were Coa Hadjo, seventy-one warriors, six women, and four Indian-Negroes. Their armament was fifty-two rifles. Flanked by mounted soldiers, the captives reached St. Augustine about sundown. There, as if they had known the outcome all along, almost the whole population of the town turned out to see the parade. The cynosure, of course, was Osceola. The most famous Seminole fulfilled expectations, dressed in a bright blue calico shirt, red leggings buttoned on the outside, one bright print shawl around his head, and another over his shoulders.* Surgeon Jarvis noticed that he looked unwell.[58]

General Jesup was responsible for this treachery. After the abduction of June 2, he had said that he would seize the abductors if a chance arose and apparently he no longer cared about the means. He could not have guessed that Osceola's capture would attract nationwide attention, characteristic American attention that would create a martyr and a villain, the latter Jesup himself. Defenders came to his aid, however, and when the matter reached the floors of Congress in the spring of 1838 about as many legislators defended him as assailed him. They advanced reasons to justify what he had done. (1) Osceola had promised in March that he would take his people across the peninsula to Tampa and there turn them in for shipment west. To that end he had drawn rations at Fort Mellon, but he had not kept his word. (2) Osceola and Coa Hadjo returned to St. Augustine to rescue Philip and massacre the white people. Jesup claimed he learned this from the Indian-Negroes. (3) Osceola agreed to the parley, knowing well that Jesup had refused to negotiate any longer and that those who came in did so for no other purpose than to give themselves up. He intended to give up voluntarily as soon as he saw that St. Augustine had been too heavily reinforced for him to achieve the rescue of Philip. (4) Jesup claimed that Osceola had killed a

---

*Moore-Willson, _Seminoles_, 27, states that an old soldier, John S. Masters, saw Osceola knocked down with a musket butt, and bound, but contemporary documents do not verify the statement.

messenger under a flag of truce and that he had abused such
a flag more than once to spy in St. Augustine. (5) The Indians
had broken the truce in August, 1837, by committing hostile
acts and by going east of the St. Johns and north of Fort Mellon, areas closed to them by the capitulation of March 6. And
(6) finally, there was the argument of expediency. The war
could go on forever unless drastic measures were employed.

General Jesup may finally have convinced himself of the
honorableness of his conduct, but he was still writing justifica-
tions of it twenty-one years later. Viewed from the distance of
more than a century, it hardly seems worthwhile to try to
grace the capture with any other label than treachery. Undoubtedly the general violated the rules of civilized warfare,
but he did so because he believed that those rules did not apply
to the Seminoles and that his orders to remove them justified
any means. Afterwards he adopted a similar practice more or
less as standard procedure, and with it he captured much of
the hostile fighting force. In consequence, the deepest inroads
on Indian strength were made during his command. On the
other hand, those Indians who held out resisted more fanati-
cally than before. Any confidence they had felt in the word of
the white leaders was utterly shattered.[59]

Soon a runner was sent into the forest, carrying Osceola's
directive to his family to come in. The runner returned with
about fifty people: two wives of Osceola, with two children, a
sister of his, three warriors, and the rest Negroes. An observer
noticed the squalid misery of the Negroes.[60]

In spite of the vituperation in the press, General Jesup
seemed much heartened. Floridians nearly to a man approved
of what he had done. By fair means or foul he now had an impressive list of Seminole leaders in his power: Philip, Coa
Hadjo, Miccopotokee, Yuchi Billy, Yuchi Jack, Coacoochee,
Osceola, Chitto Yaholo, and Holata Tustenuggee, and eighty-
one warriors besides. In time, most of these were sent to the
reservation in the West. Could he now capture Tiger Tail,
Tuskinia, Tuskegee, and Alligator, he told the Secretary of
War, he would end the conflict.[61]

As for the most famous captive, Osceola, his short life was
nearly over. First he was imprisoned in Fort Marion at St.
Augustine, then in Fort Moultrie at Charleston. All the while

his health failed rapidly. At this time George Catlin talked with him and painted his portrait. This portrait, coupled with the flattering things Catlin said of Osceola's character, helped to create the legend. The white doctors still believed they could save his life, but the intervention of a medicine man prevented their treatment. On January 31, 1838, Osceola felt his end to be near. He gathered some of his people around him and caused them to array him in his finery, including ostrich plumes and silver medals. Lying thus in state, he expired. Sentimental accounts have ascribed his death to a broken heart, but in reality it resulted from quinsy aggravated by intermittent malaria. He is known to have had malaria at least as far back as 1836, and is thought to have contracted it at Fort Drane, which the white men had abandoned because of the disease, and which the Indians had at once occupied.[62]

Micanopy, according to one observer, was unmoved when he learned of Osceola's death. The legitimate chiefs generally had not liked Osceola because they regarded him as the author of some of their worst troubles. But the reaction of the white population, outside of Florida, was different. Osceola's short life, his treacherous capture, and his death in prison had gripped the imagination of the country. Although the war went relentlessly on to drive his people out of Florida, Osceola became to many Americans a symbol of the patriot chief fighting for the land he loved. In consequence, newspaper accounts of his death referred to him as a great man, and a real Osceola fad developed. There are in the nation twenty towns, three counties, two townships, one borough, two lakes, two mountains, a state park, and a national forest bearing his name.[63]

Dr. Frederick Weedon, who had had Osceola in charge, for some reason cut off the head, embalmed it, and took it with him back to St. Augustine. If one of his three small sons was disobedient, the doctor would hang the head on the child's bedstead for the night. Later Weedon gave the relic to his son-in-law Dr. Daniel Whitehurst, who in turn gave it to Dr. Valentine Mott. No one knows what finally became of it, but the presumption is that it burned with the rest of Dr. Mott's Surgical and Pathological Museum in New York City in 1866. So the body of Osceola remains to this day without a head in its grave at Fort Moultrie.[64]

11

Okeechobee

WITH OPTIMISTIC EXPECTATIONS and about 4,000 men, General Jesup put his campaign in motion late in October, 1837. His plan had many more facets than Winfield Scott's earlier one, but the strategy was the same: trap the Indians among converging columns and force them to fight. The basic difference between the two plans was that Jesup put seven columns in the field to Scott's three, and that Jesup did not expect his columns to act in synchronization. Jesup also possessed the advantage of having better scouts than Scott's, but in spite of the scouts his ignorance of the terrain to be invaded was equal to that of any of his predecessors.

The main elements of Jesup's campaign were these: (1) Colonel Zachary Taylor, newly arrived in Florida with his First Infantry Regiment, received the command of an area between the Kissimmee River and Pease Creek. He was told to establish a depot somewhere along the Pease in order to be able indefinitely to maintain his force of 1,400 men in the interior. He actually built Forts Gardner and Bassinger, both of them close to the Kissimmee. (2) Colonel Persifor F. Smith, commanding about 600 Louisiana volunteers, was ordered to march inland from the mouth of the Caloosahatchee River, considerably south of Taylor's area. (3) Lieutenant Levi N. Powell, United States Navy, with a mixed force of 85 sailors, two companies of artillery, and a company of volunteer infantry, was assigned the task of penetrating the Everglades. These three columns were to sweep through the Seminole country; they were also to contain the bands of Indians forced against them by the main wing. (4) The main wing itself was divided into four columns, all advancing toward the headwaters of the St. Johns River: (a) the column commanded by General Joseph M. Hernandez was ordered to move by steamer to Mosquito Lagoon and to await directions there; (b) a second column, commanded by Colonel John Warren and composed of his Florida militia and two companies of dragoons, was to advance southward between the Atlantic and the St. Johns; (c) a third column, commanded by General Abraham Eustis, was to ascend the St. Johns by boat; and (d) a fourth column was to scout the country between Fort King and the Oklawaha River and then between the Oklawaha and the St. Johns, after which it was to join Eustis at Fort Mellon.[1]

Jesup, like Call, hardly knew what to do with the navy. Except for Levi Powell's detachment, it had no direct part in his grand design. Its basic assignment was to cut off the trade with Cuba and the Bahamas, by means of which the Seminoles received arms and ammunition. But Commodore Dallas could find no evidence that this trade existed. In general, when called upon, the navy gave aid cheerfully but was not as forward as it had been in the beginning. Dallas complained to Secretary of the Navy Mahlon Dickerson that the excellent service performed by naval officers had scarcely received mention in army general orders. Naturally the ardor of those officers had cooled.[2]

Heavier reinforcements than could be supported began to reach Jesup's army. In September the General had purposely summoned an excess of citizen soldiers because he was sure most of them would never arrive. They had been called in individual companies, not battalions and regiments, in order to eliminate the heavy staffs of officers typical of large units of irregulars. He called upon Tennessee, Louisiana, South Carolina, Georgia, and Alabama, as well as the Territory of Florida itself. Six hundred mounted volunteers, to be accepted as a regiment, were mustered in even from faraway Missouri.[3]

In the early fall Senator Thomas Hart Benton of Missouri had proclaimed to the Senate that none but frontiersmen could fight Indians successfully. When asked if Missourians would drop their private concerns to enter the fight in Florida, he said they would, whereupon an act was passed permitting volunteers from the western states generally. Missouri immediately raised a regiment. Richard Gentry, Senator Benton's choice for colonel, had no trouble securing recruits, for times were hard and the volunteers were promised pay in coin. Inasmuch as this was the first unit of volunteers the young state of Missouri had sent off to fight for the United States, there was a popular flurry of enthusiasm. Patriotic ladies sewed a silk standard for the unit inscribed: "First Regiment Missouri Volunteers, Gird, gird for the conflict, Our banners wave high; For our country we live; For our country we'll die." Because Benton could not bear to be left out, the outfit had to wait a few days for him to reach Jefferson Barracks and address it. His speech was the last shred of romance connected with the expedition of the Missourians. Going down the Mississippi, the regiment put to sea at New Orleans on a long and sickly voyage, which greatly weakened the men and killed the horses. At Tampa it was necessary to discharge 190 men before they ever entered the field, because their horses had been lost. The mounted remainder were attached to Colonel Taylor's command.[4]

Meanwhile other units of mounted volunteers flooded into Florida. Utterly dumbfounded by the volume, General Jesup ascribed their swarming to the enthusiasm created by the seizure of Osceola. Whatever the cause, it was impossible to support so many mounted men with the offensive wings of the army. For this reason, they were, except for the Missourians, assigned to keep the peace in the northern part of the peninsula. The Georgians, under their capable commander, General Charles H. Nelson, were established on the line of the Suwannee. Lieutenant Colonel B. K. Pierce commanded volunteer troops along the Indian River; Colonel Alexander Fanning (breveted colonel for gallantry at the Withlacoochee) had charge in the vicinity of St. Augustine. Colonel Benjamin Snodgrass of Alabama, with 950 mounted Alabamans, was directed to guard the area of Garey's Ferry. Later, his command diminished and he was given charge of the building of a fort between the Oklawaha and the St. Johns, from which continuous mounted patrols were to issue. Major William Lauderdale, in command of 500 Tennessee volunteers, was to occupy Fort Mellon until the arrival there of General Eustis.[5]

Watching costs soar with the number of volunteers, Secretary Poinsett lost his composure. So large a mounted force, he wrote Jesup, would "break down your army, [and] destroy all the resources of the country." But after a good night's sleep he was ready to admit that he had written in a panic. He certainly did not want to jeopardize the chance of victory by skimping, but since Congress was investigating costs, care must be exercised. Retain only 2,000 horsemen, he ordered, and send the balance home without delay.[6]

Jesup, for his part, did not want the horde of volunteers because citizen soldiers were not to be compared with regulars for "laborious and distant war." But the cackling about costs made him angry. Congress had broken down the army in 1821, and was therefore responsible for the high cost of Indian turmoil. It could not escape paying for its own mistakes. "People cannot go into an unexplored wilderness to catch savages," he wrote to Representative Joseph R. Underwood of Kentucky, ". . . and transfer them to another wilderness without expense —particularly when that wilderness furnishes nothing to support man or horse."[7]

General Armistead had been relieved of duty for health reasons and had left the theater. On July 25 he suddenly reappeared in Florida ready for a new assignment. With the campaign already in motion and the top commands well assigned, what could Jesup do with a brevet brigadier of the regular service? His solution was to make Armistead second in command, with the assignment of holding down the west side of the peninsula while the commanding general himself was with his main column in the east. But Armistead was given to understand that he must not interfere with Colonel Smith or Colonel Taylor.[8]

In came a delegation of Cherokee chiefs sent by the Administration. It was thought in Washington that these Cherokees might be able to persuade the Seminoles to move west. But the General trusted Cherokees no more than he did Seminoles. He would not even permit them to associate with the captives at Fort Marion unless one of the officers was present. Mutual

recriminations resulted. Jesup asserted that the Cherokee delegation delayed his campaign three weeks, while the delegation
charged him with openly opposing their mission on the grounds
that it took control out of his hands. They added that he departed for Fort Mellon without even notifying them of his intention. Moreover, when scouts brought in word that Micanopy
would talk to them, they could not get from the commander a
ruling as to whether or not they could go. When it finally
came, his permission was indirect and qualified. In spite of the
fact that they had to travel fifty miles each way to and from
the rendezvous, Jesup obliged them to be back within six days.
Accordingly, guided by Coa Hadjo, they set out for a hurried
trip. Pridefully they returned to Fort Mellon accompanied by
Micanopy himself, Yaholoochee, and eleven subchiefs. Yet General Jesup, they said, received them coolly, and on December 5
took an uncompromising position with the Seminole chiefs. He
would not even negotiate with them until they had fulfilled
conditions which left nothing to negotiate: they must give
themselves up unconditionally, they must agree to the terms of
the capitulation of March 6, they must bring in their families,
and they must give up their rifles.[9]

Nevertheless, the Cherokees plunged into the scrub once
more to try to persuade other chiefs to surrender. Sam Jones
just laughed at them and reviled them for aiding the white
men; Coacoochee (escaped from prison) spurned their advice.
When they returned from their mission to Fort Mellon on December 14 and reported their failure, General Jesup reacted in
a way which added to their frustration. He ordered Micanopy
and all who had come in with him seized and held. In vain the
Cherokees protested that these Seminoles had arrived under a
flag of truce, and that they had given their own guarantee of
safe conduct. The general denied the flag, was indifferent to
Cherokee honor, and so held his captives fast. He thus secured
Micanopy, Yaholoochee, Tuskegee, Nocose Yaholo, and seventy-
eight other Indians. Without delay they were loaded aboard a
steamer and shipped off to St. Augustine for safekeeping in
Fort Marion, the formidable old Castillo de San Marcos. Surgeon Jarvis watched Micanopy weep at the departure.[10]

Meanwhile, at St. Augustine a remarkable escape offset to
some degree the rich haul Jesup had made. Osceola had been

taken to the Castillo along with the other captives, among them
Coacoochee, the first victim of Jesup's policy of ignoring flags
of truce, and John Cowaya (John Cavalo), an Indian-Negro
leader. Osceola was too ill or too proud to be interested in
escape, but not Coacoochee and Cowaya. They were aided in
their determination by the fact that the southwest angle of
the heavy coquina fortress was deemed escape-proof and left
unguarded; no wonder, for the avenue to freedom was an aper-
ture fifteen feet from the floor, five feet long but only eight
inches wide, cut through the six-foot thickness of the walls.
Two iron bars blocked this slit, but somehow the escapers removed one of them. Tying a line to the remaining bar, they
dropped themselves down the outside wall twenty-one feet into
the ditch. During the night of November 29, 1837, Coachoo-
chee, Cowaya, sixteen warriors, and two squaws escaped. Since
such a departure seemed impossible unless there was collusion,
a board of inquiry met at once and conducted an examination.
It found no blame or collusion to charge to Captain Lucien B.
Webster, the fort commander, nor to anyone else.[11]

Coacoochee and his associates rapidly made their way southward to join the intransigents, to whom Coacoochee now added
his strong and effective leadership. He had impressive hereditary claims to authority among the Florida Indians, for his
father was Philip (probably a Mikasuki) and his mother was a
sister of Micanopy. Thus he united the hereditary leadership
of Mikasukis and Alachuas, and his hope was to succeed
Micanopy as head chief. General Jesup considered him the
ablest of the Indian leaders.[12]

Coacoochee was in his twenties when the war broke out.
Surgeon Forry described him as a real Apollo. All white observers conceded his good looks, but some thought him ferocious looking. They noticed especially his dark, full, expressive
eyes. He was perfectly aware of the impact of his own appearance. Before entering Fort Peyton—in what proved to be his
entrance also into captivity—he retired into the hammock to
deck himself out, emerging resplendent with a plume of white
crane feathers, bright scarlet leggings, and a silver band
around his turban. Although only five feet eight inches tall, he
was marvelously agile. When pursued he had been known to
stop and laugh and jeer, then take up his flight again and easily

out-distance his pursuers. In addition, he was an effective speaker with a clear, soft voice.[13]

One incident involving Coacoochee well illustrates the culture gap which lay between white and red society. While he was still a prisoner, the young Indian was released to attend a ball in St. Augustine. Although one of the enemy, he was also to the local gentry, soaked as they were in Romanticism, a prince of the forest. As a result, he was a lion in that hall, but from white standards he proved to be somewhat of a boor. When introduced to a gentleman and his very pretty new wife, he remarked blandly that the young woman was certainly a beauty and that the man no doubt enjoyed her very much, but that after she had a few children, she would hardly be worth having.[14]

In the first bitterness over Coacoochee's escape, General Jesup announced that Philip's life would be forfeit if his son and associates did not give themselves up. But in a cooler moment he reconsidered. He directed instead that Philip and the other prisoners be put in irons, but in a day or two he rescinded this order as well.[15]

In the final month of 1837 General Jesup tried to control the largest army to assemble in Florida during the Seminole wars. Official figures showed that he had 4,636 regular army, including 170 marines. The Second Dragoon Regiment was there (the balance of that regiment had marched from Jefferson Barracks, 1,200 miles in 55 days); men from all four of the artillery regiments were present, together with members of the First, Second, Third, and Sixth Infantry. At the same time there were 4,078 volunteers from Florida, Louisiana, Georgia, Alabama, and Tennessee; there was a company from the District of Columbia, two companies from Pennsylvania, one from New York, and the Missouri regiment. One hundred and seventy-eight northern Indians and 100 sailors added to the variety. The total was nearly 9,000 men, too many, in truth, for the logistical base. Here was a patent violation of that principle of war called "economy of force." Since only a limited number of them could be sustained in the wastelands which made up the south of the peninsula, the rest cluttered up what we would now call the zone of the interior.[16]

Considering that the authorized enlisted strength of the

army at this time was 7,130, and that 4,000 were in Florida, it will be appreciated that few regular troops were available for duty anywhere else. Yet there were many, many widely scattered jobs for them to do in other quarters. These considerations impelled Commanding General Alexander Macomb, in his report to the Secretary, to request that the size of the army be doubled to 15,000. Otherwise, he said, the service could not do its job "without calling out militia which is always attended with heavy expenditures, and loss of life by disease, and is highly detrimental to the concerns of individuals." Secretary Poinsett adopted Macomb's idea and incorporated it in his report to the President. Knowing the ever-present fear of a standing army, Poinsett added that there was little danger from such a force, scattered over 8,000 miles of frontier and commanded by officers indoctrinated in civil control over the military. And even if there was danger, a proper organization of the militia would guard against it. Macomb's suggestion and Poinsett's echoing of it amounted to wishful thinking in public documents, but they did in the end produce some tangible results. Seven months later Congress added an eighth regiment of infantry to the army, and at the same time nearly doubled the authorized strength of companies throughout the service. The net effect was to raise the overall authorized enlisted strength to 11,800.[17]

On the eve of great events in mid-December, 1837, the defense of northern Florida lay pretty much in the hands of citizen soldiers, in some cases under the immediate direction of regular officers. Southward the four columns of the main wing of Jesup's army had drawn together under General Eustis. Numbering close to 2,000 men, Eustis' command was directed from Fort Mellon on Lake Monroe. About ten miles south of it was Fort Lane, the center from which General Hernandez directed his column of Florida militiamen.[18]

Fortune was about to bestow upon Colonel Zachary Taylor the opportunity to direct the largest battle of the war. On December 19 Taylor received permission from General Jesup to move forward and hunt the enemy. That same day he marched from Fort Gardner (which he had built on the Kissimmee River a little south of Lake Tohopekaliga) at the head of 1,032 men. Except for 180 Missouri volunteers, 47 men organized in a company called "Morgan's Spies" of whom about 30 were Missourians, and 70 Delaware and Shawnee Indians, the force was composed of regulars. Taylor's route was southward down the Kissimmee toward Lake Okeechobee. On the evening of the first day Indians began to come in and give up. Jumper surrendered, accompanied by 63 followers. He and his party were sent back toward the fort, guarded by some Shawnees who refused to march farther. The next day 26 Indians gave up when their camp was discovered. On the third day, December 21, Taylor paused to build a small stockade in which to leave his heavy baggage and artillery, for the going was becoming increasingly severe. This stockade became Fort Bassinger. To garrison it, he detached one company and the pioneers and pontoniers, with about 85 sick men and some Indians. The main body moved out with provisions to last through December 26. Small parties of Indians surrendered to them as they advanced. By moving at daylight, the army entered one large camp in which the fires were still burning, although the Indians had fled. Then, they captured a single warrior in an open prairie (probably planted there) who showed them where the foe was settled into position ready to fight.[19]

Never had Indians prepared a battleground with greater care. They were in a hammock with about half a mile of swamp in front of them, and Lake Okeechobee not far to their rear. The sawgrass in the swamp stood five feet high, and mud and water were three feet deep. The Seminoles had cut down the grass to provide a corridor for fire, and had notched the trees in their hammock to steady their guns. Believing themselves virtually impregnable, from 380 to 480 Indians waited attack. Old Sam Jones, although not a war chief, commanded more than half of them on the right, Alligator led 120 in the center, and Coacoochee, crazy for revenge, held the left with about 80 followers. Seminoles and others were segregated, as usual, into separate groups. As a result, they were not a cohesive fighting force subject to the direction of one unifying will. And it was their misfortune that the largest body of Negro warriors was not present.[20]

Confronted by this defense, Taylor called his officers together. His plan was to charge through the swamp squarely at the front of the enemy. The Missourians later claimed that

Colonel Gentry, their commander, proposed an encirclement, whereupon Taylor asked him if he was afraid. It is not clear that there was any way to get at the Indian flanks, but Taylor was not one to make an indirect approach anyway. He put the Missourians with Morgan's spies in the first line. Only 132 men of the regiment were by this time fit for duty, a heavy attrition rate from the near 600 who had left Missouri three months before. Behind them came the Fourth and the Sixth Infantry, and the First Infantry remained in reserve. Since the attack area was impassable for horses, all the attackers dismounted. The lines advanced at 12:30 P.M. on a pleasant Christmas Day. In his official report Taylor claimed that the Missouri volunteers broke after a volley or two and went to the rear. Colonel Gentry was mortally wounded almost at the first moment, and could not rally them. The volunteers denied Taylor's claim, asserting that they had to crawl through the sawgrass, stand to fire, and drop down again, lest they be shot by the Indians in front or the Sixth Infantry in the rear. They were placed, they said, in the hottest spot. Be that as it may, the heaviest fire bored into five companies of the Sixth in the corridor cut through the sawgrass. When all but one of their company officers and most of the noncoms had been hit, these five companies retired and reformed. At this moment Colonel Ramsey Thompson of the Sixth was fatally hit. Propped against a tree facing the foe, he called out "Remember the regiment to which you belong!" and so died. Once the frontal attack was strongly pressed, Taylor ordered the First Infantry, the reserve, to reach the enemy's right and hit him in that flank. As soon as the First got into position, the Indians gave one final volley and began to retreat. Coacoochee and Alligator later asserted that Sam Jones cravenly retreated on that wing, but they did not understand the pressure he was under. The Indians withdrew toward the lake, scattered, and escaped toward the east.[21]

Even though outnumbered two to one, the Seminoles elected to stand and fight at Okeechobee only because they thought they could inflict more harm than they would receive. The casualties indicated that their estimate was right; the white force lost 26 killed and 112 wounded, compared to the Seminoles' 11 and 14. The fight was over by three o'clock. There was no pursuit because Taylor had so many dead and wounded to evacuate. He ordered a footway made over the swamp, and directed that every casualty be carried across it, except one private who could not be found. All of December 26 was occupied in tending the wounded and trying to get them in condition to travel. At the same time about 100 Indian ponies and 300 cattle were rounded up. On December 27 the column started back to Fort Bassinger. The wounded were racked cruelly as their litters swayed and jerked over the rough terrain. But on December 28 they reached their destination, and on the last day of the year re-entered Fort Gardner. From that point the wounded were sent their painful way to Fort Brooke under the escort of the Fourth and Sixth Infantries. Taylor was prepared to take the field again as soon as his horses were fit and his supplies adequate. He reported that 180 Indians were in his hands through capture or surrender, together with 600 Indian cattle and 100 of their horses.[22]

Taylor's assertion in his official report that the Missouri volunteers had retired in disorder and could not be reformed brought roars from the people of Missouri. The state legislature adopted resolutions condemning the colonel and praising the volunteers. From the floor of the United States Senate Thomas Hart Benton called upon the President for all the relevant papers. Missourians claimed that from the start of the march Taylor had given them the hard assignments to spare his precious regulars. His orders would be found to be "monuments of oppression" toward the volunteers. Moreover, it was poor tactics to put green troops in the front line as he had done. In the United States Senate Linn of Missouri said that if Taylor had thrown the reserve at one flank, and Colonel Foster's Fourth Infantry at the other, the savages would have been annihilated. (If Taylor's report is to be trusted, he had actually sent the reserve against the right flank.) Regular officers, Linn continued, were suitable for European-style warfare, but of no use when it came to Indians. They were too cautious because they were too much afraid of being beaten by a body of wretched savages.[23]

Taylor made no especial effort to defend himself, but the higher governmental powers did. To the Senate on February 20, 1838, Secretary Poinsett declared that "no blame can rightly be attached to [Taylor] . . . for placing the volunteers in the front rank. . . . The enemy occupied a position that could not be turned and from which he could only be driven by the utmost efforts of the regular force. The task of storming such defenses could not be left to volunteer troops nor would an experienced officer rely on irregulars to form the reserve, as on the steady conduct of this force the fate of the action often depends. . . ." He added that the volunteers had to be used as skirmishers or not at all. Poinsett probably stated the case correctly.[24]

12

Conclusion of Jesup's Command

THE DAY AFTER THE Battle of Okeechobee, far to the north of the lake, General Nelson's Georgia volunteers engaged in a brisk fight on the Wacasassa River. General Jesup, concluding that Nelson had fought a wandering band and that most of the fighting power of the hostiles was still before him in South Florida, continued intensive preparations in that region. He built another fort farther up the St. Johns than any before it, about eighty miles straight north of the Okeechobee battleground. Because of the date on which the work began, the new log structure was named Fort Christmas, and by December 30 it was completed and garrisoned with two companies. On January 3 General Jesup himself led the St. Johns River wing southward from the Christmas area. Surgeon Jarvis, watching the column of 70 wagons and 1,000 horses winding across the wilderness of grass, was deeply thrilled. But the temperature stood at an unseasonal 103 degrees in the sun and men and animals quickly gave out.[1]

The supply line stretched out precariously as the army moved southward. Volusia lost its importance as a supply point, then Fort Mellon, then even Fort Lane. The general directed the quartermaster to cut a road twenty-five or thirty miles from Indian River Inlet to the head of the St. Johns, and when this was completed to abandon the St. Johns as a supply line. But shoal water at the mouth of the inlet forced Jesup to retain the river line. All the while he exhorted the supply arms: get us pontoons and boats suitable for swampy country; get us gunpowder of the first quality, the Indians have a better quality than we; spare no expense, for it may be possible to end the war soon if the army is not forced to fall back on account of supplies.[2]

We have seen what Colonel Taylor's force was doing, and have watched the St. Johns wing move southward. Lieutenant Levi Powell in command of a third detachment had, pursuant to his instructions, pushed his motley force into the Everglades. Surgeon Motte was struck by the detachment's heterogeneity: "When drawn up in line they presented a curious blending of black and white, like the keys of a piano forte; many of the sailors being coloured men. There was also an odd alternation of tarpaulin hats and pea jackets, with forage caps and soldiers trip roundabouts; soldiers and sailors, white men and black, being all thrown into the ranks indiscriminately." Perhaps this expedition gathered some strength from its diversity; it certainly needed all it could find, for its service was harsh in the extreme. The season had been so dry that instead of being floated, boats often had to be dragged to some of the islands. Heat, sawgrass, and insects made living itself a hopeless toil.[3]

Powell's detachment skirmished with the Indians several times, but its fiercest action occurred on January 15, 1838, just as it was emerging from the interior. Near the head of Jupiter River a squaw was captured and forced to act as guide. She led them to where they could see smoke issuing from a swamp. Forming in silence, they charged toward an undetermined foe across unknown ground. The gunfire which met them was so hot that they were forced to fight a rear-guard action to get back to their boats. The human cost was high: two soldiers, two sailors, and Naval Surgeon Dr. Frederick Leitner killed, and fifteen wounded. Surgeon Motte especially mourned Dr. Leitner, who had been his schoolmate and who had had a promising career ahead of him. Lieutenant Powell believed that the band he had fought was led by Tuskegee; that chief apparently had escaped beforehand, for he had been detained by General Jesup some weeks earlier.[4]

Optimistic by temperament, Jesup now began to feel that he

was closing the ring around the hostiles. On January 18 the St. Johns wing made contact with Taylor's command. Westward, twenty miles from their point of meeting, stood Fort Floyd, erected by Taylor's men. It was especially important because it completed the line of posts clear across the peninsula from Tampa Bay to Indian River Inlet. The eastern anchor of that line was Fort Pierce, named for Lieutenant Colonel B. K. Pierce. Farther south on the Atlantic coast was another fort built by the Tennessee volunteers and named for Colonel William Lauderdale, their commander. Colonel Smith's column of Louisiana, Pennsylvania, and New York volunteers was in motion west of Lake Okeechobee, and was expected to prevent the Seminoles from slipping northward on that side of the lake. Therefore, Jesup reasoned, the entire fighting force of the hostiles was confined among his several mobile columns, with limited exceptions. The Tallahassees, another band he called Hitchitees, and about one hundred Mikasukis formed the roving bands General Nelson had engaged on December 26, and it was up to Nelson to continue to keep them in check.[5]

At this time General Eustis joined the St. Johns column. Starting from Fort Pierce, this main column was forced to go inland to get around the St. Lucie River, and then to turn back toward the coast to the spot where Lieutenant Powell had engaged the Indians. Artillery, wagons, and pack mules formed a center column, while one hundred yards away, on each flank, the troops marched in two other columns. Lacking roads or trails, men and animals pushed and hauled their way through the swampy ground. Sawgrass tore the horses' legs, tattered the trousers of the men, and even cut up their shoes. Clothing could be patched with old corn bags, but shoes could be neither repaired nor replaced. It was a problem to find enough dry soil for a bivouac. The night's encampment held a fascination for the literate members of the command. Surgeon Motte wrote of it in his diary: "Frequently have I deserted my blanket to wander through the tented avenues and canvass streets when midnight has thrown its deep shadows o'er the sward, and the sounds of camp are all hushed; when nothing is heard but the piping of the wind through the branches of the trees. On one side . . . a long line of horses fastened to ropes stretched from tree to tree, and extending from one extremity of camp to the other. In another direction . . . innumerable wagons drawn up in solid squares; their white and clean looking tops glancing in the light of the camp fires. . . . All around are the temporary abodes of hundreds of human beings; here today; gone to morrow."[6]

Inching its heavy way along, an alien thing in this wilderness, the army halted at noon on January 24 because of the stirring report that a force of Indians was hiding in a hammock ahead, ready to fight. This was Jesup's first chance of the war to sport himself in the glare of combat; he ordered an attack at once. The attackers had to cross a cypress swamp in which horses floundered up to their girths, and cypress knees gouged and bruised them. The dragoons dismounted and charged, the artillerymen came up and followed, while on the flanks the six-pounder blasted the hammock. Congreve rockets hissed into the thick vegetation, Indians yelled, rifles cracked, and cannon shook the surface of the water; all the noises mingled in a frightful din. Shortly the Indians retreated to a new position behind a stream about thirty yards wide. Here their fire appeared about to demoralize the Tennessee volunteers. At this moment General Jesup rode up, dismounted, drew a pistol, and ordered the Tennesseans to follow him. As he paused at the edge of the stream to see if they were coming, a bullet struck and shattered his glasses and laid open his cheek. Waving the Tennesseans on, the general carefully picked up the pieces of his glasses, and then moved to the rear. Soon thereafter the Indian opposition melted away, leaving the hammock to the whites. Thus ended the Battle of Lockahatchee. It was estimated that from two hundred to three hundred red men took part in it, their casualties unknown. Seven white men were killed and thirty-one wounded, including the commander himself.[7]

By a curious irony the House of Representatives was debating the Florida war even as this, Jesup's last, battle was fought. Representative Henry A. Wise of Virginia declared that the war was a disgrace; he would rather vote money to secure the unfortunate Indians in their hammocks than to fight them. We had recently threatened war with France, we were now talking about demanding an explanation from England, yet we could not defeat one thousand Indians. He and the world condemned Jesup's treacherous seizure of Osceola and the other captives. Up leapt Charles Downing, the delegate from Florida. Such misplaced concern as this for the "unfortunate" Seminoles, he asserted, had prolonged the war. Even while they were butchering white men, the Indians and Negroes received the whites' sympathy. It had been charged that the Floridians were keeping the war going for profit's sake. Nonsense. They would have ended it long ago if left to their own methods. Richard Biddle of Pennsylvania then announced that he would not vote a penny more for the military until he could learn better how the military's money was being used. Some of the congressmen did come to the support of the war and of General Jesup, but one wandered off into the abolition question, where he was quickly ruled out of order. Meanwhile the party spokesman urged haste in voting because some of the departments of the military were without funds. In the end, after a few more solons had had their say, all the requested appropriations were granted.[8]

With at least four hundred men shoeless because of the sawgrass, it was necessary for the army to stop at Fort Jupiter on Jupiter Inlet and wait until barrels of shoes could reach it. Providence seemed to watch over the Seminoles, for a ship loaded with rice was just at this time wrecked off the mouth of New River, and the hostiles carried off the much-needed food. The army moved southward, and on February 8 an important parley was held by the white and red men. Tuskegee and Halleck Hajo attended; Tuskegee, who said he was sick, came at Jesup's special insistence. The upshot of the talk was that the general promised to ask the government if the Indians might remain in southern Florida, where in his view the land was not worth the cost of conquering it. In return the Seminoles agreed to make camp near the army, pending a reply from Washington.[9]

Pursuant to this compromise, Jesup on February 11 sat down to compose an extraordinary letter to Secretary Poinsett. There had never before been a case in America, he wrote, in which the Indians had been pushed out before the white men needed the land. The Seminoles were not now in the way of the white advance in Florida. If the policy of immediate emigration was not soon abandoned, the war in Florida could drag

on for many years. Might not the Seminoles remain on a specified reservation?

As soon as the letter was finished, Lieutenant Thomas B.
Linnard, Jesup's aide-de-camp, hurried off to Washington,
personally carrying it to the Secretary of War. After Linnard was gone, Jesup thought up refinements to strengthen
his argument and forwarded them to Poinsett by the regular
mail. When dealing with a band of naked savages, beaten,
broken, dispirited, and dispersed, the national honor was in no
way involved. Now the Seminoles were as surely beaten as the
opponents of Wayne, Harrison, and Jackson had been. If Jesup
were allowed to offer the same terms as those commanders
had offered, he could obtain peace with the Seminoles at once.
What was more, if the Seminoles were permitted to grow one
crop and at the same time were cut off from a supply of arms
and ammunition, they would actually demand removal in a
year's time.[10]

Toward the end of February, Tuskegee attended a ceremonial council at Jesup's camp. Surgeon Motte recorded the scene.
About 10:00 A.M. Tuskegee and Halleck Hajo, "dressed in all
the paraphernalia of Indian finery," appeared at the head of a
procession. Preceding them were two warriors "cutting the
most fantastic capers." Along the way they stopped from time
to time to utter a shrill whoop in which all the Indians joined.
Arriving at the general's tent, they shook not hands but elbows
with each officer, at the same time touching the forehead of
each with a white feather attached to a stick. Next the calumet
was smoked, and then an old squaw opened the talks. All the
warriors were her children, she lamented; many were slain,
their villages burned, their children perishing. The star of her
nation had set in blood, and she desired that a perpetual peace
be arranged.[11]

The bearing of the numerous Negroes jarred Southern officers. Motte thought them "diabolical looking . . . ferocious and
oriental in aspect. They had none of the servility of our northern blacks, but were constantly offering their dirty paws with
as much hauteur . . . as if they were conferring a vast deal of
honour."[12]

About a week later the officers received an invitation to attend an Indian dance and to bring a good deal of whiskey with

them. They accepted, took the whiskey, and as it warmed their spirits, began to join in the dance. "Many of the officers . . . accepting the invitation of the master of ceremonies, took our places in the ring, and danced with the utmost gravity depicted on our faces; imitating the various grotesque evolutions . . . and chiming in with the chorus, our voices rendered awfully distinct by their rough tones amid the softness of the Indians' musical notes; like a few thorns projecting from a bouquet of roses."[13]

But in spite of savage dances, the daily round of camp life grew oppressive during the wait for the reply from Washington. In the interval a board of officers tested Samuel Colt's newly invented revolver. The inventor himself came to Florida and carried his weapons to the remotest posts in order to obtain a trial for them. Most of the officers found them too much subject to misfire, and too frequently apt to backfire. Lieutenant Colonel William S. Harney, on the other hand, liked and used Colt's rifles.[14]

At last, on St. Patrick's Day, the expected reply came from Washington. In categorical terms and tart words Secretary Poinsett denied Jesup's request to allow the Seminoles to remain in South Florida. There was nothing left to do but call a council and announce the decision to the Indians. Apparently they knew what it was, for none of them bothered to attend. When the Seminoles failed him at the council, Jesup acted in what had now come to be a characteristic manner. Right or wrong, he was not willing to see so many hostiles plunge once more into the wilderness. How many years, how many lives might it take to corral them again? On March 21, 1838, he ordered David E. Twiggs, colonel of the Second Dragoons (who had first come to Florida with General Gaines in 1836, but had stayed only briefly), to disarm all the warriors and take into custody every Indian in the adjacent camp. When Twiggs executed this assignment, he brought in the largest bag of captives since the war began, 504 to 513 Indians, of whom 151 were warriors. One wonders why the red men were at this stage off their guard when dealing with the notorious general.[15]

The Florida press lauded the government's decision not to allow the Seminoles to remain, and at the same time criticized General Jesup severely for having made such a proposal.

He had, the press then generalized, done little to end the war.[16]

Conflict now rekindled over a wide area. Under heavy pressure in the south, a few Seminole bands circumvented Jesup's several columns and worked their way back northward. There they ravaged once more the areas which had been desolated two years earlier. A rash of murders were committed in Middle Florida. Not willing to leave anything to chance, Jesup dispatched General Armistead to take command there. Soon he also sent General Eustis northward to take charge in the Suwannee region.[17]

Meanwhile in South Florida Zachary Taylor (promoted to brigadier general for his conduct at the Battle of Okeechobee) succeeded in capturing Holatoochee with forty warriors. In the same area Lieutenant Colonel James Bankhead of the Fourth Artillery found on March 22, 1838, a band of hostiles in their favorite defensive position on the edge of a hammock, and sought to achieve a double envelopment. Two companies of the Fourth were posted in front as a holding force, while four companies moved to the left in water two feet deep. On the right the water was deeper yet, and Bankhead embarked in rowboats his right flanking force, a mixture of soldiers and sailors. This amphibious detachment carried with it one four-pounder which it fired from a boat. Pressed on three sides, the Indians as usual simply melted away.[18]

Holatoochee reported that there were probably not more than two hundred warriors left at large. These no longer had an appreciable supporting force of Negro warriors because most of the latter had surrendered on Jesup's promise to free them. During the first week in April, the hostile force underwent a further very important reduction. General Jesup sent Abraham and Holatoochee into the scrub to contact Alligator. In a few days they triumphantly brought that formidable foe, with eighty-eight people including the runaway John Cowaya and twenty-seven Negroes, into Fort Bassinger to surrender. Alligator saw no future in continuing to struggle.[19]

As part of what now seemed to be the final mop-up, Jesup directed Lieutenant Colonel William S. Harney to try to run down old Sam Jones. Harney picked fifty dragoons from his own regiment, the Second, and armed them with Colt's rifles.

Fifty men were drawn from the Third Artillery and equipped with muskets. All knew that the assignment before them was a hard one. They went as far as they could on horseback, then transferred into fifteen log canoes which carried them along the coast until, led by a guide, they struck inland once more through a tangled mangrove swamp. Next the way lay across an area of coral rocks which lacerated their feet right through their shoes, "as much," said Surgeon Motte, "as if we were walking over a surface from which protruded a thick crop of sharply pointed knives." The heat was intense, and there was no good water.[20]

But on April 24, 1838, they saw in the distance the smoke of an Indian camp. Harney quietly divided his force into three detachments and sent them forward on the double. The warriors opened fire from behind trees. Harney's men also took to trees and returned the Seminole fire. After a brief gunfight, the defenders began to yield ground, and finally broke cover and ran. Whooping in pursuit, the white men became badly scattered and in danger of being attacked in fragments. At the end of two and one-half hours the fight was over, with the usual disappointing yield, one Indian known killed and one captured. The cost in fatigue was very great. The next day Surgeon Motte's strength failed him utterly, and he dropped where he stood. Some comrades loyally brought him along until he could reassume responsibility for himself.[21]

General Jesup, now willing to do anything to bring the interminable war to an end, suggested the use of bloodhounds. In addition he hinted to R. K. Call that it might be wise to let the red men draw together and plant a crop in apparent security. Once they were concentrated and entirely off guard, a swift attack would end their resistance. When reporting each action, high in expenditure of energy but low in captives or hostile lives taken, he pointed out to the Administration the long, painful grind lying ahead if the Seminoles were to be forced to migrate.[22]

Months earlier General Jesup had asked to be relieved. At Tampa on April 29 the welcome word of relief reached him. A letter of April 10 said that when affairs in Florida were in transferable order, he might surrender the command and resume his duties as the army Quartermaster General. Happily he set about making his final arrangements. The First and the Sixth Infantry regiments and four companies of the Second Dragoons would remain in Florida, the rest of the regulars would be shipped to Georgia and Alabama, to aid there in the tragic removal of the Cherokees. All these plans were completed to the general's satisfaction by mid-May, and on May 15, 1838, he turned the reins over to Zachary Taylor.

During the nearly eighteen months of Jesup's command, almost 3,000 Indians had been placed outside of combat, 100 of them killed, 2,900 captured. Lest the government take this accomplishment lightly, he flatly asserted that his job in Florida had been far harder than anything Wayne, Harrison, and Jackson, those three most redoubtable Indian fighters before him, had faced.[23]

The same thing about difficulty could have been justly said of the officers and men under Jesup. It is indeed doubtful if United States ground forces endured harsher field conditions anywhere. Protracted service in the humidity, the rank growth, and the darkness of the Florida swamps took the sunshine out of a man's life. Cypress knees, mangrove roots, and sawgrass tortured the foot soldier. Too much water, and the lack of water, made his life a torment. There was marching in water from ankle- to armpit-deep, hour after hour, with no chance to dry off, not even at night. Men slept in their clothes, often including boots, for four months running. When mules could not pull the wagons through the mud, the men on foot had to drag them. Surgeon Forry wrote, "Our position here [Fort Taylor] is indeed melancholy. After each rain we resemble Noah on the top of Mt. Ararat. Clouds of crows and blackbirds then hover around, waiting for the waters to subside, to resume their daily vocation of picking up corn. Turning your eye to the earth you then behold a score of glandered and sore backed mules! Now a mosquito buzzes in your ear, and next a flea bites you between the shoulders." At other times there were periods of drought so severe that the marching troops could find nothing but stagnant water to drink. And the temperature fluctuated wildly. The same soldier might shuffle along in 102-degree heat that killed mules in one season, and shiver all night from 30-degree cold in the next.[24]

We are "almost eaten up by fleas, ants, cockroaches and almost all manner of vermin," said Captain Joseph R. Smith. Far more dangerous of course were snakes, and the army trampled its way through areas where even the Seminoles would not live because of the rattlers. Once feeling one leg heavier than the other, a soldier glanced down to see a large rattlesnake caught by the fangs in his pants leg. Yet, strange to tell, if snake-bite killed and crippled men, the written record does not mention it so much as one time.[25]

Cut by sawgrass, made raw by insects bites, now and again reeling dizzy from dysentery and fever, the common soldier in Florida lived in a world which had no horizons. He had little relief to hope for. Why was he willing to endure such a life? Many of the regulars were foreigners who came to this country only to be caught in that sharp depression, the Panic of 1837. In a given period 906 Americans enlisted in the American army, and in the same period 811 Irishmen, 179 Englishmen, 143 Germans, 95 Frenchmen, 53 Poles, and 117 Scots. A few of these aliens came from service in some foreign army. An officer noted the case of one fine-looking enlisted man who had suffered 300 lashes in another service for attempted desertion. These old regulars made the best soldiers, but the worst men. Because of the depression (the first modern one), men with valuable skills enlisted in the army, men who would have scorned the service in other eras. Others were already on the road to debasement when they joined, and the harsh conditions in Florida tended to brutalize them further. Callousness was probably more common than not. One observer recorded the case of a boy of seventeen who died of fever in the hospital, wallowing in his own blood, while the attendants sat on the floor beside him and gambled. Sunday was just another horizonless day to many soldiers. "Oh my God," wrote the same Captain Smith, a deeply religious man, "how is this, thy holy day desecrated. Oh grant to touch the hearts of both officers and soldiers."[26]

Two regulars, presumably because they could no longer endure the hardships, deserted somewhere between Forts Bassinger and Gardner. It is not even known whether they survived the enveloping trackless wilderness.[27]

Up to February, 1838, 1,076 officers and 17,438 enlisted citizen soldiers had shared the hardships of campaigning in

Florida with the regulars. Privation was easier for them to endure because they could look forward to release in three months, six months, or at most a year. If they stayed in as much as six months, they learned discipline, but if for shorter terms, their contribution to the war effort was limited.[28]

Service side by side did not endear regulars and citizen soldiers to each other. The Southern volunteers, being used to slave help, would not labor, throwing the burden of details, such as road building and other heavy manual work, upon the regulars. In general, the regular officers thought the citizen soldiers a poor military instrument. Citizens, on the other hand, held the reverse of that view. At a banquet in Tallahassee in 1837 someone proposed a toast which expressed the citizen view. "The Army of the United States, paralyzed and powerless. Too feeble to chastize one tribe of wandering savages. How hath the mighty fallen!"[29]

Even the most anti-regular citizens nevertheless had no idea of eliminating the Seminoles without professional help. They knew it was growing difficult to enlist Floridians, even for short terms. The Legislative Council in February, 1837, thought it necessary to pay a bounty of $16.50 per month to every man who would enroll for a year, and to this end it empowered the governor to borrow $30,000. Yet it was necessary to make a draft from time to time. The citizens of Jefferson County complained bitterly that they had been called on "until the patience of our citizens has been exhausted." Many would desert the area if ordered out once more. Forgetting their scorn for regulars, they asked for a company of dragoons to be stationed in their county.[30]

Back in Washington, Andrew Jackson had an interview with retiring Territorial Delegate Joseph M. White. The latter stressed to the old man the strain which the war put upon Florida. Jackson took immediate exception. Florida, he said, had never yet put a brigadier's command in the field for her own defense. When White contradicted him, the President waxed warm. With fifty women, he vowed, he could defeat all the Indians who had been ravaging the area west of the Suwannee. Florida men ought to get themselves shot and free their women to breed up a bolder species. "Let the damned cowards defend their country!" Had he had future political ambitions, he might have controlled himself more firmly, but as it was, less than a month later he turned the helm over to Martin Van Buren. And White gave place to Charles Downing.[31]

If the white invaders endured much, the Indians bore even more. Bit by bit during Jesup's command the army probed into their remotest hiding places and captured their camps. The Seminoles lost irreplaceable, indispensable articles. They lost their crops too, and nearly starved. While waiting for word from Washington at Jupiter Inlet, close to Jesup's camp, the squaws picked up kernel by kernel the corn dropped by horses. Detractors of General Jesup have claimed that he opened the road to starvation for them by shooting all their cattle which his own army could not use. On the surface, at least, the warriors appeared to bear their privations well, but the women showed the ravages. Their ragged clothes scarcely covered their nakedness, and some were reduced to wearing the old corn sacks thrown away by the troops. White men watched them weep openly many times, yet oddly enough considered them more intransigent than their men. A squaw widowed by the conflict would sell her husband's ammunition for hunting, but give it away for war use.

The deepest sufferers of all were the Seminole children. Many did not survive, and white men claimed, but maliciously, that mothers killed their infants to relieve their misery and to be free of the encumbrance of them. It is also claimed that some mothers buried their children in the swamp to the neck and left them during the day, returning to feed them under cover of darkness. Silence was essential to survival, and the children learned to play quietly, a habit which persisted for generations afterwards.

Nor was quietness the only legacy of the war to the daily habits of the Seminoles. Certain students have advanced the theory that the "chickee" (the open-sided shelter lifted off the ground on low stilts) developed during the war. Previously the Florida Indians had lived in cabins like their Creek cousins, but the uprooting of their lives forced them to shelter themselves in something less permanent and more easily constructed. Finally, the patchwork design of Seminole clothing is said to stem from the need to sew scraps together.[32]

When Congress looked south to Florida, it divided two ways, according to sectionalism and to Jacksonism. It was, of course, sensitive to the heavy expenditures being poured out. About the time of Jesup's departure, Secretary Poinsett estimated them at $458,000 per month. The direct costs, up to that time, as far as anyone could compute them, came to $9,400,000 since the start of the war. Caleb Cushing of Massachusetts said he believed the country could thank Andrew Jackson for this great charge, as he had brought on the war. William K. Bond of Ohio opined that the war appropriations were made to delay installments due the states from the Treasury under the act which had sought to dispose of a surplus in that department. Actually the Panic had wiped out the surplus. Now, more than before, heavy expenditures were hard to justify. John Quincy Adams asserted in debate that his state received no benefits from the appropriations for the army, but that he was consistently outvoted in committee by the Southern and Western representatives whose sections were benefited. Some legislators favored a Congressional investigation of the conduct of the war. Yet debaters protested that an appointed committee would be loaded with partisans who would quash any findings that were damaging to their party. So the investigation came to little.[33]

Florida itself, in spite of the Indian war, was debating the matter of statehood. East Florida, whose leaders considered the area too poor to pay state taxes, was opposed. Let Middle and West Florida become a state, if they liked.[34]

Far off in Alton, Illinois, Elijah P. Lovejoy was murdered for agitating in favor of the abolition of slavery. This event was related to the war in Florida. There was steady awareness of hard times in the newspapers and of the government's proposal for a subtreasury bill. The Florida newspapers noticed these things; indeed from them one might have inferred that the war with the Seminoles was not the central event in Florida. All the while, a portrait painter advertised that he would work in St. Augustine, while the Reverend D. Brown displayed his prospectus for a Florida magazine. Indians or no Indians, the vitality of the society remained inextinguishable.

13

Zachary Taylor

ZACHARY TAYLOR, who in May, 1838, took up the Florida burden laid down by General Jesup, was to carry it a full two years, a period in the war longer than that of any other commanding officer. Most of the honor he was to obtain from his service against the Seminoles came while Jesup still commanded, out of the Battle of Okeechobee, which service indeed earned him promotion by brevet to brigadier general. He was four years older than his predecessor, but like him had come into the military service in the expansion of the army after the *Chesapeake-Leopard* incident of 1807. He was commissioned first lieutenant from civilian life in 1808. His greatest deficiency then and thereafter was a lack of formal schooling. Despite this handicap, his rise in the army was steady, though slow. It was Zachary Taylor's bad fortune to serve throughout the career-making War of 1812 on the remote frontier of the Mississippi Valley. While Scott and Gaines advanced to brigadier rank by brevet, he rose only to brevet major. Following the war, he left the army for one year, then returned to it and did more duty on the frontier. He became a colonel on April 4, 1832. By that time Thomas S. Jesup, who had also begun in 1808, had been a brevet major general for four years. Taylor served in the Black Hawk War and then did still more frontier work. From the frontier he was ordered on July 31, 1837, to report for duty in Florida with his First Infantry.[1]

Zachary Taylor

Fifty-four years old when he assumed control in Florida, Taylor had already earned the nickname "Old Rough and Ready" because of his dislike of uniform and panoply, and his willingness to fight. Brusque, profane, easy of access, plain in his manners, the new general was the kind enlisted men liked. He had, before Florida, never organized operations except on a small scale, but he had put together a plan for defending the frontiers which showed an ability to anticipate and to think. His attention to detail fell far below Jesup's, so did the size of his army, yet his command contained many more men than Taylor had ever commanded before. The Army of the South when he took over from Jesup came to only about 2,300, of which 1,833 were regulars.[2]

General Taylor had been in command only three days when he wrote Governor Call of his intention to end the use of citizen soldiers during the sickly season. He would rely on his twenty-six companies of regular infantry and four of regular dragoons. With these his first project was to drive the hostiles south of a line running from St. Augustine through Garey's Ferry, thence along the road from Fort King to Tampa. This would push the Indians away from "every portion of Florida worth protecting." Then by cutting off interchange between whites and Indians, he could force the latter to leave Florida. Taylor's letter irritated the governor. Much more of Florida seemed to Call worth protecting than Taylor had stipulated, and the incessant murders and depredations had to be curbed. On May 27, 1838, there was a smart action barely one mile from the Okefenokee Swamp on the Georgia border, a new trouble area. Captain Sandelung with forty Florida militiamen engaged about twenty Indians for half an hour, and suffered two wounded. So it went, season in and season out, and Governor Call did not see how the military force could be reduced.[3]

The federal government, not Taylor, dictated the reduction of force. Secretary Poinsett directed the commander to reduce the number of Florida militia on duty in order to cut down expenses. After June 1, 1838, the Secretary set the limit at 1,000. Inasmuch as the law regulating volunteers had expired one month earlier, it was necessary to accept volunteers into federal service as if they were drafted militia. Regulations concerning citizen soldiers were to be strictly enforced on a retroactive basis, and this meant, for example, that Colonel Lindsay had to dig into his own pocket for part of the pay of a volunteer officer whom he had promoted beyond the legal limit.[4]

June was filled with small desperate actions which the general ascribed to four or five hundred Mikasukis, Tallahassees, and a few renegade Creeks. Taylor believed that the "Seminoles," his term for the Alachuas, were finished. The Second Dragoons engaged in numerous forays out of Fort Brooke without the direction of their Colonel David E. Twiggs, who to Taylor's distress was absent on a leave granted by General Macomb without even notifying Taylor. One of the dragoons' sharpest fights took place on June 4, 1838, near Gaines' and Clinch's old battleground on the Withlacoochee. Heavy rain halted the pursuit, and the outcome was inconclusive. The Seminoles burned Fort Dade and tried to burn the log bridge across the Withlacoochee there. Brevet Major Benjamin L. Beall, a true *beau sabreur,* led one detachment in a fight on the Kanapaha Prairie, with a loss of militia Captain Walker of Newnansville killed and six dragoons wounded.[5]

In July, two Georgia families were murdered by Indians who then hid in the Okefenokee Swamp. The Lasley family was murdered near Tallahassee on July 28, and the Gwinns on the Santa Fe in the same month. Hogs tore the flesh of the wounded Gwinns, and a mounted volunteer claimed that the Indians had dashed out a baby's brains and laid the shattered body in its murdered mother's arms.[6]

Considering the Indians to be absolute masters of the region between the Apalachicola and the Ochlockonee Rivers, Governor Call ordered out three companies of Florida mounted men, confident that he could shame the Secretary into taking them into federal service. The regulars, he was convinced, could not do the job by themselves.[7] Under this pressure Secretary Poinsett began to soften his position toward citizen soldiers. On August 20 he directed Taylor to call five hundred mounted Florida militiamen, who knew the terrain and were acclimated, to defend Middle Florida. That area must be protected. The former inhabitants were to be encouraged to return, the returning men to be then received into federal service and formed into defensive battalions. Each battalion was to have a central depot for a rallying point. The soldier-settlers could spend some of their time growing food and the rest of their time patrolling.[8]

General Taylor applied such broad discretion to these instructions that he in fact nullified them. He had no confidence in Floridians, lacked the time to put the project into effect, and had still to find out whether the quartermaster could provision the armed settlers. He also waited for Congress to do something about land grants for such settlers. Meanwhile Taylor developed his own scheme and proposed it to the government: lay off the whole of North Florida as far south as the Withlacoochee in squares twenty miles on each side, and place in the center of each square a post garrisoned by twenty men, half of them mounted. This pattern of occupation would require four full regiments, but would use them effectively to choke off depredations. The Administration liked the proposal, and Poinsett cheerfully informed General Macomb on January 23, 1839, that it was approved.[9]

While all this went on, Taylor registered complaints about the contradictory directives relating to citizen soldiers. First he had been limited to a thousand of them, then was unlimited for a brief period, and now was apparently cut back to five hundred. But deeming it virtually impossible to refuse the militia, he directed his subordinates to enroll them if there was any apparent need.[10]

Before word reached him of the approval of his plan of squares, Taylor projected a southward expedition of four hundred men. This project was replaced by a scheme to drive the hostiles out of the area between the St. Johns and the Oklawaha. But when the approval of his squares reached him on February 15, 1839, he canceled other plans and sent out orders to the officers who were to lay out the squares. He told the officers west of the Suwannee to make the squares eighteen instead of twenty miles on each side, because townships of that size had already been platted in the area. The responsible officer was to open a road around the perimeter of each square and interlace its hammocks with trails. He was then to make a detailed map of his area and institute routine patrolling for a part of every day. The quartermaster would supply seeds for a garden in each area. "We must," Taylor said, "abandon

Map Showing Taylor's Squares in North Florida

general operations and confine ourselves to minute and specific ones."[11] The Florida press did not expect much from the new system because the number of available regulars was not sufficient to make it operate effectively.

Whenever Indians of any standing could be induced to negotiate, a parley was held with them. The few remaining Apalachicolas agreed to go west by October 1, 1838, and did so. The Tallahassees did not prove equally reliable. Two of their important chiefs contracted to bring their people in by the end of October, but did not do it. Renewed negotiations produced a new promise to turn themselves in by late November, but this too was only partially honored.[12]

Taylor arranged to ship those Indians beyond the Mississippi who were already on his hands. The major problem was not with them but with the Indian-Negroes. Although himself a slaveholder, Taylor handled the Negroes without Jesup's ambiguity. He would not, he told Secretary Poinsett, aid in depriving the Seminoles of their Negroes, nor would he do anything which would reduce the latter from comparative freedom to slavery. On the other hand, he was pledged to return any slave to his legal white owner. In practice what he did was to turn both Negroes and Indians over to the officer in charge of emigration, who happened to be Lieutenant John G. Reynolds of the Marine Corps.[13]

Reynolds had a knotty problem on his hands, especially because of the Negroes captured by the Creek Indians. General Jesup had offered $8,000 for these slaves, but the Creeks had rejected it. Poinsett then directed that the Negroes themselves be turned over to their captors, but when Indian Commissioner C. A. Harris undertook to obey, he found that Reynolds had already shipped them westward. In the meantime the Creeks, not waiting until they had possession, sold their captives to a Mr. James C. Watson of Georgia for $15,000. Watson sent his brother-in-law, Nathaniel F. Collins, to find and claim his seventy-odd slaves. Collins hastened to New Orleans, where Indians and Negroes were awaiting shipment on the last leg of their journey. Backed by the Secretary of War, he demanded his relative's property, but to no avail. Apparently the local military officers were determined to see General Jesup's promise carried out. When Collins sued, General Gaines, no less, appeared in court and testified that all the Negroes in his possession were prisoners of war, and as such could not be delivered to anyone. While Collins threatened and protested, his brother-in-law's alleged property went abroad ship and passed on toward Fort Gibson. Undismayed, Collins pursued, and caught up with the caravan at Vicksburg.[14]

His reappearance almost produced mutiny among the Seminoles. As they had been promised that their Negroes would be with them in the Indian Territory, they wanted to know what right Collins had to hover around like a vulture. The officers with them sympathized, and silently worked to fulfill the promise. This was dangerous because back in Washington neither the Indian Commissioner nor the Secretary of War wanted those Negroes to reach the reservation. Once there they would create differences between Creeks and Seminoles. Yet inexorably the expedition moved closer to its destination. Finally at Little Rock, Arkansas, Lieutenant Reynolds dared not go on without trying to turn the Negroes over to the importunate Collins. By this time, though, the Seminoles were so angered that nothing but force would separate them from their black associates. On June 3, 1838, Reynolds called on the governor of Arkansas for enough military power to enforce seizure of the Negroes. The governor responded with a denunciation. "Had the government," he said, "intended to dispose of these negroes to the Creek Indians, it should have been done in Florida, and not bring [Seminoles] and negroes into Arkansas . . . then *irritate* the Indians to madness, and turn them loose on our frontier, where we have no adequate protection—the massacre of our citizens would be the inevitable consequence." Far from giving Reynolds military aid, the governor continued, he had assured the Seminole chiefs that their Negroes would not be taken from them. Lieutenant Reynolds heaved a sigh of relief. Nevertheless, upon reaching Fort Gibson he felt duty bound to call on General Matthew Arbuckle to supply him with a force big enough to carry out his orders. Arbuckle also declined. And so between three and four hundred Negroes did reach the Indian Territory with the Seminoles.[15]

Fifty-four Indians and Negroes, among them Philip, had died on the westward trip, but Lieutenant Reynolds delivered 1,221 live bodies, red and black, to the destination. No tools, clothes, or transport awaited them there. General Jesup had promised these articles to the captives and, be it said to his credit, he had done his best to deliver them.[16]

When the cool weather came to Florida early in November, 1838, General Taylor felt he ought to put his army into the field. These were his dispositions: Colonel Twiggs (who by this time had reported for duty again) was to scour between the Atlantic and the St. Johns as far south as New Smyrna, and to erect a new post there; Colonel Fanning was to re-establish Fort Mellon on Lake Monroe; Colonel William Davenport was to re-establish Fort Clinch up from the mouth of the Withlacoochee and to operate in that area; Lieutenant Colonel Green was to police the area from St. Marks to the Suwannee; and Major Gustavus Loomis, with a mixed force of regulars and militia, was to act against the Indians in the Okefenokee area. The immediate object of the campaign was to bring security to the settled areas by driving the natives below a new line drawn from New Smyrna to Fort Brooke. To achieve this, it would be necessary to advance a complex of roads and posts as systematically as if conducting a siege. When all was completed, there would be a good road running from one end of the line of demarkation to the other with a strong post every twenty miles. But November had not come to an end before the *Florida Herald* of St. Augustine announced that Taylor's policy had failed, and asked why he had so stubbornly refused to use Florida militia.[17]

Just as Taylor laid out his cool-weather operations, Major Truman Cross took over as quartermaster to the Army of the South. While Jesup had commanded this army, Cross had been Acting Quartermaster General of the United States Army, and his coming to Florida indicated the importance of that theater. His initial directive to quartermasters was an economy manifesto. Officers were to eliminate civilian agents and issue stores themselves. Clerks and highly paid laborers were to be discharged from small supply points, leaving the troops to do their work. Officers must reduce the number of their horses. Ambulances were not to be used except for the sick and wounded. Teamsters were held accountable for supplies they took out of depots and were to be punished if they molested the citizenry. If the new quartermaster could enforce these lean regulations the taxpayers would bless him, but many citizens of Florida would hate him.[18]

Floridians continued to demand drastic action to stop Indian depredations. Governor Call pointed out to Taylor that twelve white men had been killed in one week. Even though the territorial militia was in a chaotic condition, Florida troops ought to be taken into federal service. Federal officers had hampered the development of the militia, Call claimed, and had permitted stores to spoil lying in storage while citizen soldiers suffered for lack of them.[19]

Wholly in agreement with Call, the Florida Legislative Council authorized the raising of twelve companies of volunteers. Call was to offer these to the United States, but if Taylor turned them down Call was permitted to borrow $500,000 at 8 per cent to pay and equip them. In either case their officers were to be appointed by the governor and were to report directly to him. Call acted promptly to raise this corps, and Taylor equally promptly accepted it, with the proviso that only one-half of the men be mounted. Whereas his predecessor had thought horsemen the best reliance, Taylor commented to Call that the Seminoles rarely went into the pine woods, and that mounted men were of little value in the hammocks.[20]

Meanwhile the routine of defense and Indian removal continued. Eighteen Seminoles were captured on February 2 near Fort Mellon. At about the same time eighty miles to the northwest two dispatch riders were wounded near Micanopy. Elsewhere, Major Thomas Noel of the Sixth Infantry, who had survived the Battle of Okeechobee, was killed, and far to the south Captain Samuel L. Russell was fatally shot while traveling in a boat down the Miami River. Clearly, the foe was widely dispersed and in very small bands. This being the case, General Taylor protested the order which directed him to ship the Fourth Artillery to New Orleans. This regiment occupied nine important posts, and had more platoon officers than any other regular outfit in Florida. Officers were desperately needed; five companies of the Second Infantry were commanded by second lieutenants instead of captains, and four of the lieutenants had just been appointed from civil life. Continuing the slow resettlement of Florida Indians, on February 25, 1839, Taylor shipped 196 more westward, 65 of them warriors. Some individuals of this group were Negroes, but Taylor did not distinguish between reds and blacks in his reports as Jesup had done.[21]

Up to this point five of the sixteen generals in the army (twelve of them were generals by brevet) had exercised the command in Florida. Now came the turn of the highest rank-ing general of them all, Alexander Macomb. For some reason his role in the military establishment had recently been grow-ing. On March 18, 1839, the Secretary directed him to go to Florida and do whatever was necessary to protect the citizens and to end the war. He was allowed more discretion than pre-vious commanders, but he was enjoined not to interfere with Taylor's system of squares.[22]

Next to Edmund P. Gaines, Macomb was the oldest of the generals to come to Florida. Born in Detroit in 1782, he had first obtained a commission during the pseudo war with France in 1799. In 1801 and 1802 he had gained some experience with the Indians of the Southeast, and the memory of it apparently gave him confidence in his ability to deal with them. Upon the founding of the Military Academy he became one of the first student officers to receive instruction there. Then the War of 1812 provided him his great chance. No officer rose any higher; he was brevetted a major general as a reward for his remark-able defense of Plattsburg, New York. On September 11, 1814, he arranged 1,500 men, most of them citizen soldiers, to try to stop ten times their number. Although the navy saved the day, Macomb made the most of his forces. The post of com-manding general consequently became his upon the death of Jacob Brown in 1828.[23]

General Macomb's youthful aid, John T. Sprague, historian of the Second Seminole War, asserted that Macomb was al-ways in a good humor and very fond of society. "He par-ticipates with interest and vivacity in all that's passing, and infuses into all around him a spirit of gaity and interest." Yet he was a deeply religious man who suspended business on Sun-day and read his Bible for hours on end.[24]

When the Commanding General of the United States Army reached Garey's Ferry on April 5, 1839, that drab post was spruced up in his honor. While the band of the Second Dra-goons played "Hail to the Chief," the officers stepped forward to shake hands. Taylor was there, but if he expected to be superseded, he quickly learned he would not be. Although he had been charged with the entire conduct of the war, General Macomb declined to interfere with military operations and confined himself to negotiations with the Indians. He stayed three weeks at Garey's Ferry, inspecting the installations there and trying to arrange a parley with the important Seminole chiefs. But finally, on April 25, he set out along the military road to Fort King mounted on a large gray horse named Micanopy and escorted by a company of dragoons.[25]

The commanding general's coming made little difference in the day-by-day activity of the people and the troops in Florida. On April 6 a Captain Scott and his overseer repulsed a band of trespassing Indians. A few such receptions as this, the press exulted, would make the Indians more cautious. About this time word came from Lieutenant John T. McLaughlin, United States Navy, that, in response to Taylor's orders of July, 1838, he had examined the entire east coast of Florida. Ashore at Tampa one hundred hostiles liberated thirty of their people who were waiting to be sent west.[26]

After Macomb had looked over the situation, he concluded that the Seminoles no longer attacked parties of regulars or even the unguarded wagon trains of the army. It was the Florida crackers whom they assailed at every opportunity, and for whom they felt both hatred and fear. The crackers appealed little more to Lieutenant Sprague than to the Indians. He reported them as "dirty, ragged and dusty, seated upon long-tailed and short-eared horses, with the deadly rifle resting in front and a short jacket, long beard and hair, and a broad-brim white hat."[27]

Not until May 18 could General Macomb lure enough Seminoles to Fort King to conduct a respectable council. Even if the standing of the two chiefs who finally came was questionable, the general left nothing undone to create an impressive setting. On a camp ground just west of the fort a council house was erected, and great fires of pine burned near it all night, lighting up the surrounding country. At the appointed time Macomb marched to the council house escorted by a company of dragoons in full dress, all in step to stirring marches played by the band of the Seventh Infantry. Even those Indians who remembered General Scott had seen nothing to equal this parade. They sat in silence smoking for fifteen minutes. Macomb opened with a welcoming speech interpreted by Sandy, a Negro. Chitto Tustenuggee (who the white men believed had replaced Sam Jones as head chief) responded, followed by Halleck Tustenuggee. The council continued for two days in intensely hot weather. At the end the suffering seemed to have been rewarded, for on May 20 the general issued a general order in which the war was proclaimed at an end.[28]

General Taylor and his staff had told Macomb that the conflict could be ended only by allowing the hostiles to remain in Florida. Macomb accepted this assertion as fact, and exercising the authority which Jesup had sought in vain more than a year before, he arranged the peace on that basis. The two chiefs, whom Macomb regarded as qualified to represent the Seminoles, agreed to withdraw south of Pease Creek, within specified boundaries, by July 15, 1839, and remain there, "until further arrangements were made." Bedazzled by this outcome, Lieutenant Sprague concluded that his commander had succeeded where those before him had failed because he had relied heavily on ritual and pomp.[29]

The Tallahassee *Floridian* printed the news of Macomb's agreement and framed it top and bottom in gigantic type that cried "Shame! Shame! Shame!" An insane scheme, the editor said, which could not really be intended in good faith. Inflamed by unpunished murders, Floridians would shoot Indians on sight, agreement or no agreement. Resolutions passed at a mass meeting in Tallahassee declared that Florida was the last place in the country where Indians should be left, because they had access to the ocean and could be expected to fight on the side of any foreign foe of the United States. Also they would harbor runaway slaves. Such was the majority opinion, but not by any means the only one. Two citizen soldiers who had been in the thick of the fight from the beginning, Colonel John Warren and Lieutenant Colonel W. J. Mills of the Florida militia, expressed their approval to Macomb and said they knew many persons in the country who felt the same way. Then, with the passage of time, Floridians took hope that the arrangement was not meant to be permanent. After all, the general had not entered into a formal written treaty and had told the Secretary, "Nor did I think it politic, at this time, to say anything about their emigration, leaving that subject open to such future arrangements as the government may think proper to make with them." Secretary Poinsett, writing to General Taylor, had also said that the Indians were to "be permitted to remain there until other and permanent arrangements shall be made by the Government." And a letter of Poinsett's which had been published said, "I am of the opinion that the arrangement made by General Macomb will . . . enable me to remove the Indians from the territory much sooner than can be done by force." If these expressions mollified the white men, they had the opposite effect on the Indians.[30]

Poinsett directed Taylor to help the Seminoles get within the prescribed boundaries, to see that they stayed there, and to protect them against encroachments by white men. The President declared their reservation to be Indian territory under the provisions of the Indian Intercourse Act of June 30, 1834.[31]

There were four bands of hostile Indians still roaming free in southwestern Florida alone: one band led by Sam Jones with Chitto Tustenuggee and Holata Mico (Billy Bowlegs) as war chiefs; another band led by Hospetarke with Passacka as war chief; a third led by Otalke Thlocco, known as the Prophet; and the so-called Spanish Indians led by Chakaika. Of all these chiefs, only Chitto had dealt with General Macomb. There were other bands in other areas of Florida, the one led by Coacoochee, for example, who was still dangerously at large. Since General Macomb was an intelligent man, we may assume that he made the agreement with an unrepresentative knot of Indians in the hope that it might in time touch more and more of the Indians and might lead finally to the real end of the war.[32]

The officers who had been serving in Florida were skeptical of Macomb's success. One of them couched his disbelief in the following bit of irony: "Having awaited with breathless anxiety until daybreak, we had the satisfaction of discerning something approaching the fort. I ordered the gate thrown open. A canine female, apparently in distress, came voluntarily in, and seemed to ask protection. . . . Quarters were furnished, and the subsistence department directed to issue the proper rations. In the course of the day I had the inexpressible pleasure of an addition of eight more of the same tribe, which were brought in and delivered by the aforesaid female, whose Indian name we have been unable to learn. . . .

"From the avidity with which this poor creature received our bounty, the subsistence department of our late enemy's army have been considerably reduced, and in all probability, many more will come in.

"Returning thanks to that high functionary whose diplomatic sagacity has showered blessings upon our army. . . ." General Taylor, who had no gift for irony, was equally skeptical, but at the same time ready to carry out orders. Governor Call, for his part, was determined to proceed against small bands of renegade Creeks who were moving into Florida, contending that they were not included in the agreement. Taylor gave orders to issue him the supplies he needed, but on no account to bring the regulars into the fight, as that would violate Macomb's truce.[33]

While the commanding general was in Florida, Taylor took the opportunity to ask to be relieved. Floridians, he explained, were so hostile to him and to the regulars that necessary cooperation was all but impossible. Some of them even incited the Seminoles to continue the fight in order to keep government money flowing into Florida. Moreover, Missouri had raised a shrill cry over the handling of her volunteers at Okeechobee, and he wished a court of inquiry to examine his conduct in that action. Macomb forwarded the request to Washington, but as the Secretary was not there, a reply was slow in coming. When Poinsett did answer, he denied the general's request for relief and also for a court of inquiry. Taylor need not be concerned, he wrote, because the Floridians were antiregular. This was not his fault. As for Missouri's complaints, both Missouri senators had pronounced Taylor free of blame.[34]

Events in several quarters of Florida worked rapidly to break down Macomb's peace. On June 5, 1839, thirty Indians escaped from Tampa where they had been waiting to be sent west. At once Taylor caused those remaining in custody to be put aboard ships. On July 17 marauders murdered the Chaires family and escaped undetected. The murderers were presumed to be renegade Creeks or small Seminole bands who had not heard of the new order. Combining with this hopeful presump-

William S. Harney

tion was at least one peaceful gesture, which helped to hold the agreement nominally in operation. Near Fort Lauderdale Sam Jones himself came in to hear the terms. Professing to like what he heard, he ordered his people to live up to the agreement. The conduct of other bands was neither peaceful nor overtly hostile. The commandant at Fort Andrews in Middle Florida observed that the band camping near him went off every few days and returned with powder, lead, tobacco, and clothes. Where and from whom these were procured, he could not say.[35]

Short of crisis, yet far from peaceful, affairs in Florida rocked along during the summer of 1839. On July 20 General Taylor reported the results of his activities in the last eight months: 53 new posts, 848 miles of wagon road, and 3,643 feet of causeways and bridges. It had been necessary to build a bridge 340 feet long over the Oklawaha River at a place where the stream itself was only eight yards wide. This was a measure of the engineering difficulties encountered, but a growing web of communications and strongpoints made it ever more difficult for the Indians to maintain themselves.[36]

Of course General Macomb's peace slowed down the organization of Taylor's system of squares. Even so, Taylor reported that his men had searched every hammock and swamp. Two officers and six enlisted men of the regular force had been waylaid and killed in the process, yet the general felt that the Seminoles had tried hard to avoid collision with the army. On the other hand, they harassed the native whites at every opportunity. He concluded that the only way to subdue the Indians was to prevent them from hunting and fishing.[37]

Pursuant to Macomb's agreement, it was up to General Taylor to see that a trading post was established on the Caloosahatchee River within the bounds of the Indian reservation. In July James B. Dallam, an infantryman who liked Florida and wished to remain there, was appointed trader, and a force of twenty-six men, armed with Colt's rifles, under Lieutenant Colonel William Selby Harney, Second Dragoons, was assigned to give him protection while the new post was being established. Harney was then in his prime. Thirty-nine years old, he stood six feet three inches, and was so well proportioned that Cassius M. Clay called him the finest specimen of manhood he had ever seen. Harney could command by his mere presence. Unfortunately, he displayed some qualities of the bully, especially where "inferior" races were concerned.[38]

Dallam's store was erected about fifteen or twenty miles from the mouth of the Caloosahatchee, and Harney's military detachment set up its camp a short distance away. The duty was light and boring, and on July 23, 1839, Harney took a boat to the mouth of the river to hunt wild boars. Returning to the camp about nine that night, he threw himself down somewhat apart from his men and slept heavily. A clash of arms aroused him. Soon realizing that Indians had attacked the camp and that he could do nothing to save it by himself, he sprinted down a path toward the river in shirt and underdrawers. Footsteps beat closer and closer behind him until he turned at bay, determined to defend himself with his fists. "Come on, you red devils!" he yelled furiously. He heard an Irish brogue, "Holy saints, Colonel, is it you?" too late to stop the sledgehammer blow he had aimed in the darkness. Down went one of the sergeants, but the next minute Harney picked him up, apologized, and the two escaped downstream together in a boat.[39]

The other white men were not so fortunate. There was no guard on duty, and 160 Indians, divided into two bands, had achieved complete surprise. One band led by Hospetarke attacked the store, the other under Chakaika assailed the camp. Striking simultaneously they were able to wipe out or capture eighteen men. Fourteen men escaped, including Private Luther, who, though wounded, managed to get away and to live on oysters for fifteen days until he was rescued. The survivors recorded the heroic conduct of Dallam's unusually large Irish setter. The big red dog took his stand over the body of his master and could not be moved until the Indians shot him.[40]

For the attackers the loot was substantial: $2,000 to $3,000 worth of trade goods, and $1,500 in silver coins, besides the personal effects and the Colt's rifles of many of the soldiers. On the white side there was much explaining to do. Harney blamed General Taylor who, he said, had refused to give him a big enough detachment to do the job, and had been unwilling to assign him another commissioned officer. This lack, said Harney, made it necessary to leave a sergeant in charge when he was absent. Blame for failure to post a guard rested upon Sergeant John Bigelow.[41]

Chakaika was chief of a band called Spanish Indians who up to this point had taken no part in the war. They lived in the vicinity of the Caloosahatchee, and some writers have contended that they were a remnant of the once powerful Calusas. In reality they were Seminoles set apart from the other bands largely because of their remote dwelling place.[42]

A giant Negro named Samson was wounded in the leg and captured by the raiders. If his story is to be believed, the rest of the captives would have been better off had they met sudden death. Torture was rare among the Seminoles, but Samson claimed that it was used in this instance. Because of the intervention of Holata Mico, Sergeant Simmons lived on for three months, but then was killed by very cruel means. The Negro interpreter and one other man were burned to death in an agony which lasted six hours.[43]

The assault on Harney was considered by the whites an act of unspeakable treachery and a betrayal of General Macomb's agreement. Almost beyond doubt the attacking Indians knew of that agreement, but may never have considered themselves bound by it. The two Seminole leaders who reached agreement with Macomb had no authority over numerous other bands. Be that as it may, the attack reopened the war and gave it an added bitterness. When Lieutenant W. K. Hanson, in command at Fort Mellon, heard the news, he surrounded the fifty-one Indians peacefully camping close to his installation and shipped them off to Charleston. In all quarters murder and rapine blazed up. There was a brisk action near Orange Lake and one at Fort Andrews, where seventeen men stood off forty Indians. Tiger Tail, so white reports said, ordered his followers to split up into bands of five and to kill all white men they saw. Not knowing this, four soldiers accepted an invitation to go to visit his camp. When the Indians turned on them, they leapt into the river to escape, but only one got back to his camp.[44]

Atrocities became so frequent in the settled parts of Florida that General Macomb ordered Taylor to use the regulars to drive out the Indians in the area north of a line from the mouth of the Withlacoochee to Palatka. Meanwhile Taylor had collected nearly two hundred prisoners. He let the chiefs know that these would be freed if the "murderers" who had attacked Harney's detachment were delivered up. The Tallahassee *Floridian* denounced this policy as soft, and suggested that Taylor had proved himself incompetent. There was a disposition in Florida, Taylor said, to take the command away from the army and give it to a civilian. This must not be. The war had to be conducted altogether by the people of Florida or by the government; it could not be done by both at once. Of the same mind, Colonel William Davenport asked to be relieved of the command in Middle Florida. "An evil genius seems to preside over the affairs of Florida," he wrote, "whose agency I am unable to control." One assumes that that evil genius was Governor Call. There were influential persons higher up the chain of command who had the same opinion. On November 29, 1839, Secretary Poinsett wrote President Van Buren that the transfer of hostilities to Middle Florida had brought military and civil authorities closer together. Call, he continued, had failed to win the respect of the Army of the South when he commanded it, and had been bitter against the regular service ever since his removal. With this relationship, necessary cooperation was impossible. Bluntly Poinsett asked that Call be removed as governor. The President tersely endorsed the letter, "Let Call be superceded and Judge Reid put in his place."[45]

This action brought forth from Call a memorial to Congress running to more than 6,000 words. The butt of its sharpest barbs was the Secretary of War. Call asked Congress to decide whether Poinsett "should not be held responsible to his country for the blood which has been shed through the weakness and imbecility of his administration of the War Department." Poinsett, and indeed President Van Buren himself, had deemed a campaign against political opponents in New York far more important than one against the "treacherous Seminoles" in Florida. Because Call had been critical, Poinsett had maneuvered to bring about his downfall. The only charge against him, Call said, was that he had criticized the Secretary of War. "If it be an offence requiring such a penalty, to hold the plans and policy pursued by Mr. Poinsett in prosecuting the Florida War in contempt, a policy which has desolated the fairest portion of this Territory, bankrupt the National Treasury, and covered our people with mourning . . . Your Memorialist pleads guilty. . . . If the removal from Office of Your Memorialist was necessary to sustain the political party of the President in this Territory, let this also be assigned as a reason. . . ."[46] Some Floridians agreed with Call that his removal was a consequence of dirty politics. On the other hand, David Levy congratulated Poinsett on his part in the affair.

Although contemporaries were divided, modern scholars concede that Robert Raymond Reid, the new governor, was a notable person. Call's biographer so describes him. "Reid was a remarkable man: an urbane scholar, a gentleman, an intellectual who shrewdly evaluated his fellow men; he analyzed his own mind, dissected his vices with philosophic resignation, and wrestled with religious dogma, always wanting to believe but never quite able to do so. In his calm introspection, his tact, his discretion, his humanitarian impulses, his shrinking from physical exertion, he presents a picture of a man quite opposite in temperament from Call." The substitution of Reid for Call, however, made no appreciable difference in the conduct of the war.[47]

Taylor now mounted a campaign to drive the Indians east of the Suwannee. He commanded 3,071 regulars made up of at least parts of almost every unit in the army. The force he meant to use in Middle Florida included the First and Sixth Infantry Regiments, three companies of the Third Artillery, and two companies of the Second Infantry, yet the aggregate strength of all these came only to 21 officers and 331 men. The campaign went forward, but its results, though solid, were by no means decisive.[48]

Through no initiative of Taylor's, one of the notorious episodes of the war now occurred. General Jesup, as early as July, 1837, had said that a few bloodhounds would be worth an army and had asked how the country would react to their use, but the matter had gone no further. In 1838 Secretary Poinsett authorized Taylor to procure some dogs, or so it was claimed in Congress; but the general apparently had not Jesup's opinion of them and did not bother to get the dogs. That was the state of affairs when the Territorial government of Florida took the initiative. The governor and legislative council were impressed by the story of the use of bloodhounds during the Maroon Revolt in Jamaica, 1655-1739. This war had dragged on eighty years, but it was concluded within a year after bloodhounds were introduced. Accordingly, Governor Call sent Colonel Richard Fitzpatrick to Cuba. Fitzpatrick bought thirty-three bloodhounds at $151.72 each and secured four trainers to come with them. They were established for training at Magnolia in Middle Florida under the direction of the quarter-master general for the Territory. On January 27, 1840, Governor Reid offered the dogs to the army, and Taylor accepted two of them for trial. In the fullness of time Florida billed Taylor for $2,429.52, but the general declined to pay it on the grounds that the hounds failed their tests. They were trained to track Negroes, he said, and could not be induced to nose out Indians. This caused abolitionists in Congress, such as Joshua Giddings of Ohio, to declare that they had been imported to hunt down runaway slaves, not to end the Indian War at all. The navy procured some dogs too, but derived no good from them.[49]

The importation of the dogs created a stir in Congress and across the nation out of all proportion to its importance. Congressmen introduced resolutions demanding to know if the United States had ordered them. Secretary Poinsett replied that the governor and council of Florida had imported them without the knowledge of the War Department. As soon as he learned of it, he had written to General Taylor directing that they might not be used by the army unless leashed and muzzled. But he did not forbid their use. Senator James Buchanan of Pennsylvania presented a memorial from members of the Society of Friends that such an inhuman method should not be employed. The situation was remarkable enough to provoke former President John Quincy Adams to submit the following resolution on March 9, 1840, to the House of Representatives, of which he was a member: "That the Secretary of War be directed to report to this House, the natural, political, and martial history of the bloodhounds, showing the peculiar fitness of that class of warriors to be the associates of the gallant army of the United States, specifying the nice discrimination of his scent between the blood of the freeman and the blood of the slave . . . between the blood of savage Seminoles and that of the Anglo-Saxon pious Christian. . . . Also, whether a further importation of the same heroic race into the State of

Maine, to await the contingency of a contested Northeastern boundary question is contemplated, or only to set an example to be followed by our possible adversary in the event of a conflict. Whether measures have been taken to secure exclusively to ourselves the employment of this auxiliary force, and whether he deems it expedient to extend to the said bloodhounds and their posterity the benefits of the pension laws." Other people also protested, but the system had friends as well. One friend writing in the Tallahassee *Floridian* regretted the Secretary's order to muzzle the brutes, for he hoped they would "tear to pieces" the "red devils." But in the end their employment proved neither inhuman nor useful. The hounds aided in the capture of two Indians, but no more.[50]

During the summer of 1838 Congress enacted the third enlargement of the army since its drastic cut in 1821. The First Dragoons had come into being as a result of the Black Hawk War in 1832, and the Second Dragoons because of the Seminoles in 1836. Now on July 5 the whole military establishment was given a general increase. Each of the four regiments of artillery acquired an additional company, and every company received sixteen additional privates. One sergeant and thirty-eight privates were added to each infantry company, and an entire new regiment, the Eighth United States Infantry, was authorized. The Engineering, Quartermaster, Commissary, and Ordnance Departments received permission to add a number of officers. Finally, the President was allowed to re-equip two existing infantry regiments as rifle units, and a third as light infantry. All this increased the authorized strength to 11,800 enlisted men. Since officers were in short supply, they were no longer to be loaned out for civil engineering projects nor otherwise permitted to work for private concerns. The need for them in their units was far too pressing.[51]

The act did not provide for additional medical officers, and these remained very scarce. The entire army contained 90 surgeons and assistant surgeons, of which 34 were in Florida. The navy had a total of 124, but the number of them serving in Florida is not known. Some enlisted men referred to the medics who were present as quacks. In terms of mid-twentieth-century medical knowledge most of the treatment administered was certainly more nearly quackery than medicine. General

Taylor's chief complaint was that the surgeon general left his letters unanswered. For what slight significance there may be in it, one is struck by the lack of professional material in the otherwise very revealing diaries kept by surgeons in the Florida war.[52]*

In an attempt to stimulate recruiting, Congress raised the pay of privates to eight dollars per month, with two dollars withheld each month until a tour of duty was completed. It also awarded three months' extra pay to any man who reenlisted, and 160 acres of land for ten years of faithful enlisted service. Two of these provisions lasted only a couple of days. Congress, repenting of its openhandedness, reduced the pay to seven dollars (with only one dollar withheld) and abrogated the land grant. One clause in the new act must have repelled more prospects than it attracted; it substituted sugar and coffee for the liquor ration which had been general issue for so long.[53]

Military uniforms had become so functional in the field that at fifty yards you could not tell a colonel from a second lieutenant. A wit, writing in the *Army and Navy Chronicle*, offered a system of identification: let colonels go entirely unshaven, while lieutenants shaved a track through their hair and grew a beard on one side of the face. A correspondent who saw no wit in such flippancy wrote that he observed a lamentable tendency to break down the natural barriers separating the classes. Army officers, he said, were upper class, and it was time the people stopped treating them as servants. A surgeon in St. Louis conducted his own private research on the status of enlisted men and why they entered the service. Of fifty-five recruits, nine-tenths had enlisted because of women, he found. Forty-three of them also had a problem with drink. On the other hand, one-third of them had been well placed in society: four had been lawyers, three doctors, and two ministers of the gospel.[54]

The war often seemed, it is necessary to repeat, to be primarily a struggle between regulars and citizen soldiers. A militiaman claimed in the St. Augustine *Florida Herald* that regular officers had committed many outrages upon Florida citizens. One man was made to ride the wooden horse because

* See the diaries of Forry, Jarvis, Strobel, and Motte.

he refused to work on Sunday.* Apparently willing to print both sides of the issue, another newspaper carried the statement that regulars were more reliable than militia. A reader swiftly rejoined, and the Tallahassee *Floridian* printed, "you ought to have your nose pulled and your ears cut off." To favor the regulars was to subvert republican government.[55]

Regulars, on the other hand, found the militia a feeble dependence. By Governor Call's own admission they would not turn out if they had to walk; nor would they respond, even on horseback, if obliged to travel away from home. The draft produced little from them, in one case just six men to serve out of sixty called. An officer reported that a Florida company under his command was so encumbered with women and children that it could not possibly be moved.[56]

The romantic approach to the Seminole War had died with Osceola, at least for the regulars. One subaltern serving in the sweltering heat gave terse expression to the shift in expectations. In the feverish summer, he said, the healthy soldiers were mostly occupied tending the sick and burying the dead. "And this is warfare, glorious, noble chivalrous warfare!" Adding to the soldiers' disillusionment, even in time of war promotion came slowly, if at all. To get ahead it was often necessary to enlist influential civilian aid, and the officers did not hesitate to do so. One captain begged an important citizen to intercede for him to get a promotion for which he had been waiting thirty-one years. Either he was entitled to promotion, he said, or else he should have been forced out of the service long before.[57]

Professional soldiers often thought that talk in Congress was uninformed and unjust. Congressman William Montgomery of North Carolina, for example, said that United States arms had been hopelessly disgraced in the Seminole War. There had been paper victories in Florida, but the vanquished were still present in strength. The army did not prevent depredations, but ineffectively pursued outlaws after they had gone. The congressman was convinced that regular officers could not wage this type of war successfully; they had lived elegantly in the cities too long to enter the forest and give a

---

* To ride a wooden horse was to sit astride a narrow plank with weights suspended from the feet.

good account of themselves. "We only want a Jackson for a short time to settle the whole matter." In the absence of so great a leader, the thing to do was to drill and arm the militia, for it could conquer. Increases in the army since 1821 pointed to military despotism. Moreover, army officers had done more than any single group to increase the cost of government. Montgomery admitted ruefully that he would vote for the war appropriation, but wished he could see the money paid to the people of Florida rather than to the army.[58]

Throughout the country there was a good deal of sympathy for the Indians. Most of the regular officers considered the removal of the Seminoles to be cruel and unnecessary, and sometimes they wrote as much to the folks at home. Major Hitchcock entered in his diary, "The government is in the wrong, and this is the chief cause of the persevering opposition of the Indians, who have nobly defended their country against our attempt to enforce a fraudulent treaty." Lieutenant John T. Sprague had the same reaction. "Their sin," he wrote in his diary, "is patriotism, as true as ever burned in the heart of the most civilized." Now and again such sentiments were uttered in Congress, but when this happened there was always swift rebuttal. Delegate Downing never let the House listen without an antidote to such poisonous words. Those who spoke so, he said, had read too many of James Fenimore Cooper's books. Let them go and live among the Indians, and they would change their outlook. At home in Florida newspaper utterances were not so restrained. Sympathy for the Indians, they vowed, was criminally misplaced, for the Seminoles were fiends in human shape, a disgrace to humanity. Later, new Governor Robert Raymond Reid said the war was waged against "beasts of prey," while the *Floridian* suggested that it would be a good policy to offer a reward of a thousand dollars for each Indian brought in, dead or alive.[59]

Life went on elsewhere as if there were no war in Florida. North of the peninsula the evacuation westward of the Cherokees was creating the notorious "Trail of Tears." Floridians could only envy so simple a solution as this, for their problem seemed insoluble. Farther north there was trouble between Illinoisans and Mormons. At the seat of government it was discovered that Samuel Swartwout, one of Andrew Jackson's loyal supporters, collector of the port of New York, had taken for himself more than a million dollars of public money. Disorders flourished to the south and the north of the United States. Southward the French had blockaded Mexico and on December 18, 1838, had assaulted Veracruz. Their assault cost the Mexican national hero a leg, but General Antonio López de Santa Anna was later to figure in United States history. Beyond Mexico, Chile and Peru were fighting each other. Northward there were internal disturbances in Canada which might any day have implicated the United States. In the event of a clash with France over Mexico or with England over Canada, the United States would be handicapped for having most of its military strength in Florida.[60] In June, 1837, Victoria became Queen of England and in time gave her name to an age.

Certain personnel changes in Washington were important to Florida. On the last day of June, 1838, Mahlon Dickerson stepped out as Secretary of the Navy and James K. Paulding, author and politician, stepped in. On October 22, 1838, Carey A. Harris left the post of Commissioner of Indian Affairs, and T. Hartley Crawford, an unusually energetic public servant, took his place.[61]

Considering the immediacy of the war, many aspects of life in Florida went on with surprising regularity. The population grew by 20,000 from 1830 to 1840, despite the hostilities. It was, it is true, necessary to send troops with the United States marshal to take the census in 1840, but the count was made. The greatest concentration of people was in Middle Florida where there were 15,779 in 1830 and 34,238 in 1840. The total population in 1840 was 54,477. The Southern Life Insurance and Trust Company marketed its notes, and other vendors offered town lots in Florida to investors who preferred the good earth to paper securities. Southern College prepared to begin classes in St. Augustine.[62]

Florida tradesmen were concerned that their currency had fallen into chaos in spite of the huge sums spent in the Territory. The federal government was also selective; it announced that it would take in payment for public land only twenty-dollar bills or larger from banks which were redeeming their paper in specie. In spite of everything, Florida bonds sold in Europe at 2 per cent above par. This must have startled some of the local conservatives who felt that overissue was endangering the credit of the Territory. David Levy blamed former Governor Call for much of the financial trouble. The $350,000 worth of bonds Call had caused to be issued had started Florida on the road to ruin. A contributor to the *Floridian* noted that the per capita debt in Florida had risen to $140 which was as much as that in Great Britain. Doubtless a deep-dyed Jacksonian, he inveighed against Wall Street stockjobbers and gamblers and their Florida counterparts. "By means of their rag-monied institutions, their gossamer stocks, their banks without the shadow of a soul," they had done Florida as much harm as the Indians. In the same vein, one John Branch wrote President Van Buren that he feared, "the insiduous [*sic*] encroachments of a paper aristocracy." John Branch would be the last governor of the Territory of Florida. Land speculators came into a windfall too, for in 1839 the Supreme Court found in favor of the assigns of the grantee of the Arredondo Tract, which had been in litigation since 1828. But all Floridians closed ranks when the northern press charged that they sought to prolong the war. Far from profiting because of the war, they wrote, Florida had been set back ten years by it, and those persons who made such charges were of course the tools of abolitionists and Indian lovers.[63]

Forces other than the Seminoles operated to undercut Florida's economy. After the freeze of 1835 had ruined the citrus crop, growers had tried some replanting, but in a year or two the new trees were ruined by the "purple scale," somehow transplanted from China. Tree-minded, profit-seeking Floridians planted mulberries and in 1838 went heavily into the culture of silk. For a time it seemed as if this industry might replace the wrecked citrus business. Then in the winter of 1839 the price of silk dropped ruinously, and the infant silk culture went to the wall.[64]

In November, 1839, Joseph M. White died; he had been Florida's third delegate to Congress. Two months later, in January, 1840, violence, no stranger to him, re-visited Leigh Read. As he was sitting down to dinner in the City Hotel at Tallahassee, he was attacked by Willis Alston, whose brother he had killed in a duel some years before. Alston shot him through the hips and cut him in the abdomen, yet Read lived, but from that time forward could never escape dwelling in the shadow of violent death. Alston escaped to Texas, where before long he was killed by an avenger of Leigh Read.[65]

Since 1837 there had been an active movement in the Territory to try to gain admission to the Union as a state, and there had been an almost equally brisk opposition, centered primarily in East Florida. A precondition to admission was the adoption of a feasible constitution. In January, 1839, a convention met at St. Joseph to draw one up. The sharpest division among the members was over the status of banks. Wealthy and powerful men sought to insert provisions which would make a favorable climate for banking, but they were effectively forestalled. The drafted constitution was submitted during the year to the voters, and they adopted it by a very narrow margin, about 95 votes out of 4,000. This was an essential step toward statehood, but the succeeding steps were to be delayed several years.[66]

Not all aspects of life, by any means, ran on as if there was no war. The courts had not met in Columbia County for three years because of the Indians. This recess caused many inconveniences, but none more disturbing than that suffered by John Bryan. His wife had run off and was living in adultery with another man, yet John could not obtain a divorce. To give him relief the legislature granted him a divorce by enactment.[67]

By spring, 1839, Florida was more closely tied to the rest of the nation than before. The steamer *Florida* ran twice a week from Savannah to Picolata and back. Its run made travel possible by steamer from Maine into the very heart of the peninsula. About the time this link was completed, the army bought two steamers and turned them over to the navy to operate. This was overdue economy, although on the surface it might seem an extravagance. Entire fleets of rented vessels had run up demurrage bills because their unloading was poorly organized. Marine rents were exorbitant. One small steamer was offered for sale to the government for $5,000, but was rejected. It later earned from the War Department $80,000 in rent at $300 per day. This was far from being an isolated case. It was even charged that wood for the steamers could only be bought at excessive prices.[68]

14

Walker Keith Armistead

GENERAL ZACHARY TAYLOR finally received permission to leave the Florida command, the harshest service in the United States, on April 21, 1840. Three weeks passed before he could arrange affairs well enough to depart. Even then he did not know who his successor was to be, so he installed the senior officer, Colonel David E. Twiggs, as temporary commander in Florida, and gladly left the theater. After several changes of station, he found himself assigned to Fort Gibson and then to Fort Smith, Arkansas—out of Florida, but not out of contact with the Seminoles.[1]

Meanwhile, the War Department had picked Brevet Brigadier General Walker Keith Armistead to succeed him. Armistead formally assumed control on May 5, 1840, and Taylor left on May 11, but the new commander claimed that he did not know Taylor's plans. Less is known of him than of the other Florida commanders. Even the exact date of his birth in Virginia is not known, though the year was probably 1785. If so, he was fifty-five when given the post, a year older than Taylor was when he took command. According to the *Biographical Register of Graduates of the United States Military Academy*, Armistead was appointed a cadet in that brand new institution because of good behavior as an orderly sergeant at the Battle of Fallen Timbers, on August 20, 1794. If this were true, he would have been nine years old when he took part in that historic fight. In any case, he did enter West Point in the second class (composed of three men), and graduated in 1803 at the top of it. Thereafter he proved himself an above-average engineer. Serving on the Niagara front during the War of 1812, he attained the rank of lieutenant colonel. Afterward, in 1818, he became chief of engineers with the grade of colonel. Three years later the reduction of 1821 took him out of the engineers and into the command of the Third Artillery Regiment. Then in ten years, following the regulations of that time, he was brevetted brigadier general for a decade of faithful service. He had served under General Jesup in Florida on two earlier occasions.[2]

Armistead was a more mechanical and punctilious man than either Jesup or Taylor. Unfortunately the only two associates to leave written comments on his ability were usually hypercritical of all they saw. Captain Nathaniel Wyche Hunter, also a West Pointer, referred to him as a "grey bearded and imbecile dotard." Ethan Allen Hitchcock disapproved of his methods of dealing with the Indians and labeled his character "puerile." Armistead divided Florida into two command zones, delimited by the Suwannee River, and put Colonel David E. Twiggs in command of the eastern section. Yet in later years Twiggs declined to shake his hand. This was probably more a reflection upon Twiggs than upon Armistead.[3]

It fell to Armistead to seek reward for Captain Gabriel J. Rains of the Seventh Infantry for gallantry displayed in March while General Taylor still commanded. Rains had been so severely wounded that he could not make a formal report until two months after the event. This was the story. He had led sixteen men out of Fort King on a scouting mission on March 28, 1840, when a band of ninety-three Indians opened fire from ambush. The first volley killed two men and wounded another. The soldiers got behind trees and returned the fire, but Rains soon saw that they would be encircled. He led a charge of twelve men back toward the fort. Down he went, badly wounded, but three of his men carried him to safety while three others acted as rear guard. Even before Rains made his belated report, Florida newspapers had called his action the most gallant of the war. The captain himself, who was not expected to live, received a brevet majority upon General Armistead's recommendation. He did recover and he lived long enough to become a major general in the Confederate service twenty-one years later.[4]

Like his predecessors, General Armistead projected a strategy. His hope was to strike before the extreme heat came. This action would give the troops needed occupation and destroy Seminole crops. He would continue the effort into the summer, and explore the immense section of country, never thoroughly explored before, from the Withlacoochee to the St. Johns north of Fort Mellon. The general established the headquarters of the Army of the South at Fort King. He had nine hundred men there whom he intended to employ in detachments, each one hundred strong. Meanwhile Lieutenant Colonel Green was directed to move up and down the west bank of the Suwannee to prevent infiltration into Middle Florida. Finally, the general projected an imaginary line running east and west through Fort King. His hope was to turn over the defense of the area north of that line to citizen soldiers, and thereby free the regulars to guard the line itself, and to explore, and probe, and harass the savages below it until all were finally forced to emigrate.[5]

A number of the Seminoles were north of Armistead's east-west line; indeed, within two weeks of his assuming command they had murdered four families in the populous area along the Apalachicola River, and at the same time threatened Newnansville in Alachua County. Armistead claimed that his concentration at Fort King prevented them from destroying Newnansville. It did not, however, prevent serious reverses north of the line. Coacoochee, leading from eighty to one hundred warriors, fell upon a detachment under Lieutenant James S. Sanderson on May 19, 1840, eight miles from Micanopy. He killed the lieutenant and five of the men. Around the same time Coacoochee attacked an unescorted carriage and a large baggage wagon carrying a theatrical troupe to St. Augustine from the steamboat landing at Picolata. Three actors were killed, but three escaped; one by hiding in the brush beside the road, another by snapping a pistol at his pursuers, and a third, for some unaccountable reason, by the grace or the oversight of the attackers themselves. The Negro driver of the wagon also eluded capture. While the Indians were plundering, another

Walker Keith Armistead

wagon came into view from St. Augustine, carrying a Negro driver and three white persons. Two of these whites were killed. After this incident a cry of help arose from Picolata where only nine men made up the garrison. In contrast, a yelp of joy issued from Coacoochee's band. The captured wagon contained eighteen trunks full of theatrical costumes, grander attire than the Indians had ever seen before.[6]

Notwithstanding the terror spread by this chief in the vicinity of St. Augustine, the white forces did slowly tighten a net about the Seminoles. Certain of Armistead's subordinates had a talent for guerrilla-style warfare. Their penetration of Coacoochee's hideaway at Wekiva was said to have started the chief on his orgy of vengeful attacks.* He drifted southward, and Armistead, in response, ordered the reopening of Fort Mellon to be used as a base. Especially successful was Captain B. L. E. Bonneville of the Seventh Infantry. In June, 1840, he probed into a retreat in Big Swamp, only fifteen miles from Fort King, where the Seminoles had been safe throughout the war. There he scattered a hundred Indians as they furtively tried to carry out the ritual of the Green Corn Dance. Another skillful guerrilla fighter was Lieutenant Colonel Bennett Riley, Second Infantry. He requested and received permission from Armistead to use his troops as a partisan corps. He led them in a sharp action on June 2, 1840, at Chocachatti, and destroyed an important Seminole stronghold. His reward was a brevet colonelcy. When W. S. Harney asked permission to dress his men like Indians, Armistead disapproved; army regulations, he said, would not permit it. But functioning within the limits, Armistead's lieutenants found and destroyed haunts where the Seminoles had been safe for many years. They discovered flourishing fields in Wahoo Swamp and at Chocachatti where it had been supposed the Indians would no longer dare to live. More cultivated fields were uncovered along the Oklawaha. All in all, by midsummer these ferrets had destroyed five hundred acres of the Indians' crops. The units they used were surprisingly large for such a purpose, two or two and one-half times the bands of one hundred which Armistead had projected.[7]

* This Wekiva was probably on a tributary, so named, of the St. Johns River, along what is now the border between Seminole and Lake Counties.

Late in June, Lieutenant Colonel Harney captured the mother of Coacoochee. For an unknown reason she was willing to conduct her captors to the village through which trade had been carried on with sailing vessels. Armistead pointed out acidly that the navy had denied the existence of this trade.[8]

To assure efficient supply lines, Armistead moved the main depot from Garey's Ferry to Palatka where the government purchased a sizeable plot and turned it into a service area (which lasted into the 1880's). He established general hospitals at Cedar Key and at Picolata because these towns were thought to be healthy sites. The general took a very independent attitude toward the Territorial government. He would not brook Governor Reid's trying to dictate to him how much Florida militia should be taken into federal service. His relations with Reid deteriorated so far that he asked the War Department to take over all communication with him. In addition he refused to consult any of Reid's colonels when using Florida troops. Yet distasteful as it was to him, he had to ask for a total of 1,500 Florida militiamen. These were under the command of Leigh Read, now a general and now recovered from the wounds Alston had inflicted upon him. Armistead felt certain that he could have his line of demarcation garrisoned by July 15, 1840. Accordingly, the Secretary of War relieved him of responsibility for defending the settlements in his rear and gave him permission to remove all regulars from the area north of the line.[9]

Indian Key lay roughly seventy-five miles from Cape Florida and about as many from Key West. There in 1825 Jacob Housman had founded a demesne. He made a good deal of money salvaging wrecks along the dangerous east coast of Florida, and by 1834 had invested $40,000 of it in his key. Determined to protect so heavy an investment when the Seminole War broke out, he organized a militia to defend his property. This force, unfortunately, was disbanded in 1838 when a revenue cutter made its base there. Even while the war went on, Housman was successful at having Dade County created in 1836 and his island made its county seat. He put up his own money to build the courthouse.[10]

Housman was a bold and enterprising man, but he might have died unknown had not Dr. Henry Perrine come to Indian

Key. Perrine was a horticulturist who wished to experiment with tropical plants in Florida. Congress granted him a whole township on the mainland in 1838 for that purpose, but because of the war he could not occupy it. Anxious, however, to be in the area, he took his family to live at Indian Key in December, 1838. Housman was proud to have the Perrines there even though the doctor would not let his ladies associate with the owner and the flashy woman who purported to be his wife. Twenty pleasant months passed for the Perrines, only to be barbarously terminated at dawn on August 7, 1840. A band of the so-called Spanish Indians, led by Chakaika of Harney Massacre fame, paddled in seventeen canoes the thirty miles from the mainland and landed at dawn on Indian Key. They began to pillage the island, and when Dr. Perrine tried to reason with them, they killed him. His family made a miraculous escape, hiding in the cellar of a burning house, and got to Tea Table Key where a naval detachment was based. As it happened, no naval personnel were present just then except twelve invalids and the attending surgeon. Midshipman Murray, one of the patients, loaded five of the invalids into a boat with a small cannon and set out for the hostile shore. When bullets began to whistle, he fired the cannon, which recoiled overboard. The Indians had found a six-pounder on shore, and they loaded it with musket balls and turned it upon Murray's boat. This is one of the few instances when American Indians fired an artillery piece. Of course Murray could do nothing but retreat, leaving the Indians to escape with several barrels of powder and many valuable provisions. Of the seventy souls who lived on Indian Key, only thirteen had been killed, but their houses were all in ruins. Now in a bad plight financially, Housman made the government a proposition by which he hoped to recoup his losses: he would catch or kill all Indians in South Florida at two hundred dollars a head. The Administration paid no attention. Housman was killed in an accident in May, 1841.[11]

Because murders and depredations continued in the settled parts of Florida, Secretary Poinsett authorized the acceptance of more Florida militia into federal service, and even agreed that five hundred of them might remain at home as guards. In return, the previous division of responsibility was to be strictly

adhered to; that is, it was up to citizen soldiers, without regular army help, to protect the area north of the east-west line
running through Fort King. To stimulate activity south of the
line, the Eighth Infantry was sent to Florida, where Armistead directed that it be concentrated at Fort King. With the
arrival of the Eighth the following regular regiments were
in Florida: ten companies of the Second Dragoons, headquar-
tered at Fort Heilman; nine companies of the Third Artillery
at St. Augustine; the First, Second, and Eighth Infantry at
Fort King; the Third and Sixth Infantry at Fort Brooke; and
the Seventh Infantry at Micanopy.[12]

At the end of the first week of action General Armistead
sent a notice to all commanders to avoid hostile operations lest
they upset forthcoming conferences. A council was scheduled
with two of the most important chiefs still at large, Tiger Tail
(Thlocklo Tustenuggee), a Tallahassee, and Halleck Tustenuggee, a Mikasuki. Tiger Tail was always well received because
he knew how to act in white society. His father's village had
stood on the site later occupied by the town of Tallahassee, but
Tiger Tail had practically lived at the home of Robert Gamble.
An urbane man and a banker, Gamble was one of the bank
party in Florida, a member of what we would now call the
power elite. Tiger Tail's affection for the family was such
that Gamble's home on the Wauculla River was undisturbed
throughout the conflict. Tiger Tail spoke English fluently, kept
the sabbath, and treated his family white-style. Everyone knew
him in Middle Florida because he had been a common lounger
in the streets of Tallahassee. More than six feet tall, well built,
with very dark skin and many furrows in his face, he was a
conspicuous figure. Mouth and nose were both remarkably
large. His nickname dated back to the Treaty of Moultrie
Creek, when at a ball game he had worn a strip of panther
skin dangling at his belt.

Halleck Tustenuggee came out of a different mold. He was
as tall as Tiger Tail, but his face was as smooth and delicate as
a woman's. He too had genteel manners, but the white men
who knew him felt that he had never known pity or sympathy
and were sure that he hated their race. They acknowledged
that his intellect was remarkable, but they rated his sensibili-
ties as those of a true savage. Behind his sweet smile and un-

assuming manner lurked a fierce spirit.[13] He had murdered his
own sister because she favored surrender, and had threatened
other members of the band with a similar fate. Later when
one of them accused him of selling out the Seminole cause, he
sprang upon him and tore off his right ear with his teeth.

At the all-important council which met after some delays
on November 10, 1840, Halleck wore a fine turban ornamented
with black ostrich feathers, and his followers waited on him
like a prince. General Armistead made no attempt to treacherously seize Halleck and Tiger Tail as Jesup had done with
Osceola, but he did try to bribe them. He offered each of them
$5,000 to come in and bring his band. The chiefs in turn asked
for two weeks to think it over, two weeks during which they
lingered with their forty warriors, drawing supplies and liquor. In the end they decamped. Thus in mid-November the
general ordered resumption of the conflict. Just at this time
twelve Seminoles came back from the West to persuade their
Florida kinsmen to join them, but the only visible effect was
the disappearance of some Indians who had come in to await
deportation. Captain John Page, who accompanied the western
delegation, blamed Armistead for the failure. Those Seminoles
who had fled did so, Page believed, because of ill-timed troop
movements ordered by the commander. Armistead, who according to Page knew little of Indian character, made the mistake of offering peace and war at the same time. Moreover,
he had begun his negotiations with the intractable Mikasukis
instead of with some of the more pliant bands. Influenced by
Page and certain it could do no good, the western delegation
requested permission to return west. Upon their departure,
Armistead ordered resumption of the detailed scouring of the
country. He could draw upon 4,500 regulars and 2,000 militia
in federal service, and he had divided his command into three
districts: the Atlantic with headquarters at St. Augustine; the
St. Johns with headquarters at Palatka; and the Oklawaha
with headquarters at Fort King. There ensued a period of dull,
routine service.[14]

Monotony did not sit well with Lieutenant Colonel William
S. Harney. For a year and a half he had been nursing a desire
to gain revenge on those Indians who had treacherously surprised his detachment in July, 1839, and had forced him to

run for his life in his underdrawers. At length in December, 1840, he succeeded in persuading General Armistead to give him an opportunity. On the fourth day of that month he led an expedition of ninety men out of Fort Dallas (its site is now in downtown Miami) in sixteen canoes provided by a lieutenant of marines. Twenty-one of the men, armed with Colt's rifles, were from the Second Dragoons, the balance belonged to the Third Artillery. But the most important member of all was a Negro named John who offered to serve as guide. He had been captured by the Indians in 1835. Upon appearing again before white settlements he had been put in irons and may have been willing to betray the Seminoles in order to be free of them. In any case, Harney's expedition would have been a wild-goose chase without him, for he guided it well in an area which appeared to have no distinguishing landmarks. "It seems like a vast sea, filled with grass and green trees," one soldier wrote, "and expressly intended as a retreat for the rascally Indians." As the white force threaded its way among the islands of the Everglades, it came upon parties of Seminoles in canoes. Some of these were overtaken and captured, and Harney ordered the warriors hanged on the spot. When John seemed to have lost his course, Harney is said to have tried to force the captured squaws to lead the way by threatening to hang their children if they refused. To their credit they declined to do it, and to his credit he never carried out the threat. Then John found his bearings again, and the expedition stealthily drew near Chakaika's island. In spite of General Armistead's ruling, Harney now dressed and painted his men like Indians. It was an hour or two after sunrise when these white-Indians reached the chief's island, yet Chakaika was taken completely by surprise, for he believed his band to be far beyond white detection. Chakaika himself, almost a giant, was chopping wood a little apart when the attack began. He ran, then seeing there was no escape, he stopped, grinned, and offered his hand. The nearest soldier shot him dead. A fierce fight developed, under the cover of which some Indians escaped. When the fighting was over, Harney had two of the three captured warriors hanged forthwith, but spared the third for use as a guide. Even the huge corpse of Chakaika was strung up with the other two. One of the white party described the scene. "The night was beautiful, and the bright moon rising displayed to my view as I lay on my bed the gigantic proportions of this once great and much dreaded warrior." Other persons viewing this same body dangling before the moon were Chakaika's wife, mother, and sister, all captives.[15]

Harney's expedition returned to Fort Dallas at the end of twelve days. It had wiped out Chakaika's band but had failed to find two important old Seminole leaders, Hospetarke, who had helped lead Harney's Massacre, and Sam Jones. Harney's score stood one white man dead against four Indians killed in action and five hanged. Sam Jones was said to have gone into a rage over the hangings, but the Legislative Council of Florida announced that Harney's retaliation for the massacre and for the rape of Indian Key was perfectly suited to the needs of the times. It voted him a commendation and a fine sword. Harney's fortunes were waxing. When Colonel Twiggs, who seemed to be in a perpetually aggrieved mood because he had to serve in a subordinate position in Florida, secured one of his innumerable leaves, Lieutenant Colonel Harney was directed on December 6, 1840, to take command of the Second Dragoons.[16]

Armistead passed the word to all field commanders to let Sam Jones know that he could have a tract of land and remain in Florida if he would cooperate in ending hostilities. Echo Emathla, a Tallahassee chief, turned himself in at Fort Clinch, and for a time the white commanders halted operations in that area to permit the rest of the Tallahassees to come in. Few did, and least of all those whom Tiger Tail controlled. That chief had been in white camps three different times, where he had rested a while, had been fed well, and then had absconded. As for the Mikasukis, they launched a fresh offensive. On December 28 they fell upon a small party of eleven mounted men and two lieutenants escorting an officer's wife from Fort Micanopy to Fort Wacahoota. Their first fire killed Mrs. Alexander Montgomery, Lieutenant Walter Sherwood, and three enlisted men. Pursuit issued swiftly from the fort, followed by a punitive scout, but nothing was accomplished. Coosa Tustenuggee and Halleck Tustenuggee, believed to have led these depredations, kept the area from St. Augustine to Wacahoota in constant alarm.[17]

By early February, 1841, Armistead held 270 Indians at Tampa for removal westward. Others were brought in from time to time as a result of incessant scouting. The wounded were put under the care of white surgeons. Lieutenant William Tecumseh Sherman, fresh out of West Point, commented on their stoicism. He wrote of one small girl, shot in the back, who spoke hardly at all, and of a squaw, literally riddled with buckshot, who also bore her misery in silence and in fear of the white folk.[18]

In March, 1841, General Armistead thought he saw victory ahead. The numerous brisk actions, brought about by the continual scouting, progressively weakened the power of the Seminoles. The officers directing the forays often showed great skill. The fight conducted by Lieutenant William Alburtis of the Second Infantry near Fort Brooks on the Oklawaha is a good example. Halleck sought to lure Alburtis' force out of the fort. Instead of falling into the Indian ambush, Alburtis established a counter-ambush. He worked his men to the rear of the Indian position and there opened a destructive fire. Halleck's warriors scattered. Later an approaching supply train was attacked by thirty-five of Halleck's warriors, and tree-to-tree fighting, followed by an assault, scattered them once more.[19]

Along with the attrition of Indian forces caused by scouting and fighting, the general employed bribery. He received $25,000 for this purpose, but then asked for $30,000 more. Coosa Tustenuggee, a Mikasuki and one of the murderers of Mrs. Montgomery and Lieutenant Sherwood, accepted $5,000 for coming in and bringing his band of sixty. Each of the lesser chiefs got $200 and every warrior $30 and a rifle. Even Billy Bowlegs came to Fort Brooks to parley. Wherever there seemed a chance of successful negotiation, Armistead sent word to the commanders in the sensitive areas to suspend operations until the outcome was known. Such a tractable policy did not suit some officers in the theater. They claimed that the Indians took advantage of the suspensions of hostility to plant and raise their crops, having no intention of giving up once their food was harvested.[20]

One chief who took such advantage was Coacoochee, the biggest prize of them all. On March 5, 1841, arrayed as Ham-

let in one of the costumes captured near St. Augustine the
previous May, he presented himself at Fort Cummings for a
talk. Beside him walked Horatio, while behind him crowded
Richard III, very fierce of mien and very dark. "Others were
ornamented with spangles, crimson vests, and feathers, according to fancy." Before the ceremonies were well begun, a
small daughter of Coacoochee's, whom he had supposed dead—
and whom the white men had treated well—came toward him
holding in her outstretched palms powder and bullets she had
been able to collect and hide while in captivity. At this sight
the chief wept openly. But his powers were not in the least
weakened when it came to the talks. Even the officers, fairly
hard of heart where Indians were concerned, were moved by
what he said. Sprague reported it: "The whites . . . dealt un-
justly by me. I came to them, they deceived me; the land I was
upon I loved, my body is made of its sands; the Great Spirit
gave me legs to walk over it; hands to aid myself; eyes to see
its ponds, rivers, forests, and game; then a head with which I
think. The sun, which is warm and bright as my feelings are
now, shines to warm us and bring forth our crops, and the
moon brings back the spirits of our warriors, our fathers,
wives, and children. The white man comes; he grows pale and
sick, why cannot we live here in peace? I have said I am the
enemy to the white man. I could live in peace with him, but
they first steal our cattle and horses, cheat us, and take our
lands. The white men are as thick as the leaves in the hammock; they come upon us thicker every year. They may shoot
us, drive our women and children night and day; they may
chain our hands and feet, but the red man's heart will be
always free."[21]

There was another interview in the same tenor at Fort
Brooke on March 22 at which Coacoochee agreed to bring in
his followers in May, or early June at the latest. Thereafter
he appeared first at one fort and then at another to be resup-
plied, becoming increasingly demanding as time wore on. On
May 1 he turned up at Fort Pierce with a limited following
of warriors. Displaying his pass signed by General Armistead, he demanded food and liquor. Once supplied, he complained of both, but got drunk and sank into a sodden sleep.
Awake again, he demanded a horse to ride to Tampa. Reluc-

tantly, Major Thomas Childs gave him one with supplies and five and one-half gallons of whiskey. Coacoochee heaped his own supplies on his already heavily burdened followers.[22]

Like all his predecessors, General Armistead sought relief from the Florida burden. He had heard, he wrote the Adjutant General, that the command was to be given to General Gaines. Should this occur, Armistead requested relief, for he had served two campaigns with General Jesup in addition to his own tenure. His record was good; he had shipped 450 Indians and Negroes westward and had 236 more on hand for shipment. Of those sent west, 120 had been warriors, which left, he estimated, no more than 300 fighting men in Florida. Of course there had been white men hovering about to try to gain possession of the captured Negroes, but he had handled them firmly. Some he had politely asked to leave the Tampa area because their presence kept many Indians from coming in.[23]

Early in May, Halleck Tustenuggee let it be known that he would come in and bring his band. But that event, plus the seizure of Coacoochee, occurred under another command, for on May 31, 1841, General Armistead was relieved.

Commanders came and commanders went, but for the lower-grade officers the Florida assignment went on being the worst possible. From the start of the war to the middle of 1840, some three hundred of them had resigned from the army because of poor pay. The matter came up in Congress. How can you expect the soldiers to fight with spirit and success, said Representative William Butler of Kentucky, "while you treat them as murderers and pay them but half the hire of slaves?" No colleague rose to answer him. The reactions of the officers to their lot varied. One of them felt at times very sorry for himself. "Oh how delighted I should be to see you all tonight," he wrote, "but I am here, uncomfortable, wretched water, eaten up by insects in an unhealthy climate, suffering from heat, indifferent food, scarcely any fresh meat,—and this to support my family. I say no more." Another surveyed what he saw with gray-, not rose-colored glasses. He thought the method of trying to surprise the Indians was criminally neglected, "Then that damned bugle is sounded again," he wrote, "as if the trampling of 200 horses and the shouts of 200 men and the occasional firing of a gun were not sufficient." How could you expect to sneak up on Indians that way? "What have we gained from this expedition? Seven Indians and ignominy." It was his misfortune to serve in a very wet season, "Rain, rain, rain, will it never cease its eternal patter!" His sense of duty struggled constantly with his conviction that the errand he was upon was perpetrating a cruel wrong.[24]

One of the second lieutenants of the Eighth Infantry wrote directly to the regimental colonel flatly stating that his captain had been afraid during a foray and had shown it. This earned the lieutenant a court-martial with a sentence of suspension for three months. Later in the same month, May, 1841, a major in the Quartermaster Corps struck the same captain. He too earned a trial and got a sixty-day suspension. Finally, there was the case of a lieutenant who was tried for cruelly beating two recruits. But because he had been long imprisoned (this is not explained in the records), the court did not sentence him.[25]

For an infraction not stated on the record, a soldier was sentenced to ride the wooden horse three hours a day for fifteen days. One deserter was sentenced to pay the government back for time lost and to receive fifty lashes with cowhide on his bare back. Other deserters suffered the same, in addition to six months hard labor with a ball and chain attached. Family problems, not punishment, occupied some of the soldiers. More of them had members of their families along than one would suppose. One such family man complained to his captain that the sergeant hung around his wife altogether too much. When the attentions did not stop, he shot and killed the sergeant. How he fared before the court is not recorded. There were a number of children with the Sixth Infantry and most of them had been born in the army; some had lost one parent. Lieutenant Colonel Green asked permission to carry them on the rolls at half rations, and admitted that he had already issued rations to them under the cloak of providing for the children of suffering inhabitants.[26]

No aggressive spirit of innovation agitated the military services, but inventors pushed them to try some novelties, while members of the services themselves generated a few. The experimental use of pontoons made of India rubber continued; so did the use of rockets. One John H. Sherburne even proposed balloons for reconnaissance, but General Armistead vetoed the idea without a trial—the forest, he said, was too dense for visibility. New shoulder arms received at least perfunctory trials. Lieutenant Colonel Harney seems to have been the only commander sold on Colt's rifles, but Samuel Colt himself did all a man could to establish them. In the summer of 1840 he even offered to raise a battalion of men and arm them with his rifle, but Secretary Poinsett told him this could not be done under existing regulations. Nevertheless, both the army and navy tried Colt's rifles. Not so the Ordnance Department. It began in 1840 to turn out a new model, a flintlock, notwithstanding that the chief of ordnance himself believed flint-and-steel firing mechanisms to be obsolete. European armies, he said, were converting from flintlocks to percussion, but apparently he dared not suggest that the United States do the same until the European armies had experimented some more. Yet he convinced Secretary Poinsett that percussion types were the firing mechanisms of the future, and Poinsett in his annual report for 1840 recommended that the United States adopt them. In other ways the Secretary was not so progressive. He told the President that the breechloading principle was almost certain to fail, and the revolver principle too.[27]

There was a tendency to adopt partisan methods of combat. Accordingly, Captain Joseph R. Smith experimented with lightening the soldier's load. He issued to his men a ration consisting of parched corn ground with sugar. This was half as heavy as the standard ration, and sustained a man's strength just as well.[28]

The navy could use its steamers for the first time under semi-combat conditions. Ship handlers were able to learn a good deal and at the same time were able to disprove some faulty theories. One of these errors was the belief that steam vessels purified the air and helped prevent disease. The nature of the naval service enforced the use of small boats, especially of Indian dugouts. In a flotilla of dugouts, John T. McLaughlin led an expedition from December, 1840, to mid-January, 1841, across the entire peninsula from east to west. His was the first party of white men ever to cross the full width of the Everglades.

The Florida war went on in the halls of Congress as well as in the swamps of the peninsula. In the capitol it mixed itself with some very critical issues. One such issue was the role of citizen soldiers and that of the regular forces. Senator Robert Strange of North Carolina had earlier marked out the line taken by the extreme supporters of the militia. Reliance could be placed upon the militia, he said, since history revealed that it had won all of the nation's victories. Just clear the regular army out of the way and let the citizen soldiers do the job. Delegate Downing of Florida embraced this position and embodied it in a bill which proposed that direction of the war be taken from the federal government and given to the government of Florida. He and his constituents were tired of trusting operations to regular officers, who understood neither Floridians nor Indian warfare. Yet in the last analysis Downing was a win-the-war man, and he even switched parties to adhere to this goal. For a time he followed Henry Clay and the Whigs, but when he realized that Clay was soft on the prosecution of the war, he stood by the Democratic administration.[29]

Party interest often dominated the military debates. Representative Butler of Kentucky accused the Whig members of crucifying all but Whig generals. Thomas Hart Benton of Missouri had already made similar accusations in the Senate. General Jesup, he said, had been persecuted because of his Jacksonian connections. It remained for the Whig side to carry this argument to its ultimate absurdity. Hiram Hunt of New York asserted that General Scott, a leading Whig, had been sent to Florida by a Democratic administration with the hope that he would be killed there and thus eliminated from politics. Sobered by irrational charges such as this, Senator Benton took a more statesmanlike posture. He defended the army, even though most of the officers were Whiggish, not as a politician but as a senator; for he conceded that the officers had stood to their duty regardless of party loyalty.[30]

A far deadlier difference than citizen soldier against regular and Whig against Democrat began to insinuate itself into the congressional debate over the Florida war. Up to 1840 the attitude of the nation toward slavery had been rather apathetic, but strong feelings now began to replace apathy in the Congress. William O. Butler, who had defended the Democratic conduct of the war, argued that abolitionism lay beneath the criticisms of the way the war was waged. He insisted that abolitionists, "that saintly brood of hypocrites, these exclusive friends of the red man and the black," were really interested not in defending the Seminoles, but in preventing Florida from becoming a slave state. He quoted from the *Antislavery Almanac* and from William Lloyd Garrison to demonstrate that they cared not at all what happened to the Constitution and to the Union. Butler was at least partly right. Representatives John Quincy Adams and Joshua Giddings, with some other members, had agreed to test the gag rule (passed in 1836 to forbid discussion of petitions about slavery on the floor of the House), not by openly violating it, but by raising the issue of slavery in connection with other topics. The Seminole War proved to be one of their most efficient vehicles. Indeed, the war and slavery were seen in Congress to be more and more intimately related.[31]

The slavery issue sharpened during the House debate on the Florida war in February, 1841. Ostensibly this debate began over the appropriation of money to pay Seminoles to give themselves up. Certain congressmen asserted that it was the duty of the government to subdue the Seminoles rather than to buy them off. Giddings used the discussion to make an attack upon slavery. There were attempts to rule him out of order, but he got his tirade into the record. Reviewing the causes of the Seminole War, he vowed that Georgians had been paid three times over for slaves they claimed the Seminoles had stolen from them. Here was the source of the Florida conflict, he said, for in order to extort yet more, Georgia with united Southern aid got the United States to commit its armed forces to capture runaway slaves from the Indians. Such use, he said, was unconstitutional, and his constituents objected to having to pay for it. Then he enumerated a series of high-handed and illegal actions by Georgians near the border of Florida. When he was done, the representatives from Georgia took the floor to denounce him savagely. Who would suppose, said Edward Black, that an abolition speech would result from a proposition to vote money to remove the Indians? If Giddings should have the courage to come to Scriven County in Georgia, he would be lynched. Giddings did not heed this particular challenge, but on one occasion, when threatened by Black with mayhem, he said, "Come ahead, the people of Ohio do not send cowards to Congress!" Painful as it must have been, Black and Giddings actually voted on the same side of the appropriation bill. Black voted nay because he said the government must beat the Seminoles whatever the cost, while Giddings voted the same way because he asserted that the money was not truly a war appropriation but would be used to pay slaveholders for runaway slaves. Yet, in spite of these two opponents, the appropriation bill passed.[32]

Eighteen-forty was a notable year in American politics. The Whig Party had produced a powerful contender for the Presidency, and this strength had a strong impact in Florida. For the first time two distinct political parties were beginning to emerge there. The class of men who had run the Territory ever since it had belonged to the United States were for the most part joining the Whigs. The governorship of Robert Raymond Reid seemed to them evidence that the nation was falling into the hands of irresponsible Democratic elements. Even Richard K. Call, once Jackson's "boy," was becoming a pure Whig. Speaking in New York in August, 1840, he denounced the Van Buren administration for placing the political campaign ahead of the war in Florida. There was no hope of a successful conclusion of the hostilities, he said, as long as Van Buren and Poinsett directed them.[33]

William Henry Harrison was elected President in 1840. One of the factors which defeated Martin Van Buren, at least so Joshua Giddings claimed, was the Florida war, for foes asserted that it had been waged both extravagantly and fruitlessly. The party change, of course, shook Democratic officeholders from top to bottom. Joel Poinsett was replaced as Secretary of War by John Bell of Tennessee, later to be famous as a Presidential candidate in 1860. Bell served for a few months, until John Tyler became President. Only two weeks after Poinsett left, Florida Governor Robert R. Reid was ousted and Richard K. Call, now a Whig in good standing, was reinstated.

At the end of March, 1841, all the citizen soldiers in Florida were discharged and reliance was placed entirely upon regulars. This made it necessary to increase the regulars employed in Florida to an all-time high—5,076 in April. Whether this was the policy of the new President himself, both a veteran citizen soldier and a regular, is not known. But when Harrison died after one month in office, and John Tyler took over the Administration, the policy remained the same, indeed persisted to the end of the conflict. One of the obvious reasons for the change was cost. The Paymaster General informed the Secretary of War that up to May 20, 1841, $2,525,399.29 had been paid to regulars as compared with $3,461,622.15 to citizen soldiers. The Administration felt that the latter were not worth as much as regulars, yet had cost one million dollars more. Of course, not everybody agreed. It goes without saying that Floridians opposed the shift and clamored for the renewed use of citizen soldiers.[34]

15

William Jenkins Worth

THE CONTINUAL DISBANDING of militia and volunteer units eliminated the hierarchy of general officers who went with them. Thus it no longer seemed necessary to Secretary of War Bell to send down the highest officers of the regular army to outrank the militiamen. Now for the first time a colonel was given the responsibility, and William Jenkins Worth of the Eighth Infantry became the commander in Florida. Major Ethan Allen Hitchcock, then acting as aide to the Secretary of War, alleged that he advised the Secretary to relieve Armistead and to select Worth. If true, his action goes against his private opinion of Colonel Worth, whom he called in his diary "as arrogant and domineering as pride can make a man."[1]

Worth was the second of the Florida commanders to be under fifty. Born in 1794 in a Quaker family, he was drawn away from Quaker principles (if in fact he had ever held them) by the second war with England. His commission as first lieutenant came in 1813, before he had any military experience whatsoever. It was his good fortune soon to become aide to Winfield Scott, who thereafter was his fast friend and benefactor until the two became enemies during the War with Mexico. Worth named his only son Winfield Scott. At the Battle of Lundy's Lane, July 25, 1814, Worth was so seriously wounded by grapeshot in the thigh that he was not expected to live. Bedridden and confined to a room for one long year, he emerged from the ordeal permanently lame. For his good conduct during the war he was brevetted major. After the peace he survived the army cut of 1821 and served as commandant at West Point from 1820 to 1828, although not himself a graduate. In 1838 he became a colonel and received command of the new Eighth Infantry. In November, 1840, he led his regiment to Florida from the upper Mississippi valley.[2]

Considered one of the handsomest men in the army, Worth was of middle height, had a martial bearing, a trim figure, and the appearance of physical strength. He showed to best advantage when mounted, for he was one of the finest of horsemen. During combat he radiated confidence. Could he have remained forever on the battlefield there probably would not have been a more famous officer in the service. Unfortunately he had a petty streak mingled with overweening vanity, which cropped up when he was not in a fight. Rash and impetuous, he often said and did things he regretted afterward. His mind was intense and narrow; he was self-centered. Vanity glares forth in the statement ascribed to him after the Battle of Monterey during the Mexican war: "I am satisfied with myself. The most vindictive foes crouch at my feet, and my friends choke with joy and delight." Yet in spite of this quality, or perhaps because of it, Worth was a capable soldier who drove hard, and the mood of the Florida war changed sharply when he took charge of it.[3]

In his history of the Florida war, John T. Sprague, Worth's aide-de-camp and later to be his son-in-law, vividly put the new commander's problem this way: "Forty-seven thousand square miles in the territory of Florida, was occupied by an enemy by nature vindictive and revengeful, treacherous and subtle, striving for their rights, and for the soil made sacred by those superstitious influences which became part of an Indian's nature, by his duty to the *Great Spirit,* and the injunctions of parents and prophets. Every hammock and swamp was to them a citadel, to which and from which they could retreat with wonderful facility. Regardless of food or the climate, time or distance, they moved from one part of the country to the other, in parties of five and ten; while the soldier, dependent upon supplies, and sinking under a tropical sun, could only hear of his foe by depredations committed in the

William Jenkins Worth

section of the country over which he *scouted* the day before."
Nevertheless Colonel Worth, like all his predecessors, offered a
preliminary plan: first rid the country of Indians between the
Withlacoochee and the frontier settlements, and then strike at
the bands known to be in the South. He intended to use his
troops as partisans and to keep them campaigning right on
through the sickly season. The War Department approved of
this strategy and undertook to keep enough regulars at his
command to carry it out. Thus the force remained above 4,800
through July, dropped by 500 when the First Infantry left
Florida in August, then rose to about 5,000 in October and
stayed as high until February, 1842.[4]

The Indians continued their raids and depredations, and
many Floridians and Georgians ascribed their success to the
inability of the regulars to handle Indian warfare. Indeed the
grand jury of Madison County in Florida issued a presentment setting forth that proposition. Veteran hunters were required to do the job, the jurors found, not the kind of men
who entered the army. The solution of course was militia.
Properly officered and free of party spirit—which, by the way,
was ruining the country—militiamen could end the war. Naturally the regular officers disagreed with such opinions. They
believed that the Floridians were frequently frightened by
imaginary Indians, and that the Floridians' object in criticizing the army was not so much to end the war as to get themselves on the federal payroll.[5]

The governor of Georgia protested the discharge of four
companies of Georgia militia which had been doing duty on
the border. These men, believing they would serve for the duration of the war, had not planted a crop, had expended their
ready money, and had all contracted debts. "They are now to
be coolly turned off; the protection of their homes confided to
strangers, with whom they hold not one feeling in common."
Finally relations between Georgia and the army reached the
ultimate strain. The governor sent evidence to the Secretary
of War that regulars had committed depredations in his state.
They had, he said, killed hogs and cattle, had beaten a man
and had taken a barrel of whiskey from him, and had killed
another man for demanding to see the brand on a beef they
had slaughtered. The soldiers contended that the man was

drunk and was menacing them, and that they had killed him in self-defense. What really lay behind the charges, said the captain whose men were involved, was that the people near his camp had it in for him because he restrained his company from buying their whiskey. Also, they were frantic to be drawing federal pay themselves. Colonel Worth's response to all this was to remove the regular units, but he made it clear that threats from the governor had not influenced him at all.[6]

War expenses were running at $92,300 per month, not counting the pay of the regulars, and the fact drove Colonel Worth to do other things which made him unpopular with the whites in Florida. These expenses paid 1,060 civil employees, and supported 1,373 horses, 1,260 mules, 380 wagons, 5 steamers, and 3 sailing vessels. Worth set about to reduce costs, primarily by cutting civilians off the payroll. The quartermaster estimated the savings during the year ended April 30, 1842, at $174,923.90, but this included savings which resulted from the removal of three regiments of infantry and five companies of the Second Dragoons. Naturally many local folk were hurt. Some were so determined to stay on the payroll, at least so John T. Sprague believed, that they did all they could to prolong the war. He cited 40 highly paid Negro interpreters and guides as the worst offenders.[7]

Lieutenant William Tecumseh Sherman was sent out on May 1, 1841, to escort Coacoochee into Fort Pierce. Wary of this crafty chief, Sherman would not dismount to greet him, and also took pains to secure all the Indians' guns. For his part, Coacoochee prepared to make a ceremonial entrance. He stripped, washed himself in a pond, then commenced to put on one shirt after another, and several vests. One of the vests was marked with blood and a bullet hole. The chief had the effrontery to pull a one-dollar bill on the Tallahassee Bank from a pocket, and ask Sherman to give him silver for it. As soon as Coacoochee had donned his finery, the procession moved into the fort. At the ensuing council Major Childs agreed to give the chief thirty days to ready his people for migration. During the thirty days, the Indians freely came and went at Fort Pierce. Bit by bit Childs became convinced that Coacoochee did not mean to keep his agreement. He applied for permission to seize the chief, and received it. On June 4 he made prisoners of Coacoochee and fifteen of his tribesmen. Lieutenant Colonel William Gates ordered that the captives be shackled and shipped at once to New Orleans. Colonel Worth, who intended to use Coacoochee to bring in other Seminoles, angrily countermanded this order and had the chief brought back to Tampa. At the same time he ordered the arrest of Gates, but when that officer explained the reasons for his action, Worth allowed him to go free. Sprague described the Indians' return to Tampa on July 3. "Coacoochee and his warriors came up slowly to the quarterdeck . . . their feet-irons hardly enabling them to step four inches, and arranged themselves according to rank. As they laid their manacled hands upon their knees before them, in the presence of so many whom they had so long hunted as foes, they hung their heads in silence."

Colonel Worth went aboard their ship, two miles from shore, and gave them a cheerful greeting. He described himself as Coacoochee's friend, but delivered a most unfriendly message. Coacoochee must bring in his entire band. If he failed, the chief and his fellow captives would be hanged. When Worth had finished, Coacoochee is reported to have spoken these words: "I was once a boy; then I saw the white man afar off. I hunted in these woods, first with a bow and arrow; then with a rifle. I saw the white man, and was told he was my enemy. I could not shoot him as I would a wolf or a bear; yet like these he came upon me; horses, cattle, and fields, he took from me. He said he was my friend; he abused our women and children, and told us to go from the land. Still he gave me his hand in friendship; we took it; whilst taking it, he had a snake in the other; his tongue was forked; he lied, and stung us. I asked but for a small piece of these lands, enough to plant and to live upon, far south, a spot where I could place the ashes of my kindred, a spot only sufficient upon which I could lay my wife and child. This was not granted me. I was put in prison; I escaped. I have been again taken; you have brought me back; I am here; I feel the irons in my heart."

Nothing was left but for the Indian to "play ball." Thereafter, for considerations which came to about $8,000, Coacoochee did his best to get the remaining Florida Indians to move west. Refused freedom to go himself, he sent out messengers with instructions. "The sun shines bright today, the day is clear; so let your hearts be: the Great Spirit will guide you. At night, when you camp, take these pipes and tobacco, build a fire when the moon is up and bright, dance around it, then let the fire go out, and just before the break of day, when the deer sleeps, and the moon whispers to the dead, you will hear the voices of those who have gone to the Great Spirit; they will give you strong hearts and heads to carry the talk of Coacoochee."[8]

The intractables knew the appeal Coacoochee would have as an advocate of migration and they tried to offset it. In a meeting held in Long Swamp east of Big Hammock and close to Fort King, Halleck Tustenuggee, Tiger Tail, Nethlockemathla, and Octiarche, with 120 warriors, agreed to put to death any messenger from the white side. Although the southern chiefs were not present at this meeting, they seem to have learned of it and to have approved. Even so they did not carry it out to the letter, for when Solemico, an emissary from the white men, made contact with a council composed of Holata Mico, Sam Jones, Otulkethlocko (the Prophet), Hospetarke, Fuse Hadjo, and Passacka, he was made prisoner but not killed. Later he escaped and returned to the white men. The northern chiefs did little better.[9]

During June Colonel Worth set on foot a concerted drive from Fort Brooke, Fort King, and Fort Harrison (at what is now Clearwater harbor) to round up the Indians in the vicinity of the Cove of the Withlacoochee and the Homosassa and Crystal Rivers. It seemed as if the war had reverted to the pattern of five years earlier when the same area had been the object of a concentric movement. The colonel's plan was not unlike General Scott's, though on a much smaller scale, and he pushed it with a zealot's energy. His instructions were explicit and detailed. Each command of 200 men was to be broken up into detachments of 20, and was to have a troop of dragoons with it. "Scorn the exposed points in every direction,—keep the men in constant motion—tax their strength to the utmost." Officers must set examples of endurance. He was a thorough exponent of the strenuous life. Although there were 2,428 soldiers on the sick list in July, the colonel told the Adjutant General that this was not a consequence of continuous campaigning. On the contrary it was a result of garrison duty with its lack of excitement, its heavy food, and its easy access to indulgence.[10]

Governor Call complained that much of Middle Florida lay defenseless. Travelers along the main routes, which had here- tofore been safe, were in mortal peril. In the past the Indians had attacked only white men, but now they were murdering Negro slave drivers at their work. Heretofore the planting of crops could go ahead, but the new policy of the Seminoles jeop- ardized it. Six hundred mounted Florida volunteers, the gov- ernor concluded, would overcome these dangers. But Worth, who had no confidence in citizen soldiers, would not enroll them.[11]

On June 25, 1841, Alexander Macomb died, and shortly thereafter Winfield Scott, Worth's friend and mentor, was appointed to the post of commanding general of the United States Army.

Colonel Worth's attempt to drive the remaining Seminoles out of the field by force was supplemented by a policy of white resettlement. Settlers were encouraged to return to their hold- ings and assured that the army would help them. All aban- doned forts were put at the disposal of the settlers, while the military stood ready to aid them with transport and the build- ing of new forts and cabins. One officer was assigned to the job of securing settlers and abetting their resettlement. His first success came on August 9, 1841, when a band of thirteen white people with eight slaves tried to establish themselves at Cedar Hammock, twelve miles northeast of Fort White. Soon thereafter another group of thirty-one whites and two Negroes planted themselves at the Natural Bridge. By the following March (1842) there were 164 white men, 137 white women, and 192 children together with 103 slaves and 56 slave chil- dren clustered in twelve resettlement points. The army issued them rations, just as it had been doing for so long for the "suffering inhabitants" of Florida. Lieutenant Marsena R. Patrick, the resettlement officer, good laissez faire devotee that he was, felt sure that this issue would sap the vitality of the settlers and pauperize them.[12]

Coacoochee was not the only Seminole whose life depended on his cooperation with the whites. When Waxihadjo—who had done a good deal of murdering along the roads—was killed, two of his warriors fell into white hands. They were offered a fearsome choice: to get their people to come in within fifteen days, or to suffer execution. Meanwhile on August 8, Coacoochee's messengers had brought in all of his band except five men and fifteen women. This was enough to save his life. "Take off my irons," he said, "that I may once more meet my warriors like a man." When this was done, he went ashore, resplendent with three ostrich plumes set in a crimson turban, silver ornaments bespangling his breast, a many-colored frock, a sash, and red leggings.[13]

Thereafter General Worth allowed him to penetrate the backcountry in person, bringing the gospel of removal to the intransigents. Such was Coacoochee's station and personal force that he was successful. He persuaded Hospetarke to come in and even to board a vessel for a council. Once aboard, "the shrill bugle gave the preconcerted signal, each soldier was at his post, the doors of the cabin were closed by bayonets, officers drew their swords from the scabbards, and the drum in camp beat to arms." Colonel Worth seized Hospetarke under the pretext that the chief had come in with only fifteen warriors, no women or children, and that he obviously intended to obtain much-needed supplies and then go back to the woods. Hospetarke, bent and white-haired, being close to eighty-five, gave the impression that he did not mind capture; he was too tired anyway to carry on. Coacoochee, for his part, by pretending that he had been drunk, convinced the captives that he had not knowingly lured them into a trap. Worth finally freed five of the party upon their promise to bring in the rest of their band, said to number 320. They fulfilled their word in the fall. After some time had passed, Coacoochee asked that the Seminoles gathered for emigration be shipped forthwith, because he could no longer keep them occupied. Recognizing the wisdom of this advice but saving a few out as guides, Colonel Worth embarked 211 of them, including Coacoochee, on October 12, 1841.[14]

In mid-August three friendlies went forth to try to locate Halleck's camp. All commanders were directed to help them and to make only limited movements as long as they were out. Meanwhile, the Indians at large went on committing the never-ending depredations. During the fall three men were murdered along that treacherous lane from Micanopy to Wacahoota where Mrs. Montgomery and Lieutenant Walter Sherwood had been killed in the previous year. Charitably, the colonel commanding chose to ascribe these murders to Seminole youths who had never known anything but war.[15]

The quasi-armistice did not apply to the southernmost parts of the peninsula. At this time a joint army-navy expedition entered the Everglades. "There was at one time to be seen in the Everglades," wrote Lieutenant Sprague, "the dragoon in water from three to four feet deep, the sailor and marine wading in the mud in the midst of cypress stumps, and the soldiers, infantry and artillery, alternately on the land, in the water, and in boats." Their efforts were directed especially at trying to bring in Sam Jones by fair means or foul. That old man had become a symbol of the Seminole intransigents, as this poor but amusing doggerel shows.

> *Ever since the creation*
> *By the best calculation*
> *The Florida War has been raging*
> *And 'tis our expectation*
> *That the last conflagration*
> *Will find us the same contest waging.*
>
> *And yet 'tis not an endless war*
> *As Facts will plainly show*
> *Having been "ended" forty times*
> *In twenty months or so.*
>
> *Sam Jones! Sam Jones! thou great unwhipped*
> *Thou makest a world of bother*
> *Indeed, we quite expect thou art*
> *One Davy Jones's brother.*
>
> *"The war is ended" comes the news*
> *"We've caught them in our gin:*
> *The war is ended past a doubt*
> *Sam Jones has just come in!"*
>
> *But hark! Next day the tune we change*
> *And sing a counter strain*
> *"The war's not ended," for behold!*
> *Sam Jones is out again.*

And ever and anon we hear
Proclaimed in cheering tones
"Our General's had a battle?"—no,
A "talk with Samuel Jones."

For aught we see while ocean rolls
(As though these crafty Seminoles
Were doubly nerved and sinewed)
Nor art nor force can e'er avail
But, like some modern premium tale,
The war's "to be continued."[16]

In the fall Worth gave orders to occupy a line running from Punta Rassa to Fort Denaud, thence to Lake Okeechobee, and across it to Fort Pierce or Fort Dallas. There had been heavy rains and due to the deluged condition of the country he intended to move along this line in boats or canoes. Accordingly, a joint expedition under the command of Lieutenant John T. McLaughlin, United States Navy, passed up the Caloosahatchee to Lake Okeechobee and then south to reach the ocean at Fort Lauderdale. This trek occupied two months and was so grueling that some of McLaughlin's men collapsed from a "regular cave-in" of their constitutions. Thirty of them carried Colt rifles which, as far as the commander was concerned, had also caved in. Five rifles had burst upon firing, injuring the sailors who handled them. McLaughlin said he fully intended to return to muskets.[17]

Worth was determined to mop up the Indians who had fled south. Following the general's orders, Major Childs' command found cultivated fields along the Indian River so extensive that 80 of his men had to work two days to destroy them. A part of the overall plan was to bring back Seminole leaders who had already been shipped away (Congress had voted $15,000 for this purpose), and they would try to coax the irreconcilables to surrender. In October a delegation of seven chiefs, headed by the once formidable Alligator, arrived at Tampa. Successful at the start, Alligator persuaded Tiger Tail and his brother Nethlochemathla to come in with their people. These two leaders, with 52 men and 110 women and children, set up their camp at Fort Brooke on October 19, 1841. Few other such attempts, however, ended so successfully; two of the friendlies were murdered for their pains. But two Seminole villages were uncovered in the vicinity of Fort Lauderdale by the time-honored method of capturing an Indian and forcing him to lead the way. In this case the technique resulted in the capture of 29 adults and 31 minors, the death of 6 warriors, and the destruction of provisions and 20 canoes.[18]

Meanwhile, the commanders of the three military districts to the north—the Oklawaha, the Micanopy, and the Western—were told to keep two-fifths of their garrisons in the field at all times. The mobile portion was to stay well toward the Indian frontier, to cover the settlements at the same time, and to observe all known Indian routes. Worth also ordered his commanders to change position often.

The Seminoles themselves kept them moving. Mikasukis led by Halpatter Tustenuggee and Chitto Hadjo harassed Middle Florida. (This Halpatter was of course not Alligator of the Alachua band, who was then in Florida persuading his erstwhile brethren to migrate.) Bands of Creeks, slipping in from the north, also harried the settlements. Octiarche, the Creek chief, could not be induced to visit on board a steamer, although the friendlies did their best to persuade him. On December 20 fifteen warriors led by Halleck Tustenuggee left Haw Creek near Dunn's Lake, headed north, and struck at the Mandarin settlement on the east bank of the St. Johns River thirty-five miles northwest of St. Augustine. Mandarin was in an area where there had been no Indian incursions—where indeed there had been no Indians—for the last three years. Meeting no opposition, Halleck's raiders murdered four people, burned two buildings, and gathered a great haul of loot. They even stayed in Mandarin all night before bothering to depart. The regular officer who investigated the affair said that a better local organization could have prevented the depredations. The usual cry went up in Florida for a militia force to insure greater local protection. Very much against such a solution, Colonel Worth himself went north to take charge.[19]

Under his supervision the army in the north fanned out in all directions. Major Joseph Plympton, commanding a detachment of 102 men of the Second Infantry, caught up with Halleck's band camped in a hammock near Dunn's Lake east of the St. Johns on January 25, 1842. At 9:30 A.M., forming his men in a single line with six-foot intervals between them, Plympton charged the camp. But the Mikasukis had hastily abandoned the place and were waiting under cover to the rear. It took a sharp gun fight of an hour and a quarter to dislodge them and the pursuit did not catch any prisoners. The campaign was severe, as Plympton's report attests: "If about six weeks of constant marching over the worst part of a bad country—and, on an average ⅔ds of the time in water, from ankle to waist deep; sleeping without fires at night with cheerful expressions,—and without a solitary instance of discontent, —entitles troops to the favorable notice of their superiors, then [these] are richly entitled to the reward."

Now began a frenetic converging movement by several white detachments to surround and take Halleck's band. No success. Farther west a systematic search was being made for Octiarche's group of Creeks. Colonel John Garland directed the Fourth Infantry operating out of Fort Fanning, Lieutenant Colonel Gustavus Loomis led the Sixth Infantry in Wacasassa Hammock, and Lieutenant Colonel William Whistler worked the Seventh Infantry from Micanopy and Wacahoota. All the while persuasion too was being practiced. Nethlochemathla took thirty warriors and went off to find Octiarche and reason with him. Tiger Tail, who John T. Sprague claimed was jealous of his brother, not only refused to accompany the expedition but even escaped on January 21, 1842 with two men and two women. He proceeded to persuade the Creeks not to give themselves up. So it went: the efforts were prodigious, the results small.[20]

To the south the campaign also played itself out. Major William G. Belknap, who had taken command when Worth went north, pushed parties out to try for contact with the foe. On December 20, 1841, he stirred up a fight with bands directed by Bowlegs and the Prophet. The Indians had chosen their spot well. Water, studded with cypress knees, stood two or three feet deep all around them. The best opening was exactly where the defenders had their front. Assault brought the usual results: some casualties, some prisoners, and the main force of the enemy out of reach. Nevertheless, three months later this effort and his general good conduct earned Belknap a promotion to lieutenant colonel. By the end of February

Worth believed that Big Cypress Swamp was cleared of hostiles and thus called back northward all but two companies of
the troops in the south. The Third Artillery was now relieved
of duty in Florida.[21]

The Indians were much reduced. Colonel Worth estimated
that there were 301 of them left at large in Florida, and of
these 143 were in the far south and had never joined in the
hostilities. This thin population, including only 112 men, was
scattered widely in tiny bands, never exceeding 20 warriors
each. Notwithstanding their small numbers, violence continued, although it too revealed the Indians' loss of power. A
family was murdered with arrows alone, indicating a scarcity
of ammunition. But the Seminole spirit was not yet extin-
guished, for when the murderers were tracked down and
surrounded in a swamp, the warriors literally hurdled their
encirclers and escaped.[22]

Colonel Worth informed Washington on February 5, 1842,
that he had just shipped 230 Seminoles, 68 of them warriors.
Here in one shipment went nearly as many as remained in the
entire Territory. What the colonel next said caused a cry of
rage when it became known in Florida. Small as the remainder
was, it could not be brought in by force. His recommendation
was to reduce the military strength in Florida and place what
was left so as to give absolute protection to the settlements.
This done, he would let the 300 Indians remain and plant and
come undisturbed to any post, but all the while continually
attempt to persuade them to go west. So crucial was this
proposal that the Secretary of War convened a council of high-
ranking officers to consider it. They rejected it, and only General Jesup supported Worth's position.[23]

Accordingly, the intransigents were relentlessly pursued.
Fast-moving detachments followed trails like bloodhounds,
killing a few warriors and capturing some every week. The soldiers were offered a hundred dollars for every warrior captured or slain. Finally, Halleck himself, with a band of forty
fighting men, was brought to bay on April 19, 1842, southeast
of Peliklakaha near Lake Ahapopka. Halleck made his stand
in a hammock surrounded by water. The Indians had cleared
a field of fire, as had been done at Okeechobee, and had thrown
a log barricade across the front. Colonel Worth himself di-

rected the white force of about four hundred, and at his order
the Second, Fourth, and Eighth Infantry regiments fired and
began their approach, two lines in extended order. They first
had to pass through heavy mud and then into a dense mass of
vegetation which stank so badly that some men vomited. The
hostiles concentrated their fire upon the Negroes and the
friendlies, for they knew who had led the army to every otherwise inaccessible hideaway. Worth also sent a detachment of
the Second Dragoons against the Indians' rear, and when it
made contact the defenders left their position and seemed to
evaporate. Their main camp and most of their gear were taken
at a cost of one white killed and three wounded.[24]

This action, the last one of the Florida war which might be
called a battle, was the beginning of the end for Halleck's band.
Although most of the warriors escaped, they could no longer
hold body and soul together. As a result, Halleck came ten days
later into the colonel's camp at Warm Springs for a conference. With him came two of his wives and two children. For
several days Worth permitted him to demand beef, corn, flour,
and whiskey in an insulting way and to come and go as he
pleased, but the plan was to seize him and all of his followers.
The commander took Halleck with him on a visit to Fort King
and instructed Colonel Garland to wait three days and then
round up all the Indians. Garland concentrated the Indians by
giving them a feast with the promise of much liquor. When
they were all secured, the word was sent to Worth who sprang
the trap on the chief. One officer recorded that Halleck stormed
like a madman. Sprague wrote, "He stood erect quivering with
excitement, brushing his fingers through his long black hair,
his eyes sparkling with fire, his breast heaving in agony."
Then he dropped to the floor unconscious.[25]

By thus employing the method which had earned General
Jesup obloquy, Colonel Worth captured 43 warriors, 37 women,
and 34 children. This was more than one-third of the total
he had estimated to be left in Florida. Halleck accepted a
thousand dollars for himself, which brought reproaches from
some of his followers. In response he knocked down two warriors, kicked a third in the chest with both feet, leapt upon
him like a beast of prey, pummeling him, and tore one ear
from his head with his teeth. "I am your chief," he screamed,

"whether prisoner or not!" Because Coacoochee was gone, Worth turned now to Halleck to contact the remaining intransigents. Through him word went out that they could plant unmolested if they would go south of Pease Creek. In offering them this chance, Colonel Worth was apparently falling back upon the broad discretion given him as on-the-spot commander. He had no specific authorization to allow the Indians to remain; indeed the members of the Administration seemed to carefully avoid a positive statement on so explosive an issue.[26]

A trace of humor here enters an otherwise grim story. It had seemed suitable to Captain Henry McKavett to name a new post Fort Repose, but the headquarters of the Florida army was not amused. Such a name would be seized on by the harpies in Congress who hated the war and took every opportunity to discredit the army.[27] The fort was renamed.

Meanwhile, at Washington, there had been noteworthy personnel alterations. Secretary of War Bell had resigned with the rest of President Tyler's cabinet when Tyler revealed himself to be a Democrat, not a Whig, by vetoing the Whig bill to establish a third United States Bank. John C. Spencer took the post on October 12, 1841. He could not change operations to any degree, but with Winfield Scott to prompt him he was more likely than not to accept Colonel Worth's suggestions about the Florida theater. At the colonel's recommendation, one by one the regular regiments left Florida. Finally only the Third and Eighth and six companies of the Fourth Infantry remained.[28]*

The date May 10, 1842, was a historic one. It was the day on which Secretary Spencer notified General Scott that the Ad-

*The First Infantry arrived in Florida, November, 1837, departed, August 5, 1841, lost 6 officers, 135 enlisted men; the Second Dragoons arrived June, 1836, 5 companies departed October 17, 1841, 5 companies May, 1842, the regiment lost 5 officers to disease, 2 in battle, 172 enlisted men to disease, 20 in battle; the Third Artillery arrived 1836, departed March, 1842, lost 8 officers to disease, 3 in battle, 125 enlisted men to disease, 33 in battle; the Second Infantry arrived June, 1837, departed May, 1842, lost 2 officers, 131 enlisted men; the Sixth Infantry arrived September, 1837, departed February 20, 1842, lost 6 officers to disease, 4 in battle, 110 enlisted men to disease, 19 in battle; the Seventh Infantry arrived May, 1839, departed July 20, 1842, lost 2 officers to disease, 2 in battle, 88 enlisted men to disease, 28 in battle. Sprague, *Origin*, 526-50, lists by regiment all the men who died in Florida during the war.

ministration desired an end to hostilities as soon as possible. The exact moment was left up to the field commander. With this directive, Colonel Worth for the first time received authority to end the war in any way he thought proper. If necessary, he assured the Adjutant General, he would allow the Seminoles to remain for the time being in the area south of Pease Creek.[29]

Naturally the navy also began to lighten its operations in Florida. During the command of Colonel Worth the navy had been more than usually active, for the theater commander, Lieutenant John T. McLaughlin, had taken pains to establish good army-navy relations. Under his command, he had a force of 7 vessels, 50 officers, 385 enlisted men (100 of them marines), and 140 dugout canoes, and had from the first kept all hands busy carrying out the colonel's strategy. Even before Worth began his command, McLaughlin had early in 1841 personally led a naval expedition in the first crossing of the peninsula via the waterways of the Everglades and Big Cypress Swamp. It did not much alter his duties when President Tyler's apostasy produced a vacancy at the head of the Navy Department in Washington as it had done in the War Department. Secretary Paulding, like Bell, had resigned, and Abel P. Upshur had taken his seat. In the end the small flotilla serving in the Florida war (which was never designated a squadron) was formally dissolved on August 3, 1842.[30]

As after every other war in American history, Congress quickly took up the matter of the reduction of force. In the forensic struggle Florida was represented by a new delegate who was to achieve more personal fame than any before him. It would be hard to have a more exotic background than David Levy's. A staunch Democrat, he stood across the path of the Whiggism of Governor Call and his entourage, and upon him fell the defense of the attitude of Floridians in the windy debate which occurred during the spring and summer of 1842.[31]

As might be expected, Secretary Spencer's directive to declare the war at an end as soon as possible drew the first bursts of talk. David Levy objected to stopping the conflict as long as there was one Indian left in Florida. He concluded that President Tyler merely sought credit for ending the unpopular war. Then Caleb Cushing of Massachusetts asked him whether he wanted four regiments of regulars in Florida to chase eighty warriors. Inasmuch as two regiments were to be kept there even after the war was declared ended, what difference did the declaration make? Levy favored armed occupation in Florida and cared little whether the army was cut back or kept up. His oratory was applied to the purpose of securing complete removal of the Seminoles and at the same time clearing his constituents of blame for the war. To make his points, he undertook to prove that the Seminoles were not aborigines, and so had no just claim to the land. As for the policy of pacification without removal, this could not work unless the savages were metamorphosed into something else. "If you can root from the heart of the Seminole its ferocity and scorn of faith; if you can lay the tiger in his nature; then you may essay pacification." He asserted that his constituents were virtually free of blame. "I regard the conduct of the people of Florida toward their savage neighbors to be eminently entitled to the praise of the country." After citing some acts of barbarity and displaying the head of a spear which he said had been taken from the body of a child the Indians had tormented, his peroration went thus, "let us hear no more of sympathy for these Indians. They know no mercy. They are demons, not men. They have the human form, but nothing of the human heart. . . . If they cannot be emigrated, they should be exterminated."[32]

No one specifically replied to Levy, as congressmen were less concerned with race relations in Florida than with regulating the military establishment. The House passed a proposal to cut the army back to the level of 1821. It was not a party matter; there were Whigs for and against the cut, and Democrats too. In the main, those representatives who spoke against the army and in favor of its reduction were, believe it or not, from the South: Cave Johnson of Tennessee, James A. Meriweather, Edward J. Black, and Lott Warren of Georgia, Thomas Gilmer of Virginia, and John Pope of Kentucky. They argued that an enlarged army was advocated by high-tariff men, and they disliked high tariffs. They warned of the dangers of a steadily enlarging military establishment. One of their northern allies, John Reynolds of Illinois, even advocated once more the abolition of the Military Academy. The Georgians had a particular grievance against the service; they claimed that the soldiers stationed in Georgia during the Seminole War had harassed the population instead of the Indians. Finally, most of them insisted that the militia could guarantee the security of the nation, even if the foe were formidable England herself. Edward Black voiced their conviction: "I believe the best army we can have is the militia—the armed people—the citizen soldiers of the country who . . . will fight for a great stake—for their wives and children, their homesteads and their honor. Upon these, and the navy, I confidently rest the defense and protection of the American people." There was also a scattering of northern support for the army cut; one of the most important representatives in that camp being John Quincy Adams of Massachusetts who agreed with Black concerning the militia. Rarely found voting with the Southerners, he did so in this case.[33]

Supporting the enlargement of the army were such Northerners as Millard Fillmore, Francis Granger, and Aaron Ward of New York, Caleb Cushing of Massachusetts, Joshua Lowell and William Pitt Fessenden of Maine, and William Halstead of New Jersey. They had some support in the debate from William Cost Johnson of Maryland and Edward Cross of Arkansas. The men of the Northeast were concerned lest the United States appear weak during the negotiations going on at that very moment between Webster and Ashburton concerning the Maine-Canada boundary line. Hostilities could easily result. Citing the northeast boundary dispute (specifically the burning of the *Caroline*), Mexico, affairs in Oregon, the seizure of one of our ships on the west coast of Africa, and of fishing ships in the Bay of Fundy, they contended that in so troubled a world the United States ought to remain strong. As for reliance on militia in the midst of such uncertainties, Aaron Ward spelled out in great detail the decline of that institution, and Caleb Cushing spoke to clear up the reverse side of the militia argument, the fear of a standing army. He stated that the nation ought to support a force of 10,000 men, and that if it did so, many conflicts would be prevented. There was nothing to fear from such an army; no American officer had ever tried to overthrow civilian control. There was one soldier for every 2,500 people, and how could one regular overcome 2,500 citizens? "Why the old ladies of the country would brain them with distaffs if need be."[34]

In August an act was passed to regulate the military establishment. Naturally it was a compromise. The House had eliminated the Second Dragoons, but the Senate converted it into a rifle unit instead. Being infantry, a rifle unit was much cheaper to maintain than horse troops, hence more acceptable to the legislators. In addition, the act provided for the reduction of the size of companies from fifty to forty-two. Otherwise the army held its strength. At the same time the appropriation for the navy was enlarged. This support of the navy and the fate of the Second Dragoons brought a fulmination from Senator Thomas Hart Benton. "We protect Africa from slave-dealers and abandon Florida to savage butchery." Doubtless he overstated the case, but the men of the Second Dragoons felt humiliated at being put down on foot.[35]

Also in August, 1842, an Armed Occupation Bill for Florida was enacted into law. The idea for such a system traced at least as far back as 1838, when Governor Richard K. Call had suggested that the only way to overcome the Seminoles was to establish colonies of settlers to work the land and hold it. Early in 1839 Senator Benton of Missouri had picked up the concept and advanced it as a bill. Debate over this bill ebbed and flowed in both houses of Congress for three years. There was a brisk clash early in 1840. Benton, being chairman of the Senate Committee on Military Affairs, was the principal proponent, with his colleague Lewis F. Linn of Missouri and Clement Comer Clay of Alabama in support. The protagonists insisted that armed occupation would be cheapest in the long run, because there was nothing for a high-priced army, whether of regulars or militia, to fight in Florida. Then the Seminole Indians preyed upon wrecks along the coast, and in some cases lured vessels in to despoil them. Benton appealed to New England members for their support to eliminate this hazard to commerce. In response, opponents argued that it would be ruinous to give away so much. Those for whom the government provided clothes, medical care, seeds, and ammunition would do nothing; indeed the idle from the cities would be attracted. Benton's rebuttal was that the settlers were not being given anything at all; what they received was in payment for military services, and would certainly be earned. He cited the support of men who had struggled in the theater: Call, Jesup, Surgeon General Thomas Lawson, and Joseph M. Hernandez. The opposition replied by attacking these individuals for not having ended the war. They also asserted that small landholders of the sort who were winning the West would not come to Florida, for it was slave territory. But Benton insisted that the bill was designed to lure yeomen, who were needed because Florida, a peninsula, was especially vulnerable to invasion. People for defense, not large plantations, was the need. Some New England legislators feared that the measure would serve to stimulate slavery. Aside from the ever more sensitive slavery issue, there appeared the fear of what a giveaway might do to the nation and to the people. It might create a nation of dependents as well as a national juggernaut. If you could give away 3,000,000 acres of Florida land, John Robertson of Virginia asked, what would prevent you from doing the same elsewhere?[36]

In spite of opposition the Armed Occupation Act became law in 1842. Any head of a family could obtain title to 160 acres in Florida subject to the following stipulations: (1) his land must be south of a line running east and west about three miles north of Palatka and ten miles south of Newnansville; (2) he must reside on the land for five years; (3) he must build a house and clear five acres; and (4) he must not settle within two miles of a military post. The act was to expire at the end of one year, and the grants under it could not exceed a total of 200,000 acres. There were two land offices, Newnansville and St. Augustine. Newnansville was then a town of about 1,000 persons, which had managed to survive in spite of the war. The office of this hamlet issued 942 land patents, while St. Augustine issued only 370. Here was the precedent for homestead donations of public land, the direct forebear of the Homestead Act of twenty years later. Under it, as amended, 210,720 acres were patented. Only 43 permits were issued in 1842, but 1,274 the next year. Assuming five persons per permit, the addition to the population in those two years would have been nearly 6,500, which was more than one-tenth of the entire population.[37]

The tapering off of the war burdened the commander nearly

as much as had waging it. Military personnel became restless from inactivity and the desire to get out of Florida. A Lieutenant Baker was reported to have led his detachment in flight from the Indians, leaving the wounded to be mutilated. "This is the most scandalous transaction of the war," said Worth and ordered the officer's arrest. Captain Nathaniel Hunter of the Second Dragoons, whose critical diary we have noticed before, was accused of writing an anti-army petition circulated in Georgia. Besides such disagreeable personnel problems as these, there was the matter of ending aid to settlers, the closing of several army posts, and the shipment of regular regiments out of the Territory. Lieutenant Patrick, the resettlement officer, was directed to notify the recipients that public aid would end on August 31 in all but a few cases. Regarding the Indians, peace could be extended to all who remained in an assigned area. Meanwhile the shipment of those already in the army's control went forward. On July 14 Halleck's band of forty warriors and eighty women was shipped out. "I have been hunted like a wolf," Halleck said, "and now I am sent away like a dog."[38]

The opening days of August, 1842, were occupied with conferences between the colonel and the chiefs still at large. Because of guarantees which they apparently felt really protected them, most of these came in for talks. Holata Mico and two sub-chiefs, Fuse Hadjo and Nocosemathla, from the Indians who had gone far south, came to Cedar Key (where the headquarters of the Army of the South then was) on August 5. On the ninth, Tiger Tail, the Tallahassee, and Octiarche, the Creek, entered into talks. Colonel Worth told them that every warrior agreeing to go west would receive a rifle, money, and one year's rations. A few took the offer, but others procrastinated, for they had an alternative: they could settle within the limits of a reservation and be left alone, at least for the present. The boundaries of the reservation were the same as those drawn by the late General Macomb in 1839: from the mouth of Pease Creek up its left bank to the fork and along the south branch to the head of Lake Istokpoga; thence down the eastern margin of that lake to the stream which emptied from it into the Kissimmee; then down the left bank of the river to Lake Okeechobee; then south through the lake and the Everglades to the Shark River; and along the right bank of that river to the Gulf; thence, along the shore, excluding the islands, to the starting point. On this basis Colonel Worth on August 14 declared the war at an end. At the same time he asked for ninety days' leave. He was granted the leave and rewarded with a brevet as brigadier general. Not everybody was happy over his promotion. Major Hitchcock brooded in his diary that Worth had gained his star on a policy he, Hitch-cock, had recommended two years before. "This almost makes me exclaim against the humbug of the world."[39]

Now for a time the command devolved on Josiah H. Vose, colonel of the Fourth Infantry. He had at his disposal six com-panies of his own unit together with the Third and the Eighth Infantry Regiments, a total of 1,890 regulars. These occupied posts from Tallahassee to Fort Brooke and then across to Palatka, with the headquarters of the army at Cedar Key. The Third Infantry had arrived in Florida in October, 1840, and had lost 3 officers and 65 enlisted men; the Fourth had lost 6 officers (including Major Dade) and 128 enlisted men; while the Eighth Infantry had entered Florida in No-vember, 1840, and subsequently lost 4 officers and 66 enlisted men.[40]

Murder and rapine continued even in Middle Florida, and embittered the native whites against the army and the govern-ment. In the whites' view, no Indian should have have been left on the soil of the Territory. Even in September some of the major chiefs had not decided finally what they intended to do. Vose reported that Octiarche seemed determined to remain in Florida, whereas Tiger Tail was willing to move. Sentiment in Florida finally coerced the War Department to order Colonel Vose on September 12 to take the field. Now Vose was forced to make one of those lonely decisions which render hard the lot of leaders. His decision and the grounds for it are stated in his own words. The Indians "have so far fulfilled, though slowly, every promise they have made & it was with no less astonishment than mortification that I suddenly found myself instructed . . . to forfeit every pledge I had made to the Indians & pursue a course which in the present state of affairs would in my opinion not only disperse those assembled, under the proclamation for peace, but incite the entire Indian population

to acts of retaliation & revenge, inevitably tending to repro-
duce a state of War. After much reflection upon the subject, I
have determined, in view of all the circumstances which surround me, and under the most unprejudiced conviction that it
will be for the good of the country, to suspend the execution
of the Secretary's instructions. . . ." The War Department accepted his judgment.[41]

Colonel Vose, like the long line of regulars who had preceded
him, held the conviction that the trouble in Florida was not
the fault of the "Savages" alone. He reported to the War Department "a spirit of implacable resentment towards the Indians in the vagabond class of the citizens of this territory.
. . ." These people were threatening to assemble in large bodies
to make war on the small knots of Seminoles who remained.
Most of them had not evinced a disposition to defend their
own firesides earlier when the Indians were more formidable.
Should such a lawless band begin to move, he reminded the
Department, he had no authority to restrain them. The Secretary remedied this condition by endorsing Vose's letter. "If
any citizens of Alachua or others attack such Indians, [Vose]
must repel such attack by force, and he will cause it to be
known that such will be his course."[42]

Fate itself seemed to make Colonel Vose's tenure a difficult
one. On October 4 and 5 a destructive hurricane struck Cedar
Key, and the damage was so great that the post had to be
abandoned. The Indians, convinced that the Great Spirit had
struck the blow, would no longer visit the Key.[43]

General Worth reassumed the command on November 1,
1842. Colonel Vose's regiment had left Florida on September
30, and its commander asked and was granted permission to
follow it. It soon appeared that Tiger Tail and Octiarche had
delayed too long in making up their minds. The general, after
some inconclusive parleying with them, sent out word that
they should both be captured and brought in with their bands.
Here, again, he followed the pattern General Jesup had established. Once taken, Tiger Tail had to be carried on a litter
(Lieutenant Sprague said because he was lacerated from injuries received while drunk, but another officer reported that
his weakness resulted from disease). This left Halpatter, Chitto
Hadjo, and Cotsa Fixico Chopca still at large outside the

boundaries of the reservation. General Worth on December 11 offered a reward of $300 for each chief and $100 for every warrior. He then shipped off the captured, who with those halted at New Orleans totaled 250. While waiting for shipment from New Orleans to the Indian country, Tiger Tail died, halfway between the old and the new home of his people.[44]

1843

After April, 1843, the Eighth Infantry was the only regular force left in Florida. As for the Indians, in November, 1843, General Worth reported that there remained in the Territory 42 Seminole warriors, 33 Mikasukis, 10 Creeks, and 10 Tallahassees, totaling 95. Adding the women and children, the whole figure was about 300. Worth asserted that Bowlegs, whom he called Hotate-mathlochee, a nephew of Micanopy, was the acknowledged chief, with Ossinawa, Otulkethlocko, and Halpatter Tustenuggee as sub-chiefs. He asserted that these were not a menace; indeed since the pronouncement of the end of the war on August 14, 1842, they had observed perfect good faith, had planted and hunted diligently, and had taken their skins and game as agreed to the post at Tampa. Nor had the settlers under the Armed Occupation Act offered them any harm. The settlers, he said, had neither arms nor any desire to use them. Even so, there still were a few depredations.[45]

The conditions of service while William J. Worth commanded were, if possible, worse than before, because Worth pressed his men hard and sent them into remote areas. Water created a large measure of the hardship—officers and men all but lived in it. Sprague described an officer in command of a detachment of thirty to forty on one of Worth's scouts as being without socks or shoes, having a brace of pistols in his belt, without coat or vest, and the leather flap of his cap turned to the rear. "The only stars over his head were the stars of heaven, the only stripes were lacerated feet." Lieutenant Edward Ord on one of the Everglades expeditions wrote about wading waist deep in water tugging a canoe, getting cold and wet and being obliged to sleep that way. "We ought to be brevetted for our sufferings," he wrote home, "and have a year's leave of absence when the war is over to polish up and see the ladies." Captain George A. McCall told of operating in water from six inches to two feet deep for two and a half days, hard put to find swells of dry ground on which to rest. Pack mules carried supplies, but as often as not they caused more labor than they saved. It took six men to drag one mule through some of the bogs. As much as five hours in water no less than knee-deep, beating one's feet and legs against logs, snags, and cypress knees while seeking traction in the slime, moving in a sunless medium—all this was hard for white men to bear. In this particular campaign, McCall said, only 200 men out of 800 remained fit for duty. The rest were incapacitated by fever, diarrhea, or swollen feet and ankles from the endless water.[46]

Ensign George H. Preble, United States Navy, recorded his experiences on an Everglades expedition in 1842 in one of the most interesting diaries to be preserved. The expedition consisted of officers, marines, sailors, one Indian, one Negro, one squaw, and one Indian child, totaling eighty-seven persons. Eighteen canoes served as home to this fragment of humanity for sixty days. The canoes were thirty feet long and four feet wide, hollowed out of great cypress logs. The officer in charge of each slept on a locker in the stern containing the stores, but the men slept on their oars. Ammunition had to be carried in glass bottles to prevent dampness. Being a gourmand, Preble relieved the drudgery by looking forward to meals. He and his shipmates tried everything in the bountiful variety offered by the Everglades. They enjoyed crow, blackbird, and woodpecker, shot wild hogs and ate them, downed omelets of crane's eggs, and tried with satisfaction a "stewzie" of young cranes and water turkeys. Gator tails and turtles proved excellent fare. These were followed by wild turkey, broiled and fried curlew, plover, teal, stewed crane, and stewed anhingas (water turkeys which Preble called "Grecian Ladies"). Perhaps most exotic of all, but delicious, was rattlesnake meat, and trout literally jumped into the canoes. "The Astor House," said Preble, "could not have supplied such a dinner or such appetites."[47]

In this expedition the brutal and the beautiful were mingled. Even in the empty stretches of the Everglades it was thought necessary to lash some of the men. Two of them deserted, which would seem to indicate that conditions were more than they could bear, for who would willingly leave the support of the group and the knowledge of guides in that trackless wilderness? Preble recorded that a squaw went off into the scrub by herself and bore a child, dead at birth, and then rejoined the caravan. The nights, he said, were thunderous with the screaming of cranes and herons, the bellowing of frogs, and the hooting of owls. He had an eye for natural beauty. "The sunset very beautiful, dark-purple clouds piled up and tinged gold. The sun's lower disk, just before it reached the horizon, appeared below the lower edge of a large cloud, and shot up its brilliant rays far about it; the ruddy sky beneath, and the dark pines reflected in the placid Lake, and a light fleecy cloud soaring above all, invested by our fancies with the shape of our eagle emblem, completed a beautiful scene."

The diarist bore up well until the expedition returned to Fort Lauderdale, then he fell sick. Where the saw grass had cut them and mud filled the wounds, his legs ulcerated and they did not fully heal for two years. Sometimes during that period he feared it might be necessary to amputate one or both legs.[48]

Fortunately unaware of what the next two decades held, Lieutenant W. T. Sherman wrote to the girl he later married that here was the sort of war a young United States soldier ought to know since "The Indian is most likely to be our chief enemy in time to come." So far as hardship constituted valuable training, he was certainly right. This service was as hard as any the American military has ever had to endure. It took a heavy toll in sickness. In the nine months ending February 28, 1842, in Florida 15,794 soldiers were entered on sick rolls. Of these 234 died and 117 were discharged for disability. Small wonder that there was a problem with drinking, especially when the high command, however hard it tried, could not stop the sale of whiskey to the troops. At one time Lieutenant Colonel Bennet Riley reported to the commander that he had 90 men on sick list and 50 in the guardhouse because of liquor. He had reasoned with the citizens of Micanopy where he was stationed, but the respectable citizens had told him flatly that they could not stop the sale.[49]

16

Conclusion

IN SPITE OF General Worth's designating a date for the end of hostilities, the Seminole War did not come to an abrupt end. It simply dragged itself out. The few Seminoles remaining in Florida withdrew into the Everglades. There is no way to be sure how many of them perished during the war, but 3,824 had been shipped westward by the end of 1843. Thereafter their numbers in Florida slowly declined, and a count in 1844 showed only 3,136 remaining in the western Indian Territory. The remnant in Florida was unfortunate enough to be involved in the decade of the 1850's in what is known as the Third Seminole War. This reduced their numbers to less than one hundred. For two decades after that disturbance the Florida Seminoles dropped from the white man's sight. No effort was made to keep contact with them in their Everglades fastness. They came out to trade from time to time at Fort Myers and other towns on the borders of the great swamp, but otherwise they had nothing to do with white men. Beginning in the 1880's their isolation was slowly broken down. Later too the decline in population decelerated and then reversed itself. As of 1962 there were 1,000 Seminoles in Florida and 2,343 in Oklahoma.[1]

The effect of the Second Seminole War upon the military service was substantial, especially on the army. Seventy-four commissioned officers were killed, while a much larger number left the service in part because of this grueling, gloryless war. Those who saw it through gained invaluable field experience in the hardest duty they were ever to know. Some of them went on to command, only three years later, in the War with Mexico; indeed the two top commanders in that conflict were Winfield Scott and Zachary Taylor. Oddly enough, Taylor was the only officer to come out of the Seminole War with an enhanced reputation. His Battle of Okeechobee, though by no means a work of genius, caught the popular imagination. Americans then as now expected a war to be made up of battles. Only by battles, they reasoned, could the nation end a war and get back to the normal pursuits of peace. To Americans war was, and is, abnormal. And while Okeechobee was by no means decisive, it was at least recognizable as a battle in a war which produced few such major confrontations. Taylor profited by chance on an American characteristic.

Beyond the War with Mexico loomed the Civil War, and numerous veterans of the Seminole War lived to command in that one too, on one side or the other. Enumeration of but a few will demonstrate how important they were: William T. Sherman, Samuel Heintzelman, Edward Ord, George H. Thomas, Braxton Bragg, William S. Harney, George Gordon Meade, Joseph E. Johnston, and John C. Pemberton. These men and others necessarily learned something from the Florida war which they employed later. Surely, too, they caught a glimpse of how grim the practice of their profession could be.

The navy also gained valuable training. It played a larger role in this than in any other Indian war, for here the combat zone was surrounded on three sides by water. Probably the most important lesson for the navy was the close liaison which had to be maintained with the army. In no previous conflict had the two services been called on to do so much together. And if the relationship between the officers of the two services was not always perfectly cordial, at best it was excellent and productive of efficient results. Unified command was not achieved at the top, but farther down there were several instances of it, such as Lieutenant Levi Powell's expedition into the Everglades. Moreover, the army turned its vessels over to the navy to operate, and the navy loaned its sailors and marines to the army. In fact, during more than half of the war the naval flotilla in Florida operated under the direction of the Secretary of War.

Unfortunately scandal came close to disfiguring the navy's contribution. Some years after the war ended, Congress forced an inquiry into the high cost of naval operations under Lieutenant John T. McLaughlin. Certainly it could not find fault with McLaughlin's zeal, for although he had been severely wounded during the fight at the head of Lake Monroe on February 8, 1837, needing nineteen months to recover, he had asked for duty in Florida again. He received command of the Florida "Expedition" late in 1838, a command he continued to exercise until the naval effort came to an end. The investigating committee found that the navy had expended $510,988.01 during the Florida war, of which $343,937.00 had been handled by McLaughlin. It found extravagance and the payment of some prices of as much has 800 per cent above the market. For example, whereas the army had bought dugout canoes for $10 to $15 each, the navy averaged $226; and whereas the cost of treating an illness in the army came to 70.5 cents per head, it equaled $20.60 in the Florida flotilla. Liquor purchased for hospital stores alone cost $2,125.97. Yet when the committee weighed its findings, it exonerated McLaughlin of collusion with his suppliers and also of willfully wasting supplies and money. George Bancroft, Secretary of the Navy at the time (1845-46), wrote the Speaker of the House of Representatives that he thought the inquiry ought to stop there. And it did.[2] If there was equivalent waste in the army in Florida, no investigation ever uncovered it.

The ground force naturally had to carry the main burden. In so doing, it was obliged to relearn some very hard lessons about Indian warfare. War against the Seminoles was not very different from other North American Indian fighting, except in climate and terrain. Knowing their numerical inferiority and utilizing their terrain, the Seminoles were less willing to engage in battles than some tribes, and were more difficult to corner and to force to fight because of their semi-tropical home. The commanders had to adopt a technique as old as Indian warfare: to strike at the nerve centers of the native society, their villages, crops, and herds.

At the start of the war the white commanders used large

columns of troops. With these they brought the foe to bay and made him fight on several occasions because they chanced to be close to vital settlements, and had to be delayed, whatever the cost, until Indian women, children, and essential gear could be moved out. The battles of Wahoo Swamp and Lockahatchee were examples. In time the commanders found that the big columns were not equally successful in finding and destroying crops and villages. Thus, as the war went on, the trend was toward smaller units, minus supply trains, with the troops carrying what they needed on their backs.

One ingredient necessary to the destruction of the vital centers of Seminole culture was knowledgeable scouting and guiding. Many villages, well protected by nature, went undiscovered for years, even though close to white strongholds. These, and the Seminoles' remotest hideaways, might never have been found, except for the guides who had lately been with the Indians. Sometimes the guides were Seminoles; more often they were Negroes. It may be that some of the latter were coerced into betraying their former allies (evidence on the point is scanty), but more probably they were following self-interest. At the start of the war the Indian-Negroes had nothing to expect from white men but bondage, so they sided with the Seminoles. But as time passed, the Negro leaders, who had "patriotic" devotion to the red cause, were captured and shipped west. As the remaining Negroes saw that their allies could not prevail, they began to turn to the white man for such advantages as might accrue. In addition to self-interest, an essential factor was operating. The Indian-Negro culture, because of the war, was in the process of disintegration, and the values which it supported were weakening. Thrown into an utterly unstable situation, the Negroes acted opportunistically.

This war confirmed two tactical operations which a few studious soldiers knew had been demonstrated in previous Indian wars. At the rare times when the Seminoles could be brought to battle, the best system was to pour upon them a heavy fire, preferably augmented by cannon and rockets, and then charge with the bayonet. Naturally, if a flank of the Indian position was open, it was the most sensitive point to attack. Even though this operation was hampered by terrain and climate, it could nearly always be employed. To aid it, horses and mules dragged cannon into seemingly inaccessible spots, though the animals died by the hundreds in doing so. Sometimes it was necessary to put part of the assault force into small boats, but the effect was the same.

The second operation, at least two hundred years old, stemmed from the inveterate unwillingness of the Indians of North America to mount guard at night. Attackers could creep up on a village in the dark, wait for the first light of dawn, and then pour in a devastating fire. The fire in the Seminole War issued in the main from flintlocks. This was a flintlock war. Except for Colt's weapons, the hand and shoulder guns on both sides were fired by flint and steel.

The Second Seminole War is important in American military history because of its development of guerrilla, or partisan-style, warfare. If organized white forces were to force the Seminoles out of Florida, they had to find ways to penetrate inaccessible areas, live in part off the land, recruit guides from among the natives or erstwhile allies of the natives, destroy the enemy's food supply, track him down in his deepest lairs, learn to endure severe privation, and all the while protect friendly settlements. The fact that they finally were forced to permit a handful of unconquered Seminoles to remain in the Everglades stands as an eternal reminder of the difficulties of combating guerrilla-style operations.

The price paid in casualties for the lessons learned and for the ground liberated was high. The regular army suffered 1,466 deaths, of which 328 were killed in action. Deaths in the navy totaled 69. Less than one-quarter of the losses were from battle; as it is in most wars, disease was the greatest murderer. If 10,169 be taken as the number of individuals who did duty in the regular services in Florida, the death rate for regulars equals 14 per cent. There is no way to be sure about the citizen soldiers. Of around 30,000 of them who served, only 55 were killed in action; but much larger numbers almost certainly died of disease. The wounded as often as not either died or were permanently crippled. There did not exist any type of welfare system to aid the handicapped. Ransom Clarke, famous as the only white survivor of Dade's Massacre, was too badly shocked and injured to work. He was obliged to write accounts of his escape in order to obtain food. When this source began to fail, he appealed for government grants and for charity. But precious little came to him from anywhere. And there was the widow of Major Dade. Her pension of half-pay for five years ended in 1840, and destitution threatened her and her family if added bounty was not forthcoming. The Legislative Council of Florida could do no more than direct the delegate to introduce into Congress a bill for her relief.[3]

Money costs of the war are given variously at from $30 million to $40 million. As far as is known, no analytical study of costs has ever been made. One difficulty of such a study lies in the fact that the appropriation bills often included a lump sum for the suppression of Indian hostilities, without stipulating any details. This makes it nearly impossible to separate the costs of the Creek uprising of 1836 from the Seminole War. It is also hard to prorate the costs of the two military services so as to assign to a given Indian war an accurate share.[4]

Obviously the Second Seminole War was connected intimately with the nation's number one problem of slavery. At the start the connection was not generally apparent, but as the war progressed, and the slavery issue grew year by year more deadly, the relationship became crystal clear. Indeed, in the end the war did a good deal to add to the bad feelings on both sides of the question.

The national policy of Indian removal met its fiercest opposition from the Seminoles.

It is all but impossible to measure the net impact of the conflict upon the Territory of Florida. Even though the destruction of property was appalling, population increased slowly throughout the war. And the Armed Occupation Act provided an incentive to settle not available anywhere else in the United States. Moreover, the war brought what had been virtually an unknown land into public notice. In consequence the map of the peninsula was filled out, and almost all portions of the wilderness explored. Only three years after General Worth proclaimed the end of the war, Florida entered the union as a state.

There is one final and important way in which the Second Seminole War became a milestone in American history. At the end of the War of 1812 the federal government had all but lost the power to repel an enemy. It could scarcely raise money, supplies, and men. Impressed by this debility, the states undertook to regain some of the decisive powers vested by the Constitution in the federal government. They sought to secure for themselves the power to tax and the power to raise and maintain military forces. Andrew Jackson's phenomenal victory at New Orleans probably saved these powers for the Union. When the war was over, a surge of nationalism swept the United States, and the federal government began to regain strength and efficiency. By the time of the war with the Seminoles, two decades later, it had advanced so far that it could wage war much more smoothly than before. The Seminole War was a step in the progression, and when it was over, the United States was better able to convert its economic and social strength into wartime military power.

Notes

(The following abbreviations are used for convenience in the citations and in the location of records cited.)

AG	Adjutant General, U.S. Army
AGLR	Adjutant General, Letters Received
AGLS	Adjutant General, Letters Sent
ASPFR	*American State Papers: Foreign Affairs*
ASPIA	*American State Papers: Indian Affairs*
ASPMA	*American State Papers: Military Affairs*
CG	Commanding General
CO	Commanding Officer
Cong.	U.S. Congress
DAB	*Dictionary of American Biography*
FHQ	*Florida Historical Quarterly*
GHQ	General Headquarters
GO	General Order
Hq.	Headquarters
HR Doc.	U.S. House of Representatives document
OIALR	Office of Indian Affairs, Letters Received
OIALS	Office of Indian Affairs, Letters Sent
OWRS	Old War Records Section, National Archives
QM	Quartermaster
SW	U.S. Secretary of War
Sen. Doc.	U.S. Senate document
sess.	session (of Congress)
TP: Florida	Clarence E. Carter, *The Territorial Papers of the United States*, Vols. XXII-XXVI: *Florida Territory*
USSL	*United States Statutes at Large*
WOLR	War Office, Letters Received
WOLS	War Office, Letters Sent

CHAPTER 1

1. *Cong. Globe*, XI, Appendix, 499-500. For complete information on the sources see the Bibliography.

2. Cohen, *Notices*, 31.

3. Statement of Seminole chiefs in *TP: Florida*, XXIII, 549.

4. McReynolds, *Seminoles*, 5; Boyd, *Florida Aflame*, 4; Brinton, *Notes*, 112-34; Swanton, *Early History*, 320-21; Fairbanks, "Report," 7.

5. Sturtevant, "Spanish-Indian Relations," 69-70.

6. *Ibid.* Boyd, *Florida Aflame*, 21, and Swanton, *Early History*, 27, 344, say the Spanish Indians were Calusas; for the contrary see

Neill, "Identity," 43-57; Sturtevant, "Chakaika."

7. Fairbanks, "Report," 98; "Oconee" in Hodge, *Handbook;* McReynolds, *Seminoles*, 5.

8. Boyd, "Documents"; Swanton, *Early History*, 12, 183.

9. Harper, *Bartram*, 117-18; Boyd, *Florida Aflame*, 14; Swanton, *Early History*, 80 ff., 101, 106-7; Brinton, *Notes*, 139-40; Woodward, *Reminiscences*, 130 ff.; "Yamassee" in Hodge, *Handbook*; Foreman, *Indian Removal*, 364; Fairbanks, "Report," 100-101; Crane, *Southern Frontier*, 162-86.

10. Swanton, *Early History*, 180-81, 398-99; Harper, *Bartram*, 117-18; McReynolds, *Seminoles*, 5.

11. Sturtevant, "Seminole Personal Document," 59-60; Swanton, *Early History*, 12, 183, 401 ff.; Boyd, *Florida Aflame*, 15-16.

12. Boyd, *Florida Aflame*, 13.

13. *Ibid.*, 5; Swanton, *Early History*, 172-73, 178-79.

14. Swanton, *Early History*, 110.

15. Boyd, *Florida Aflame*, 13.

16. Swanton, *Early History*, 286-87, 304, 312; McReynolds, *Seminoles*, 121; Young, "Topographical Memoir," 85.

17. Halbert and Ball, *Creek War, passim.*

18. Varying figures for the number of Indians in Florida will be found in McReynolds, *Seminoles*, 62; Cotterill, *Southern Indians*, 232; Boyd, "Dexter," 81; Brinton, *Notes*, 149; Swanton, *Early History*, 403; Bell to Metcalf, 1822, *TP: Florida*, XXII, 463-65; Fairbanks, "Report," 83, 211.

19. Porter, "Founder"; Boyd, *Florida Aflame*, 5; Stuart to Gage, Dec. 14, 1771, quoted in Fairbanks, "Report," 83, 211; evidence in Krogman, "Racial Composition," has been rejected as being patently in error.

20. Swanton, *Early History*, 216.

21. *Ibid.*, 286-87, 317 ff.; Swanton, *Social Organization*, 310, 327 ff.; Harper, *Bartram*, 313; Caughey, *McGillivray*, 1-68.

22. Pound, *Benjamin Hawkins*, 162.

23. Harper, *Bartram*, 313; Swanton, *Social Organization*, 276, 314-15; Boyd, "Dexter," 83; Debo, *Road to Disappearance*, 12; Adair, *History*, 379, 428, 430; Caleb Swann as quoted in Schoolcraft, *Historical Information*, Part 5, 279; Hawkins, "Sketch," 65-66; Young, "Topographical Memoir," 89, 93; Boyd, *Florida Aflame*, 7.

24. Boyd, *Florida Aflame*, 10-12; Porter, "Origins," 39; Goggin, study of the lineage of the Alachua chiefs in "Source Materials."

25. Debo, *Road to Disappearance*, 12 ff., 25; Swanton, *Social Organization*, 405, 425-26; Hawkins, "Sketch," 66; DuVal to SW, Oct. 26, 1824, *TP: Florida*, XXIII, 91; Boyd, *Florida Aflame*, 7-8.

26. Boyd, *Florida Aflame*, 12, 18; Swanton, *Early History*, 401; Porter, "Origins," 39; Debo, *Road to Disappearance*, 25.

27. Debo, *Road to Disappearance*, 15; Swanton, *Social Organization*, 166, 168.

28. Swanton, *Social Organization*, 345, 384-88; Debo, *Road to Disappearance*, 14-16.

29. Swanton, *Social Organization*, 345, 384-88; Simmons, *Notices*, 83; Boyd, "Dexter," 84; Spoehr, *Camp, Clan and Kin*, 88-94.

30. Schoolcraft, *Historical Information*, Part 5, 272; Adair, *History*, 380 ff.

31. Swanton, *Social Organization*, 364-65; Spoehr, *Camp, Clan and Kin*, 21; Tallahassee *Floridian*, March 30, 1839; Schoolcraft, *Historical Information*, Part 5, 273.

32. Schoolcraft, *Historical Information*, Part 5, 275; Neill, *Florida's Seminole Indians*, 68.

33. Capron, *Medicine Bundles*, 155-210; Sturtevant, "Medicine Bundles and Busks."

34. Adair, *History*, 379-80, 387-

88; Simmons, *Notices*, 81; Swanton, *Social Organization*, 366, 408, 424, 426, 428.

35. Swanton, *Social Organization*, 408 ff.; Adair, *History*, 381-83; Swanton, *Religious Beliefs*, 538-39; St. Augustine *Florida Herald*, May 12, 1836.

36. Swanton, *Religious Beliefs*, *passim*.

37. *Ibid.*, 617-18, 620, 625, 638.

38. Swanton, *Social Organization*, 456-70.

39. Pope, *Tour*, 62-63.

40. Simmons, *Notices*, 75; Young, "Topographical Memoir," 92.

41. Cotterill, *Southern Indians*, 12-13, 124-25; Dexter to DuVal, Aug. 26, 1823, WOLR, Indian Affairs, Record Group 75.

CHAPTER 2

1. Patrick, *Florida Fiasco*, 104, 180.

2. Harper, *Bartram*, 134-35; Mowat, *East Florida*, 113-14, 120-21.

3. Cotterill, *Southern Indians*, 127-37; *DAB*; Fairbanks, "Report," 199 ff.; McAlister, "Bowles."

4. Mitchell to Sen. Committee, Feb. 23, 1819, *ASPMA*, I, 748-49.

5. Porter, "Negroes and the Seminole War, 1817, 1818," 251n.

6. *Ibid.*, 249-80; McCall, *Letters*, 160; Sturtevant, "Accomplishments," 30.

7. Giddings, *Exiles*, 32.

8. Kappler, *Indian Affairs*, II, 46-50; Mitchell to SW, Dec. 14, 1817, *ASPIA*, II, 161.

9. This invasion, called the Patriot War, is definitively dealt with in Patrick, *Florida Fiasco*.

10. *Ibid.*, 170 ff.

11. *Ibid.*, 199-207; Pound, *Benjamin Hawkins*, 220.

12. Patrick, *Florida Fiasco*, 225-33.

13. Halbert and Ball, *Creek War*.

14. Paine, "Seminole War," 50-52; Fairbanks, "Report," 218;

Hugh Pigot to Alex. Cochrane, June 8, 1814; Cochrane to Nicolls, July 4, 1814, Admiralty Papers, Class 1, folio 506, 394-97, 480-82, Public Record Office, London.

15. McReynolds, *Seminoles*, 76.

16. *Ibid.*, 76-78; Paine, "Seminole War," 54 ff.

17. Fairbanks, "Report," 224-27; Young, "Topographical Memoir," 85; Perryman to Sands, Feb. 24, 1817, *ASPMA*, I, 681-82.

18. Gaines to SW, Dec. 2, 1817; to Jackson, Nov. 21, 1817; to SW, Nov. 26, 1817; Mitchell to Sen. Committee, Feb. 23, 1819, *ASPMA*, I, 686-87, 748-49.

19. SW to Jackson, Dec. 26, 1817, *ASPMA*, I, 439; to Gaines, Dec. 2, Dec. 9, Dec. 16, 1817, *HR Doc. 173*, 15 Cong., 1 sess., 23-24, 28.

20. Arbuckle to Gaines, Dec. 29, 1817; to Jackson, Jan. 12, 1818, *ASPMA*, I, 691, 695.

21. Paine, "Seminole War," 69, 74, 80; Jackson to SW, Mar. 25, 1818, *ASPMA*, I, 699; Jackson to SW, March 25, 1818, *HR Doc. 14*, 15 Cong., 2 sess., 50; Fairbanks, "Report," 266; Porter, "Negroes, 1817, 1818," 274.

22. Monroe to Cong., March 25, 1818, *ASPFR*, IV, 183; see also *ASPMA*, I, 680-81, and Jackson to CO, St. Marks, April 6, 1818, 704-5.

23. Jackson to SW, April 8, 1818; Butler to AG, May 3, 1818; *ASPMA*, I, 700, 703.

24. James, *Andrew Jackson*, 314.

25. Butler to AG, May 3, 1818; SW to Gaines, Aug. 14, 1818, *ASPMA*, I, 703-4, 696; see also 739-43.

26. Porter, "Negroes, 1817, 1818," 277 ff.; Fairbanks, "Report," 230.

27. Griffin, "Comments."

CHAPTER 3

1. Concerning censure of Jackson see *Sen. Report 100*, 15 Cong., 2 sess., also in *ASPMA*, I, 739-43;

"Memorial of Andrew Jackson," Aug. 3, 1820, *HR Doc. 73*, 16 Cong., 1 sess.; Parton, *Andrew Jackson*, II, 550, 570; James, *Andrew Jackson*, 321.

2. "Treaty of Amity, Settlement, and Limits Between the United States and His Catholic Majesty," Feb. 22, 1819, *ASPFR*, IV, 623-25.

3. "An Act to Reduce and Fix the Military Peace Establishment," March 2, 1821, 3 USSL 615; Ganoe, *History*, 158-59; Mahon, "History," 59.

4. Bell to SW, Jan. 22, 1822; White to SW, Dec., 1822, *ASPIA*, II, 416, 411; Hernandez to SW, March 11, 1823, *TP: Florida*, XXII, 644; Simmons, *Notices*, 89; see Patrick, *Florida Fiasco*, for details on the Patriot War.

5. Vignoles, *Observations*, 129, 134.

6. Simmons, *Notices*, 47, 84; Brinton, *Notes*, 149; "Statement of Commissioners," *ASPIA*, II, 439; Bell to Metcalfe, n.d., 1822, *TP: Florida*, XXII, 463-65.

7. Jackson to Secretary of State, April 2, 1821; to SW, Sept. 20, 1821, *TP: Florida*, XXII, 29, 211; Abel, "History of Events," 328-29.

8. Ganoe, *History*, 158-59.

9. SW to Jackson, March 31, 1821; to Pénières, March 31, 1821, *TP: Florida*, XXII, 25-28.

10. Bell to SW, Aug. 14, July 17, 1821, *TP: Florida*, XXII, 126, 170-71; Pénières to Jackson, July 19, 1821, *ASPIA*, II, 412; Boyd, "Dexter," 69.

11. Boyd, "Dexter," 80; Brevard, *History of Florida*, I, 269.

12. Boyd, "Dexter," 66-67; Jackson to SW, Sept. 17, 1821; Dexter and Wanton to Eustis, Oct. 5, 1821, *TP: Florida*, XXII, 207, 244.

13. SW to Bell, Sept. 28, 1821; Bell's court-martial and acquittal, *TP: Florida*, XXII, 220, 409n.

14. Jackson to SW, Sept. 20, 1821; SW to Pénières, March 31, 1821; SW to Bell, Sept. 28, 1821;

Worthington to SW, Dec. 4, 1821, *TP: Florida*, XXII, 211, 27, 220, 294.

15. SW to Jackson, Nov. 16, 1821, *TP: Florida*, XXII, 278.

16. SW to Pelham, Oct. 29, 1821; DuVal's commission, April 17, 1822; Humphreys' commission, May 8, 1822; SW to Bell, June 1, 1822; to DuVal, June 11, 1822, *TP: Florida*, XXII, 264, 469, 429, 429n, 450, 453; Boyd, "Dexter," 73.

17. Knauss, "DuVal."

18. SW to Mitchell, Oct. 26, 1818, March 11, 1819, WOLS; DuVal to SW, June 21, July 18, n.d., Aug., Sept. 22, 1822; SW to Bell, Sept. 28, 1821; to DuVal, Aug. 19, 1822, *TP: Florida*, XXII, 471, 491, 501, 533, 534, 220, 508.

19. White to Commissioner, Fla. Land Titles, Dec. 1, 1822, *ASPIA*, II, 411; "Proclamation," July 29, 1822, *TP: Florida*, XXII, 501.

20. SW to DuVal, July 17, Aug. 19, Aug. 28, 1822, *TP: Florida*, XXII, 488, 508, 518.

21. Bell to SW, Jan. 22, 1822, *ASPIA*, II, 416; DuVal to SW, Aug. 3, 1822, *TP: Florida*, XXII, 501.

22. Eustis to SW, July 23, 1822; Walton to SW, Nov. 4, 1822, *TP: Florida*, XXII, 495, 557.

23. Wright to Walton, Dec. 7, 1822, *TP: Florida*, XXII, 578.

24. Perryman to Sands, Feb. 24, 1817, *ASPMA*, I, 681-82.

25. Walton to Humphreys, Jan. 21, 1823; DuVal to Secretary of State, March 16, 1823, *TP: Florida*, XXII, 602, 649.

26. Committee on Indian Affairs to HR, Feb. 21, 1823, *ASPIA*, II, 408-10; Message of the President, Dec. 3, 1822, *Sen. Doc. 1*, 17 Cong., 1 sess., 7.

27. Hernandez to SW, March 11, 1823; DuVal to Secretary of State, March 16, 1823; SW to Hernandez, March 19, 1823; Gadsden to SW, June 11, 1823, *TP: Florida*, XXII, 644, 649, 652, 695.

28. *DAB*; Gannon, *Cross*, 129; Commissions of Gadsden and Segui, April 7, 1823, *TP: Florida*, XXII, 42*n*, 659-60.

29. Agreement marked by Micanopy and Jumper, June 4, 1823, *ASPIA*, II, 432; "Proclamation," June 7, 1823, *TP: Florida*, XXII, 649 (see also 659*n*).

30. Gadsden to SW, June 11, 1823, *ASPIA*, II, 433-34.

31. SW to Gadsden, June 30, 1823, *ASPIA*, II, 434.

32. Jackson to SW, July 14, 1823, *TP: Florida*, XXII, 719-20.

33. Gadsden to SW, June 11, 1823, *TP: Florida*, XXII, 696.

34. Interchange between DuVal and Erving, Aug. 26, Aug. 27, 1823, *ASPIA*, II, 436.

35. For location of treaty grounds, see St. Augustine *Florida Herald*, Sept. 6, 1823.

36. *Ibid.;* Boyd, "Dexter," 86; DuVal to Dexter, May 10, 1823, *TP: Florida*, XXII, 681.

37. DuVal to SW, Jan. 12, March 19, 1824, *TP: Florida*, XXII, 832, 904; Boyd, *Florida Aflame*, 32; Minutes of Council; Humphreys to DuVal, April 7, 1824, *ASPIA*, II, 437, 617.

38. Glenn, "Diary," 148.

39. Minutes of Council, *ASPIA*, II, 437; Kappler, *Indian Affairs*, II, 203-5.

40. Minutes of Council, *ASPIA*, II, 437-38.

41. *Ibid.*, 438-39.

42. *Ibid.*, 439; Treaty of Moultrie Creek, Kappler, *Indian Affairs*, II, 203-5; Commissioners to SW, Sept. 26, 1823, *ASPIA*, II, 440.

43. Minutes of Council, *ASPIA*, II, 439; Kappler, *Indian Affairs*, 203-5; Commissioners to SW, Sept. 26, 1823, *TP: Florida*, XXII, 747-51; for extensions of the reservation see Gadsden to Editor, St. Augustine *News*, July 3, 1839, reprinted in *FHQ*, VII (April, 1929), 350-56; McKenney to DuVal, Sept. 15, 1825; SW to Delegation of Indians, May 10, 1826, *TP: Florida*, XXIII, 192-93, 318, 539.

44. Gadsden to SW, June 11, 1823; Commissioners to SW, Sept. 26, 1834, *ASPIA*, II, 433-34, 440.

45. *TP: Florida*, XXII, 747*n*.

46. Neamathla's list is in Minutes of Council, *ASPIA*, II, 439.

47. Gadsden to SW, Sept. 29, 1823, *TP: Florida*, XXII, 752.

48. McKenney to Commissioners, Dec. 15, 1825, *ASPIA*, II, 642; DuVal to McKenney, Jan. 22, 1826, *TP: Florida*, XXIII, 422.

49. On ratification see *TP: Florida*, XXII, 747*n*.

50. SW to President, Jan. 24, 1825, *ASPIA*, II, 543-44.

51. Commissioners to SW, Sept. 26, 1823, *TP: Florida*, XXII, 750; Gadsden to Jackson, Nov. 14, 1829, Jackson Papers, Library of Congress.

52. Abel, "History of Events," 330, 332.

53. 8 Wheaton 572-90.

CHAPTER 4

1. DuVal to SW, Sept. 26, 1823, *TP: Florida*, XXII, 747; Certificate, Chaires, May 20, 1824, *ASPIA*, II, 688.

2. DuVal to SW, July 12, 1824, *TP: Florida*, XXIII, 13.

3. DuVal to SW, July 29, 1824; vice versa, Aug. 17, 1824, *TP: Florida*, XXIII, 22, 43.

4. DuVal to SW, Jan. 12, 1824, *TP: Florida*, XXII, 832.

5. DuVal to SW, July 29, 1824, *ASPIA*, II, 620-21; for the romanticized version see Martin, *Territorial Days*, 66; Brevard, *History of Florida*, I, 89; Irving, "Conspiracy of Neamathla."

6. McCall, *Letters*, 148-49.

7. Brooke to CG, April 6, 1824; DuVal to SW, July 29, Oct. 26, 1824, May 26, 1825, *TP: Florida*, XXII, 918, XXIII, 22, 90, *ASPIA*, II, 629.

8. Humphreys to DuVal, April 7, July 26, 1824, *ASPIA*, II, 616-17, *TP: Florida*, XXIII, 77.

9. SW to DuVal, April 20, 1824; vice versa, Aug. 31, 1824; DuVal to Walton, Sept. 30, 1825, *TP*: *Florida*, XXII, 926, XXIII, 45*n*, 329-31.

10. DuVal to Bellamy, Sept. 1, 1824; to SW, Oct. 2, Oct. 26, 1824, *TP*: *Florida*, XXIII, 63-64, 78, 89; McKenney to DuVal, Dec. 26, 1825, *ASPIA*, II, 643.

11. DuVal to SW, Oct. 2, 1824, *TP*: *Florida*, XXIII, 78.

12. Gadsden to SW, Jan. 27, 1824; Monroe endorsement, July 29, 1824; Chaires to DuVal, Jan. 13, 1825; Executive Order, Feb. 24, 1825; Walton to McKenney, Oct. 18, 1825, *TP*: *Florida*, XXII, 841, XXIII, 21, 192, 343-44; Chaires to DuVal, Jan. 13, 1825, *ASPIA*, II, 629.

13. Abel, "History of Events," 331; SW to President, Jan. 24, 1825, *ASPIA*, II, 543-44; Gadsden to SW, March 25, 1826, *TP*: *Florida*, XXIII, 489-92; to Jackson, Nov. 14, 1829, OIALR, Seminole Agency, Emigration, microfilm roll 806; Gadsden to Editor, St. Augustine *News*, July 3, 1839.

14. Schmeckebier, *Office of Indian Affairs*, 26-27; *DAB*; Prucha, "McKenney."

15. Monroe to Sen., Jan. 27, 1825, *ASPIA*, II, 541-42.

16. Abel, "History of Events," 344-60; for the Georgia controversy see Doc. 249, *ASPIA*, II, 727-862.

17. Humphreys to McKenney, Aug. 20, 1825; Walton to McKenney, Oct. 6, 1825; White to SW, Jan. 31, 1826; Gadsden to SW, March 25, 1826; DuVal to McKenney, Feb. 22, 1826, *TP*: *Florida*, XXIII, 310, 335, 432-35, 489-92, 445-48. For maps showing Big Hammock and Big Swamp, besides the one in this book, see *TP*: *Florida*, XXIII, 192, 862.

18. Humphreys to Walton, May 14, 1825; Brooke to Gibson, Dec. 20, 1825, *ASPIA*, II, 632-33, 655.

19. Same letters as note 18; Du-Val to SW, Dec. 16, 1825, *ASPIA*, II, 642; DuVal to SW, Dec. 12, 1825; Rodman to SW, July 11, 1826; DuVal to SW, Aug. 29, 1826, *TP*: *Florida*, XXIII, 385, 603-5, 635-37.

20. DuVal to SW, Dec. 16, 1825, *ASPIA*, II, 642.

21. Alberti to Gaines, June 27, 1825; Hernandez to SW, Aug. 9, 1825; to Gaines, June 27, 1825, *TP*: *Florida*, XXIII, 273-74, 291-93; Humphreys to Smith, July 8, 1825, in Sprague, *Origin*, 30-33.

22. Humphreys to SW, March 2, 1825; Brooke to Scott, Aug. 29, 1825, *TP*: *Florida*, XXIII, 202-3, 314.

23. DuVal to McKenney, Jan. 10, 1826, *TP*: *Florida*, XXIII, 409; Brooke to Humphreys, May 2, May 6, 1828; McKenney to DuVal, May 5, 1828, in Sprague, *Origin*, 52-54; Boyd, "Dexter," 87; Walton to Humphreys, May 22, 1825, *ASPIA*, II, 634.

24. DuVal to McKenney, Jan. 12, March 2, March 17, 1826, *TP*: *Florida*, XXIII, 414, 452-54, 472-73.

25. DuVal to McKenney, March 20, 1826, *TP*: *Florida*, XXIII, 483.

26. DuVal to McKenney, July 27, 1826, *TP*: *Florida*, XXIII, 624-25.

27. DuVal to SW, Oct. 26, 1824; Resolve, Legislative Council, Jan. 1, 1826; Memorial, Alachua, n.d.; DuVal to McKenney, Feb. 22, March 20, April 5, 1826—compare the letters cited so far with those below to see the change in DuVal's outlook—DuVal to McKenney, July 27, 1826; Humphreys to DuVal, Sept. 6, 1827, *TP*: *Florida*, XXIII, 89, 403, 406, 445-48, 482, 500-501, 624-25, 911-12; McKenney to Du-Val, Dec. 26, 1826; DuVal to Mc-Kenney, Jan. 23, 1826, *ASPIA*, II, 643, 686.

28. Talks, DuVal and John Hicks, *ASPIA*, II, 689-91.

29. Talk, delegation of Florida Indians, May 17, 1826, *TP*: *Florida*, XXIII, 548-51.

30. McCall, *Letters,* 153-60; Cubberly, "Fort King," 139, 142.
31. Cubberly, "Fort King"; Clinch to AG, Oct. 20, 1826; Duval to McKenney, Nov. 9, 1826; vice versa, Dec. 7, 1826; DuVal to SW, Dec. 8, 1826, *TP: Florida,* XXIII, 651-52, 661, 682-85; Bellamy to DuVal, July 22, 1826, OIALR, "Calendar of Manuscripts."
32. McKenney to DuVal, Nov. 6, 1826; vice versa, Nov. 30, 1826; Rodman to SW, July 11, 1826; DuVal to SW, Aug. 29, 1826, *TP: Florida,* XXIII, 656-57, 671-73, 603-5, 635-37.
33. McKenney to DuVal, March 22, 1827; vice versa, April 17, 1827, *TP: Florida,* XXIII, 801, 816-18; Acts, Legislative Council, Jan. 15, Jan. 17, 1827.
34. CG to Clinch, Jan. 4, 1827, *TP: Florida,* XXIII, 706-7.
35. *Biographical Directory of the American Congress;* Bemrose, *Reminiscences,* 20, 34, 54, 59, 75.
36. Clinch to CG, Feb. 13, 1827, *TP: Florida,* XXIII, 757-59.
37. Cubberly, "Fort King"; Motte, *Journey,* 276.
38. Clinch to AG, June 8, 1827; Scott to AG, April 5, 1828; White to SW, April 16, 1828; military correspondence cited, *TP: Florida,* XXIII, 856-57, 1059-61, 1066, 1067*n;* Clinch to CG, Jan. 4, 1830; vice versa, Jan. 28, 1830, *TP: Florida,* XXIV, 319-21, 339-40.
39. McCall, *Letters,* 183; Boyd, *Florida Aflame,* 30.
40. Martin, *Territorial Days,* 125-26; McCall, *Letters,* 183, 185.
41. White to SW, June 15, 1827, *TP: Florida,* XXIII, 864-67; White talk to Indians, May 20, 1827, OIALR, Seminole Agency, Emigration, microfilm roll 806.

CHAPTER 5

1. Humphreys to DuVal, Feb. 8, 1827, in Sprague, *Origin,* 39-40; to McKenney, Jan. 24, 1827, OIALR, "Calendar of Manuscripts."

2. DuVal to McKenney, Jan. 9, April 17, 1827; vice versa, March 20, 1827, *TP: Florida,* XXIII, 721-22, 816-18, 794-95.
3. DuVal to SW, April 22, 1827, *TP: Florida,* XXIII, 822; Sprague, *Origin,* 43-44.
4. DuVal to Humphreys, Sept. 22, 1828; Humphreys to SW, Oct. 10, 1828, in Sprague, *Origin,* 60-62; McKenney to SW, Nov. 1, 1828; Alachua County Memorial to SW, March 15, 1829; DuVal to SW, May 4, 1829; March to DuVal, May 29, 1829, *TP: Florida,* XXIV, 94, 97, 164-66, 232-34.
5. Report of Adair to SW, April 24, 1829; DuVal to Jackson, April 21, 1829; Humphreys to Adair, April 27, 1829, *TP: Florida,* 209-10, 197-98, 212-14; DuVal to Humphreys, Sept. 22, 1828, in Sprague, *Origin,* 60; Gadsden to Jackson, Nov. 14, 1829, OIALR, Seminole Agency Emigration, microfilm roll 806.
6. McKenney to DuVal, March 18, 1830, *TP: Florida,* XXIV, 381.
7. Talk of John Hicks, Jan. 14, 1829, in Sprague, *Origin,* 66-69.
8. DuVal to McKenney, Jan. 29, 1829, OIALR, Seminole Agency Emigration, microcopy 234, reel 806; Indian Removal Act, May 28, 1830, 4 USSL 411-12; Foreman, *Indian Removal,* 21; Abel, "History of Events," 379; *Register of Debates in Congress,* VI, 995-1120; Prucha, "McKenney."
9. Westcott to Bellamy, Feb. 2, 1832, *TP: Florida,* XXIV, 668-70.
10. Jefferson County Petition to DuVal, Jan. 18, 1832; Legislative Council Memorial to Congress, Feb., 1832; Alachua County Petition to Congress, March 26, 1832, *TP: Florida,* XXIV, 632, 667, 678-80.
11. See James Gadsden, *DAB;* SW to Gadsden, Jan. 30, 1832, *ASPMA,* VI, 473.
12. *ASPMA,* IV, 472; Thompson to DuVal, Jan. 1, 1834, *HR Doc. 271,* 24 Cong., 1 sess., 7-11.

13. Boyd, *Florida Aflame*, 44.

14. Gadsden to Editor, St. Augustine *News*, July 3, 1839.

15. Abel, "History of Events," 393n; "Abstract of Council," Oct. 25, 1834, *Sen. Doc. 152*, 24 Cong., 1 sess., 25-26.

16. "Abstract of Council," 26; Treaty of Payne's Landing, Kappler, *Indian Affairs*, II, 344-45.

17. Croffut, *Fifty Years*, 79-80.

18. For an illustration of the Seminole attitude toward the Creeks, see Worthington to SW, Dec. 4, 1821, *TP: Florida*, XXII, 294.

19. McKenney, *Memoirs*, 274-75; Dovell, *Florida*, I, 242; Moore-Willson, *Seminoles*, 13; Croffut, *Fifty Years*, 122.

20. Gadsden to SW, June 2, 1832, Nov. 1, 1834, *ASPMA*, VI, 505, OIALR, "Calendar of Manuscripts."

21. Anonymous letter to Editor, *Niles' Register*, June 18, 1829, LVI (July 7, 1839), 289; Croffut, *Fifty Years*, 78-79; Gadsden to SW, June 2, 1832, *ASPMA*, VI, 505; Cullum, *Biographical Register*.

22. Boyd, *Florida Aflame*, 6.

23. "Abstract of Council," Oct. 25, 1834, *Sen. Doc. 152*, 26; Gadsden to SW, May 15, 1832, *ASPMA*, VI, 503; to Editor, St. Augustine *News*, July 3, 1839.

24. SW to McDuffie, May 31, 1832, *TP: Florida*, XXIV, 713; Report of SW to President, Dec. 4, 1832, *ASPMA*, V, 23.

25. Gadsden to SW, Aug. 30, 1832; DuVal to SW, Oct. 11, 1832, *TP: Florida*, XXIV, 728, 740.

26. Gadsden to SW, May 31, 1832, *TP: Florida*, XXIV, 713-14.

27. Kappler, *Indian Affairs*, II, 352; Table by Thompson, n.d.; DuVal to Sheffield, Feb. 4, 1833; vice versa, Feb. 23, 1833; DuVal to Commissioner of Indian Affairs, March 3, 1833; Westcott to SW, April 27, 1833, OIALR, "Calendar of Manuscripts."

28. Gadsden to Herring, July 25, 1833, OIALR, "Calendar of Manuscripts"; Herring to DuVal, Dec. 13, 1833, *TP: Florida*, XXIV, 890n, 917.

29. Table by Westcott, Nov. 9, 1833, OIALR; Covington, "Federal Relations."

30. Malin, *Indian Policy*, 18; Abel, "History of Events," 392; Kappler, *Indian Affairs*, II, 390; 4 USSL 564.

31. "Proceedings of a Council Held with a Delegation of Florida Indians at Fort Gibson," National Archives, Sen. Records 23B-C1, Record Group 46; Treaty of Fort Gibson, Kappler, *Indian Affairs*, II, 394-95; "Abstract of Council," Oct. 24, 1834, *Sen. Doc. 152*, 23; Foreman, *Pioneer Days*, 101.

32. Sprague, *Origin*, 80; Croffut, *Fifty Years*, 80-82; Abel, "History of Events," 393; Dovell, *Florida*, I, 242; "Abstract of Council," Oct. 25, 1834, *Sen. Doc. 152*, 26.

33. "Abstract of Council," Oct. 25, 1834, 24; McCall, *Letters*, 301.

34. Kappler, *Indian Affairs*, II, 344, 394.

35. Report, Commissioner of Indian Affairs, West, Feb. 10, 1834, *HR Report 474*, 23 Cong., 1 sess., 79.

36. Westcott to Herring, Nov. 5, 1833, *HR Doc. 271*, 24 Cong., 1 sess., 96; Thornton to SW, Aug. 29, 1833; Thompson to SW, Dec. 2, 1833; White to President, Jan. 18, 1832; to SW, Jan. 23, 1832, *TP: Florida*, XXIV, 873, 916-18, 633-37.

37. *Journal of the Executive Proceedings of the Senate . . ."* IV, 338-39, 382, 385-87; Kappler, *Indian Affairs*, II, 344; *Register of Debates in Congress*, X, Part 4, Appendix, 233.

38. DuVal to SW, Aug. 21, 1832, *TP: Florida*, XXIV, 726; "Abstract of Council," Oct. 24, Oct. 25, 1834, *Sen. Doc. 152*, 23, 25.

39. "Abstract of Council," 26-27.

CHAPTER 6

1. Graham to SW, Nov. 20, 1833; to Herring, Nov. 22, 1833, *HR Doc. 271*, 24 Cong., 1 sess., 97-98.

2. Gadsden to SW, Dec. 4, 1833, *HR Doc. 271*, 97.

3. Herring to Thompson, Aug. 29, 1833, *HR Doc. 271*, 132-33; DuVal to Thompson, Nov. 23, 1833, OIALR, "Calendar of Manuscripts"; Bemrose, *Reminiscences*, 14; *DAB*.

4. Thompson to DuVal, Jan. 1, 1834, *HR Doc. 271*, 8 ff.

5. Report of Commissioners of Indian Affairs, West, Feb. 10, 1834, *HR Report 474*, 23 Cong., 1 sess., 79; Report of Legislative Council, Feb. 13, 1834, *TP: Florida*, XXIV, 970; St. Augustine *Florida Herald*, April 1, 1835.

6. Eaton to SW, March 8, 1835, *HR Doc. 271*, 100; Attorney General to SW, March 26, 1835, *TP: Florida*, XXV, 122-23.

7. 4 USSL 729-38; Prucha, *American Indian Policy*, 250-73.

8. Herring to Thompson, July 10, 1834, *TP: Florida*, XXV, 33-34; St. Augustine *Florida Herald*, Dec. 3, 1834.

9. Thompson to Herring, May 6, 1834, *HR Doc. 271*, 71; "Abstract of Council," Oct. 23, 1834, *Sen. Doc. 152*, 24 Cong., 1 sess., 20-21. See also Cohen, *Notices*, 57-63 (Cohen received some information from David Levy, who was present); Potter, *War in Florida*, 50-70 (Potter seems to have had access to official memoranda never published and not now available).

10. Thompson to Herring, Oct. 28, 1834, *Sen. Doc. 152*, 14-18; Boyd, "Osceola," 252, 261.

11. Bemrose, *Reminiscences*, 20-21; Jarvis, "Surgeon's Notes," 4; Motte, *Journey*, 141; Boyd, "Osceola," 251.

12. Potter, *War in Florida*, 53-55.

13. "Abstract of Council," Oct.

24, 1834, *Sen. Doc. 152*, 23-24.

14. *Ibid.*, 25-28; Cohen, *Notices*, 62.

15. Boyd, *Florida Aflame*, 47; Thompson to Herring, Oct. 28, 1834, *Sen. Doc. 152*, 14-18.

16. *Sen. Doc. 152*, 18.

17. Jackson's endorsement on Thompson to Herring, Oct. 28, 1834, *TP: Florida*, XXV, 63.

18. Thompson to Eaton, Jan. 10, 1835, *TP: Florida*, XXV, 90-91; to Gibson, Jan. 27, 1835; to SW, Dec. 12, 1834, *HR Doc. 271*, 161, 154-57; Call to Jackson, March 22, 1835, *Sen. Doc. 152*, 31.

19. St. Augustine *Florida Herald*, April 1, 1835; Davis, "Early Orange Culture."

20. Eaton to SW, March 8, 1835, *HR Doc. 271*, 100; SW to Clinch, April 14, 1835, *Sen. Doc. 152*, 37.

21. Boyd, *Florida Aflame*, 85-86; Potter, *War in Florida*, 84.

22. Thompson to SW, March 31, 1835, *HR Doc. 271*, 79; Harris and Clinch to SW, April 24, 1835, *Sen. Doc. 152*, 38-39; Bemrose, *Reminiscences*, 20.

23. Boyd, *Florida Aflame*, 51-52; Bemrose, *Reminiscences*, 23-24; "Acknowledgment of Validity of Paynes Landing," April 23, 1835, OIALR, Seminole Agency Emigration, microcopy 234, reel 806; Thompson, DuVal, and Harris to SW, April 24, 1835, *Sen. Doc. 152*, 37-40.

24. Acting SW to Thompson, Clinch, and Harris, May 20, 1835, *Sen. Doc. 152*, 42; *Army and Navy Chronicle*, I (May, 1835), 159.

25. Thompson to Gibson, June 3, 1835, *Sen. Doc. 152*, 43.

26. Boyd, "Osceola," 273-74.

27. Fanning to AG, April 29, 1835; "Permission Granted," June 5, 1835, *TP: Florida*, XXV, 132-33, 133n; Thompson to Gibson, April 27, 1835; to SW, April 27, 1835, *HR Doc. 271*, 182-83; Jackson's Directive, July 7, 1835, OIALS; Sprague, *Origin*, 86-88.

28. Clinch to AG, June 30, 1835; Walker to Thompson, June 22, 1835; Thompson to SW, Aug. 1, 1835, *Sen. Doc. 152*, 44, 48, 45; Potter, *War in Florida*, 18-23.

29. St. Augustine *Florida Herald*, Aug. 27, 1835; Thompson to Gibson, Sept. 21, 1835; SW to Thompson, Oct. 28, 1835, *HR Doc. 271*, 213, 225; Clinch to AG, Oct. 8, Oct. 17, Sept. 12, 1835, *TP: Florida*, XXV, 182-84, 186-87, *Sen. Doc. 152*, 51.

30. Hernandez to Eaton, Oct. 26, 1835, *TP: Florida*, XXV, 189-90; Boyd, *Florida Aflame*, 61; *Biographical Dictionary of the American Congress*.

31. Thompson to Gibson, Nov. 30, 1835, *Sen. Doc. 152*, 52; Fanning to Clinch, Nov. 27, 1835; Clinch to AG, Dec. 9, Dec. 16, 1835, *TP: Florida*, XXV, 200, 209, 213-14; Boyd, *Florida Aflame*, 85-86; Potter, *War in Florida*, 94-97 (Potter asserts that the friendlies fled to Brooke even before Charley Emathla's murder); Sprague, *Origin*, 88n.

32. Walker to SW, Dec. 8, 1835; Call to Jackson, Dec. 22, 1835, *TP: Florida*, XXV, 205, 216-17; SW to Secretary of Treasury, Dec. 13, 1835, WOLS, No. 14, 433.

33. Call to Jackson, Dec. 22, 1835, *TP: Florida*, XXV, 216-17; Boyd, *Florida Aflame*, 56-57; "Jacksonville and the Seminole War," 17-19; Potter, *War in Florida*, 100-101.

34. Boyd, *Florida Aflame*, 59-65; Motte, *Journey*, 277-79; St. Augustine *Florida Herald*, Jan. 6, 1836.

35. Jackson's endorsement on Call to Jackson, Dec. 22, 1835, *TP: Florida*, XXV, 217; "Summary of Events," *Sen. Doc. 152*, 2.

36. Clinch to AG, Oct. 8, 1835, *TP: Florida*, XXV, 183, 189n.

37. Fanning to Clinch, Nov. 27, 1835, *TP: Florida*, XXV, 200; Thompson to Gibson, Dec. 7, 1835;

Harris to Thompson, Dec. 30, 1835, *HR Doc. 271*, 243, 245-50; Sprague, *Origin*, 89; Potter, *War in Florida*, 109-11.

38. The best analysis of all known material on Dade's Massacre is in Boyd, *Florida Aflame*, 84-109; see also Roberts, "Dade Massacre."

39. Roberts, "Dade Massacre," 133n; McCall, *Letters*, 300; Boyd, *Florida Aflame*, 88; Potter, *War in Florida*, 103; Cohen, *Notices*, 77-78.

40. Sprague, *Origin*, 90-91; *Niles' Register*, L, 419; Roberts, "Dade Massacre," 125.

41. Roberts, "Dade Massacre," 135; Sprague, *Origin*, 91; *Niles' Register*, L, 419.

42. Belton to AG, Jan. 9, 1836, *HR Doc. 271*, 250-51; Barr, *Narrative*, 10-11; McCall, *Letters*, 305-7; *Niles' Register*, L, 419-20; Cubberly, "Dade Massacre," 5; Wells, "Osceola," 77-79; Hitchcock to Gaines, Feb. 22, 1836, G970/418, AGLR.

43. Sprague, *Origin*, 91.

44. Bemrose, *Reminiscences*, 31-34.

45. *Ibid.*, 32, 35-36, 80.

46. *Ibid.*, 36; Harris to Gibson, Dec. 30, 1835, *HR Doc. 271*, 245-50.

47. Harris to Gibson, Dec. 30, 1835, 245-50; AG to SW, Feb. 9, 1836, *Sen. Doc. 152*, 1-5; Lewis Cass to the Public, in *The Florida War*, a bound volume in the Office of War Records, National Archives; Clinch to Cass, May 13, 1837, *Niles' Register*, LII, 315, 318; Clinch to AG, Jan. 4, 1836, AGLR.

48. Same sources as note 47.

49. Bemrose, *Reminiscences*, 42-43.

50. Clinch to AG, Jan. 4, 1836, AGLR; Potter, *War in Florida*, 112-16; Bemrose, *Reminiscences*, 48; Parkhill to Call, July 18, 1837, in St. Augustine *Florida Herald*, Aug. 25, 1837; Call to Macomb,

Aug. 3, 1837, in St. Augustine *Florida Herald*, Nov. 13, 1837; Call to Editor, Tallahassee *Floridian*, July 20, 1837, in *Niles' Register*, LII, 395-96.

51. Parkhill to Call, July 18, 1837, in *Niles' Register*, LII, 397-98; Account by "Brevet," *Army and Navy Chronicle*, III, 323-25; Potter, *War in Florida*, 112-16; St. Augustine *Florida Herald*, Jan. 13, 1836.

52. Bemrose, *Reminiscences*, 32-33, 48-50; Potter, *War in Florida*, 112-16.

53. Potter, *War in Florida*, 112-16; Clinch Reply to Cass, May 13, 1837; Call to Editor, Tallahassee *Floridian*, July 20, 1837, in *Niles' Register*, LII, 315-18, 395-96; Clinch to AG, Jan. 4, 1836, AGLR; Mills, "General Circular to All the Good Citizens of DuVal and Nassau Counties," in "Jacksonville and the Seminole War," 23-24; Parkhill to Call, July 18, 1837; Call to Macomb, Aug. 3, 1837, St. Augustine *Florida Herald*, Aug. 25, 1837.

54. Sprague, *Origin*, 92-94; Williams, *Territory*, 221-23; *Niles' Register*, XLIX, 369.

55. Potter, *War in Florida*, 152.

56. Clinch to AG, Jan. 4, 1836; Humphreys to Flotland, Jan. 4, 1836, AGLR; Bemrose, *Reminiscences*, 51, 54; Eaton, "Returns."

57. Call to Editor, Tallahassee *Floridian*, July 20, 1837, in *Niles' Register*, LII, 395-96; Boyd, *Florida Aflame*, 79-84.

58. St. Augustine *Florida Herald*, Jan. 20, 1836; Putnam to Hernandez, Jan. 18, 1836, AGLR.

59. Hernandez to Porter, Jan. 20, Jan. 22, 1836; to SW, Jan. 24, 1836; vice versa, Jan. 20, Jan. 23, AGLR.

CHAPTER 7

1. CG to Cass, Jan. 13, 1836, in GHQ Letterbook III, 72; Report of SW, Nov. 30, 1835, *HR Doc. 2*, 24 Cong., 1 sess., 52-58.

2. McLaughlin, *Lewis Cass*; *DAB*; Allan Nevins, *Ordeal of the Union* (2 vols., 1947), I, 193.

3. SW to President, April 7, 1836, WOLS to President.

4. *Army and Navy Chronicle*, I, 324-25; "Army Register, 1835," ASPMA, V, 607-24.

5. Smith to spouse, March 6, 1838, Smith, "Letters," 340; Motte, *Journey*, 1; *Army and Navy Chronicle*, I, 388, VII, 117.

6. Bemrose, *Reminiscences*, 42, 54, 86; *Military and Naval Magazine*, I, 98-99.

7. *Military and Naval Magazine*, VI, 166; *Army and Navy Chronicle*, I, 188, 277; Bemrose, *Reminiscences*, 61; Motte, *Journey*, 11; F. P. Todd, Director, West Point Museum, to J. K. Mahon, June 22, 1962.

8. Chief of Ordnance to SW, Nov. 20, 1835, *HR Doc. 2*, 229; *Ordnance Reports*, I, 426c; *Army Regulations*, 1835, 160; *Army and Navy Chronicle*, I, 178, V, 202; Potter, *War in Florida*, 147.

9. Potter, *War in Florida*, 152, 280; *Army and Navy Chronicle*, III, 299; Sprague, *Origin*, 460; St. Augustine *Florida Herald*, Jan. 20, Jan. 22, 1836; Bemrose, *Reminiscences*, 52-53; Call to SW, Jan. 21, 1836, AGLR.

10. Data on Hall's rifles from interview with Craddock Goins, firearms expert, Smithsonian Institution, Dec. 29, 1961. There were Hall's rifled carbines Models 1833 and 1836, caliber .54, and one Model 1838 which was smoothbore.

11. Report of Secretary of Navy, Dec. 5, 1835, *HR Doc. 2*, 368-70; Metcalf, *Marine Corps*, 105.

12. AG to SW, Feb. 9, 1836, *Sen. Doc. 152*, 24 Cong., 1 sess., 5; *Niles' Register*, XLIX, 313, 329; Crawford to SW, Jan. 20, 1844, *HR Doc. 82*, 28 Cong., 1 sess., 2; Coe, *Red Patriots*, 160.

13. Indian Commissioner to SW, March 26, 1836, in *Niles' Register*,

L, 62; Report of Indian Commissioner, Nov. 22, 1837, *Army and Navy Chronicle*, VI, 68; Report, Commissary of General Subsistence, Nov. 12, 1835, *HR Doc. 2*, 296.

14. Eaton to SW, Feb. 10, 1836, AGLR; Fanning to Clinch, Nov. 27, 1835, *TP: Florida*, XXV, 201.

15. Interview with Major E. J. Keenan, March 31, 1961.

16. Coe, *Red Patriots*, 30; Bemrose, *Reminiscences*, 22, 52-53; Moore-Willson, *Seminoles*, 48; Cohen, *Notices*, 151.

17. Bemrose, *Reminiscences*, 15, 17, 25; Paine, "Seminole War," 3; Simmons, *Notices*, 88; Childs, "Correspondence," 280.

18. Interview with Major E. J. Keenan, March 31, 1961; Moore-Willson, *Seminoles*, 114; Simmons, "Recollections"; Simmons, *Notices*, 83; Castelnau, "Essay," 249.

19. Motte, *Journey*, 164; Bemrose, *Reminiscences*, 52-53.

20. Simmons, "Recollections"; Simmons, *Notices*, 64; Neill, *Florida's Seminole Indians*, 59.

21. Evidence of Seminole harshness in St. Augustine *Florida Herald*, May 19, 1836; Castelnau, "Essay," 245-46; McKay, *Pioneer Florida*, II, 511, 522; Fairbanks, "Report," 326. Contrary evidence in Simmons, *Notices*, 60; Canova, *Life*, 87; Knowles, "Torture of Captives," 179-80; McCall, *Letters*, 220-21; Porter, "Relations," 303.

22. Jarvis, "Surgeon's Notes," 452; Simmons, *Notices*, 33; Gifford, "Five Plants"; Adair, *History*, 406-15; McCall, *Letters*, 220-21; Bemrose, *Reminiscences*, 17.

23. Clinch to AG, March 9, 1835, *Sen. Doc. 152*, 34; Porter, "Cowkeeper Dynasty," 346; Childs, "Correspondence," 280-81.

24. Childs, "Correspondence," 169; Porter, "Cowkeeper Dynasty," 346; Bemrose, *Reminiscences*, 23; Foreman, *Indian Removal*, 28;

Simmons, *Notices*, 92; Sprague, *Origin*, 97.

25. Sprague, *Origin*, 97, 286; Porter, "Origins"; Childs, "Correspondence," 280.

26. Childs, "Correspondence," 170; Porter, "Cowkeeper Dynasty," 346.

27. Porter, "Origins."

28. Foreman, *Indian Removal*, 350*n*; McKay, *Pioneer Florida*, II, 512; Rodenbough, *Everglade to Cañon*, 28; Bemrose, *Reminiscences*, 20; Sprague, *Origin*, 99.

29. Interview with Major E. J. Keenan, March 31, 1961; Moore-Willson, *Seminoles*, 107; Irving, "Conspiracy of Neamathla," 294-95; Simmons, *Notices*, 76; Neill, *Florida's Seminole Indians*, 6.

30. Porter, "Negro Abraham."

31. Porter, "John Caesar."

32. Cohen, *Notices*, 28; Martin, *Territorial Days*, 90. For examples of early maps see those made by J. S. Tanner, Philadephia, 1823.

33. Williams, *Territory*, 121; Castelnau, "Essay," 209-16; Martin, *Territorial Days*, 140.

34. Martin, *Territorial Days*, 97; Cohen, *Notices*, 27; *Biographical Dictionary of the American Congress*.

35. Williams, *Territory*, 121; Motte, *Journey*, 112.

36. St. Augustine *Florida Herald*, May 7, June 19, 1834.

37. *Ibid.*, Jan. 10, 1835.

38. Indian Commissioner to Gamble, Feb. 21, 1835, OIALR, "Calendar of Manuscripts"; Knauss, *Florida Journalism*; Dovell, *History of Banking*.

39. Williams, *Territory*, 144; Martin, *Territorial Days*, 125-26; Motte, *Journey*, 105; Advertisement for post route, July 10, 1834, *TP: Florida*, XXV, 35.

40. Bemrose, *Reminiscences*, 60; Hollingsworth, "Tennessee Volunteers," 347-48; Pickell, "Journals," 159; Castelnau, "Essay," 220-21, 232-33; Williams, *Territory*, 65.

41. Williams, *Territory*, 303; Bemrose, *Reminiscences*, 12; Castelnau, "Essay," 236-40.

42. Jarvis, "Diary," 73; Sprague, "Macomb's Mission," 166; Motte, *Journey*, 90; Bemrose, *Reminiscences*, 42.

43. Pickell, "Journals," 160; Motte, *Journey*, 199; Barr, *Narrative*, 23; McCall, *Letters*, 194.

CHAPTER 8

1. Sprague, *Origin*, 106; Barr, *Narrative*, 4; St. Augustine *Florida Herald*, March 9, 1836; Meek, "Journal," 307-8; Belton to AG, Jan. 2, 1836, AGLR.

2. Boyd, *Florida Aflame*, 65-66; Douglas, *Autobiography*, 121.

3. Casey to Bassinger, n.d., Southern Historical Collection, University of North Carolina; "Jacksonville and the Seminole War," 25-27; SW to Bank of Charleston, Feb. 15, 1836, WOLS, No. 15, 127; for letters to rejected volunteer units see WOLS, No. 15, 69-70, 76, 80, 84-85.

4. Smith, *Sketch*, 114-15, 128, 135-38, 140, 197, 211, 244; Cohen, *Notices*, 135-36; Potter, *War in Florida*, 127-32; see also Barr, *Narrative*.

5. Barr, *Narrative*.

6. Williams, *Territory*, 224; Eaton, "Returns."

7. *Cong. Globe*, III, 76; Acts of Jan. 14, Jan. 29, 5 USSL 1; Cass to the Public, March 6, 1837, *The Florida War*.

8. AG to SW, Feb. 9, 1836, *Sen. Doc. 152*, 24 Cong., 1 sess., 4.

9. SW to Scott, Jan. 21, 1836, *Sen. Doc. 152*, 15; Cass to the Public, March 6, 1837; SW to governors of South Carolina, Georgia, Alabama, Florida, Jan. 21, 1836, WOLS, Nos. 15, 23; Elliott, *Scott*, 292; Scott's Defense in "Proceedings of the Military Court of Inquiry in the Case of M. G. Scott and M. G. Gaines," *Sen. Doc. 224*, 24 Cong., 2 sess., 130; AG to SW,

Feb. 9, 1836, *Sen. Doc. 152*, 4; SW to Eustis, Jan. 17, 1836, WOLS, No. 14.

10. Clinch Reply to Cass, May 13, 1837, in *Niles' Register*, LII, 318; AG to Clinch, Feb. 1, 1836, AGLS, No. 12, 131.

11. St. Augustine *Florida Herald*, Jan. 6, 1836; Hernandez to Eustis, Jan. 7, 1836, AGLR; An Act to Amend an Act to Organize and Regulate the Militia of the Territory of Florida, Jan. 15, 1836.

12. Bemrose, *Reminiscences*, 78-79; Smith, *Sketch*, 115; Cohen, *Notices*, 208.

13. Scott to Searight, March 10, 1836; to AG, Jan. 31, 1836; to Eustis, Feb. 9, 1836; to Assistant QM at New Orleans, Feb. 14, 1836; to AG, Feb. 20, 1836, *Sen. Doc. 224*, 279-80, 215-17, 231, 235-44; SW to HR Committee on Military Affairs, Feb. 10, 1836, SW Reports to Cong., III, 403.

14. *Sen. Doc. 224*, 65 ff., 130-68; *Army and Navy Chronicle*, II, 190; *Niles' Register*, L, 54.

15. Scott to AG, Feb. 6, 1836; Scott's Defense, *Sen. Doc. 224*, 231, 132-34.

16. Same sources as note 15.

17. Scott to AG, Jan. 31, 1836, *Sen. Doc. 224*, 217; Cass to the Public, March 6, 1837.

18. Silver, *Gaines, passim*; McCall, *Letters*, 299-333; Potter, *War in Florida*, 133 ff.

19. Potter, *War in Florida*, 133, 136, 143; Hitchcock to Lyon, March 11, 1836; McCall to New Orleans *Bulletin*, May 18, 1836; Testimony of Lawson, *Sen. Doc. 224*, 375-78, 381-88, 686-87; Barr, *Narrative*, 27; McCall, *Letters*, 299-333; Croffut, *Fifty Years*, 88-91.

20. Croffut, *Fifty Years*, 88-89; McCall, *Letters*, 299-333; Hitchcock to Lyon, March 11, 1836; Testimony of Hitchcock, *Sen. Doc. 224*, 376, 518-31.

21. Jesup to *Globe*, April 8, 1836; Hitchcock to Washington

Globe, June 4, 1836, *Sen. Doc. 224*, 710, 713; McCall, *Letters*, 299-333; Potter, *War in Florida*, 140.

22. Potter, *War in Florida*, 144; McCall to New Orleans *Bulletin*, May 18, 1836; Testimony of McCall; Testimony of P. F. Smith; Gaines to Clinch, Feb. 28, Feb. 29, 1836, *Sen. Doc. 224*, 381-90, 533-35, 568, 262-64; McCall, *Letters*, 299-333.

23. Same sources as note 22.

24. Potter, *War in Florida*, 146; Gaines to Clinch, Feb. 22, Feb. 29, 1836, *Sen. Doc. 224*, 263-64, 650.

25. Gaines' Defense, *Sen. Doc. 224*, 588; Silver, *Gaines*, 178.

26. Silver, *Gaines*, 178; Elliott, *Scott*, 302; Bemrose, *Reminiscences*, 74.

27. Potter, *War in Florida*, 156; Croffut, *Fifty Years*, 93-94; Sprague, *Origin*, 112.

28. Same sources as note 27.

29. SW to Macomb, March 11, 1836, WOLS, No. 15, 202.

30. Bemrose, *Reminiscences*, 79; *Niles' Register*, L, 97.

31. Scott to Crane, March 20, 1836; to Clinch, March 4, 1836, *Sen. Doc. 224*, 301, 269-70.

32. Scott to Eustis, March 14, 1836, *Sen. Doc. 224*, 284-86.

33. Clinch to Scott, April 8, 1836, *Sen. Doc. 224*, 312-14; Simmons, "Recollections"; Bemrose, *Reminiscences*, 88-89; Cohen, *Notices*, 188-89; Foster to AG, April 9, 1836, *AGLR*; Barr, *Narrative*, 19.

34. Barr, *Narrative*, 7-13; Meek, "Journal"; Potter, *War in Florida*, 167.

35. Eaton to Jackson, April 10, 1836, *TP: Florida*, XXV, 269; Doherty, *Call*, 78.

36. Potter, *War in Florida*, 170; Williams, *Territory*, 333; Lindsay to Scott, April 10, 1836, AGLR.

37. Lindsay to Scott, April 10, 1836, AGLR.

38. Bemrose, *Reminiscences*, 81-82; Cohen, *Notices*, 173-74; Eustis

to Scott, April 10, 1836, *Sen. Doc. 224*, 315-16.

39. Eustis to Scott, March 22, April 10, *Sen. Doc. 224*, 303, 315-16; Cohen, *Notices*, 173-74.

40. Cohen, *Notices*, 169; Smith, *Sketch*, 247.

41. Scott to AG, April 12, April 30, 1836, AGLR; Lindsay to Scott, May 7, 1836; P. F. Smith to Scott, April 26, April 27, 1836, *Sen. Doc. 224*, 327-30, 347-50, 355-58.

42. Clinch to Scott, April 27, 1836, *Sen. Doc. 224*, 337; *Niles' Register*, L, 311, 435; Cohen, *Notices*, 195-96; Smith, *Sketch*, 243-47.

43. Heitman, *Historical Register*; Cullum, *Biographical Register*.

44. Testimony of Mitchell; Testimony of Drane; Gaines' Defense, *Sen. Doc. 224*, 554-55, 604, 627; St. Augustine *Florida Herald*, May 12, 1836.

45. St. Augustine *Florida Herald*, July 9, 1836; Walker to McLemore, June 11, 1836, in *Niles' Register*, L, 258, 265; Bemrose, *Reminiscences*, 91-92; Tallahassee *Floridian*, Nov. 9, 1839; Scott to Clinch, May 1, 1836, AGLR; Read to Call, May 30, 1836; Walker *et al.* to Read, May 30, 1836, in *Niles' Register*, L, 322; Macomb to SW, June 21, 1836, GHQ Letterbook III, 108; *Sen. Doc. 278*, 26 Cong., 1 sess., 38-41, 47-48; Cohen, *Notices*, 198.

46. Cohen, *Notices*, 194-95; Lindsay to Scott, May 7, 1836, *Sen. Doc. 224*, 347-50; Foster to Lindsay, April 29, 1836, AGLR.

47. Foster to Lindsay, April 29, 1836; to AG, Dec. 8, 1836, AGLR.

48. GO 48, Hq., Army of Florida, May 17, 1836, *Sen. Doc. 224*, 363-64; Elliott, *Scott*, 309; St. Augustine *Florida Herald*, May 19, 1836; *Niles' Register*, L, 260.

49. Clinch to AG, April 26, 1836, AGLR; SW to Scott, April 15, 1836, WOLS, No. 15, 327; to

Clinch, May 16, 1836, *HR Doc. 267*, 24 Cong., 1 sess., 21.

50. Doherty, *Call*, 98-102; Call to SW, April 30, 1836; to Jackson, May 12, 1836, AGLR; SW to Call, May 14, 1836, WOLS, No. 15, 435; White to Jackson, May 14, 1836, *TP: Florida*, XXV, 283.

51. Scott to AG, May 20, 1836, *Sen. Doc. 224*, 372-73; Scott to AG, May 11, 1836, AGLR.

52. SW to Call, May 16, May 25, 1836, WOLS, No. 9, pp. 15-16, 442; Call to Jackson, May 30, 1836, AGLR; Williams, *Territory*, 225; SW to Call, May 26, 1836; Call to Jackson, May 30, June 1, 1836, *Sen. Doc. 278*, 1-3, 54-56.

53. Scott to Eustis, May 20, 1836; White to Jackson, May 28, 1836, *Sen. Doc. 224*, 375, 367-69; Eustis to AG, May 22, 1836, AGLR; St. Augustine *Florida Herald*, June 7, July 2, 1836.

54. White to SW, March 12, 1836; SW to White, March 22, 1836, *TP: Florida*, XXV, 257-58, 262-64; Act of April 29, 1836; Act of May 23, 1836, 5 USSL 7-8, 17, 131-33; *Army and Navy Chronicle*, II, 300 ff.; *New York Star* reprinted in St. Augustine *Florida Herald*, April 6, 1836.

55. For criticism of Gaines see Testimony of Gadsden (15-21), Testimony of Lindsay (24-32), Testimony of Bankhead (54-56); Gaines' Defense (583, 588, 590, 609), *Sen. Doc. 224*.

56. Testimony of Clinch; Scott's Defense; Gaines' Defense, *Sen. Doc. 224*, 62, 130, 661.

57. Silver, *Gaines*, 171, 190.

CHAPTER 9

1. SW to Call, May 25, June 13, 1836, *Sen. Doc. 278*, 26 Cong., 1 sess., 1-4; SW to President, May 25, 1836, *HR Doc. 267*, 24 Cong., 1 sess., 1-3; Call to Jackson, and endorsement, C282, May 30, 1836; to AG, June 21, 1836; Clinch to AG, June 13, 1836, AGLR.

2. Doherty, *Call*, 27.

3. Doherty, *Call*, 4-24, 28, 34, 42.

4. Doherty, *Call*, 24-25.

5. Doherty, *Call*, 102; McKensie to AG, Aug. 3, 1836; Call to SW, July 31, 1836, AGLR; Call to Jesup, Sept. 8, 1836, *Sen. Doc. 278*, 77-80; SW to Call, Oct. 7, 1836, WOLS, No. 16, 367; Call to Dallas, Sept. 14, 1836, National Archives, "Territorial Papers," Box 4.

6. Foster to Scott, June 15, 1836, AGLR; Hollingsworth, "Tennessee Volunteers," II, 176, 239.

7. Motte, *Journey*, 62-63; Colonel of 83d Ga. Militia to Governor of Georgia, May 30, 1836, Georgia Military Affairs, State Archives of Georgia, 412.

8. Call to Jesup, Sept. 8, 1836, *Sen. Doc. 278*, 77-80; Hollingsworth, "Tennessee Volunteers," 271-72; AG Report to CG, AG Reports, II, 479; SW to Scott, June 20, 1836, WOLS, No. 16, 104.

9. Harris to Gibson, Feb. 7, 1836; to SW, Feb. 15, 1836; GO 34, Hq., Army of Florida, April 9, 1836, *HR Doc. 271*, 24 Cong., 1 sess., 258 ff.

10. GO, Hq., U.S. Army, March 14, 1836, *ASPMA*, VI, 618; Phelps, "Letters," 69.

11. Bankhead to Scott, May 17, 1836; Heilman to Eustis, June 9, 1836, AGLR.

12. Gates to Heilman, June 12, 1836, AGLR.

13. Heilman to Eustis, June 9, 1836, AGLR; Williams, *Territory*, 245; Lee to Call, July 12, 1836, *Army and Navy Chronicle*, II, 123.

14. Call to Heilman, June 9, 1836; Heilman to Eustis, June 12, 1836, AGLR.

15. Heilman to Eustis, June 12, 1836; Call to SW, July 3, 1836, AGLR; Williams, *Territory*, 246.

16. Williams, *Territory*, 247; Rodenbough, *Everglade to Cañon*, 22; *Niles' Register*, L, 383; Maitland to Call, July 19, 1836, AGLR.

17. Merchant to Call, July 19,

1836, AGLR; Williams, *Territory*, 247.

18. Bankhead to Scott, May 17, 1836, AGLR; *Niles' Register*, L, 361; Childs, "Correspondence," 301.

19. Childs, "Correspondence," 302-3.

20. *Niles' Register*, LI, 181-82.

21. Herbert to AG, July 29, 1836, AGLR; Williams, *Territory*, 249.

22. Williams, *Territory*, 251-52; Childs, "Correspondence," 302-3; Crane to AG, July 24, 1836; Pierce to Crane, Aug. 21, Aug. 27, 1836, AGLR.

23. St. Augustine *Florida Herald*, Oct. 27, 1836; Call to Jackson, Oct. 22, 1836, *TP: Florida*, XXV, 335-36.

24. Pierce to Crane, Aug. 23, 1836, AGLR; Fairbanks, *History of Florida*, 300; Call to Jesup, Sept. 8, 1836, *Sen. Doc. 278*, 77-80.

25. *Sen. Doc. 278*, 77-80; "Statement of Steam Vessels," *ASPMA*, VII, 994-96.

26. Hollingsworth, "Tennessee Volunteers," 347-50; Doherty, *Call*, 103.

27. Doherty, *Call*, 103; Call to Jackson, June 1, 1836, *Sen. Doc. 278*, 55; Call to SW, Sept. 18, 1836, AGLR.

28. Warren to Call, Sept. 18, 1836, AGLR; *Niles' Register*, LI, 85; Williams, *Territory*, 255.

29. Williams, *Territory*, 258; *Niles' Register*, L, 66, LI, 181; *Army and Navy Chronicle*, III, 319.

30. Call to SW, Dec. 2, 1836, *ASPMA*, VI, 993-97; Guild, *Old Times*, 130; Hollingsworth, "Tennessee Volunteers," 351-56, 363-64, 61-64.

31. Hollingsworth, "Tennessee Volunteers," 64-67, 365; Williams, *Territory*, 257; Call to SW, Dec. 2, 1836, *ASPMA*, VI, 993-97; to SW, Oct. 10, 1836, AGLR; *Niles' Register*, LI, 145.

32. Same sources as note 31.

33. Hollingsworth, "Tennessee Volunteers," 68-70; Call to SW, Dec. 2, 1836, *ASPMA*, VI, 993-97.

34. Williams, *Territory*, 259; Call to SW, Oct. 22, 1836; Brown to Call, Oct. 22, 1836, AGLR.

35. SW to Call, Nov. 4, 1836, *TP: Florida*, XXV, 339-41; to Jesup, Nov. 4, 1836, *ASPMA*, VI, 993; Jesup to AG, Oct. 13, 1836, AGLR.

36. Call to SW, Nov. 27, 1836, *Sen. Doc. 278*, 92-98; Williams, *Territory*, 260; Sprague, *Origin*, 162.

37. Same sources as note 36.

38. Williams, *Territory*, 261; Sprague, *Origin*, 162; *Niles' Register*, LI, 261; Call to SW, Nov. 27, 1836, *Sen. Doc. 278*, 92-98.

39. *Sen. Doc. 278*, 92-98; Sprague, *Origin*, 162-67; Williams, *Territory*, 263; Guild, *Old Times*, 135-36; Pierce to Call, Nov. 26, 1836, in Sprague, *Origin*, 163-65; Jesup to Call, March 8, 1837, AGLR; Porter, "Negroes, 1835-1842," 427 ff.

40. Same sources as note 39.

41. Sprague, *Origin*, 162-67.

42. Gardner to Call, Sept. 18, 1838, AGLR.

43. Hollingsworth, "Tennessee Volunteers," 70-73, 164, 166-67, 170-71, 178, 236.

44. Call to SW, Dec. 2, 1836, *TP: Florida*, XXV, 344-59.

45. *Ibid.*; SW to Call, Dec. 30, 1836, Jan. 14, 1837, WOLS, No. 17, 38, *Sen. Doc. 278*, 19.

46. Call to Jackson, Oct. 22, 1836, *TP: Florida*, XXV, 336; "Officers Resigned in 1836," *HR Doc. 183*, 24 Cong., 1 sess., 1-2, 8; SW to Macomb, Oct. 15, 1836, WOLS, No. 16, 388.

47. AG Report to SW, Jan. 18, 1837, *ASPMA*, VI, 1051; Hollingsworth, "Tennessee Volunteers," 236.

48. *Niles' Register*, LI, 67; Jarvis, "Surgeon's Notes," 3.

49. St. Augustine *Florida Herald*, Nov. 24, 1836.

CHAPTER 10

1. "Chronology for Court of Inquiry"; "Army Register," 1838, *ASPMA*, VII, 180, 928.
2. "Chronology for Court of Inquiry"; Scott to Jesup, June 16, 1836; Scott's Defense; Jesup to Scott, June 17, June 19, 1836, *ASPMA*, VII, 180, 331, 210, 334.
3. Jesup to Scott, June 19, 1836; to Blair, June 20, 1836; to SW, June 25, 1836, *ASPMA*, VII, 334, 336, 346-48.
4. Scott's Defense, *ASPMA*, VII, 205.
5. Jesup to Blair, Sept. 3, 1836, *ASPMA*, 362; *Cong. Globe*, IV, 191-92, VI, 130.
6. *DAB*; Heitman, *Historical Register*; McKay, *Pioneer Florida*, II, 496.
7. SW to Jesup, Nov. 4, 1836, *ASPMA*, VI, 993; vice versa, Nov. 28, 1836, AGLR; Jesup to SW, Dec. 5, 1836, *HR Doc. 78*, 25 Cong., 2 sess., 49.
8. Jesup to SW, Dec. 9, Dec. 12, 1836, *HR Doc. 78*, 51-52.
9. Hollingsworth, "Tennessee Volunteers," 243-53.
10. Jesup to Governor of Georgia, Dec. 9, 1836, AGLR; AG to governors, Dec. 24, 1836, AGLS, No. 13, 191 ff.
11. Jesup to Dallas, Dec. 24, 1836, J47, AGLR; *Army and Navy Chronicle*, III, 12, IV, 47, 79.
12. Jesup to Armistead, Dec. 21, 1836, J47; to Call, Dec. 29, 1836, J48; to Armistead, J72, AGLR.
13. Jesup to AG, Jan. 12, Jan. 17, Jan. 19, 1837, AGLR.
14. Porter, "Florida Slaves," 401-2; St. Augustine *Florida Herald*, March 29, 1837.
15. Childs, "Correspondence," 372; Jesup to Call, Jan. 20, 1837, AGLR; to AG, Feb. 7, 1837, *HR Doc. 78*, 66.
16. Jesup to AG, Feb. 7, 1837; Henderson to Jesup, Jan. 28, 1837, *HR Doc. 78*, 66, 70.

17. Jesup to AG, Feb. 7, 1837, *HR Doc. 78*, 66.
18. *Ibid.*; Williams, *Territory*, 269; Motte, *Journey*, 100-101; Jesup to Call, March 8, 1837, J63, AGLR; Giddings, *Exiles*, 136-37.
19. Same sources as note 18.
20. Jesup to SW, Feb. 17, 1837, *HR Doc. 78*, 76-77.
21. Jesup to AG, Feb. 25, 1837, *HR Doc. 78*, 78-80; Porter, "Notes Supplementary," 300; Porter, "Abraham," 23; Childs, "Correspondence," 281; *Niles' Register*, LII, 50.
22. Jesup to Hernandez, March 29, 1837, J65, AGLR.
23. Jesup to Call, March 8, April 18, 1837; to Crabbe, March 31, 1837, J63, J65, AGLR.
24. Jesup to Brown, April 26, 1837, J79, AGLR; Citizens to SW, March 18, 1837, *HR Doc. 225*, 25 Cong., 3 sess., 7; St. Augustine *Florida Herald*, April 27, 1837.
25. Jesup to McClintock, May 1, 1837, *HR Doc. 225*, 13; "List of Negroes," *HR Doc. 78*, 113-18.
26. GO 79, Hq., Army of Florida, April 5, 1837, *HR Doc. 225*, 2.
27. Jesup to Warren, March 29, 1837, AGLR; to Harney, April 8, 1837, in Giddings, *Exiles*, 148; to Harney, May 25, 1837, in Coe, *Red Patriots*, 78; Porter, "Florida Slaves," 405.
28. Boyd, "Osceola," 291-92; Jesup to Armistead, April 15, 1837, J72; to Call, April 18, 1837; to Hernandez, April 29, 1837, J79, AGLR.
29. Jesup to Harney, April 8, 1837, *ASPMA*, VII, 837; to Brown, April 26, 1837, J79; to J. Q. Smith, April 27, 1837, J79; to Call, May 21, 1837, J90; to Bunce, May 15, 1837, J90; to Harney, May 20, May 28, 1837, J90, AGLR; Covington, "Trade," 127-28.
30. Same sources as note 29.
31. Boyd, "Osceola," 293-94; Jesup to Harney, June 1, 1837,

J117, AGLR; to SW, June 7, 1837, *HR Doc. 78*, 157-58.

32. Forry, "Letters," 133.

33. McKay, *Pioneer Florida*, II, 497; Jesup to Armistead, June 6, 1837, J117, AGLR.

34. Macomb to Jesup, June 22, 1837, *HR Doc. 78*, 5; Jesup to Chambers, July 10, 1837, J125, AGLR; SW to Gaines, Aug. 14, 1837, WOLS, No. 17, 372; to Scott, Oct. 4, 1837, WOLS, No. 18, 11.

35. Jesup to Call, Feb. 7, 1837, J60; to Chambers, July 10, 1837, J125, AGLR.

36. Porter, "Negroes, 1835-1842," 427 ff.; Motte, *Journey*, 116.

37. Foreman, *Indian Removal*, 161; Giddings, *Exiles*, 158-63; GO 160, Hq., Army of the South, Aug. 3, 1837, *HR Doc. 225*, 4; Porter, "Negroes, 1835-1842," 427 ff.

38. Porter, "Negroes, 1835-1842," 427 ff.; GO 175, Hq., Army of the South, Sept. 6, 1837, *HR Doc. 225*; Jesup to Commissioner of Indian Affairs, Sept. 24, 1837, J186, AGLR.

39. Rippy, *Poinsett*, Chaps. 12, 13; *DAB*.

40. SW to Jesup, July 25, 1837, *HR Doc. 78*, 33-35.

41. Jesup to SW, June 15, 1837, *HR Doc. 78*, 161-62.

42. Jesup to SW, Sept. 13, 1837; to AG, Aug. 13, 1837, Sept. 2, 1837; to SW, Aug. 10, 1837, *HR Doc. 78*, 42, 101, 107, 171 ff.; SW to Jesup, Aug. 18, 1837, WOLS, No. 17, 382.

43. Same sources as note 42.

44. Jesup to Armistead, April 24, 1837, J72, AGLR; SW to Jesup, July 25, Aug. 18, 1837, *HR Doc. 78*, 35, 38; SW to Jesup, Aug. 3, 1837, WOLS, No. 17, 353.

45. Same sources as note 44.

46. Forry, "Letters," 133; Jesup to Armistead, June 6, 1837; to Harney, June 8, 1837, J117; to Clark, June 11, 1837; to Childs, Aug. 2, 1837, J151; to Thompson, Aug. 6, 1837, J167, AGLR.

47. Jesup to Casey, July 18, 1837, J145, AGLR.

48. Jesup to AG, Aug. 2, July 10, 1837; to Call, July 26, 1837; to Thompson, Aug. 6, 1837, J167, AGLR.

49. St. Augustine *Florida Herald*, July 22, 1837; Statement of Fla. Volunteers, Jan. 17, 1837, J65; Jesup to Warren, June 14, 1837, J117; to Hernandez, July 7, 1837, J125; to Mills, July 15, 1837, J145, AGLR.

50. Jesup to Fanning, March 6, 1837, J63; to Cross, June 24, July 30, 1837, J118, J151, AGLR.

51. Jesup to CO, Garey's Ferry, Jan. 10, Aug. 10, 1837, J47, J167; to Gibson, Aug. 10, 1837; to Harney, Aug. 11, 1837, J179; to Bomford, Aug. 15, 1837, AGLR.

52. Motte, *Journey*, 116-20; Forry, "Letters," 215; Hernandez to Jesup, Sept. 16, 1837, *HR Doc. 78*, 108-12.

53. Hernandez to Jesup, Sept. 16, 1837, *HR Doc. 78*, 108-12; Motte, *Journey*, 120-23.

54. Jesup to Hernandez, n.d., 1837, J186, AGLR; vice versa, Sept. 16, 1837, *HR Doc. 78*, 108-12.

55. Jesup to SW, Oct. 22, 1837, *HR Doc. 78*, Supplement, 188; Motte, *Journey*, 137-38; Hernandez to Jesup, Oct. 22, 1837, *HR Doc. 227*, 25 Cong., 2 sess., 5-6; Jarvis, "Diary," 6-9; *Cong. Globe*, VI, 127-31.

56. Jarvis, "Diary," 6-9.

57. "The White Flag," Osceola Issue, *FHQ*, 225-31.

58. *Ibid.*; Jarvis, "Surgeon's Notes," 4.

59. Motte, *Journey*, 140; Sprague, *Origin*, 214-19; Boyd, "Osceola," 295-97; "The White Flag," Osceola Issue, *FHQ*, 225-31; Jesup in Washington *Daily Intelligencer*, Oct. 13, 1858; Fairbanks, *History*, 309-10, 317; Benton, *Thirty Years' View*, II, 79-80; Jesup to Cross, Nov. 17, 1837, J264, AGLR.

60. Pickell, "Journals," 159-71.

61. Jesup to SW, Oct. 22, 1837, *HR Doc. 78*, Supplement, 188.

62. McReynolds, *Seminoles*, 209; Motte, *Journey*, 287-88; "Recollections of a Campaign in Florida," 131.

63. Same sources as note 62.

64. "Disappearance," Osceola Issue, *FHQ*, 198-201.

CHAPTER 11

1. SW to Jesup, Sept. 13, 1837, *HR Doc. 78*, 25 Cong., 2 sess., 42, Supplement, 123; Jesup to Taylor, Oct. 27, 1837, J218; to Eustis, Oct. 29, 1837, J218; to Hernandez, Nov. 19, 1837, J264, AGLR.

2. Dallas to Secretary of Navy, Sept. 18, 1837, *TP: Florida*, XXV, 422.

3. Jesup to Governor of Georgia, Sept. 6, 1837, J183; to Cross, Sept. 6, 1837, AGLR; SW to Jesup, Sept. 6, 1837, WOLS, No. 17, 404.

4. SW to Gentry, Sept. 8, 1837, WOLS, No. 17, 410; AG to CG, April 25, 1838, AG Reports to SW, No. 2, 352; Gentry, *Full Justice*, 4-11.

5. Jesup to Whiting, Nov. 22, 1837, AGLR.

6. SW to Jesup, Dec. 1, Dec. 2, 1837, WOLS, No. 18, 128, 133.

7. Jesup to SW, Aug. 10, Nov. 21, 1837, *ASPMA*, VII, 874, *HR Doc. 78*, Supplement, 192 ff.; to Whiting, Nov. 22, 1837; to Underwood, Nov. 3, 1837, J218, AGLR.

8. Jesup to Armistead, Nov. 17, 1837; to Taylor, Nov. 27, 1837, AGLR.

9. Boyd, "Osceola," 301; Brown to Webster, Nov. 9, 1837, Webster Papers; Foreman, "Report of the Cherokee Deputies."

10. Foreman, "Report of the Cherokee Deputies"; Boyd, "Osceola," 301; Pickell, "Journals," 162-63; Jarvis, "Diary," 22.

11. Proceedings, Board of Inquiry, Nov. 30, 1837, Webster Papers; Porter, "Seminole Flight."

12. Jesup to SW, April 9, 1837, *HR Doc. 78*, Supplement, 143.

13. Sprague, *Origin*, 3, 98, 324; Motte, *Journey*, 134; Forry, "Letters," 89; Jarvis, "Surgeon's Notes," 5.

14. Jarvis, "Surgeon's Notes," 3.

15. Jesup to AG, Dec. 2, 1837; Order, Dec. 4, 1837, J277, AGLR.

16. AG to Jesup, Nov. 10, 1837, *HR Doc. 78*, 135-36; CG to SW, Report for 1837, *Sen. Doc. 1*, 25 Cong., 2 sess., 171.

17. SW Report to President, Nov., 1837, *Sen. Doc. 1*, 171.

18. Jesup to Taylor, Dec. 9, 1837, J278; to Nelson, Dec. 18, 1837, J53; to Snodgrass, Dec. 19, 1837, J53, AGLR.

19. Gentry, *Full Justice*, 18; Taylor to Jesup, Jan. 4, 1838, *Sen. Doc. 227*, 25 Cong., 2 sess., 2-5.

20. Taylor to Jesup, Jan. 4, 1838; Jesup to Cross, March 16, 1838, J70, AGLR.

21. Gentry, *Full Justice*, 18, 22, 26; Pickell, "Journals"; Buchanan, "Journal," 145-51; *Army and Navy Chronicle*, VI, 74; Sprague, *Origin*, 203-13, 325; Porter, "Negroes, 1835-1842," 427 ff.; Backus, "Diary," 280-81; Taylor to Jesup, Jan. 4, 1838, *Sen. Doc. 227*, 5-6.

22. Taylor to Jesup, Jan. 4, 1838.

23. *Cong. Globe*, VI, 182, VII, 165-66.

24. SW to Senate, Feb. 20, 1838, War Office Reports to Cong., No. 4, 220.

CHAPTER 12

1. Eaton, "Returns"; Jarvis, "Diary," 37.

2. Jesup to Whiting, Jan. 9, 1838, J48, AGLR.

3. Motte, *Journey*, 168, 182-84.

4. *Ibid.*; Powell to Jesup, Jan. 16, March 15, 1838, J24, J67, AGLR.

5. Jesup to AG, Jan. 18, 1838, J13, AGLR; GO 74, Hq., Army of the South, National Archives, Record Group 94.

6. Motte, *Journey*, 190; Jarvis, "Surgeon's Notes," 452; Jesup to Whiting, Jan. 18, 1838, J56; Powell to Jesup, Jan. 31, 1838, J26, AGLR.

7. Bankhead to Eustis, Jan. 24, 1838, J20, AGLR; Motte, *Journey*, 193-96; Jesup to AG, Jan. 26, 1838, *HR Doc. 219*, 25 Cong., 2 sess., 1-4; Jarvis, "Surgeon's Notes," 1-3.

8. *Cong. Globe*, VI, 126-32.

9. Jarvis, "Diary," 52; Jesup to Taylor, Feb. 3, 1838, J56; to AG, Jan. 31, 1838, J26, AGLR.

10. Jesup to Hernandez, Jan. 15, 1838, J56; to SW, March 4, 1838, J59, AGLR; to SW, Feb. 11, 1838, *HR Doc. 219*, 52.

11. Motte, *Journey*, 209.

12. *Ibid.*, 210.

13. *Ibid.*, 213-17.

14. GO 71, Hq., Army of the South, March 11, 1838, National Archives, Record Group 94; Jesup to Colt, March 11, March 12, 1838, AGLR.

15. Jesup to Eustis, March 21, 1838, J84; to SW, July 6, 1838, J138, AGLR; Foreman, *Indian Removal*, 362.

16. St. Augustine *Florida Herald*, March 22, April 5, 1838.

17. Jarvis, "Diary," 62; Jesup to Call, Feb. 18, 1838, J54; to Eustis, March 6, 1838; to AG, March 11, 1838, J50; to Harney, n.d., J91; Nelson to Armistead, March 11, 1838, J69, AGLR; GO 68, Hq., Army of the South, March 7, 1838, National Archives, Record Group 94.

18. Bankhead to Jesup, March 25, 1838, J78, AGLR; *Army and Navy Chronicle*, IV, 268.

19. Foreman, *Indian Removal*, 362; Porter, "Negroes, 1835-1842," 427 ff.; Taylor to Jesup, April 2, 1838, J82; to SW, July 6, 1838, J138, AGLR.

20. Harney to Jesup, April 24, 1838, AGLR; Motte, *Journey*, 231.

21. Same sources as note 20.

22. Jesup to Call, March 15, 1838, J70, AGLR.

23. GO 7, Hq., United States Army, April 10, 1838; GO 119, Hq., Army of the South, May 15, 1838, National Archives, Record Group 94; Jesup to Harney, April 6, 1838, J91; to Twiggs, April 6, 1838, J91; to Taylor, May 15, 1838; to SW July 6, 1838, J138, AGLR.

24. Smith to Jesup, March 17, 1838; Bankhead to Jesup, March 25, 1838, AGLR; Forry, "Letters," 96.

25. Forry, "Letters," 96; Smith, "Letters," 337; Jarvis, "Diary," 42-43.

26. "Recollections of a Campaign in Florida," 75-77; *Niles' Register*, LVIII, 339.

27. Backus, "Diary," 279.

28. Jesup to AG, Dec. 12, 1836, *HR Doc. 78*, 25 Cong., 2 sess., 52; to Gov. Clay, May 9, 1836, J82, AGLR; "Abstract of Militia and Volunteers," March 16, 1838, AGLS, No. 14, 195.

29. St. Augustine *Florida Herald*, July 22, 1837.

30. An Act to Provide for the More Effective Protection of the Frontiers, Feb. 12, 1837; Resolution of Jefferson County, Jan. 30, 1838, Acts and Resolutions of the Legislative Council, Territory of Florida, microfilm.

31. White to Knowles, Feb. 15, 1837, *TP: Florida*, XXV, 378.

32. Old settlers quoted by Moore-Willson, *Seminoles*, 72; Jesup to AG, June 15, 1837, *HR Doc. 78*, 161-62; Foreman, *Indian Removal*, 381 ff.; Tallahassee *Floridian*, March 30, 1839; Croffut, *Fifty Years*, 172; Motte, *Journey*, 207; St. Augustine *Florida Herald*, May 19, 1836; Blassingame, *Seminoles*; Neill, *Florida's Seminole Indians*, 39; *Seminole Indians*, WPA, 33.

33. *Cong. Globe*, V, 42-43, 46, 50-52, 55-56, 63-65, 108-10, 112-13, 126-27, 142-43, 148.

34. St. Augustine *Florida Herald*, running through many issues, Jan.-March, 1838.

CHAPTER 13

1. *DAB*; Dyer, *Taylor*.
2. AG to SW, Feb. 22, 1841, AG Reports to SW, II, 497.
3. Taylor to Call, May 18, 1838, T135; Smith to Dearborn, May 30, 1838, T173, AGLR.
4. SW to Taylor, June 1, 1838, WOLS, No. 19, 159; to HR Committee on Military Affairs, June 1, 1838, War Office Reports to Cong., No. 4, 280.
5. Tompkins to Twiggs, June 5, 1838, T173; Twiggs to AG, June 13, 1838, T130; Taylor to AG, June 16, 1838, T137, AGLR.
6. *Niles' Register*, LIV, 290, 369, 386, LV, 19, 256.
7. Call to Green, July 31, 1838, T205, AGLR; to Taylor, Aug. 21, 1838, *TP: Florida*, XXV, 528-31.
8. SW to Taylor, Aug. 20, Oct. 8, Oct. 20, 1838, WOLS, No. 19, 342, 399, 426.
9. Taylor to AG, Jan. 5, 1839, T13, AGLR; SW to Macomb, Jan. 23, 1839, *TP: Florida*, XXV, 568.
10. Taylor to Twiggs, June 1, 1838, T136; to Dearborn, Aug. 27, 1838, T230, AGLR.
11. Taylor to McLaughlin, Jan. 22, 1839, T49, AGLR.
12. Taylor to AG, Sept. 21, Oct. 21, 1838, T248, T272; to Davenport, Nov. 10, 1838, T307, AGLR.
13. Taylor to AG, June 2, 1838, *HR, Doc. 225*, 25 Cong., 3 sess., 30; Giddings, *Exiles*, 244.
14. Giddings, *Exiles*, 195, 201-40; *HR Doc. 225*, 30-39, 43-53, 80-97, 100-125.
15. Same sources as note 14.
16. McReynolds, *Seminoles*, 214, 229.
17. Taylor to AG, Jan. 17, 1838, T297; to Twiggs, Nov. 23, 1838, T319, AGLR; St. Augustine *Florida Herald*, Nov. 28, 1838.
18. Bulletin by Truman Cross, Nov. 11, 1838, *Army and Navy Chronicle*, VII, 362; Taylor to Twiggs, Jan. 26, 1839, T49; to Ful-

ton, Feb. 15, 1839, T60; to Green, Feb. 16, 1839, T72; to Davenport, Feb. 28, 1839, March 12, 1839, T72, T99, AGLR; Tallahassee *Floridian*, March 2, 1839; Sprague, *Origin*, 227.
19. Call to Legislative Council, reported in Tallahassee *Floridian*, Feb. 7, 1839; An Act to Authorize the Governor of Florida to Raise Troops, March 2, 1839, microfilm records of the States of the U.S., 106, Florida B2, Reel 1; Call to Taylor, March 6, 1839, T111; vice versa, March 11, 1839, T99, AGLR.
20. Same sources as note 19.
21. Taylor to AG, March 9, 1839, T75; to Davenport, March 12, 1839, T99; to AG, March 19, 1839, T88, AGLR; *Niles' Register*, LVI, 49.
22. SW to Macomb, March 18, 1839, *TP: Florida*, XXV, 597-99.
23. *DAB*.
24. Sprague, "Macomb's Mission," 142, 151, 153, 160, 173.
25. *Ibid.*, 153, 157; Taylor to Call, April 9, 1839, T126, AGLR.
26. Tallahassee *Floridian*, April 6, 1839; McLaughlin to SW, April 20, 1839, in *Army and Navy Chronicle*, VIII, 298; *Niles' Register*, LVI, 113, 194; Macomb to SW, May 6, 1839, GHQ Letterbook, III, 489; Sprague, "Macomb's Mission," 162, 166.
27. Sprague, "Macomb's Mission," 173; other sources as note 26.
28. Sprague, "Macomb's Mission," 145, 175, 178-81, 184-85; Sprague, *Origin*, 228-32.
29. Same sources as note 28.
30. Warren and Mills to Macomb, June 15, 1839, in *Niles' Register*, LVI, 289, 265; Tallahassee *Floridian*, June 1, June 15, 1839; Sturtevant, "Chakaika," 44.
31. SW to Macomb, May 25, 1839; to Taylor, June 4, 1839, *TP: Florida*, XXV, 612-15.
32. Sturtevant, "Chakaika, 44-45.

33. *Niles' Register*, LVI, 283; Sprague, "Macomb's Mission," 162; Taylor to Call, April 9, 1839, T126, AGLR.

34. Taylor to SW, Aug. 1, 1839, T236, AGLR; SW to Taylor, Aug. 17, Oct. 8, 1839, WOLS, No. 21, 90, 153.

35. *Niles' Register*, LVI, 373; Tompkins to Taylor, June 22, 1839; Belger to Green, June 30, 1839, T237, AGLR.

36. Taylor to AG, July 20, 1839, T234, AGLR; Sprague, "Macomb's Mission," 168.

37. Taylor to AG, July 20, 1839, T234, AGLR.

38. Reavis, *Harney*, iii, 35, 44; Hoyt, "Soldier's View," 356-62; Cantrell, *Kissimmee*, 13-14; Sturtevant, "Chakaika," 51.

39. Sturtevant, "Chakaika," 46; Reavis, *Harney*, 134-37; McKay, *Pioneer Florida*, II, 509-14; Sprague, *Origin*, 233-36, 316-19; Gonzalez, *Caloosahatchee*, 41.

40. Same sources as note 39.

41. Sturtevant, "Chakaika," 46; Gonzalez, *Caloosahatchee*, 41; Reavis, *Harney*, iii, 35, 44.

42. Sturtevant, "Chakaika"; Neill, "Identity."

43. McKay, *Pioneer Florida*, II, 509-13.

44. Tallahassee *Floridian*, Sept. 28, 1839; *Niles' Register*, LVII, 168-69.

45. *Niles' Register*, LVII, 44, 80, 82; Taylor to AG, Aug. 28, 1839, T306; Davenport to Taylor, Sept. 2, 1839, T316, AGLR; Macomb to Taylor, Oct. 17, 1839; SW to President, Nov. 29, 1839, *TP: Florida*, XXV, 643-44, 656-57.

46. Call to Cong., Feb. 26, 1840, *TP: Florida*, XXVI, 89-109.

47. Doherty, *Call*, 81; Poinsett, *Calendar*, 76.

48. Taylor to AG, Dec. 20, 1839, T434, AGLR.

49. Giddings, *Exiles*, 264-65; Tallahassee *Floridian*, Feb. 1, 1840; Jesup to Read, July 25, 1837,

J145, AGLR; Reid to Taylor, Jan. 16, March 17, 1840, National Archives, Department of Florida, Box 1; Covington, "Cuban Bloodhounds."

50. Covington, "Cuban Bloodhounds"; *Niles' Register*, LVIII, 51, 279; *Cong. Globe*, VIII, 131, 183, 203-4, 252.

51. An Act to Increase the Military Establishment, July 5, 1838; Act of July 7, 1838, 5 USSL, 257-60, 308.

52. Taylor to Lawson, Sept. 17, 1838, T259, AGLR; *Army and Navy Chronicle*, VIII, 223, 303; Hunter, "Captain Hunter," 71*n*.

53. Same sources as note 51.

54. *Army and Navy Chronicle*, IX, 150, 256, VIII, 382.

55. St. Augustine *Florida Herald*, April, 28, May 12, 1838; Tallahassee *Floridian*, Nov. 2, Nov. 11, 1839.

56. Davenport to Taylor, May 1, 1839, AGLR.

57. *Army and Navy Chronicle*, VI, 217, VII, 117, VIII, 124.

58. *Cong. Globe*, VII, 268-70.

59. *Ibid.*, VI, 345, 408; Tallahassee *Floridian*, March 30, Dec. 7, 1839, Jan. 12, 1840; Croffut, *Fifty Years*, 120; Sprague, "Macomb's Mission," 132, 171.

60. *Army and Navy Chronicle*, VI, 410.

61. *Ibid.*, VIII, 68.

62. Secretary of Treasury to Call, Oct. 23, 1838, *TP: Florida*, XXV, 542; St. Augustine *Florida Herald*, June 30, 1838.

63. Branch to President, Feb. 5, 1839, *TP: Florida*, XXV, 584; Sprague, "Macomb's Mission," 160; *Niles' Register*, LVII, 205; Martin, *Territorial Days*, 90; Tallahassee *Floridian*, April 6, 1839, Feb. 1, 1840; AG to Read, Aug. 3, 1840, AGLS, No. 16, 358.

64. Davis, "Early Orange Culture," 240.

65. *Niles' Register*, LVII, 193; Cash, *Story of Florida*, I, 400;

Tallahassee *Floridian,* Jan. 11, 1840.

66. Tallahassee *Floridian,* June 1, 1839; Dovell, *Florida,* II, 269-84; Martin, *Territorial Days,* 272.

67. An Act for the Relief of John Bryan, Feb. 14, 1840.

68. *Niles' Register,* LVI, 142, 373; SW to Secretary of the Navy, April 4, 1839, *TP: Florida,* XXV, 601-2; Howard to SW, Dec. 23, 1839, National Archives, Territorial Papers, No. 3; *Army and Navy Chronicle,* IX, 14.

CHAPTER 14

1. Armistead to AG, May 6, 1840, AGLR; Dyer, *Taylor,* 125.

2. *American Annual Cyclopedia;* Cullum, *Biographical Register.*

3. Hunter, "Captain Hunter," 73*n*; Croffut, *Fifty Years,* 123, 132-33; GO 7, May 10, 1840, GO 20, June 12, 1840, Hq., Army of the South, National Archives, Record Group 94.

4. Rains to Twiggs, May 29, 1840; Armistead to AG, May 30, 1840, A130, AGLR; *Niles' Register,* LVIII, 179.

5. *Niles' Register,* LVIII, 193; Armistead to AG, May 11, May 19, 1840, A113, A180, AGLR.

6. Armistead to AG, May 28, 1840, A124; Riley to Twiggs, n.d., A124; Churchill to Armistead, May 23, 1840, A124; Gates to Twiggs, May 28, 1840, A132, AGLR; *Niles' Register,* LVIII, 200, 210.

7. *Niles' Register,* LVIII, 243; Armistead to AG, June 6, 1840, A132; Bonneville to CO, Second Dragoons, June 4, 1840, A133; Armistead to AG, June 9, 1840, A136; Harney to Twiggs, June 5, 1840; Armistead to SW, June 29, 1840, A161; to AG, June 27, 1840; to Harney, July 18, 1840, A204, AGLR; Armistead to AG, June 27, 1840; Riley to Twiggs, June 9, 1840, in *Niles' Register,* LVIII, 260.

8. Armistead to SW, June 29,

July 9, 1840, A161, A192, AGLR.

9. Armistead to SW, May 28, June 18, June 22, July 9, 1840, A134, A155, A159, A192; to Hunt, June 10, 1840, A175, AGLR; SW to Armistead, July 18, 1840, WOLS, No. 22, 354.

10. Dodd, "Jacob Housman"; Walker, "Massacre at Indian Key"; *Niles' Register,* LVIII, 406, LIX, 3.

11. Same sources as note 10.

12. *Niles' Register,* LVIII, 362; SW to General of the Florida Militia, Sept. 8, 1840, WOLS, No. 22, 447; Armistead to Hunt, Sept. 20, 1840, A273; to Gamble, Sept. 14, 1840, A273, AGLR.

13. Armistead to Florida commanders, Oct. 7, 1840, A306; to SW, Oct. 7, 1840, A287, AGLR; "Old Tiger Tail Dead," *FHQ,* IV (April, 1926), 192-94; McCall, *Letters,* 405, 409, 413; Sprague, *Origin,* 99, 252, 312, 429, 483, 502-4.

14. Sprague, *Origin,* 248 ff.; Armistead to SW, Nov. 15, 1840, A312, AGLR; GO 57, Nov. 15, 1840, GO 64, Nov. 23, 1840, Hq., Department of Florida, National Archives, Department of Florida, AGO 1; SW to President, Dec. 5, 1840, WOLS to President, No. 4; Page to Office of Indian Affairs, Dec. 9, 1840; OIALR, Florida Superintendency, Emigration, microfilm roll 291; Croffut, *Fifty Years,* 123.

15. Gonzalez, *Caloosahatchee,* 41; Sturtevant, "Chakaika," 51-53; Anonymous, "Notes on the Passage Across the Everglades"; Harney to Acting AG, Dec. 29, 1840, H34, AGLR; Reavis, *Harney,* 144-45; Coe, *Red Patriots,* 156.

16. Sturtevant, "Chakaika," 54; Extract from Journals of the Legislative Council, Jan. 21, 1841, National Archives, Florida Territorial Papers, Box 3; Twiggs to SW, Sept. 29, 1840, Poinsett, *Calendar,* 128; Aide de Camp to Harney, Dec. 6, 1840, H357, AGLR.

17. Armistead to Florida commanders, June 2, 1840, A175; Aide de Camp to Belknap, Dec. 21, 1840, A357; Nelson to Armistead, Dec. 28, 1840, A5, AGLR; Sprague, *Origin*, 249-50, 252.

18. Armistead to SW, Feb. 14, 1841, A43, AGLR; Sherman, *Sherman Letters*, 16.

19. Armistead to AG, Feb. 20, 1841, A50; Barnum to Acting AG, March 7, 1841, A67; Armistead to SW, March 7, 1841, A78; to Gates, March 6, 1841, A141; Acting AG to Capers, March 20, 1841, A141, AGLR; Page to Office of Indian Affairs, Jan. 24, 1841, OIALR, Florida Superintendency, Emigration, microfilm roll 291; Sprague, *Origin*, 253-56.

20. Same sources as note 19.

21. Worth to Armistead, March 5, 1841, A66; Armistead to SW, March 28, 1841, A90, AGLR; Sprague, *Origin*, 258-60.

22. Childs to Armistead, May 1, 1841, in Sprague, *Origin*, 259; Worth to Armistead, March 5, 1841, A66; Armistead to SW, March 28, 1841, A90, AGLR.

23. Armistead to Brown, Feb. 27, 1841, A52; to SW, March 7, 1841, A77; to AG, April 30, 1841, A140; to Call, April 25, 1841, A141; to AG, May 31, 1841, AGLR.

24. *Cong. Globe*, VIII, Appendix, 667; *Niles' Register*, LVIII, 339; Smith, Letters," 346; Hunter, "Captain Hunter," 68-70, 74.

25. Cases No. 21, 23, 26, May 10, May 13, May 26, 1841, National Archives, Department of Florida, Court-Martial Records, AGO 1.

26. Cases No. 14, 32, May 24, Aug. 3, 1840, *loc. cit.*; Green to Armistead, July 5, 1840, National Archives, Department of Florida, Box 2; Sherman, *Memoirs*, I, 20.

27. Poinsett to President, Dec. 5, 1840, WOLS to President, No. 4, 258; SW to Colt, June 11, 1840, WOLS, No. 22, 428; Colonel of Ordnance to SW, Nov. 30, 1840,

Ordnance Reports, I, 378; Armistead to SW, Dec. 12, 1840, A362, AGLR.

28. Smith to Riley, Jan. 23, 1841, AGLR.

29. *Cong. Globe*, VIII, Appendix, 74-75, 77-80, 84, 663; Doherty, "Florida Whigs," Chaps. 1, 2.

30. *Cong. Globe*, VIII, 94-99, 510-11, 523, 528, Appendix, 659-67, 704-7, IX, 155, 161, Appendix, 346-52, 165-67, 170-72; Benton, *Thirty Years' View*, II, 76-81.

31. Giddings, *Exiles*, 281, 282n; *Cong. Globe*, VIII, Appendix, 660-67, 704-7.

32. *Cong. Globe*, IX, Appendix, 346-52, 165-67, 170-72.

33. *Niles' Register*, LVIII, 407, LIX, 5-6; Reid to Poinsett, Aug. 12, 1840; Jesup to Heintzelman, Oct. 9, 1840, Poinsett, *Calendar*, 120, 129; *Cong. Globe*, VIII, 663; Doherty, "Florida Whigs," Chaps. 1, 2.

34. Giddings, *Exiles*, 274-75; SW to Armistead, March 11, 1841, WOLS, No. 23, 259; Poinsett to President, March 2, 1841, WOLS to President, No. 4; Paymaster General to SW, May 20, 1841, National Archives, PMG Digest, 395.

CHAPTER 15

1. Croffut, *Fifty Years*, 130-31.

2. Wallace, *General Worth*, passim.

3. Croffut, *Fifty Years*, 126.

4. Sprague, *Origin*, 273; AG to SW, Report for 1842, *HR Doc. 247*, 27 Cong., 2 sess., 13; Worth to AG, May 31, 1841, W215, AGLR.

5. Memorial of Jurors, Madison County, April, 1842, *HR Doc. 262*, 27 Cong., 2 sess., 27.

6. McKavett to Sprague, April 15, 1842, *HR Doc. 262*, 34-35; Tracy to Governor of Georgia, April 26, 1841; Bliss to AG, Nov. 9, 1841; Governor of Georgia to SW, March 2, 1842; Day to AG, Feb. 24, 1842, *HR Doc. 200*, 27

Cong., 2 sess., 10, 41, 53, 63; Deposition of Six Georgia Men, Jan. 22, 1842, W130; Long to Casey, March 22, 1842; Casey to Acting AG, March 22, 1842; Scriven to Worth, Dec. 11, 1842, W640, AGLR; Sprague, *Origin*, 403-23.

7. Sprague, *Origin*, 268-70; "Report of Retrenchments," April 30, 1842, *HR Doc. 262*, 47.

8. Giddings, *Exiles*, 295-96, 301; Sherman, *Memoirs*, I, 24-25; Sprague, *Origin*, 263, 287-89; Worth to AG, June 15, 1841, W228, AGLR.

9. AG to Riley, July 5, 1841, W275, AGLR; Sprague, *Origin*, 281, 295-96, 314.

10. Worth to COs, June 16, 1841, W230; to Whiting, July 6, 1841, W275; to Wilson, July 10, 1841, AGLR.

11. Call to Wilson, June 28, 1841, W276; to Worth, June 29, 1841, W276; Worth to AG, July 24, 1841, W304, AGLR; AG to Worth, Aug. 20, 1841, AGLS, No. 17, 281; Giddings, *Exiles*, 310; Sprague, *Origin*, 398.

12. Sprague, *Origin*, 402; Worth to Wilcox, July 10, 1841, W275; Roll by Lt. Patrick, n.d., W97; Worth to Wilcox, July 17, 1841, W327, AGLR.

13. Seawell to Riley, July 21, 1841, W306; Worth to AG, Aug. 8, 1841, W319, AGLR.

14. Sprague, *Origin*, 293, 299-303, 320-21; Aide de Camp to Childs, Aug. 8, 1841; Worth to AG, Aug. 27, 1841, W364, AGLR.

15. Sprague, *Origin*, 319-20, 333, 354, 378-80; Worth to Riley, Aug. 12, 1841, W369; to Fauntleroy, Aug. 13, 1841; to AG, Oct. 9, 1841, W438; McLaughlin to Worth, Dec. 26, 1841, AGLR.

16. Rodenbough, *Everglade to Cañon*, 27-28.

17. Same sources as note 15.

18. Sprague, *Origin*, 330, 347; Act of March 2, 1841, *HR Doc. 247*, 11; Childs to Worth, Sept. 18, 1841, W438; Worth to AG, Oct. 25, Nov. 1, 1841, W459, W474; Wade to CO, Nov. 13, 1841, W516; Worth to Belknap, Dec. 10, 1841, W9, AGLR.

19. Worth to AG, Nov. 4, 1841, W480; Acting AG to COs, Nov. 15, 1841; Alburtis to Riley, Dec. 30, 1841, W5, AGLR; Worth to AG, March 16, 1842, *HR Doc. 262*, 15; Sprague, *Origin*, 396, 399-400.

20. Sprague, *Origin*, 429, 431, 433, 435; Plympton to Riley, Feb. 11, 1842, in Smith, "Letters," 349-51; Worth to AG, Jan. 31, 1842, *HR Doc. 262*, 8-9.

21. Worth to AG, Jan. 31, 1842, W47, AGLR; Sprague, *Origin*, 355.

22. Sprague, *Origin*, 440-45.

23. Worth to Scott, Feb. 14, 1842, in Sprague, *Origin*, 441-45 (see also 450); to AG, Feb. 5, 1842, AGLR.

24. Acting AG to Whiting, March 30, 1842, W126, AGLR; Worth to AG, Feb. 18, 1842, *HR Doc. 262*, 12; Sprague, *Origin*, 456-60.

25. Worth to AG, April 29, 1842, W184, AGLR; Worth to AG, April 21, April 29, 1842, *HR Doc. 262*, 21, 26; McKay, *Pioneer Florida*, II, 517; McCall, *Letters*, 402, 406-8, 413, 463-67.

26. McCall, *Letters*, 413; Sprague, *Origin*, 468-72; Worth to AG, May 6, 1842, *HR Doc. 262*, 30.

27. Acting AG to Riley, April 10, 1842, W180, AGLR.

28. Worth to AG, May 24, 1842, *HR Doc. 262*, 37; Sprague, *Origin*, 298, 331, 436, 446, 473, 475-76, 483.

29. Sprague, *Origin*, 480; SW to Scott, May 10, 1842, *HR Doc. 82*, 28 Cong., 1 sess., 4-5.

30. Flannery, "Naval Operations," 51-52; Hanna, *Golden Sands*, 124; McLaughlin to Worth, July 18, 1841, National Archives, Department of Florida, Box 4.

31. Yulee, "Senator Yulee"; Doherty, *Whigs of Florida*, 11.

32. *Cong. Globe*, X, 503-5, 566, 618-19, 630, 818, XI, 497-503.

33. *Ibid.*, X, 527-31, 542, 551-54, 557-60, 575, 582, 585-86, 591-92, 594-95, 665, 785, 901-2, XI, 418-20, 426-28, 442-43, 480-82.

34. Same sources as note 33 (see also XI, 829-30).

35. Benton, *Thirty Years' View*, II, 449-50; An Act to Perfect the Organization of the Army, Aug. 23, 1843, 5 USSL 512-13.

36. Call to Taylor, Aug. 21, 1838; Surgeon General to Benton, Dec. 30, 1838; Jesup to Benton, Jan. 19, 1839, *TP: Florida*, XXV, 528-31, 554-57, 563-65; *Cong. Globe*, VII, Appendix, 162-63, 204, 215, 227-28, 249.

37. Armed Occupation Act, Aug. 4, 1842, 5 USSL 502; Dodd, "Letters from East Florida," 51-52, 54; Covington, "Armed Occupation Act"; Yoshpe, *Preliminary Inventory*, 27; Donaldson, *Public Domain*, 295.

38. Worth to Whistler, May 23, 1842, W254; to Patrick, May 26, June 6, 1842, W270; Patrick to Worth, June 13, 1842, W295; Acting AG to Hunter, June 1, 1842, AGLR; Sprague, *Origin*, 482-83.

39. Sprague, *Origin*, 485-86; Giddings, *Exiles*, 314; Croffut, *Fifty Years*, 163-64; Worth to Wright, June 17, 1842, AGLR; Minutes of Talk, July 21, 1842; GO 9, Hq., Military Department, Aug. 14, 1842, *HR Doc. 82*, 28 Cong., 1 sess., 8-9.

40. Sprague, *Origin*, 487-88.

41. Long to SW, Nov. 16, 1842, *HR Doc. 253*, 28 Cong., 1 sess., 2; Vose to AG, Aug. 20, Aug. 23, Sept. 6, Sept. 8, 1842, V44, V45, V52, V54, AGLR; Vose to AG, Sept. 26, 1842, *TP: Florida*, XXVI, 548-49; Call to Vose, Nov. 3, 1842, V596, AGLR.

42. Vose to AG, Sept. 29, 1842, *TP: Florida*, XXVI, 551-53.

43. Sprague, *Origin*, 495-97.

44. Worth to AG, Oct. 31, 1842, W560; Vose to AG, Sept. 21, 1842, V69; Barbour to Vose, Nov. 2, 1842, V596; Worth to Belknap, Dec. 11, 1842, W622, AGLR; Sprague, *Origin*, 498, 500-502.

45. Dozier to Belknap, Nov. 26, 1842, W640 (also in same packet letters for Forrester, Richardson, Edwards, Treyvant, and Dexter); Worth to AG, Nov. 17, 1843, W10, AGLR; Nunes to Brown, Jan. 16, 1844, *HR Doc. 253*, 8-9; Sprague, *Origin*, 507.

46. Sprague, *Origin*, 285; McCall, *Letters*, 381-98; E. O. Ord to P. Ord, Dec. 21, 1841, Alexander Collection, Washington.

47. Preble, "Canoe Expedition."

48. *Ibid.*

49. Worth to Riley, July 26, 1841, W309, AGLR; vice versa, Aug. 5, 1841, in McKay, *Pioneer Florida*, II, 526-27; Sherman to Ellen Ewing, Sept. 7, 1841, in Sherman, *Home Letters*, 14; Sprague, *Origin*, 447.

CHAPTER 16

1. Crawford to SW, Jan. 20, 1844, *HR Doc. 82*, 28 Cong., 1 sess., 2 ff.; for history of the Seminoles after 1842, see McReynolds, *Seminoles;* for population of 1962, see Indian Affairs Bureau, "United States, Indian Population and Land," March, 1963.

2. "The Late Florida Squadron Expenditures," *HR Reports*, No. 582, 28 Cong., 1 sess.

3. Upton, *Military Policy*, 190; *Soldiers of Florida in the Seminole Indian, Civil, and Spanish American Wars*, Live Oak, Fla., 1903; Flannery, "Naval Operations," 56; Resolution of the Legislative Council, Jan. 28, 1841.

4. Coe, *Red Patriots*, 161; Silver, *Gaines*, 167.

Appendix

In the citations below, the term Mahon, Bibliography, refers to the bibliography in the first printing, and Mahon, History, to the text of that printing.

Adams, George R. "Caloosahatchee Massacre: Its Significance in the Second Seminole War," *FHQ*, XLVIII (April, 1970), 368-80. Adds useful information to the event described in Mahon, History, pp. 261-63.

Bittle, George C. "The First Campaign of the Second Seminole War," *FHQ*, XLVI (July, 1967), 39-45. Adds original information on the actions of the Florida militia along the east coast in the early months of the war. Bittle completed a dissertation at Florida State University in 1965 on "The Organized Florida Militia, 1821-1920" (unpublished).

————. "The Florida Militia's Role in the Battle of Withlacoochee," *FHQ*, XLIV (April, 1966), 303-11.

————. "R. K. Call's 1863 Campaign," *Tequesta*, XXIX (1964), 67-72.

Brown, Harvey. Letterbooks. MSS New York Public Library; microfilmed copies in P. K. Yonge Library of Florida History, University of Florida, Gainesville. Brown sent reports from St. Augustine from July 1826 to March 22, 1829, when he was transferred out of the peninsula. He began writing again from St. Augustine in February 1837 and continued to August 25, 1838. He was assistant quartermaster for Florida, so his letters deal almost entirely with supply. After the suicide of Colonel John F. Lane, however, he received command of a regiment of Creek warriors, commanding it in the campaign that culminated in the Battle of Wahoo Swamp, November 21, 1836. Only two letters among hundreds refer to his combat command, and they only obliquely.

Brown, M. L. "Notes on United States Arsenals, Depots, and Martial Firearms of the Second Seminole War," *FHQ*, LXI (April, 1983), 445-58. Brown is a leading authority on weapons, and his contribution here is useful.

Buker, George Edward. "Lieutenant Levin M. Powell, U.S.N., Pioneer of Riverine Warfare," *FHQ*, XLVII (Jan., 1969), 253-75.

————. "The Mosquito Fleet's Guides and the Second Seminole War," *FHQ*, LVII (Jan., 1979), 308-26.

————. *Swamp Sailors: Riverine Warfare in the Everglades, 1835-1842.* Gainesville, Florida, 1975. A major contribution, as it tells for the first time the part the Navy played in this conflict, the largest role it ever played in an Indian war.

Clark, Ransom. *Narrative of Ransom Clark, the only survivor of Major Dade's command in Florida, containing brief descriptions of what befel him from his enlistment in 1833, til his discharge in 1836; with an account of the inhuman massacre by the Indians and Negroes of Major Dade's detachment.* Binghampton, N.Y., 1839. 16 pp. Clark was so gravely wounded in the Dade battle that he had to support himself afterward by lecturing and writing about his experiences. Some of what he tells seems stretched for dramatic effect, but that he miraculously survived and crawled and limped his way back to Ft. Brooke is well establshed.

Cooper, Major Mark Anthony. Memoirs. Dictated to a stenographer about 1884. Typescript in the P. K. Yonge Library of Florida History, Gainesville. Cooper commanded five companies of Georgia Volunteers formed into a battalion that served with Winfield Scott. Cooper includes an account of Scott's battle of March 31, 1836, not covered in Mahon, History. Also contains interesting anecdotes of the relations of citizen soldiers with regulars.

Covington, James W. "Migration into Florida of the Seminoles, 1700-1820," *FHQ*, XLVI (April, 1968), 340-57. Covington has written numerous articles on the Florida Indians; six of them are listed in Mahon, Bibliography, and others deal with different periods of tribal history.

Craig, Alan K., and Christopher Peebles. "Ethnohistorical Change among the Seminoles, 1740-1840," *Geoscience and Man*, V (June 10, 1974), 83-96. Stresses the Florida Indians' ability to adapt to various radically changed living conditions imposed upon them by nature or by white men.

Dobyns, Henry. *Their Number Became Thinned: Native American Population Dynamics in Eastern North America.* Knoxville, Tennessee, 1983. Uses data on epidemics and food supply to assert that Florida before the whites came supported a population of around 697,000 (p. 41). This figure far exceeds that given in Mahon, History, p. 7, and all other estimates. See figures in Mahon, History, p. 321. Estimates of the present population of Indians native to Florida are 1,800 officially enrolled in the Seminole Tribe, Inc., and around 300 Miccosukees in their federally recognized tribe.

Dowd, John T. "The Investigations of the Vandalized Graves of Two Historical Personages: Osceola, Seminole War Chief, and Colonel William L. Shy," *Tennessee Anthropologist*, V (Spring, 1980), 47-72. Otis Shriver of Miami, in the dead of night on January 7, 1966, dug into the grave of Osceola at Ft. Moultrie and brought back a lead box purported to contain Osceola's remains. His object, he said, was to return the remains to the soil where they belonged. Later, when the Park Service excavated to check the grave, they found Osceola's wooden coffin deeper than Shriver had dug. Dr. John Griffin was in charge of this official exhumation, and the paper cited here is based on what he reported. The headless skeleton was reburied on January 15, 1969. The story of the head missing from the skeleton is told in Ward, cited below.

Downs, Dorothy. "British Influence on Creek and Seminole Men's Clothing, 1733-1858," *Florida Anthropologist*, XXXIII (June, 1980), 46-65. Downs modifies the theory that the style of Seminole dress resulted largely from the hardships of the Seminole Wars.

Duffner, Michael Paul. "The Seminole-Black Alliance in Florida: An Example of Minority Cooperation." Master's thesis, George Mason University, 1973. Microfilm in the P. K. Yonge Library, Gainesville.

Fairbanks ,Charles H. *Ethnohistorical report on the Florida Indians*. Photo-offset by the Garland Publishing Company, New York, 1974. In Mahon, Bibliography, this item was listed as a stencil prepared for the Indian Claims Commission, Washington, in 1957. It carries the story up to the Treaty of Moultrie Creek.

————. *The Florida Seminole People*. Indian Tribal Series, Phoenix, 1973. Although this has only a short treatment of the Florida wars, it is a fine overview of the Seminole culture by an important student of it.

Fatio, Louis. "Louis Fatio's Thrilling Story," *Jacksonville Times-Union*, Oct. 31, 1892. The story, told by himself, is of the man referred to in Mahon, History, as Louis Pacheco. This document had not been studied when the history was written.

Francke, Arthur E. Jr. *Fort Mellon, 1837-1842*. Miami, 1977.

Hammond, E. Ashby. "Bemrose's Medical Case Notes from the Second Seminole War," *FHQ*, XLVII (April, 1969), 401-13. The original notes are in the possession of Mrs. Dorothy Donovan, Knowle, Warwickshire, England; she is the great-granddaughter of John Bemrose. See the Bemrose entry in Mahon, Bibliography.

Hartley, William, and Ellen Hartley. *Osceola: Unconquered Indian*. New York, 1973. These authors stress Osceola's skill as a general, a quality they found to be rare in Indians.

Hickox, Ron G. *United States Military Edged Weapons of the Second Seminole War, 1835-1842*. Gainesville, Fla., 1984. Illustrated by Raymond E. Giron. Although cut-and-thrust weapons were not significant in this war, the booklet deals with a dimension that cannot be ignored.

Kieffer, Chester. *Maligned General: The Biography of Thomas Sidney Jesup*. San Rafael, Calif., 1979. The first full-scale life of Jesup to be printed, this book fills a long-standing gap.

Kirk, Cooper. *William Lauderdale: General Andrew Jackson's Warrior*. Ft. Lauderdale, Fla., 1982.

Koerper, Phillip, and David T. Childress. "The Alabama Vounteers in the Second Seminole War, 1836," *Alabama Review*, XXXVII (Jan., 1984), 1-12.

Laumer, Frank. "Encounter by the River," *FHQ*, XLVI (April, 1968), 322-39. A detailed account of the Withlacoochee Battle, Dec. 31, 1835.

————. "The Incredible Adventures of Ransom Clark," *Tampa Bay History* III (Fall/Winter, 1981), 5-18. Clarke's name is spelled differently in different places, even by Laumer. The best version in Ransom Clarke.

————. *Massacre!* Gainesville, Fla., 1968. Note 38 on p. 337 of Mahon, Bibliography, is no longer correct; Laumer's book is the definitive account of the Dade Battle.

McCall, George A. *Letters from the Frontiers*. A facsimile reproduction of the 1868 edition, Gainesville, Fla., 1974. Cited in Mahon, Bibliography, in its original edition only.

Meek, Alexander B. "The Florida Expedition, Feb. 21–April 23, 1836," MS, Meek Papers, Duke Univ. Library. The significant parts of this manuscript were printed in *FHQ*; see Meek entry in Mahon, Bibliography.

Matthews, Janet Snyder. *Edge of Wilderness: A Settlement History of the Manatee River and Sarasota Bay, 1558-1885.* Tulsa, Okla. Pp. 79-124 deal with the war period, adding interesting detail, particularly on the so-called Spanish Indians.

Milanich, Jerald T., and Charles H. Fairbanks. *Florida Anthropology.* New York, 1980. These authors estimate the aboriginal population to have been 100,000. See Dobyns entry above.

Monk, J. Floyd. "Christmas Day in Florida, 1837," *Tequesta*, XXXVIII (1978), 5-38. The best account of the Battle of Okeechobee in print.

Moulton, Gary E. "Cherokees and the Second Seminole War," *FHQ*, LIII (Jan., 1975), 296-305.

Patrick, Rembert W. *Aristocrat in Uniform: Duncan L. Clinch.* Gainesville, Fla., 1963. An essential source not studied at the time Mahon, History, was written.

Prince, Henry. Diary, 1836-39, 1842. MS, P. K. Yonge Library, Gainesville. MS has been transcribed and typed by Frank Laumer. Invaluable for detailed information on the terrain, with many finely drawn maps. Firsthand information on Scott's Battle of March 31, 1836, not adequately treated in Mahon, History. Had this action been fought by whites with a better knowledge of the terrain, it might have seriously crippled the Indian fighting power early.

Schene, Michael G. "Georgia Volunteers at Ft. Cooper" and "Archeological Invesigations at Ft. Cooper," *Bulletin Number 5*, Florida Bureau of Historical Sites and Properties, 1976, pp. 15-20, 21-46. This bulletin, with Prince and Cooper (see citations above), helps fill out the story of the Battle of March 31, 1836, and tells the story of the founding of Ft. Cooper.

Sturtevant, William C. "Creek into Seminole," *North American Indians in Historical Perspective*, ed. Eleanor B. Leacock and Nancy O. Lurie. New York, 1971, pp. 92-128. A superior cross-disciplinary account of the development of a separate Seminole culture.

Thurman, Melburn D. "Seminoles, Creeks, Delawares and Shawnees: Indian Auxiliaries in the Second Seminole War," *Florida Anthropologist* (Dec., 1977), 143-65.

Ward, Mary McNeer. "Disappearance of the Head of Osceola," *FHQ*, XXX (1955). Not fully cited in Mahon, Bibliography. See Dowd entry above.

Welsh, Michael E. "Legislating a Homestead Bill: Thomas Hart Benton and the Second Seminole War," *FHQ*, LVII (July, 1978), 157-72. An excellent legislative history of the Armed Occupation Act.

West, Jeffrey. "Old Hickory and the Seminoles," *American History Illustrated* (Oct., 1980), 28-35.

White, Nathan W. *Private Joseph Sprague of Vermont: The Last Soldier Survivor of Dade's Massacre, 28 December 1835.* N.p., 1981. Three men left the Dade battlefield alive. Clarke saw one of them run down and killed by the Indians, and he stated in his lectures that the third man, Joseph Sprague, had died. White denies the death, contending that Sprague lived on long after Clarke died. He continued as an enlisted man in the U.S. Army, leaving it sometimes but always re-enlisting. Apparently he could not write, so he never undertook to live by his story as Clarke did.

Annotated Bibliography

Manuscript Material

Adjutant General's Office. "Letters Sent." Record Group 94, National Archives. These letters are in bound volumes with numbered pages.

————. "Letters Received." Record Group 94, National Archives. This is far and away the most useful body of records, for it contains letters and reports from the field, to the Secretary of War as well as to the Adjutant General. There is an alphabetical register of the letters. Each piece is identified by a letter of the alphabet, usually the beginning letter of the last name of the writer, and a number. Each year the series begins anew with number 1; thus, one needs to use the date along with the identifying letter number when calling for a specific piece of correspondence.

————. "Reports to Congress." Record Group 94, National Archives. These also are bound volumes with numbered pages.

Bemrose, John. "Reminiscences of the Second Seminole War." Florida Historical Society Library, University of South Florida, Tampa. Though written many years after the experiences it relates, this is a vivid narrative of many events of the first year of the war. A typescript of it was sold in 1939 by its owner, Dr. Arthur Freeman of England, to Mr. Robert Charles Stafford of West Richfield, Ohio (as of August, 1962). The original manuscript has not been found. The "Reminiscences" were published in 1966, and the citations herein are to the published work. See the Bemrose entry under "Non-Manuscript Material."

Department of Florida. "Court-Martial Records." Record Group 94, National Archives.

————. "Records." Record Group 98, National Archives, War Records Division, Early Wars Branch.

Eaton, J. H. (compiler). "Returns of Killed and Wounded in Battles or Engagements with the Indians, British, and Mexican Troops, 1790-1848." Compiled in 1850-51. A manuscript in the National Archives, War Records Division, Early Wars Branch.

General Headquarters of the Army. "Letterbooks." Record Group 108, National Archives.

General Land Office Records. Record Group 49, National Archives. Among the records are six volumes of letters sent relating to the

Armed Occupation Act; there are also registers of letters received and the files of those letters.

Jarvis, Nathan S. "Diary Kept While a Surgeon with the Army in Florida, 1837-1839." New York Academy of Medicine. Microfilmed.

Office of Indian Affairs. "Calendar of Manuscripts in the Indian Office, 1797-1849." P. K. Yonge Memorial Library of Florida History, University of Florida, Gainesville. This record contains items relating to Florida Indians and was compiled by Dr. James A. Robertson.

————. "Letters Received, Florida Superintendency, 1824-1850." Microfilmed from Record Group 75, National Archives. Microcopy No. 234, rolls 286-89.

————. "Letters Received, Florida Superintendency, Emigration, 1828-1853." Microcopy No. 234, rolls 290-91.

————. "Letters Received, Seminole Agency, Emigration, 1827-1846." Microcopy No. 234, roll 806.

————. "Letters Sent, 1835-1843." Microcopy No. 21, rolls 17-33.

Office of the Secretary of War. "Letters Sent." Record Group 107, National Archives. These letters are bound in large volumes with numbered pages.

————. "Reports to Congress." Record Group 107, National Archives.

Territorial Papers Commission. "Florida." Record Group 92, National Archives. This file consists of five boxes of records relating to Florida, selected by the Territorial Papers Commission.

United States Navy Department. "Records Relating to the Services of the Navy and Marine Corps on the Coast of Florida, 1835-1842." National Archives, Office of Naval Records. Microfilmed.

Webster, Lucian B. "Papers." St. Augustine Historical Society, St. Augustine, Fla. A small collection of papers of this United States Army captain who was for a time commandant of Fort Marion at St. Augustine.

Non-Manuscript Material

Abel, Annie Heloise. "The History of Events Resulting in Indian Consolidation West of the Mississippi," in American Historical Association, *Annual Report*, 1906. Washington, 1908. I, 233-450.

Acts of the Legislative Council of the Territory of Florida 1822-1845. Tallahassee. The acts were printed each year.

Adair, James. *History of the American Indians.* London, 1775. John R. Swanton calls this a superb account of Indian modes of warfare in the late eighteenth century, but Adair devoted half of his book to proving that the Indians descended from the tribes of Israel.

American State Papers: Indian Affairs. 2 vols. Washington, 1832-1834. No effort is made here to designate the parts of these volumes used. They contain most of the vital documents for the period prior to 1832.

American State Papers: Military Affairs. 7 vols. Washington, 1832-1860. The sections used are listed below.

Vol. VI, pp. 56-80. "Causes of the War." Identical with *Sen. Doc. 152*, 24 Cong., 1 sess. (see, below, *United States Congress Serial Set*).

VI, 406-10. "Claims by States for Reimbursement."

VI, 433-43. "Efforts by U.S. to Control Hostiles." Contains mostly the same documents as *HR Doc. 267*, 24 Cong., 1 sess.

VI, 450-574. "Indian Hostilities in Florida." Identical with *HR Doc. 271*, 24 Cong., 1 sess.

VI, 574-783. "Causes of Hostilities." In spite of the title this document relates only to the Creek War.

VI, 788-91. "Estimates of Cost, 27 June 1836."

VI, 965-66. "Estimates of Cost, 21 Dec. 1836."

VI, 992-1002. "Operations of the Army under R. K. Call."

VI, 1026-69. "Militia and Volunteers." Same as *HR Doc. 140*, 24 Cong., 2 sess.

VI, 1075-78. "Claims of Tennessee Volunteers."

VI, 1080-81. "Estimates of Cost, 14 Feb. 1837."

VI, 1082-83. "Claims of Supernumerary Officers."

VII, 110-15. "Resignation of Officers." Same as *HR Doc. 183*, 24 Cong., 2 sess.

VII, 115-16. "Claims of Augusta, Ga. and Washington, Ga."

VII, 125-465. "Court of Inquiry of Scott and Gaines." Same as *Sen. Doc. 224*, 24 Cong., 2 sess., and *HR Doc. 78*, 25 Cong., 2 sess.

VII, 518-25. "Employment of Indians Against the Seminoles."

VII, 745-63. "Claims of Volunteers with Gaines."

VII, 794-894. "Documents Pertaining to T. S. Jesup's Command." Same as the Supplement to *HR Doc. 78*, 25 Cong., 2 sess.

VII, 918-24. "Troops in Service." Identical with *HR Doc. 133*, 25 Cong., 2 sess.

VII, 985-92. "Taylor's Report of Battle of Okeechobee." Same as *Sen. Doc. 227*, 25 Cong., 2 sess.

Anonymous. "Notes on the Passage Across the Everglades." St. Augustine *News*, Jan. 8, 1841; reprinted in *Tequesta*, No. 20 (1960), 57-65.

Army and Navy Chronicle (Washington). Published under that title from Jan., 1835, to May, 1842. There are hundreds of invaluable items scattered through this periodical.

Backus, Electus. "Diary of a Campaign in Florida in 1837-1838," *Historical Magazine* (Sept., 1866), 279-85.

Barr, James [Captain]. *Correct and Authentic Narrative . . . of the Indian War in Florida, with a Description of Major Dade's Massacre.* New York, 1836. Barr was a Louisiana Volunteer, and his account is first hand.

Bartram, William. "Observations on the Creek and Cherokee Indians, 1789," in *Transactions*, American Ethnological Society, Vol. III, Part 1 (New York, 1853; reprinted, 1909). For the edition cited herein see the Cruickshank entry below.

_____. *Travels Through North and South Carolina, Georgia, East and West Florida, the Cherokee Country, the Extensive Territories of the Muscogulges or Creek Confederacy and the Country of the Choctaws.* Philadelphia, 1791. For the edition cited herein see the Harper entry below.

Bemrose, John. *Reminiscences of the Second Seminole War*, ed. John K. Mahon. Gainesville: University of Florida Press, 1966. This published edition is cited herein.

Benton, Thomas Hart. *Thirty Years' View*, 2 vols. New York, 1854, 1856.

Blassingame, Wyatt. *Seminoles of Florida*. Tallahassee, 1959. Published by the Florida Department of Agriculture, this is a brief, popular, workmanlike account.

Boyd, Mark F. "Asi-Yaholo, or Osceola," Osceola Issue, *FHQ*, XXXIII (Jan. and April, 1955), 249-305.

_____. "Documents Describing the Second and Third Expeditions of

Lieutenant Diego Peña to Apalachee and Apalachicola in 1717 and 1718," *FHQ*, XXXI (Oct., 1952), 109-39.

————. *Florida Aflame: Background and Onset of the Seminole War, 1835*. Tallahassee, 1951. Reprinted from *FHQ*, XXX (July, 1951), 1-115. This work is an excellent and invaluable bit of scholarship.

————. "Horatio S. Dexter and Events Leading to the Treaty of Moultrie Creek with the Seminole Indians," *Florida Anthropologist*, XI (Sept., 1958), 65-95.

Brevard, Caroline Mays. *History of Florida*, 2 vols. DeLand, Fla., 1924.

————. "Richard Keith Call," *FHQ*, 1st series, I (July, Oct., 1908), 3-12, 8-20.

Brinton, Daniel G. *Notes on the Floridian Peninsula, Its Literary History, Indian Tribes and Antiquities*. Philadelphia, 1859. This work is one of the most useful of the early accounts.

Brown, George M. *Ponce de Leon Land and Florida War Record*. 4th ed. St. Augustine, 1902. A tourist guide to Florida, this small book is useful because a list of the regular soldiers who lost their lives during the Seminole War is printed on pp. 119-80.

Buchanan, Robert C. "A Journal of Lieutenant R. C. Buchanan During the Seminole War," ed. Frank F. White, Jr., *FHQ*, XXIX (Oct., 1950), 132-51.

————. "A Scouting Expedition Along Lake Pansoffkee," ed. Frank F. White, Jr., *FHQ*, XXXI (April, 1953), 282-89. This gives more of Buchanan's journal.

Canova, Andrew P. *Life and Adventures in South Florida*. Palatka, Fla., 1885. The work is strong on the Third Seminole War, but gives little on the Second.

Cantrell, Elizabeth. *When Kissimmee Was Young*. Kissimmee, Fla., 1948. I drew an anecdote or two about W. S. Harney from this book; otherwise it adds nothing.

Capron, Louis. *The Medicine Bundles of the Florida Seminole and the Green Corn Dance*. Smithsonian Institution, Bureau of American Ethnology, Bulletin 51 (Washington, 1953), pp. 155-210.

Cardwell, Guy A., Jr. "W. H. Timrod, the Charleston Volunteers and the Defense of St. Augustine," *North Carolina Historical Review*, XVIII (1941), 27-37.

Carter, Clarence E. (ed.). *Territorial Papers of the United States*, Vols. XXII-XXVI: *Florida Territory*. Washington, 1956-1962. Carter has put in this series a superb and indispensable collection of documents.

Cash, W. T. *The Story of Florida*, 4 vols. New York, 1938. The first two volumes are devoted to history, the others to contemporary biography.

Castelnau, Comte de. "Essay on Middle Florida, 1837, 1838," *FHQ*, XXVI (Jan., April, 1948), 199-255, 300-324. Other contemporary evidence often contradicts Castelnau's.

Catlin, George. *North American Indians, Being Letters, Notes on Their Manners, Customs and Conditions During Eight Years' Travel Among the Wildest Tribes of Indians in North America, 1832-1839*, 2 vols. London, 1866; reprinted in Edinburgh, 1926. In this ambitious work only five pages, 247-51, pertain to the Seminoles.

Caughey, John W. *McGillivray of the Creeks*. Norman: University of Oklahoma Press, 1938.

Chaffer, H. J. "Florida Forts Established Prior to 1860." Typescript in the P. K. Yonge Memorial Library of Florida History, Gainesville.

Chaney, Margaret A. "A Tribal History of the Seminole Indians." Master's thesis, University of Oklahoma, Norman. Since the publication of McReynolds, *The Seminoles*, there is no need to refer to this thesis.

Childs, General [Thomas]. "General Childs, U.S.A.: Extracts from His Correspondence with His Family," *Historical Magazine*, 3rd series, II (1873), 299-304, 371-74, III, 169-71, 280-84. Childs' observations were of great help in the present work.

Churchill, Franklin Hunter. *Sketch of the Life of Brevet Brigadier General Sylvester Churchill*. New York, 1888. Nothing useful was found in this book.

Cobb, Samuel E. "The Florida Militia and the Affair at Withlacoochee," *FHQ*, XIX (Oct., 1940), 128-39. This article reproduces the account of a participant in the battle, originally printed in the Tallahassee *Floridian*, Feb. 20, 1836.

————. "The Spring Grove Guards," *FHQ*, XXII (April, 1944), 208-16.

Coe, Charles H. "The Parentage and Birthplace of Osceola," *FHQ*, XVII (April, 1939), 304-11. Coe concludes Osceola was not part white.

————. *Red Patriots: The Story of the Seminoles*. Cincinnati, 1898. Coe here develops the theme of white persecution of the Indians. His work offers much useful data, especially the list of battles and forts on pp. 263-69.

Cohen M[yer] M. *Notices of Florida and the Campaigns*. Charleston, S.C., 1836; reprinted with an Introduction by O. Z. Tyler, Jr., in the Floridiana Facsimile and Reprint Series, University of Florida Press, Gainesville, 1964. Cohen was one of the literate early volunteers who rushed his experiences into print. His work affords many details which would otherwise be lost.

Congressional Globe, Containing the Debates and Proceedings, 1833-1873, 109 vols. Washington, 1833-73. Vol. 1, 23 Cong., 1833, through Vol. XII, 28 Cong., 1844, were used for this work.

Cooper, Samuel. *A Concise System of Instructions and Regulations for the Militia and Volunteers of the United States*. Philadelphia, 1836.

Cotterill, Robert S. "Federal Indian Management in the South, 1789-1825," *Mississippi Valley Historical Review*, XX (Dec., 1933), 333-52. The article is duplicated and expanded in the book listed next below.

————. *The Southern Indians: The Story of the Civilized Tribes Before Removal*. Norman: University of Oklahoma Press, 1954. The work is so condensed as often to be hard to follow, but it is written with humorous irony.

Covington, James W. "The Armed Occupation Act of 1842," *FHQ*, XL (July, 1961), 41-52.

————. *The British Meet the Seminoles: Negotiations Between British Authorities in East Florida and the Indians, 1763-1768*. Contributions of the Florida State Museum, Social Science No. 7, Gainesville, 1961.

————. "Cuban Bloodhounds and the Seminoles," *FHQ*, XXXIII (Oct., 1954), 111-19.

———— (ed.). "The Establishment of Fort Brooke: From Letters of Colonel George M. Brooke," *FHQ*, XXXI (Jan., 1953), 273-78.

————. "Federal Relations with the Apalachicola Indians, 1823-1838," *FHQ*, XLII (Oct., 1963), 125-41.

————. *The Story of Southwestern Florida*, 2 vols. New York, 1957.

————. "Trade Between Southwest Florida and Cuba," *FHQ*, XXXVIII (Oct., 1959), 114-28.

Crane, Verner W. *The Southern Frontier, 1670-1732.* Ann Arbor: University of Michigan Press, 1929.

Croffut, W. A. (ed.). *Fifty Years in Camp and Field: Diary of Major General Ethan Allen Hitchcock, U.S.A.* New York, 1909. If Hitchcock is to be trusted, he offers some of the most telling information on crucial points to be found in any contemporary material.

Cruickshank, Helen G. (ed.). *John and William Bartram's America.* New York, 1957, pp. 346-67.

Cubberly, Frederick. "The Dade Massacre," in *Sen. Doc. 33,* 67 Cong., 1 sess. Washington, 1920.

————. "Fort King," *FHQ,* V (Jan., 1927), 139-52.

Cullum, George Washington. *Biographical Register of the Officers and Graduates of the United States Military Academy . . . 1802-1890,* 3 vols. Boston, 1891.

Davis, Hilda J. "The History of Seminole Clothing and Its Multi-Colored Design," *Florida Anthropologist,* VII (Oct., 1955). The author does not mention the possible war origin of the bright patterns.

Davis, T. Frederick. "Coacoochee." This is a sixteen-page extract in the P. K. Yonge Memorial Library of Florida History, University of Florida, Gainesville. Its source is unknown, but it was probably printed in the *Florida Review.*

————. "Early Orange Culture in Florida and the Epochal Cold of 1835," *FHQ,* XV (April, 1937), 232-41.

————. "The Seminole Council, October 23-25, 1834," *FHQ,* VII (April, 1929), 330-50. Published in connection with this article was James Gadsden's letter to the editor of the St. Augustine *News,* July 3, 1839, pp. 350-56.

Debo, Angie. *The Road to Disappearance.* Norman: University of Oklahoma Press, 1941. There is very little in this book directly pertaining to the Seminoles.

Dictionary of American Biography. Eds. Allen Johnson and Dumas Malone. New York, 1928-37, 1944, 1958.

Dodd, Dorothy. "Captain Bunce's Tampa Bay Fisheries, 1835-1840," *FHQ,* XXV (Jan., 1947), 246-56.

————. "Florida in 1845," *FHQ,* XXIV (July, 1945), 3-29.

————. "Jacob Housman of Indian Key," *Tequesta,* No. 8 (1948), 3-19.

————. "Letters from East Florida," *FHQ,* XV (July, 1936), 51-64. The letters are concerned with the Armed Occupation Act.

Doherty, Herbert J., Jr. *Richard Keith Call: Southern Unionist.* Gainesville: University of Florida Press, 1961.

————. "R. K. Call Versus the Federal Government on the Seminole War," *FHQ,* XXXI (Jan., 1953), 163-80.

————. "The Florida Whigs." Master's thesis, University of Florida, Gainesville, 1949.

————. *The Whigs of Florida, 1845-1854.* Gainesville: University of Florida Press, 1959. A revision and condensation of the thesis.

Donaldson, Thomas. *The Public Domain: Its History and Statistics.* Washington, 1884.

Douglas, Thomas. *Autobiography of Thomas Douglas, Late Judge of the Supreme Court of Florida.* New York, 1856. Only the last fifteen pages deal with the Seminoles. Douglas never completed this work which would have been a valuable source, for he lived in St. Augustine and was a participant in the war.

Dovell, Junius E. *Florida: Historic, Dramatic, Contemporary*, 4 vols. New York, 1952. The first two volumes offer history, the others contemporary biography.
_____. *History of Banking in Florida, 1828-1954*. Orlando, Fla., 1955.
_____. "A History of the Everglades of Florida." Doctor's dissertation, University of North Carolina, Chapel Hill, 1947.
Drew, Frank. "Notes on the Origin of the Seminole Indians of Florida," *FHQ*, VI (July, 1927), 21-24. The notes are not accurate.
Dyer, Brainerd. *Zachary Taylor*. Baton Rouge: Louisiana State University Press, 1946.
Elderkin, James D. *Biographical Sketches and Anecdotes of a Soldier of Three Wars as Written by Himself*. Detroit, 1899. Elderkin served with the Fourth Infantry in the Seminole War, and pp. 16-38 contain interesting personal observations.
Elliott, Charles W. *Winfield Scott: The Soldier and the Man*. New York, 1937.
Ellsworth, Henry Leavitt. *Washington Irving on the Prairie, or a Narrative of a Tour of the Southwest in the Year 1832*, ed. Stanley T. Willimas and Barbara D. Simison. New York, 1937. This work supplies some data on the Treaty of Fort Gibson.
Emerson, William C. *The Seminoles*. New York, 1954. This is primarily an analysis of the twentieth-century Seminoles in a popular vein.
Fairbanks, Charles H. "Ethnohistorical Report of the Florida Indians." Presentation before the Indian Claims Commission, Dockets 73, 151. Stencil reproduction. Washington, 1957.
Fairbanks, George R. *History of Florida from Its Discovery by Ponce de Leon in 1512 to the Close of the Florida War in 1842*. Philadelphia, 1871. Fairbanks was not at all objective as regards the Indians, but he reflected the attitude of contemporary Floridians.
Fenton, William N. *American Indian and White Relations to 1830*. Chapel Hill: University of North Carolina Press, 1957. This is a bibliography.
Flannery, Edmund P. "Naval Operations During the Second Seminole War, 1835-1842." Master's thesis, University of Florida, Gainesville, 1958.
Forbes, James Grant. *Sketches, Historical and Topographical, of the Floridas; More Particularly of East Florida*. New York, 1821; reprinted with an Introduction by James W. Covington in the Floridiana Facsimile and Reprint Series, University of Florida Press, Gainesville, 1964. Though Forbes wrote to attract settlers to Florida, he did include interesting descriptions of the new territory.
Foreman, Grant. *The Five Civilized Tribes*. Norman: University of Oklahoma Press, 1934. Foreman deals partly with the Seminoles in the Indian Territory.
_____. *Indian Removal: The Emigration of the Five Civilized Tribes of Indians*. Norman: University of Oklahoma Press, 1953.
_____. *Pioneer Days in the Early Southwest*. Cleveland, 1926.
_____ (ed.). "Report of the Cherokee Deputies in Florida, February 17, 1838, to John Ross, Esq.," *Chronicles of Oklahoma*, IX (Dec., 1931), 423-38.
_____ (ed.). *A Traveller in Indian Territory: The Journal of Ethan Allen Hitchcock*. Cedar Rapids, Iowa, 1930.
Forry, Samuel. "Letters of Samuel Forry, Surgeon, U.S. Army, 1837,

'38." *FHQ*, VI (Jan., April, 1928), 133-48, 206-19, VII (July, 1928), 88-105.

Foster, Lawrence W. *Negro-Indian Relationships in the Southeast.* Philadelphia, 1935. This is a thin contribution.

Fundaburk, Emma L. (ed.). *Southeastern Indians: Life Portraits; a Catalogue of Pictures, 1564-1860.* Luverne, Ala., 1958. This is the definitive collection of pictures of the southeastern Indians.

Gannon, Michael V. *The Cross in the Sand: The Early Catholic Church in Florida, 1513-1870.* Gainesville: University of Florida Press, 1965.

Ganoe, William A. *The History of the United States Army.* New York, 1942.

Gentry, William R. *Full Justice: The Story of Richard Gentry and His Missouri Volunteers in the Seminole War.* St. Louis, 1937.

Giddings, Joshua R. *The Exiles of Florida: Or, the Crimes Committed by Our Government Against the Maroons, Who Fled from South Carolina and Other Slave States, Seeking Protection Under Spanish Law.* Columbus, Ohio, 1858; reprinted with an Introduction by Arthur W. Thompson in the Floridiana Facsimile and Reprint Series, University of Florida Press, Gainesville, 1964. An abolitionist, Giddings set out to prove that slavery was the dominant cause of the Second Seminole War. He was much biased, but there is much useful source material in his book.

Gifford, John C. "Five Plants Essential to the Indians and Early Settlers of Florida," *Tequesta*, No. 4 (1944), 36-44.

Glenn, Joshua N. "A Diary of Joshua Nichols Glenn: St. Augustine in 1823," *FHQ*, XXIV (Oct., 1945), 121-61.

Goggin, John M. "Source Materials for the Study of the Florida Seminole Indians." Laboratory Notes No. 3 (mimeographed), Anthropology Department, University of Florida, Gainesville, Aug., 1959.

Gonzalez, Thomas A. *The Caloosahatchee.* Estero, Fla., 1932. There is little here on the Second, but the work is good on the Third Seminole War.

Griffin, John W. (ed.). "Some Comments on the Seminoles in 1818," *Florida Anthropologist*, X (1957), 41-49. Griffin gives us a useful contemporary document.

Griswold, Oliver. "William Selby Harney: Indian Fighter," *Tequesta*, No. 9 (1949), 73-80. The account is dramatized, and not scholarly.

Guild, Jo C. *Old Times in Tennessee.* Nashville, 1878.

Halbe, James M. *Tales of the Seminole War.* Okeechobee, Fla., 1950. The tales are not scholarly, and add nothing to the basic fund of knowledge.

Halbert, Henry S., and T. H. Ball. *The Creek War of 1813 and 1814.* Chicago and Montgomery, Ala., 1895.

Halsey, Francis W. (ed.). *Great Epochs in American History.* New York, 1916. Section V was contributed by James Parton on the First Seminole War, and Section VI by Thomas Hart Benton on the Second Seminole War.

Hammond, E. Ashby (ed.). "Dr. Strobel Reports on Southeast Florida, 1836," *Tequesta*, No. 21 (1961), 65-75.

Hanna, Alfred J. *Fort Maitland: Its Origin and History.* Maitland, Fla., 1936.

Hanna, Alfred J., and Kathryn Abbey Hanna. *Florida's Golden Sands.* Indianapolis, 1950. This is a history of Florida's east coast.

✓   ————. *Lake Okeechobee*. Indianapolis, 1948. Chapter 3 contains a
    short, skillful account of the Battle of Okeechobee.
Harper, Francis (ed.). *The Travels of William Bartram*. New Haven:
    Yale University Press, 1958.
Harrison, Benjamin. "Home Life of the Florida Indians," *FHQ*, III
    (July, 1924), 17-28.
        ————. "Indian Races of Florida," *FHQ*, III (Oct., 1924), 29-37. These
    accounts are interesting, but not scholarly.
Hawkins, Benjamin. *Letters of Benjamin Hawkins, 1796-1806*. "Collec-
    tions of the Georgia Historical Society," Vol. IX. Savannah, 1916.
        ————. *A Sketch of the Creek Country in 1798 and 1799*. "Collections
    of the Georgia Historical Society," Vol. III, Part 1, 1848.
Heitman, Francis B. *Historical Register and Dictionary of the United
    States Army . . . to March 2, 1903*, 2 vols. This valuable record is *HR
    Doc. 446*, 57 Cong., 2 sess., published by the Government Printing
    Office, 1903.
Herring, James. *National Portrait Gallery of Distinguished Americans*.
    Philadelphia, 1835. The writing is too superficial to be of help.
Hill, Dorothy E. "Joseph M. White, Florida's Territorial Delegate, 1825-
    1837." Master's thesis, University of Florida, Gainesville, 1950.
Hirschhorn, Howard H. "An Ethnomedical Description of Indian
    Health." Master's thesis, University of Florida, Gainesville, 1958. The
    thesis is not historical in approach.
Hodge, Frederick W. (ed.). *Handbook of American Indians North of
    Mexico*, 2 vols. Smithsonian Institution, Bureau of American Eth-
    nology, Bulletin 30, Washington, 1907, 1910.
Hollingsworth, Henry. "Tennessee Volunteers in the Seminole Campaign:
    The Diary of Henry Hollingsworth," ed. Stanley F. Horn, *Tennessee
    Historical Quarterly*, I (Sept., Dec., 1942), 269-74, 344-66, II (March,
    June, Sept., 1943), 61-73, 163-78, 236-56.
Hoyt, William D., Jr. (ed.). "A Soldier's View of the Seminole War:
    Three Letters of James B. Dallam," *FHQ*, XXV (April, 1947), 356-62.
    Dallam was killed in Harney's Massacre.
Hrdlicka, Ales. *The Anthropology of Florida*. DeLand, Fla., 1922.
Hunter, Nathaniel W. "Captain Nathaniel Wyche Hunter and the Flor-
    ida Indian Campaigns, 1837-1841," ed. Reynold M. Wik, *FHQ*, XXXIX
    (July, 1960), 62-75.
Huse, Harriet P. "An Untold Story of the Florida War," *Harper's
    Magazine*, LXXXIII (Sept., 1891), 591-94. This is an account of the
    Indian Key episode.
Irving, Washington. *Works*, 12 vols.; Vol. XII: "The Seminoles," "Origin
    of the White, the Red and the Black Man," and "The Conspiracy of
    Neamathla." New York, 1882.
"Jacksonville and the Seminole War, 1835, 1836," *FHQ*, III (Jan., April,
    1925), 10-14, 15-21, IV (July, 1925), 22-30. The articles contain ex-
    tracts from the Jacksonville *Courier*.
James, Marquis. *Andrew Jackson: The Border Captain*. Indianapolis,
    1933.
Jarvis, Nathan S. "An Army Surgeon's Notes on Frontier Service, 1833-
    1848," *Journal of the Military Service Institution of the United States*
    (July, 1906), 3-8, (Sept., Oct., 1906), 275-86.
Journals of the Florida Territorial Legislative Council. Tallahassee. The
    journals were printed each year.

Judson, E. Z. C. [Ned Buntline]. "Sketches of the Florida War—Indian Key, Its Rise, Progress and Destruction." Pensacola *Gazette,* March 29, 1845, reprinted from the *Western Literary Journal and Monthly Review.*

Kappler, Charles J. *Indian Affairs, Laws and Treaties,* 2nd ed., 2 vols. Washington, 1904. This collection was published as *Sen. Doc. 319,* 58 Cong., 2 sess.

Knauss, James Owen. *Territorial Florida Journalism.* DeLand, Fla., 1926.

————. "William Pope DuVal," *FHQ,* XI (Jan., 1933), 95-139.

Knowles, Nathaniel. "The Torture of Captives by Indians of Eastern North America," in American Philosophical Society, *Proceedings,* LXXXII (1940), 151-225.

Krogman, Wilton M. "The Racial Composition of the Seminole Indians of Florida and Oklahoma," *Journal of Negro History,* XIX (Oct., 1934), 412-30.

Lee, Arthur Tracy. *Army Ballads and Other Poems.* New York, 1871.

Ludlum, Robert P. "Joshua Giddings, Radical," *Mississippi Valley Historical Review,* XXIII (1936), 49-60.

McAlister, Lyle N. "William Augustus Bowles and the State of Muskogee," *FHQ,* XL (April, 1962), 317-28.

McCall, George A. *Letters from the Frontiers.* Philadelphia, 1868. McCall's letters constitute one of the very useful works by a participant in the war.

McCarthy, Joseph E. "Portraits of Osceola and the Artists Who Painted Them." Jacksonville (Fla.) Historical Society, *Papers,* II (1949), 23-45.

MacCauley, Clay. *The Seminole Indians of Florida.* Smithsonian Institution, Bureau of American Ethnology, Fifth Annual Report, 1883, 1884, published Washington, 1887.

McDermott, John F. (ed.). *Seth Eastman, Pictorial Historian of the American Indians.* Norman: University of Oklahoma Press, 1961.

———— (ed.). *The Western Journals of Washington Irving.* Norman: University of Oklahoma Press, 1944.

McKay, D. B. *Pioneer Florida,* 3 vols. Tampa, Fla., 1959. McKay publishes some reminiscences and some documents; all of them are interesting, but not all are reliable.

McKenney, Thomas L. *Memoirs, Official and Personal.* New York, 1846.

McKenney, Thomas L., and James Hall. *The Indian Tribes of North America, with Biographical Sketches and Anecdotes of the Principal Chiefs,* 3 vols. Philadelphia, 1836-44. The three volumes contain magnificent reproductions of paintings of Indians; the original paintings were burned in a fire in the Smithsonian Institution in 1865.

McLaughlin, Andrew C. *Lewis Cass.* Boston, 1891.

McMaster, John B. *A History of the People of the United States from the Revolution to the Civil War,* 8 vols. New York, 1883-1913. Vol. IV contains an account of the First Seminole War, Vol. VI has one of the Second; neither account adds anything to the basic knowledge of the story.

McReynolds, Edwin C. *The Seminoles.* Norman: University of Oklahoma Press, 1957. Being the only comprehensive history of the Seminoles, this book is indispensable, but it is disappointing because of the very thin treatment of important episodes.

Mahon, John K. "History of the Organization of the United States Infantry," in *The Army Lineage Book*, pp. 1-61. Washington: Government Printing Office, 1953.

Malin, James C. *Indian Policy and Westward Expansion*. Bulletin of the University of Kansas, Humanistic Studies, II, No. 3, Lawrence, 1921.

Manucy, Albert C. "Some Military Affairs in Territorial Florida," *FHQ*, XXV (Oct., 1946), 202-11. The piece adds nothing to the basic fund of knowledge.

Martin, Sidney Walter. *Florida During the Territorial Days*. Athens: University of Georgia Press, 1944. The work contains many errors of fact.

————. "Richard Keith Call, Florida Territorial Leader," *FHQ*, XXI (April, 1943), 332-51.

————. *Sectional Aspects of Seminole Conflict*, "Studies in Georgia History and Government," ed. James C. Bonner. Athens: University of Georgia Press, 1940. The work is not at all reliable.

Meek, A. B. "The Journal of A. B. Meek and the Second Seminole War, 1836," ed. John K. Mahon, *FHQ*, XXXVIII (April, 1960), 302-18.

Metcalf, Clyde H. *History of the United States Marine Corps*. New York, 1939.

Milford, Louis LeClerc de. *Memoir of a Cursory Glance at My Different Travels and My Sojourn in the Creek Nation*, trans. Geraldine de Courcy. Published 1802; reprinted, Chicago Lakeside Press, 1956.

Military and Naval Magazine, ed. Benjamin Homans. 6 vols., March, 1833, to February, 1836.

Miller, David Hunter (ed.). *Treaties and Other International Acts of the United States of America*, 8 vols. Washington, 1931-48. The series does not include Indian treaties.

Moore-Willson, Minnie. *The Seminoles of Florida*. New York, 1896; reprinted, 1920. The volume is more sentimental than historical.

Motte, Jacob Rhett. *Journey into Wilderness: An Army Surgeon's Account of Life in Camp and Field During the Creek and Seminole Wars, 1836-1838*, ed. James F. Sunderman. Gainesville: University of Florida Press, 1953. Motte's journal is perhaps the best of all those relating to the Second Seminole War. There are also comprehensive notes by the editor.

Mowat, Charles Loch. *East Florida as a British Province, 1763-1784*. Berkeley: University of California Press, 1943; reprinted in the Floridiana Facsimile and Reprint Series, University of Florida Press, 1964.

"The Muskogees and Seminoles," by an Officer of the Medical Staff, U.S. Army, *Monthly Magazine of Religion and Literature* (1840), pp. 137-47.

Nash, Roy. *A Survey of the Seminole Indians of Florida*. Washington, 1931. This survey is *Sen. Doc. 314*, 71 Cong., 3 sess. It is of course not a historical account of the Seminoles, but it is very interestingly written.

Neff, Jacob K. *The Army and Navy of America*. Philadelphia, 1845. This is a thin, popularized account of the military of the time.

Neill, Wilfred T. *Florida's Seminole Indians*. Silver Springs, Fla., 1952. Although a small booklet for sale to tourists at Ross Allen's Reptile Farm at Silver Springs, this is a generally accurate account.

————. "The Identity of Florida's 'Spanish Indians,'" *Florida Anthropologist*, VIII (June, 1955), 43-57.

Niles' Weekly Register (Baltimore), 1811-1849. The title varies. This is a prime source for the war, as it is for so much American history of its time.

"Old Tiger Tail Dead," *FHQ*, IV (April, 1926), 192-94, reprinted from the Tallahassee *Floridian*, Oct. 25, 1881, apparently quoting Tiger Tail's son.

Ordnance Reports, 4 vols. Washington, 1878-90.

"Osceola Issue," *FHQ*, XXXIII (Jan. and April, 1955). The entire issue, by various writers, is devoted to Osceola.

Paine, Charles R. "The Seminole War of 1817-1818." Master's thesis, University of Oklahoma, Norman, 1938. This is the most compact but thorough account of the First Seminole War that I have seen.

Parrish, J. O. *Battling the Seminoles: Featuring John Akins, Scout.* Lakeland, Fla., 1930. There is little history but much adventure.

Parton, James. *Life of Andrew Jackson*, 3 vols. New York, 1860. Although Jackson was President for two years of the war, there is in the three volumes not a word concerning the Second Seminole War.

Patrick, Rembert W. *Florida Fiasco: Rampant Rebels on the Georgia-Florida Border, 1810-1815.* Athens: University of Georgia Press, 1954. Patrick's is the definitive study of events for the years covered.

Peithmann, Irvin M. *The Unconquered Seminole Indians.* St. Petersburg, Fla., 1957. A booklet prepared for sale to the tourist trade, it is decently accurate and thorough.

Phelps, John W. "Letters of Lieutenant John Phelps, U.S.A., 1837, 1838," *FHQ*, VI (Oct., 1927), 67-84.

Pickell, John. "The Journals of Lieutenant John Pickell, 1836, 1837," ed. Frank F. White, Jr., *FHQ*, XXXVIII (Oct., 1959), 142-71.

Poinsett, Joel R. *Calendar of the Joel R. Poinsett Papers in the Henry D. Gilpin Collection.* Philadelphia, 1941. Owned by the Historical Society of Pennsylvania, these are the main body of all the extant Poinsett papers.

Pond, Fred. E. *Life and Adventures of "Ned Buntline."* New York, 1919. Ned Buntline (E. Z. C. Judson) was a navy lieutenant who was on the *Otsego* off the Florida coast in 1840.

Pope, John. *A Tour Through the Southern and Western Territories of the United States of North America; the Spanish Dominions on the River Mississippi and the Floridas; the Countries of the Creek Nation and Many Uninhabited Parts.* Richmond, Va., 1792; reprinted, New York, 1888.

Porter, Kenneth W. "The Cowkeeper Dynasty of the Seminole Nation," *FHQ*, XXX (April, 1952), 341-49.

_____. "The Episode of Osceola's Wife: Fact or Fiction?" *FHQ*, XXVI (July, 1947), 92-98.

_____. "Florida Slaves and Free Negroes in the Seminole War, 1835-1842," *Journal of Negro History*, XXVIII (April, 1943), 390-421.

_____. "The Founder of the 'Seminole Nation,' Secoffee or Cowkeeper?" *FHQ*, XXVII (April, 1949), 362-84.

_____. "John Caesar, Seminole Negro Partisan," *Journal of Negro History*, XXXI (April, 1946), 190-207.

_____. "The Negro Abraham," *FHQ*, XXV (July, 1946), 1-43.

_____. "Negro Guides and Interpreters in the Early Stages of the Seminole War, December 28, 1835-March 6, 1837," *Journal of Negro History*, XXXV (April, 1950), 174-82.

_____. "Negroes and the Seminole War, 1817, 1818," *Journal of Negro History*, XXXVI (July, 1951), 249-80.

_____. "Negroes and the Seminole War," *Journal of Southern History*, XXX (1964), 427-50. This article presents the Negro story in more complete and compact form than any other account.

_____. "Notes Supplementary to Relations Between Negroes and Indians . . ." *Journal of Negro History*, XVIII (July, 1933), 282-321.

_____. "Origins of the St. Johns River Seminoles: Were They Mikasuki?" *Florida Anthropologist*, IV (1951), 39-45.

_____. "Relations Between Negroes and Indians Within the Present Limits of the United States," *Journal of Negro History*, XVII (July, 1932), 287-367.

_____. "Seminole Flight from Fort Marion," *FHQ*, XXII (Jan., 1944), 113-33.

_____. "Three Fighters for Freedom: Maroons in Massachusetts; John Caesar, a Forgotten Hero of the Seminole War; Louis Pacheco," *Journal of Negro History*, XXVIII (Jan., 1945) 53-72.

_____. "Tiger Tail," *FHQ*, XXIV (Jan., 1946), 216-17.

[Potter, Woodburne]. *The War in Florida, Being an Exposition of Its Causes and an Accurate History of the Campaigns of Generals Clinch, Gaines, and Scott.* Baltimore, 1836. Potter is a useful source for the onset of the war and for its early stages.

Pound, Merritt B. *Benjamin Hawkins, Indian Agent.* Athens: University of Georgia Press, 1951.

Preble, George Henry. "A Canoe Expedition into the Everglades," *Tequesta*, No. 5 (1945), 30-51. This is a fascinating first-hand account of campaigning in the swamps.

Prucha, Francis P. *American Indian Policy in the Formative Years: The Indian Trade and Intercourse Acts, 1790-1834.* Cambridge: Harvard University Press, 1962.

_____. "Thomas L. McKenney and the New York Indian Board," *Mississippi Valley Historical Review*, XLVIII (March, 1962), 635-55.

Read, William A. *Florida Place Names of Indian Origin and Seminole Personal Names.* Louisiana State University Studies, No. 11, Baton Rouge, 1934.

Reavis, Logan U. *Life and Military Services of General William Selby Harney.* St. Louis, 1878. It is an adulatory biography.

"Recollections of a Campaign in Florida," *Yale Literary Magazine*, XI (1846), 72-80, 130-37.

Register of Debates in Congress, 1825-1837, 29 vols. Washington, 1825-37.

Ridaught, Horace. *Hell's Branch Office: Florida's Choctaw Indians.* Citra, Fla., 1957. This is an interesting book, but its authenticity is highly questionable.

Rippy, James F. *Joel R. Poinsett.* Durham, N.C.: Duke University Press, 1935.

Roberts, Albert H. "The Dade Massacre," *FHQ*, V (Jan., 1927), 123-38.

Rodenbough, Theophilus. *From Everglade to Cañon with the Second Dragoons.* New York, 1875.

Romans, Bernard. *A Concise Natural History of East and West Florida.* New York, 1775; reprinted with an Introduction by Rembert W. Patrick in the Florida Facsimile and Reprint Series, University of Florida Press, Gainesville, 1962. Romans did not distinguish the Florida Indians from all the rest in the lower Mississippi Valley.

Rouse, Irving, and John M. Goggin. *Anthropological Bibliography of the Eastern Seaboard.* New Haven: Yale University Press, 1947.

Rowles, W. P. "Incidents and Observations in Florida in 1836," *The Southron* (Gallatin, Tenn., 1841), 54-55, 106-10, 116-18, 157-61, 199-204; a photostatic copy is in the P. K. Yonge Memorial Library of Florida History, University of Florida, Gainesville.

Royce, Charles C. *Indian Land Cessions.* Washington, 1898. The compilation was *HR Doc. 736,* 56 Cong., 1 sess.; it includes the Seminole cession at Moultrie Creek.

St. Augustine *Florida Herald* 1822-45.

Schmeckebier, Lawrence F. *The Office of Indian Affairs.* Service Monographs of the United States Government, No. 48. Baltimore, Johns Hopkins University, 1927.

Schoolcraft, Henry R. *Historical and Statistical Information Respecting the History, Condition and Prospects of the Indian Tribes of the United States,* 6 parts. Philadelphia, 1851-57.

Schoolcraft's "Indian Tribes of the United States," Index to. Compiled by Frances S. Nichols. Smithsonian Institution, Bureau of American Ethnology, Bulletin 152, Washington, 1954.

The Seminole Indians in Florida. Compiled by workers of the Federal Writers' Project of the Work Projects Administration; published by the Florida Department of Agriculture, Tallahassee, 1951. The compilation is useful, but it is not perfectly reliable.

The Seminole Indians of Florida vs. the United States. Hearings before the Indian Claims Commission, Dockets 73, 151. Washington: Government Printing Office, 1961.

Shappee, Nathan D. "Fort Dallas and the Naval Depot on Key Biscayne, 1836-1926," *Tequesta,* No. 21 (1961), 13-40.

Shaw, Helen Louise. *British Administration of the Southern Indians, 1756-1783.* Lancaster, Pa., 1931.

Sherman, William T. *Home Letters of General Sherman,* ed. M. A. deW. Howe. New York, 1909.

————. *Memoirs,* 2 vols. New York, 1889.

————. *The Sherman Letters: Correspondence Between General and Senator Sherman from 1837 to 1891,* ed. Roche S. Thorndike. New York, 1894.

Silver James W. "A Counter Proposal to the Indian Removal Policy of Andrew Jackson," *Journal of Mississippi History,* IV (1942), 207-15. General Gaines proposed to leave the Indians where they were.

————. *Edmund Pendleton Gaines.* Baton Rouge: Louisiana University Press, 1949.

Simmons, James W. "Recollections of the Late Campaign in East Florida," *National Atlas and Sunday Morning Mail* (Philadelphia), July 31, 1836-Aug. 28, 1836.

Simmons, William H. *Notices of East Florida, with an Account of the Seminole Nation of Indians.* Charleston, 1822. This is another basic source.

Simpson, J. Clarence. *A Provisional Gazeteer of Florida Place Names of Indian Derivation,* ed. Mark F. Boyd. Florida Board of Conservation, Special Publication No. 1, Tallahassee, 1956.

Sleight, Frederick W. "Kunti: A Food Staple of the Florida Indians," *Florida Anthropologist,* VI (1953), 46-52.

Smith, Hale G. "The Development of Knowledge Regarding the Florida

Indians," *FHQ*, XXXVII (Oct., 1958), 156-60. Smith is concerned with the prehistoric Indians of the Florida region.

Smith, Joseph R. "Letters from the Second Seminole War," ed. John K. Mahon, *FHQ*, XXXVI (April, 1958), 331-52.

[Smith, W. W.]. *Sketch of the Seminole War and Sketches During a Campaign*, by a Lieutenant of the Left Wing. Charleston, S.C., 1836. Another of the early volunteers, Smith is an additional basic source for the first year of the war.

Spoehr, Alexander. *Camp, Clan and Kin Among the Cow Creek Seminoles of Florida*. Field Museum of Natural History, Anthropological Series, Vol. XXXIII, No. 1. Chicago, 1941.

_____. *The Florida Seminole Camp*. Field Museum of Natural History, Anthropological Series, Vol. XXXIII, No. 3. Chicago, 1944.

_____. *Kinship System of the Seminoles* [of Oklahoma]. Field Museum of Natural History, Anthropological Series, Vol. XXXIII, No. 2. Chicago, 1942.

Sprague, John T. "Macomb's Mission to the Seminoles: John T. Sprague's Journal Kept During April and May, 1839," ed. Frank F. White, Jr., *FHQ*, XXXV (Oct., 1956), 130-93.

_____. *The Origin, Progress, and Conclusion of the Florida War*. New York, 1948; reprinted with an Introduction by John K. Mahon in the Floridiana Facsimile and Reprint Series, University of Florida Press, Gainesville, 1964. This work has been until now the only full-scale history of the war and is of course an indispensable source.

Stafford, Robert C. "The Bemrose Manuscript on the Seminole War," *FHQ*, XVIII (April, 1940), 285-92. Stafford here prints a very small fraction of the manuscript.

Sturtevant, William C. "Accomplishments and Opportunities in Florida Indian Ethnology," in *Florida Anthropology*, ed. Charles H. Fairbanks. Florida Anthropological Society, Publication No. 4. Tallahassee, 1958.

_____. "Chakaika and the 'Spanish Indians': Documentary Sources Compared with Seminole Tradition," *Tequesta*, No. 13 (1953), 35-73.

_____. "The Medicine Bundles and Busks of the Florida Seminoles," *Florida Anthropologist*, VII (May, 1954), 31-70.

_____ (ed.). "R. H. Pratt's Report on the Seminoles in 1879," *Florida Anthropologist*, IX (1956), 1-24.

_____. "A Seminole Personal Document," *Tequesta*, No. 16 (1956), 55-75.

_____. "Spanish-Indian Relations in Southeastern North America," *Ethnohistory*, IX (Winter, 1962), 41-94.

Swanton, John R. *Early History of the Creek Indians and Their Neighbors*. Smithsonian Institution, Bureau of American Ethnology, Bulletin 73, Washington, 1922.

_____. *Religious Beliefs and Medical Practices of the Creek Indians*. Smithsonian Institution, Bureau of American Ethnology, 42nd Annual Report, 1924-1925, Washington, 1928.

_____. *Social Organization and Social Usages of the Indians of the Creek Confederacy*. Smithsonian Institution, Bureau of American Ethnology, 42nd Annual Report, 1924-1925, Washington, 1928.

Tallahassee *Floridian*, 1829-45.

United States Congress Serial Set, Washington. The documents used are listed below.

"Report of the Commissioners of Indian Affairs, West," *HR Report 474*, 23 Cong., 1 sess., Feb. 10, 1834.

"Hostilities in Florida," *Sen. Doc. 152*, 24 Cong., 1 sess., Feb. 10, 1836.

"Report on Causes of Hostilities," *HR Doc. 267*, 24 Cong., 1 sess.

"Supplemental Report on Causes of Hostilities," *HR Doc. 271*, 24 Cong., 1 sess., June 2, 1836.

"Proceedings of the Military Court of Inquiry in the Case of Major General Scott and Major General Gaines," *Sen. Doc. 224*, 24 Cong., 2 sess., March 2, 1837.

"Calls for Irregulars," *HR Doc. 140*, 24 Cong., 2 sess., Feb. 8, 1837.

"Resignation of Officers, etc.," *HR Doc. 183*, 24 Cong., 2 sess., March 2, 1837.

"Number of Troops Employed," *Sen. Doc. 226*, 25 Cong., 2 sess., Feb. 21, 1838.

"General Taylor's Report of Okeechobee," *Sen. Doc. 227*, 25 Cong., 2 sess., Jan. 4, 1838.

"General Jesup's Report of His Command," *Sen. Doc. 507*, 25 Cong., 2 sess., July 7, 1938.

"Trial of Scott and Gaines," but there is a supplement of General Jesup's correspondence, *HR Doc. 78*, 25 Cong., 2 sess.

"Troops in Service," *HR Doc. 133*, 25 Cong., 2 sess., Jan. 30, 1838.

"Jesup's Conduct of the War," *HR Doc. 219*, 25 Cong., 2 sess., March 12, 1838.

"Memorial of Cherokee Mediators," *HR Doc. 285*, 25 Cong., 2 sess., March 26, 1838.

"Forces in Florida," *HR Doc. 299*, 25 Cong., 2 sess., April 4, 1838.

"Indian Prisoners of War," *HR Doc. 327*, 25 Cong., 2 sess.

"Captured Negroes," *HR Doc. 225*, 25 Cong., 3 sess., Feb. 27, 1839.

"Correspondence Between R. K. Call and the War Department," *Sen. Doc. 278*, 26 Cong., 1 sess., March 12, 1840.

"Expenditures in the War," *HR Doc. 8*, 26 Cong., 2 sess., Dec. 15, 1840.

"Petition of General Jesup," *Sen. Doc. 231*, 26 Cong., 2 sess., March 3, 1841.

"Depredations in Georgia," *HR Doc. 200*, 27 Cong., 2 sess., April 22, 1842.

"Slaves Captured," *HR Doc. 55*, 27 Cong., 2 sess., Jan. 29, 1842.

"Expenditures," *HR Doc. 247*, 27 Cong., 2 sess., June 18, 1842.

"Correspondence of the Secretary of War with the Commander in Florida," *HR Doc. 262*, 27 Cong., 2 sess., July 7, 1842.

"Small Arms Manufacture," *HR Doc. 3*, 27 Cong., 3 sess., Dec. 13, 1842.

"Indians Remaining in Florida, *HR Doc. 82*, 28 Cong., 1 sess., Jan. 27, 1844.

"Indians Remaining in Florida," *HR Doc. 253*, 28 Cong., 1 sess., May 9, 1844.

"Expenditures of the Florida Squadron," *HR Report 582*, 28 Cong., 1 sess., June 14, 1844.

"Naval Court of Inquiry," *HR Doc. 130*, 29 Cong., 1 sess., Feb. 19, 1846.

"Report of the Commissioner of the Land Office on the Armed Occupation Act," *Sen. Doc. 39*, 30 Cong., 1 sess., April 28, 1848.

"Information Regarding Difficulties with Creek and Seminole Indians," *HR Doc. 15*, 33 Cong., 2 sess., Dec. 18, 1854.

Upton, Emory. *Military Policy of the United States*. Washington, 1907.

Vignoles, Charles. *Observations upon the Floridas*. New York, 1823.

Walker, Hester Perrine. "Massacre at Indian Key, August 7, 1840, and the Death of Dr. Henry Perrine," *FHQ*, V (July, 1926), 18-42. This is the narrative of one of Dr. Perrine's daughters, herself a victim.

Wallace, Edward S. *General William Jenkins Worth, Monterey's Forgotten Hero*. Dallas, Texas, 1953.

Wells, W. Alva. "Osceola and the Second Seminole War." Master's thesis, University of Oklahoma, Norman, 1936. Wells draws very heavily on Giddings, and so adds little.

Williams, John L. *The Territory of Florida*. New York, 1837; reprinted with an Introduction by Herbert J. Doherty, Jr., in the Floridiana Facsimile and Reprint Series, University of Florida Press, Gainesville, 1962. This is an important early source.

Wiltse, Charles M. *John C. Calhoun, Nationalist, 1782-1828*. Indianapolis, 1944.

Woodford, Frank B. *Lewis Cass*. New Brunswick, N.J.: Rutgers University Press, 1950. Only one paragraph in the entire book refers to the Seminole War.

Woodward, A. L. "Indian Massacre in Gadsden County," *FHQ*, 1st series, I (April, 1908), 17-25. Woodward reminisces of a personal experience in 1840 of an Indian attack.

Woodward, Thomas S. *Woodward's Reminiscences of the Creek or Muscogee Indians, Contained in Letters to Friends in Georgia and Alabama*. Montgomery, Ala., 1859; reprinted, 1939. There is more on the period 1812-20 than on the Second Seminole War.

Yoshpe, Harry B., and Phillip P. Brower (compilers). *Preliminary Inventory of the Land Entry Papers of the General Land Office*. Washington, 1949.

[Young, Hugh]. "A Topographical Memoir on East and West Florida . . ." ed. Mark F. Boyd, *FHQ*, XIII (July, Oct., 1934, Jan., 1935), 16-50, 82-104, 129-64. This man was with Jackson in 1818 and supplies useful data.

Young, Rogers W. "Fort Marion During the Seminole War," *FHQ*, XIII (April, 1935), 193-223.

Yulee, C. Wickliffe. "Senator Yulee," *FHQ*, 1st series, II (April, July, 1909), 26-43, 3-22.

Index

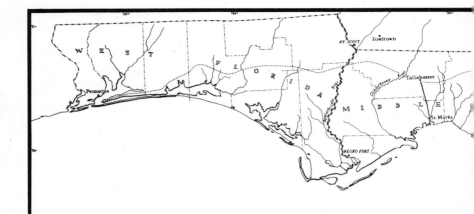

FLORIDA — 1835-1842

to accompany

History of the Second Seminole War

by John K. Mahon

DRAWN FROM CONTEMPORARY SOURCES

SCALE 1 : 1,000,000

(U S GEOLOGICAL SURVEY BASE MAP)

Legend

.... Seminole Reservation Boundary, 1823

· · · · · · · · · Seminole Reservation Boundary at War's end

.... Road

—··—··— County Boundary, 1962

Drawn by J.E. Massey - 1962